BEHIND THE GREEN CURTAIN

Ireland's Phoney Neutrality
During World War II

BEHIND THE GREEN CURTAIN

Ireland's Phoney Neutrality
During World War II

T. RYLE DWYER ~

Gill & Macmillan

Gill & Macmillan Ltd
Hume Avenue, Park West, Dublin 12
with associated companies throughout the world
www.gillmacmillan.ie

© T. Ryle Dwyer 2009, 2010
First published in hard cover 2009
First published in paperback 2010
978 07171 4650 5

Index compiled by Helen Litton
Typography design by Make Communication
Print origination by O'K Graphic Design, Dublin
Printed by J F Print Ltd, Somerset

The paper used in this book comes from the wood pulp
of managed forests. For every tree felled, at least one
tree is planted, thereby renewing natural resources.

A CIP catalogue record for this book is available from
the British Library.

5 4 3 2 1

To Denis, Johanna, Arthur, Tiffany, Lucy and Ryle Hassett

CONTENTS

PREFACE

In 1973, while defending my doctoral dissertation, 'Irish Neutrality and the USA, 1939–1945', at North Texas State University (now the University of North Texas), it transpired one of the external professors had been a member of the British Royal Air Force during the war. He said that he had heard of stories of U-boat bases in Ireland. I contended there were none, because all of Ireland's oil was supplied by Britain and the British did not supply the kind of heavy diesel oil that U-boats required. As a result, even if the Irish had wished to re-fuel the U-boats, they did not have the means to do so. The British government admitted this at the time. 'Yes,' the professor replied, 'but you and I know that governments sometimes lie.' Indeed, therein lay the problem.

In relation to Irish neutrality, the United States and British governments distorted Ireland's role for their own political purposes. More than half a century after the end of the war, my brother Seán traced a fellow officer who was with my father on the day he was killed-in-action in Germany, in January 1945, while serving with the US Army. When Seán mentioned that we had been reared in Ireland after my father's death, the man expressed surprise that my mother would go to Ireland in view of Ireland's role during World War II.

Many believed Ireland was anti-British to the point of being pro-Nazi. Some people undoubtedly were; other Irish people have expressed shame that the country adopted an amoral policy in refusing to help the Allies. In truth, Ireland was not neutral in wartime. From the very outset the Irish Taoiseach (leader), Éamon de Valera, secretly assured the British that he was prepared to give all possible help, short of involving Ireland in the conflict.

An extraordinary level of cooperation was established, first with the British, later with the Americans. Irish coast-watchers cooperated with the British from the initial weeks of the conflict, but this was never enough for Winston Churchill, who was an imperialist hardliner. He tried to persuade the British war Cabinet to seize Irish bases in October 1939. But even Churchill backed off because of the likely impact this would have on American opinion at a critical time. De Valera managed to keep Churchill at bay by exploiting the disruptive political potential of Irish-American opinion, much to the annoyance of President Franklin D. Roosevelt.

J. Russell Forgan—the acting head of American Intelligence in Europe at the height of the distortion surrounding an American demand for the expulsion of Axis diplomats from Dublin in the spring of 1944—later explained that the Irish cooperated with the United States on intelligence matters as if they were allies. 'They have never received the credit due to them,' he explained. Details of that cooperation went beyond anything that has ever been openly admitted. The aim of this book is to get behind the curtain of secrecy and distortion in order to provide an accurate picture of Irish policy during World War II. The book explains why officials on the ground were satisfied with the level of Irish cooperation and why Churchill and Roosevelt were never content, and hence conspired to distort the true record.

TRD
Tralee

Chapter 1 ❧

| **BACKGROUND**

Nobody should have been surprised when Éamon de Valera announced, in September 1939, that he was determined to keep Ireland out of the war. There were a number of reasons behind his decision.

Keeping the country out of the war afforded an opportunity to demonstrate Irish independence, which had been an imperative of Irish politics since the Anglo-Irish Treaty of 1921 accorded the Irish Free State the same *de facto* status as Canada, but allowed the British to retain control of three ports (Lough Swilly, Berehaven and Queenstown (now Cobh)) and the right to whatever other Irish bases they might desire in time of war. The Treaty was approved by a majority of Dáil Éireann, but de Valera opposed it, which led to the civil war of 1922–3.

Having been on the losing side in that conflict, de Valera spent almost a decade in the political wilderness, during which time he broke with Sinn Féin and the IRA and set up his own party: Fianna Fáil. Although the partition issue had essentially nothing to do with the Treaty controversy, de Valera later harped on the issue to such an extent that he managed to generate the impression that partition had been a central issue in the dispute. He was the first person to suggest in the Dáil that it was necessary to accept partition in some form. 'The minority in Ulster had a right to have their sentiments considered to the utmost limit,' he told a private session of the Dáil on 22 August 1921.[1] To attempt to coerce the majority in Northern Ireland would be to make the same mistake the British had made with the Irish people as a whole. In December 1921 de Valera presented the Dáil with his alternative to the Treaty, which included the partition clauses *verbatim*.

The Treaty controversy centred on the issue of independence, with the result that demonstrating independence became the imperative of the country's foreign policy in succeeding years. Different Irish governments demonstrated it in many ways over this time: by registering the Anglo-Irish Treaty as an international agreement at the League of Nations, over the objections of the British; by appointing an Irish Minister to the United States, thus becoming the first British dominion to send a diplomatic representative to a country outside the British Commonwealth. The Dublin government also appointed diplomatic representatives to the League of Nations, France, and Germany. Irish representatives played a major role in the negotiations leading to the Balfour Declaration of 1926 and the resulting Statute of Westminster, which formally proclaimed that dominions were autonomous in their own affairs.

On coming to power in 1932, de Valera admitted he had underestimated the benefits of the 1921 Treaty: 'I am quite prepared to confess that there have been advances made that I did not believe would be made at the time.'[2] He told the Dáil:

> The recognition of co-equal status has been fully recognised by the British Parliament in the Statute of Westminster. We are, therefore, to-day quite free to do anything here without any violation of the Treaty, anything they can do in Canada, anything they can do in Australia or New Zealand, anything they can do in Britain as regards relations with the Crown.[3]

De Valera used that freedom to demonstrate further independence by abolishing the controversial oath of fealty to the British King prescribed in the 1921 Treaty. He also pursued independent policies at the League of Nations, where he distinguished himself in September 1932, at a particularly critical time. The Japanese had flouted the League's Covenant by invading Manchuria the previous year. It was the first real test of the League's ability to prevent war, and it was the Irish Free State's turn to provide the President of the Council, in line with the practice of rotating the position every three months. De Valera seized an opportunity to shine on an international stage.

He arrived in Geneva with the reputation of being an enemy of the League, the result of his actions in the United States during 1919 and 1920 when he opposed American ratification of the Versailles Treaty, which contained the Covenant for the League of Nations. However, he quickly confounded his critics by presiding effectively at the opening session of the Council, on Saturday, 24 September 1932. Two days later he delivered the opening address to the Assembly, as President of the Council. He wrote his own speech for the occasion, spotlighting the League's shortcomings and emphasising the need to strengthen the organisation in order to provide it with the necessary influence to achieve its worthy goals:

> No state should be permitted to jeopardise the common interest by selfish action contrary to the Covenant and no state is powerful enough to stand for long against the League if the governments in the League and their

peoples are determined that the Covenant shall be upheld.[4]

The address was well received by the diplomats and reporters present. 'In the lobbies the speech received nothing but praise,' the correspondent of the London *News Chronicle* reported. 'It was the most candid piece of criticism that within my recollection any League chairman has ever dared to utter. Yet the speech was moderate in tone, entirely without bitterness and, indeed, indicative of the speaker's sympathy with the work and aims of the League.'[5] De Valera 'had rendered a service to the League', according to an editorial in *The Times* of London.[6]

'Rarely has Geneva heard such a speech,' the prestigious *New York Times* reported on its front page. 'It is Mr de Valera's personal work, and together with the way he presided over the Council on Saturday, it unquestionably made him the outstanding personality of this session.'[7]

De Valera continued to speak out boldly and to adopt an independent approach to international affairs. In 1934 he suggested the League of Nations should intervene to stop the Chaco War between Bolivia and Paraguay, much to the annoyance of the United States, which would consider such intervention a violation of the Monroe Doctrine. As Italy prepared to invade Ethiopia in 1935, de Valera urged his colleagues that the League was being given a last chance to prove its effectiveness. On 16 September 1935 he told the Assembly:

> The final test of the League and all that it stands for has come. Our conduct in this crisis will determine whether it is better to let it lapse and disappear and be forgotten. Make no mistake, if on any pretext whatever we were to permit the sovereignty of even the weakest state amongst us to be unjustly taken away, the whole foundation of the League would crumble into dust.[8]

Initially, the British took a strong stand against Italy's threatened aggression, but the Italians proceeded to invade Ethiopia, on 3 October 1935. The following day de Valera went on 2RN, the Irish radio station, to warn that Japan's earlier violation of the Covenant had shaken the League to its foundations and that if a second, similar successful violation were allowed, the League of Nations would disappear as an effective safeguard for individual members. He not only supported a British call for economic sanctions against Italy but also suggested military action should be taken, if the economic measures failed. He had already warned his Cabinet that it would be 'contrary to the spirit of the Covenant' to refuse to take part in any 'collective military actions to be taken by the League'.[9]

'Whether or not one accepts Mr de Valera's views on these grave issues,' one long-standing critic wrote, 'one must realise that he has approached them sincerely and in no petty spirit, and that he is prepared to carry his opinions to their logical conclusions.'[10] His unequivocal support of the League met with some criticism at home, even from within his own party. Kathleen Clarke, the widow of Tom Clarke, one of the main leaders of the Easter Rebellion of 1916, contended the Dublin government should have used its stand at the League 'for bargaining purposes' in order to extract economic concessions from the British in return for supporting their call for sanctions against Italy.[11]

De Valera was unequivocal in his response:

If we want justice for ourselves, we ought to stand for justice for others. As long as I have the honour of representing any government here outside, I stand, on every occasion, for what I think is just and right—thinking thereby I will help the cause of Ireland, and I will not bargain that for anything.[12]

In the light of subsequent history, de Valera's behaviour during the various crises of the early and mid-1930s stands out as both brave and wise. Indeed, it could be contrasted favourably with the behaviour of some of his greatest critics. 'Churchill had been obsessed by German ambitions to the exclusion of all other perils,' according to historian R.R. James. 'On virtually all the major international crises of the 1930s involving unilateral belligerence by other totalitarian regimes his position was somewhat equivocal. In effect he condoned Japanese aggression in Manchuria; his attitude to the Abyssinia question was something less than heroic; he supported the Franco regime in the Spanish Civil War.'[13]

The Fine Gael opposition pilloried de Valera. 'They have tried to rally all our abysmal ignorance of foreign affairs against him,' said former Irish diplomat Seán Lester, who was serving in the secretariat of the League of Nations and who would eventually become its second, and last, Secretary General.[14] Lester was not the only former critic who admired de Valera's foreign policy. Frank MacDermot, who was one of the deputies of the Centre Party when it amalgamated with Cumann na nGaedheal and the Blueshirts to form Fine Gael in 1933, broke with the party over its opposition to de Valera's foreign policy during the Ethiopian crisis.

Although often accused of exploiting anti-British feelings at every opportunity, de Valera made no effort to do so during the various international crises of the 1930s. He blamed the League itself, especially for the Ethiopian debacle. 'There was never a better chance for the League of Nations to be successful against a great power as there was in that case,' he explained. 'If it failed in the case of Italy, it was bound to fail in the case of other powers.'[15]

He abandoned his own outspoken support of collective security within the League of Nations and announced that Ireland would remain neutral in the war, which he now felt was virtually inevitable. He became a logical supporter of appeasement. Speaking in Geneva on 2 July 1936, for instance, he called for the lifting of the sanctions against Italy: 'We have now to confess publicly that we must abandon the victim to his fate. Despite our judicial equality here, in matters such as European peace the small states are powerless.'[16] And he told the Assembly:

> Peace is dependent upon the will of great states. All the small states can do, if the statesmen of the greater states fail in their duty, is resolutely to determine that they will not become the tools of any great power, and that they will resist with whatever strength they may possess every attempt to force them into a war against their will.[17]

On 14 December 1937 de Valera announced the appointment of an Irish Minister to Italy, whose credentials were addressed to the 'King of Italy and Emperor of Ethiopia'. This afforded *de facto* recognition of Italy's annexation of Abyssinia, before Britain or any of the other dominions. It was another symbolic step in demonstrating dominion independence.[18] Throughout the 1930s de Valera espoused democracy. In fact, Ireland was one of the few countries in Europe with a Roman Catholic majority that remained truly democratic throughout his sixteen years in power, from 1932 to 1948.

Despite the near-hysterical stance taken by political opponents and by Catholic Church leaders during the Spanish civil war, de Valera refused to support the forces of Francisco Franco. Instead, he endorsed the non-interventionist approach of the League of Nations.

In the midst of the deteriorating international situation, British Prime Minister Neville Chamberlain's first concern was to secure Irish goodwill. In the Anglo-Irish talks which began in London in January 1938, he was ready to hand over the three Treaty ports and to renounce all other rights gained under the 1921 Treaty. Privately, he described partition as an anachronism that he could do nothing about against the will of the majority in Northern Ireland, because the British public would not stand for putting pressure on Belfast.

Chamberlain was hopeful from the outset of the talks. He described de Valera as a 'queer creature' in many ways, but no enemy of Britain; 'I shall be grievously disappointed if we don't get an all-round agreement on everything except partition,' he added. 'That is the difference that cannot be bridged without the assent of Ulster.'[19]

De Valera appealed to President Franklin D. Roosevelt for help: 'I am writing to ask you to consider whether you could not use your influence to get the British Government to realise what would be gained by reconciliation and to get them to move whilst there is time. In a short while, if the present negotiations fail, relations will be worsened.'[20] Roosevelt realised that an Anglo-Irish settlement would be a good thing all round. He asked Joseph P. Kennedy, the newly appointed US Ambassador to Britain, to tell Chamberlain privately that the President of the United States was anxious for an Irish settlement. He wrote to de Valera:

> You will realise, I know, that I cannot officially or through diplomatic channels accomplish anything or even discuss the matter. But I have taken the course of asking my friend, Mr Joseph P. Kennedy, who sails today for England to take up his post as Ambassador, to convey a personal message from me to the Prime Minister, and to tell the Prime Minister how happy I should be if reconciliation could be brought about.[21]

De Valera concentrated on the need to resolve partition. In the past he had used the issue for his own political purposes. He was largely responsible for generating the delusion that the civil war had been fought over partition, but having fooled the people in order to lead them, he was now forced to serve the folly he had promoted. His negotiating tactics in relation to Northern Ireland disturbed his Finance Minister, Seán MacEntee, who was a member of the four-man Irish delegation. 'I feel that the Partition problem cannot be solved,' MacEntee wrote in January 1938, 'except with the consent of the majority of the Northern non-Catholic population. It certainly cannot be solved by their coercion. Hitherto, we as the Government here have done nothing of our selves to secure a solution, but on the contrary have done and are doing certain things which have made a solution more difficult.'[22]

Over the years de Valera had repeatedly complained about partition, but never took any practical steps to do anything about it. In March 1933 he told the Dáil that 'The only policy for abolishing partition that I can see is for us in this part of Ireland to use such freedom as we can secure to get for the people in this part of Ireland such conditions as will make the people in the other part of Ireland wish to belong to this part.'[23] Five years later, he had still made no effort to appeal to Northern unionists.

'In regard to partition, we have never had a policy,' MacEntee complained. The government consistently maintained that it did not wish to coerce Northern unionists into a united Ireland, but it did nothing to win them over. 'With our connivance every bigot and killjoy, ecclesiastical and lay, is doing his damnedest here to keep them out,' MacEntee argued.[24]

When Ambassador Kennedy delivered President Roosevelt's message to Chamberlain on 7 April, the Anglo-Irish talks were deadlocked. The Prime Minister later told his Cabinet that Kennedy 'had spoken strongly to him of the valuable effect on opinion in America of an agreement with Éire.'[25] The impasse was overcome when the British dropped their demand for the Dublin government to make trade concessions to Northern Ireland. The two governments formally concluded an agreement to hand over the Treaty ports and to renounce Britain's rights to Irish bases in time of crisis.

'A more feckless act can hardly be imagined,' Winston Churchill later wrote.[26] He was bitterly opposed to the defence concessions. 'Mr de Valera has given no understanding,' Churchill complained. 'The ports may be denied to us in the hour of need and we may be hampered in the greatest manner in protecting the British population from privation, and even starvation. Who would wish to put his head in such a noose?'[27]

'Over and above the improved relations between Britain and Éire,' Home Secretary Samuel Hoare noted, 'there was the great gain of a more friendly atmosphere in the United States, where hostile Irish opinion has so persistent and dangerous an influence.'[28] The move was really aimed at improving Anglo-American relations, according to Dominions Secretary Malcolm MacDonald. Because 'Irishmen take a great part in foreign affairs and politics' of the United States, he argued, the agreement would improve 'the friendly relations which exist between the United States and this country'.[29]

'There has been no bargain,' de Valera assured the Dáil. 'There are no conditions. There is no secret understanding, but there is a belief, I am certain—a belief which I have tried, over 20 years, to get into the minds of British Governments and of the British people, in so far as I could—that it is far better for Britain, far more advantageous for Britain, to have a free Ireland by its side than an Ireland that would be unfriendly because of liberties which Britain denied.'[30]

A few months later, on 31 August 1938, Joseph P. Walshe and John Dulanty suggested a secret liaison be established between MI5, the British intelligence service, and G2, Irish Army Intelligence. MI5 appointed Cecil Liddell, a brother of Captain Guy M. Liddell, one of the leading figures in MI5's counterintelligence division, to take charge of the organisation's liaison with G2, which was represented by its Director, Colonel Liam Archer. The British got on so well with Archer they believed he was more sympathetic than his political masters, but the liaison was conducted with the full approval of de Valera, given that all correspondence went through his Department of External Affairs and the Irish High Commission in London.

De Valera credits Roosevelt with playing a vital part in the success of the Anglo-Irish negotiations. 'The knowledge of the fact that you were interested came most opportunely at a critical moment in the progress of the negotiations,' de Valera wrote. 'Were it not for Mr. Chamberlain personally the negotiations would have broken down at that time, and I am sure the knowledge of your interest in the success of the negotiations had its due weight in determining his attitude.'

Feeling that he was already being criticised for being on 'too friendly terms with the British',[31] de Valera deliberately played down the significance of the agreement, but capitalised on its popularity at home by calling a general election in June 1938. Fianna Fáil had a resounding victory at the polls, getting 52 per cent of the first preference votes and winning an overall majority of fifteen seats. His political standing was further boosted in September when he was elected President of the Assembly of the League of Nations.

The League met that autumn under the cloud of the Munich crisis. Germany was demanding the annexation of the Sudetenland of Czechoslovakia, with its German majority. De Valera believed Hitler had a valid claim because the Versailles Treaty had cut off the German majority in the Sudetenland from Germany without regard for the principle of self-determination. The Taoiseach saw a similarity between the Sudeten problem and the situation in Northern Ireland. On his way to Geneva, he told the British Attorney General, Sir Thomas Inskip, that Dublin had its 'own Sudetens in Northern Ireland' and he sometimes considered 'the possibility of going over the boundary and pegging out the territory, just as Hitler was doing'.[32]

De Valera warmly welcomed Chamberlain's decision to go to Berchesgaden to meet Hitler. 'One person at least is completely satisfied that you are doing the right thing no matter what the result,' he telegraphed Chamberlain. [33]

'Whatever happens I shall not regret what I have done,' Chamberlain replied. 'I am convinced that I was only just in time to prevent a disaster.' He told de Valera he 'would be very grateful for any steps' to mobilise opinion within the Assembly for a settlement.[34]

The following day de Valera appealed to Roosevelt in a broadcast over Radio Nations, the League's radio station: 'The time for something like a general European Peace Conference, or at least a conference between the greater powers, is overdue. If nations be called to make certain sacrifices at such a conference, these will be far less than the sacrifices they will have to make in the event of war.' Hitler might not be satisfied with that to which Germany was justly entitled, but if the Germans then went to war, their wanton aggression would be clearly exposed. 'If by conceding the claims of justice or by reasonable compromise in a spirit of fair play we take steps to avoid the latter kind of war,' de Valera said, 'we can face the possibility of the other kind with relative equanimity.'[35]

In his capacity as President of the League's Assembly, de Valera sent an open telegram to Chamberlain on 27 September. 'Let nothing daunt you or defeat you in your effort to secure peace,' he urged. 'The tens of millions of innocent people on both sides who have no cause against each other, but who are in danger of being hurled against each other, with no alternative to mutual slaughter are praying that your efforts may find a way of saving them from this terrible doom.'[36]

The ill-fated Munich Agreement was signed in the early hours of 30 September 1938. De Valera delivered the closing address to a greatly relieved Assembly later that day. Having avoided giving Chamberlain public credit for the Anglo-Irish Agreement earlier in the year, he was now effusive in his praise of the British leader, whom he described as a 'knight of peace' who had 'attained the highest peak of human greatness, a glory greater than that of all the conquerors'.[37]

On his return journey, de Valera met Chamberlain in London and tried to persuade him to move decisively on the partition question, but the Prime Minister said it was politically impossible. While de Valera had talked, on his way to Geneva, about 'pegging out' nationalist territory in Northern Ireland he now dismissed the idea of simply claiming nationalist territory. 'A plebiscite would give us territory, but it would not solve the problem of partition,' he told Helen Tiltmann of the London *Evening Standard*.[38] Redrawing the border 'would leave in Belfast alone a minority of a hundred thousand nationalists permanently cut off from the common life with their motherland'. He held out the possibility of concluding an alliance with Britain in return for an end to partition. 'No Irish leader will ever be able to get the Irish people to cooperate with Great Britain while partition remains,' de Valera said. 'I wouldn't attempt it myself, for I know I should fail.'[39]

'Keep your local Parliament with its local powers if you wish,' the Taoiseach was saying to the people of Northern Ireland. 'The Government of Éire ask for only two things of you. There must be adequate safeguards that the ordinary rights of the Nationalist minority in your area shall not be denied them, as at present, and that the powers at present reserved to the English Parliament shall be transferred to the all-Ireland Parliament.'[40]

At the Fianna Fáil Árd Fheis in November 1938, de Valera announced that he was asking friends in America and the two ethnic Irish newspapers that had consistently supported him—the New York *Irish World* and San Francisco *Leader*—to inform the American public of 'the nature of partition and the wrong done by it to the Irish nation'.[41] He was embarking on a propaganda campaign to marshal Irish-Americans to put pressure on Washington to in turn persuade the British to end partition.

The issue posed a real enough political threat to the de Valera government.

The IRA, which was getting financial backing from sympathisers in the United States, declared war on Britain in January 1939.[42] This involved a sporadic bombing campaign in English cities. The bombs—mostly made up in small packages and transported by bicycle to pillar-boxes—were intended to force the British to abandon Northern Ireland. Over 100 small bombs were set off, but they never had a chance of achieving the objective—as would become painfully evident when infinitely heavier German bombing only strengthened the British resolve to resist. By comparison with the forthcoming German Blitz, the IRA's outrages were mere pinpricks.

Even though de Valera ruled out the use of force as a means of ending partition, he appeared to pander to militancy by indicating that he would favour violence, if he thought it would be successful. 'I am not a pacifist by any means,' he said. 'I would, if I could see a way of doing it effectively, rescue the people of Tyrone and Fermanagh, South Down, South Armagh and Derry City from the coercion which they are suffering at the present time, because I believe that, if there is to be no coercion, that ought to apply all round.' Yet he admitted he never asked the British to transfer those nationalist areas, 'because I think the time has come when we ought to do the thing properly. That would only be a half measure.'[43] He preferred to have the grievance of the contiguous nationalist areas being compelled to remain within Northern Ireland, because this afforded legitimacy to his complaints about partition and, anyway, he thought 'natural forces', in the form of the higher birth-rate among Catholics, would ultimately allow for partition to be settled in a democratic way.[44]

When speaking in Geneva in 1934 about the problem of European minorities, de Valera had said that the best solution would be to transfer the minority to its ancestral homeland, if possible. He was considering transferring Protestant Unionists of Scottish extraction to mainland Britain and replacing them with a similar number of Catholics of Irish extraction from Britain, and he was planning an international propaganda campaign on the issue. He could hardly have chosen a more offensive setting, in the eyes of Northern Protestants, to launch his initiative. While visiting the Vatican for the coronation of Pope Pius XII in March 1939, de Valera delivered a St Patrick's Day address over Vatican Radio. He appealed to 'the millions of our race scattered throughout the world' to join in a campaign to end partition, which he described as 'an open wound'. [45]

He planned to visit the United States in early May, ostensibly to open the Irish pavilion at the World's Fair in New York, but also arranged a six-week, coast-to-coast tour of American cities. It was a time of rising international tensions. Hitler had violated the Munich Agreement in March 1939 by seizing the rump of Czechoslovakia to which Germany had no claim. As a result, de

Valera predicted a major war following the next harvest, in the autumn of 1939. He was hoping for a partition settlement before the war, for fear Northern nationalists might otherwise revolt during the war and the whole island could once again be dragged into a conflict with Britain.

Roosevelt famously asked Hitler for an 'assurance that your armed forces will not attack or invade the territory or possessions of the following independent nations: Finland, Estonia, Latvia, Lithuania, Sweden, Norway, Denmark, The Netherlands, Belgium, Great Britain and Ireland, France, Portugal, Spain, Switzerland, Liechtenstein, Luxemburg, Poland, Hungary, Rumania, Yugoslavia, Russia, Bulgaria, Greece, Turkey, Iraq, the Arabias, Syria, Palestine, Egypt and Iran'.[46]

Robert Brennan, the Irish Minister to the United States, protested against the lumping of 'Great Britain and Ireland' together, as if they were one country.[47]

'I must also draw Mr. Roosevelt's attention to one or two mistakes in history,' Hitler replied in an address to the Reichstag. 'He mentioned Ireland, for instance, and asks for a statement that Germany will not attack Ireland. Now, I have just read a speech delivered by de Valera, the Irish Taoiseach, in which, strangely enough and contrary to Mr. Roosevelt's opinion, he does not charge Germany with oppressing Ireland but reproaches England with subjecting Ireland to continuous aggression.'[48]

'With all due respect to Mr. Roosevelt's insight into the needs and cares of other countries,' the Führer continued, 'it may nevertheless be assumed that the Irish Taoiseach would be more familiar with the dangers which threaten his country than would the President of the United States.'[49]

De Valera's planned visit to the United States was cancelled when a political crisis erupted in Northern Ireland over British plans to introduce conscription. Under pressure from de Valera, Northern Ireland was excluded from the Conscription Act, and Irish people living in Britain were exempted, unless they had been living in Britain for a certain number of years. The Taoiseach's American visit was rescheduled for September 1939, but was cancelled when war broke out following the German invasion of Poland in August.

Chapter 2 ∿

'FRIENDLY TO ENGLAND'

'It will be a long war,' de Valera told James A. Farley, the American Postmaster-General, 'but in the final analysis, the Allied powers should win. From our point of view it will be best to stay out of the war. By doing so we will be able to keep intact and at the same time be friendly to England. We are desirous of being helpful, in this or any other crisis in so far as we are able, short of actual participation in the war. That would be ruinous for us and injurious to England.'[1]

On the eve of the invasion of Poland, Edouard Hempel, the German Minister to Ireland, called on de Valera to pass on an assurance that Germany would respect Ireland's neutrality. Ireland desired peace, but due to economic necessity, she would have to show 'a certain consideration' for the British, de Valera explained.[2] In the event of war, de Valera candidly told the Dáil, after the return of the ports Ireland would have to continue trading with Britain out of economic necessity, which could lead to difficulties with Britain's enemies.

'Did I understand the Prime Minister correctly when I believe him to have said that if we continue to send foodstuffs to Great Britain in time of war it would be folly to pretend that we can maintain our neutrality?' James Dillon asked.[3]

'I fear it would be so, in fact,' de Valera replied. 'The truth is, of course, that in a modern war there is no neutrality.'[4] Although he publicly characterised his policy as 'neutrality', it should more appropriately have been described as non-belligerency, because it always favoured the Allies.

Years later de Valera stated that his main reason for trying to keep Ireland out of the war was his belief that the country could not affect the outcome of the conflict:

We tried to keep out of involvement in the last war because we believed that war would be made in spite of us and without consulting us, that war would be ended without consulting us and that the terms on which the war would be ended would not be the terms we would have wished for but the terms which would suit the interests of the large Powers engaged in the war.[5]

By not following Britain into the war, the Dublin government demonstrated its independence in determining its own foreign policy, notwithstanding the remaining ties with the British Commonwealth. The only dominion to adhere to the doctrine that the King's declaration of war committed it to the conflict was Australia. Prime Minister Robert Menzies merely signed and published a notice in the *Commonwealth Gazette* that Great Britain had declared war on Germany and that, as a result, Australia was also at war. New Zealand acted just as quickly by endorsing the British ultimatum to Hitler and announcing that, once the ultimatum had expired, New Zealand would be at war with Germany. The Union of South Africa and Canada stood briefly aloof as their governments sought parliamentary approval for their actions. Prime Minister J.B.M. Hertzog, who was of a German-Jewish background, advocated South Africa declare neutrality, but his proposals were rejected by his Cabinet and the Union parliament. Hertzog was replaced as Prime Minister by Jan C. Smuts, who carried the Cabinet and parliament in favour of a declaration of war. Thus South Africa stayed out of the war for only three days, while Canada remained aloof for a little longer—it was seven days before the Canadian parliament declared war on Germany.

Edouard Hempel reported that neutrality 'visibly strengthened Irish national self-consciousness'. It was the most conclusive demonstration of Irish independence.[6]

The fact that Ireland was relatively defenceless reinforced arguments against involvement in the conflict. In addition, there was the belief that as long as partition was in place, the Dublin government could not openly ally with Britain without provoking civil strife in Ireland. However, de Valera's subsequent refusal to risk involvement in the war even in return for an end to partition suggested that he considered staying out of the conflict more important than ending partition.

Having anticipated the war and decided to stay out of it from as early as 1936, de Valera's government spent only 5 per cent of its annual budget on defence; countries like Holland and Denmark were allocating between 20 and 25 per cent of their budgets to defence. He realised it would be in Britain's interest to help defend Ireland against attack. 'Would Britain just stand aside and allow us to be attacked by an outside State?' de Valera asked the Dáil in July 1938. 'If we should be attacked by an outside State, Britain would, if she felt that she was going to be affected by the result, be interested in giving to us any aid that we might ask.'[7]

Once the war began, however, the comparatively defenceless state of the country made it all the more necessary to stay out of the conflict. The Irish Army consisted of 7,263 regular soldiers. They were only intended to deal with the internal threat posed by the IRA; they were not equipped to resist an invasion by a modern military force. Military reserves were called up and the Army's ranks swelled to over 19,000 by the end of September 1939, but there were hardly enough rifles for all of them. The Navy consisted of two small fishery protection vessels, *Muirchú* and *Fort Rannock*, which had only light armaments and 12-pounder guns. The Air Corps did not yet exist; there were only eight light anti-craft guns to cover the whole country, and just four aircraft searchlights. Since the full extent of the evil of Fascism would not become apparent until much later, there was an overwhelming Irish consensus in favour of avoiding involvement in the war.

On Saturday, 2 September 1939, a special sitting of the Oireachtas (Parliament) was held, not to debate whether Ireland should declare war but to pass emergency legislation to facilitate efforts to keep the country out of the conflict. The government proclaimed an emergency and legislation was rushed through the Dáil and Senate during the one-day sitting. The Constitution permitted the use of Emergency Powers in time of war, but legislation was necessary to stipulate that 'in time of war' applied to the existing situation, even though Ireland was not actually at war.

'In this country there are sympathies, very strong sympathies, in regard to present issues, but I do not think that anybody, no matter what his feelings might be, would suggest that the Government policy, the official policy of the State, should be other than what the Government suggests,' de Valera told the Dáil.[8] Only two members of the Oireachtas—Sir John Keane and Frank MacDermot, both Senators—expressed reservations about the government's policy, but each admitted the government was doing what the electorate desired.

'I quite admit, as a practical politician, that the vast majority of the people of this country are in favour of a policy of neutrality, and that it would not be practicable at present for any Government to follow any other policy,' MacDermot told the Senate. 'I do not think it is right,' he added.[9] Keane and MacDermot mounted only token opposition and all stages of the legislation were passed without difficulty.

Many of the Irish in Britain clearly agreed with the Irish decision to stay out of the war and they expressed their approval with their feet. There were mass scenes of confusion at Paddington and Euston railroad stations in London and at the ports of Fishguard and Holyhead as thousands of Irish women and their English-born children headed for Ireland. A special correspondent of the *Cork Examiner* depicted 'pathetic scenes at the stations as young husbands said 'good-bye' to their wives and children', but as the trains drew out, he noted, 'there was relief in the knowledge that they would be comparatively safe in Éire'.[10]

'It's a great relief to get my wife and five-month-old baby away to her people in Cavan,' one air-raid warden explained. 'I would be worrying about her and the baby while on duty in air raids in London and wondering if anything happened to them. In Cavan she has her people to take care of her.'[11]

Adding to the confusion, the two stations were blacked out and the trains had only a few small blue lights. The mail train from Euston to Holyhead ran in four separate sections to accommodate more than 5,000 passengers, and there were three special trains running from Paddington to Fishguard. These were so crowded that there was no segregation between first-, second- and third-class passengers. People just grabbed any space they could get in carriages that bore more than double their normal complement. Passengers were mostly women and children, bringing meagre belongings with them, including cots and prams.

There was even more confusion at the various ports. The luggage of some passengers had to be carried on a later boat, which added greatly to the disorder at the other end. The B&I steamer from Liverpool arrived at the North Wall, Dublin, more than five hours late after two people fell overboard, in separate incidents, and had to be rescued.

The next morning, Sunday, 3 September, Neville Chamberlain announced in a radio broadcast that the deadline for the withdrawal of German forces from Poland had expired without any communication from Hitler, and therefore Britain was at war with Germany. Within minutes a Royal Air Force (RAF) seaplane set down in Irish waters, in Dun Laoghaire harbour, about 10 miles south of Dublin. It had been flying from Pembroke to Stranraer with another plane when they became separated. Nobody attempted to disembark; the plane just sat there for over two hours.

At around 2.00 p.m. another plane set down, this one off the seaside village of Skerries, north of Dublin. The pilot, Squadron Leader M.C. Collins, went ashore and made some telephone calls from the local Garda station. The plane at Dun Laoghaire then flew to Skerries and set down beside the other aircraft. Rumours spread through Dublin that a British invasion force was just off the coast. Numerous people went out to the two aircraft in small boats and were given guided tours, while Squadron Leader Collins waited onshore as the Irish authorities decided what to do next. It had never occurred to the pilot that he and his crew might be interned; they had taken off before Chamberlain's broadcast. After consulting de Valera, it was decided that the airmen should be treated as distressed mariners and allowed to leave. Collins returned to his aircraft and at about 5.00 p.m. the two planes then took off.

It was a busy day in Dublin—the All-Ireland Hurling final was being played in Croke Park between Kilkenny and Cork, which was captained by future Taoiseach Jack Lynch, who later said that he was much more concerned that day about Cork's defeat than the outbreak of war abroad. That evening de Valera went on Radio Éireann to explain his policy and announce an extensive Cabinet reshuffle. Two new ministries were established to deal with the special problems caused by the war. Seán Lemass was appointed Minister for Supplies and Frank Aiken was named Minister for Co-ordination of Defensive Measures, while Gerald Boland went to Justice and Oscar Traynor to Defence. With the lone exception of James Ryan at Agriculture, de Valera moved all his ministerial colleagues to different portfolios, but he retained External Affairs himself. Despite the extensive nature of the changes, he only introduced one new face into the Cabinet—P.J. Little, as Minister for Posts and Telegraphs.

A number of special trains were put on to cater for people coming from England and those attending the hurling final. At the various stops along the way there were chaotic scenes as women tried to get off the trains, dragging their belongings and trying to cope with cranky and crying children who had been travelling for more than twenty-four hours. To make matter worse, the trains and stations were blacked out. Notwithstanding the numbers who got off at the various stations along the way, the trains were still crowded on reaching the end of the line.

'When the special excursion train to Dublin for the all-Ireland hurling final arrived in Tralee last night, it was packed to suffocation with Irish people returning from England,' the *Kerry Champion* reported. 'All those arriving showed signs of exhaustion and particularly the children.'[12]

The same evening another drama was playing out some 250 miles off the Irish coast, when a German submarine torpedoed the passenger liner *Athenia*, sailing from Glasgow to Montreal. The sinking of the ship, with the loss of 112 lives, revived haunting memories of the sinking of the *Lusitania* off the Cork coast in 1915. Several ships raced to the scene to pick up 1,306 survivors. The *Knut Nelson*, an oil tanker, picked up 430 people and headed for Galway, where it docked two days later.[13]

German authorities welcomed the Irish decision to remain neutral because it meant Irish facilities would be denied to British naval vessels, submarines and military aircraft. On 5 September the British Cabinet was told that de Valera 'had expressed the desire to help', but Winston Churchill—who had just been appointed First Lord of the Admiralty and was, as such, the minister in charge of naval affairs—was highly sceptical.[14] He asked the First Sea Lord for a report on the issues 'arising from the so-called neutrality of the so-called Éire'.[15] He stipulated the report should cover two areas in particular:

Firstly, what does Intelligence say about possible succouring of U-boats by Irish malcontents in West of Ireland inlets? If they throw bombs in London, why should they not supply fuel to U-boats? Extreme vigilance should be practiced. Secondly, a study is required of the reduction to the radius of our destroyers through not having the use of Berehaven or other South Irish anti-submarine bases; show also the advantages to be gained of our having these facilities.[16]

In short, Churchill was looking for a report that would be critical of the denial of Irish bases.

'What is the position on the West coast of Ireland?' he asked the Director of Naval Intelligence the following day. 'Are there any signs of succouring U-boats in Irish creeks or inlets? It would seem money should be spent to secure a trustworthy body of Irish agents to keep most vigilant watch. Has this been done?'[17]

John Dulanty presented the British with an *aide-memoire* on 12 September, emphasising that Irish territorial waters and bases would be closed to all aircraft and vessels of war. The British wished to voice their disapproval to de Valera personally, but they had no representative in Ireland.

De Valera's cabinet had agreed the previous week to approach the British about appointing a representative. The Chamberlain government decided to appoint Sir John Maffey, who had retired a short time earlier after a distinguished career in the colonial service and at the Colonial Office, where he had risen to post of Permanent Under-Secretary. It was first necessary, however, to settle a diplomatic impasse between Dublin and London over the title of his post. Maffey arrived at the Department of Agriculture on 14 September, using an arranged pseudonym, and was taken to de Valera's office at the other end of Government Buildings for a secret meeting. De Valera wished that Maffey be called Ambassador or Minister, like the German representative, but the British preferred the title of High Commissioner—the diplomatic term used by representatives of one dominion accredited to another. John Dulanty, for instance, had the title of Irish High Commissioner in London. The Chamberlain government proposed a compromise by designating Maffey as 'British Representative in Ireland' and agreed to de Valera's amendment, calling him 'British Representative to Ireland'. De Valera told Maffey he was trying to avoid handing the IRA and extremist elements grounds for shouting that 'Dublin Castle' was back again.[18]

This was not the time for squabbling. Maffey reported the discussion was 'very natural and easy, and certainly more cordial that I expected'.[19] The main issue he sought to address at the time concerned a neutrality memorandum presented by Dulanty in London a couple of days earlier. This had provoked 'a grave difficulty' at Whitehall. 'It was fully understood that Éire had adopted a policy of neutrality and the emphasising of that policy in general terms must be expected,' Maffey explained. 'But this rigid *aide-memoire*, dotting the "i's" and crossing the "t's" in the way of stringent rules affecting British ships and aircraft, had been read with profound feelings of disappointment.'

Maffey pleaded that the document should not be released as it would add to Chamberlain's difficulties. De Valera reacted immediately to the reference to Chamberlain. 'He expressed the deepest admiration for and sympathy with the Prime Minister,' Maffey noted.

'He has done everything that a man could do to prevent this tragedy,' de Valera said. 'There was a time when I would have done anything in my power to help destroy the British Empire. But my position has changed.'[20]

De Valera talked 'at some length of the difficulties of his position', with his every action being scrutinised by men who were bitterly opposed to any rapprochement with Britain and who were particularly 'critical of any wavering from the straight path of neutrality', according to Maffey. 'All this happens because you maintain the principle of partition in this island,' de Valera argued. He pointed to a map on the wall with Éire in 'jet-black', while Northern Ireland was 'a leprous white'. According to Maffey's report, de Valera continued:

> Why did not our Prime Minister put his foot down and stop the follies and oppressions of Northern Ireland? Look at what a picture we might have! A united, independent Ireland. Think of the effect in America where the Irish element had ruined and would ruin any possibility of Anglo-American understanding! Why could we not see where the flaw in our armour lay? It was not a matter of religion. The Protestant minority in Éire today were happy and contented. The Northern element would be of real use to England as part of the whole body politic of the island. The petty tyrannies and oppressions now going on in Northern Ireland must lead to disaster. 'If I lived there,' he exclaimed, 'I should say "I'll be damned if I'll be ruled by these people"'.

As de Valera saw it, the longer the war went on, the greater the danger would be of a physical clash over Northern Ireland. There was naked discrimination against the Roman Catholic minority in Northern Ireland in the areas of employment and housing. 'My friends in America say to me,' he added, 'Why don't you take a leaf out of Hitler's book and work the Sudeten-Deutsch trick in Northern Ireland?'[21]

The Irish-Americans were important because they provided Ireland with the best protection, especially against the British. In the following weeks

Churchill would advocate violating Irish neutrality, but in the last analysis both he and his Cabinet colleagues would draw back from the brink, for fear of provoking Irish-Americans and the damage this could do to Anglo-American relations.

The Taoiseach said that he could not rule out the possibility of German submarines receiving some Irish assistance, but 'he would do his utmost to prevent it'. He wished to help the British in relation to submarines, so he was adopting strict rules towards them. But if he only made orders against submarines, this would be seen as purely anti-German; therefore he was going to apply a similar policy to naval vessels and aircraft.

'Why tie your hands?' Maffey asked.

When the British aircraft set down at Dun Laoghaire and Skerries on the day Britain declared war, the Taoiseach said he had turned a blind eye and the newspaper editors were instructed not to report the incidents, but those were still the subject of widespread comment.

'How could this continue?' de Valera asked.

Suddenly the telephone rang and, after a brief telephone conversation, de Valera turned to Maffey. 'There you are!' he said. 'One of your planes is down in Ventry Bay. What am I to do?'

An RAF seaplane, with twelve men on board, had set down in Ventry Harbour, near Dingle, in County Kerry, at 9.00 a.m. that morning. The pilot and a mechanic went ashore with a broken fuel pipe and a passing motorist took them to Dingle, where the mechanic repaired the pipe in a garage.

De Valera said he would have to intern the crew. 'It was quite obvious he found this course most unpalatable,' Maffey reported. 'I said that in view of the Skerries precedent he should warn the British Government before introducing internment in any such cases. The men concerned had probably had no warning of any such possibility.'

According to Maffey, both he and de Valera 'were much relieved when the telephone rang again an hour later to report that the plane had managed to get away—or rather had been allowed to get away.' Maffey left convinced that even though de Valera planned to stay out of the war, he wished 'to help us within the limits of that neutrality to the full extent possible'.

The British were not only unwilling to guarantee to respect Irish neutrality, they even refused to accept that the country had a right to remain neutral. 'We do not want formally to recognise Éire as neutral while Éire remains a member of the British Commonwealth,' Dominion Secretary Anthony Eden wrote on 16 September. 'To do this would be to surrender the hitherto accepted constitutional theory of the indivisibility of the Crown. Equally we do not want to take the line that Éire is no longer a member of the British Commonwealth.'[22] The London government had, in fact, accepted the principle of the divisibility of the Crown in 1937, when the King authorised the formal appointment of the Irish Minister to the court of the King of Italy as Emperor of Ethiopia, at a time when Britain was still refusing to recognise Italy's annexation of Ethiopia. Now the British were trying to reverse things, by grasping at straws.

Eden realised that any infringement of Irish neutrality might provoke unfortunate repercussions, 'particularly on United States opinion'.[23] But Maffey was nonetheless instructed to tell de Valera 'that the present situation might rapidly become a very grave one in which the questions at issue would not be a matter of politics but of vital concern to this country'.[24]

In time, the British would become particularly concerned about German people in Ireland. Among the influx from Britain were a couple of Germans who would later be arrested for spying for their home country. The British already suspected Werner Unland, who was married to an English woman; the pair had fled to Dublin just before the outbreak of the war. Another, Wilhelm Preetz, claimed that he arrived in Ireland on 2 September. He was married to an Irish woman, Sarah Josephine Reynolds of Tuam, County Galway. He had previously visited Ireland in 1937 and 1938 and stayed with his in-laws, so his presence did not attract attention initially.

Irish Military Intelligence (G2) had already set up links with its British counterpart (MI5), and there was concern over contacts between the IRA and some of the German colony. There was considerable relief, therefore, when most of the recognised Nazis decided to return to Germany. The British facilitated more than fifty of these Germans by allowing them to travel through Britain. 'Some of them are technicians who will be useful to the enemy but I think that we should be well-advised to let them go through,' Guy Liddell, head of counter-intelligence at MI5, advised. Otherwise they would probably remain in Ireland, which 'would be extremely undesirable'.[25]

The Germans being repatriated included Colonel Fritz Brase, the director of the Irish Army's school of music; Friedrich Herkner, professor of sculpture at the National College of Art; Otto Reinhard, director of forestry in the Department of Lands; Froed Weckller, chief accountant of the Electricity Supply Board; Heinz Mecking, an adviser with the Turf Development Board; and Helmut Clissmann, who was in charge of the German Academic Exchange Service in Dublin. Hempel saw them off at Dun Laoghaire as they departed for Holyhead, whence they were taken across England by train, in sealed carriages guarded by British military, before boarding a boat bound for the Continent. Some of them played roles within the German bureaucracy in the formulation of policy towards Ireland in the following years.

Meeting de Valera for a second time, on 20 September 1939, Maffey warned that Irish bases might become essential for Britain's survival. 'If such action is vital, we shall have to take it,' Maffey said. 'But we must think twice and count the gain and the loss.'[26] In the hope of staving off that fateful day, he advocated joint Anglo-Irish patrols.

Although de Valera rejected such patrols, he did come up with an idea to help Britain while at the same time preserving the appearance of strict neutrality. Once Irish authorities located any submarine or belligerent aircraft, the information of its whereabouts would be reported on radio. 'Not to you especially,' he said. 'Your Admiralty must pick it up. We shall wireless it to the world. I will tell the German Minister of our intention to do this.'[27] This would be of no assistance to the Germans because they were too far from Ireland to use such information; the British, on the other hand, were close enough to react.

'The whole fabric of neutrality is beginning to look healthier from our point of view,' Maffey wrote. Before the meeting ended, Maffey was again given the map treatment. De Valera led him to the black map of Ireland with its white blemish on the north-east corner. 'There's the real source of all the trouble,' he said.

'He could not let me go without that,' wrote Maffey.[28]

'All this talk about partition,' Churchill wrote to the Deputy Chief of Naval Affairs on 24 September, 'and the bitterness that would be healed by a union of Northern Ireland and Southern Ireland will amount to nothing. They will not unite at the present time, and we cannot in any circumstances sell the loyalists of Northern Ireland.' Ever a man to rely on his own intuition, Churchill dismissed the 1938 judgment of the Chiefs of Staff that naval facilities in southern Ireland were not important to Britain. He railed against Irish neutrality, which he refused to believe had the support of the vast majority of the Irish people. 'Three-quarters of the people of Southern Ireland are with us, but the implacable, malignant minority can make so much trouble that de Valera dare not do anything to offend them,' Churchill contended.[29]

The Irish were really interfering with a grand plan that Churchill had in his own mind of the United States and Britain constructing a strong navy to protect the world against Nazism, but he realised that too many American isolationists were opposed to the idea—'too many Irish haters of England, too many people that would prefer to remain outside England's sphere'.[30] As Secretary of the Navy during World War I Roosevelt was the American counterpart of Churchill, who had also served as First Lord of the Admiralty. In September 1939 Churchill was barely back in the office a week when Roosevelt wrote to him: 'It is because you and I occupied similar positions in the World War that I want you to know how glad I am that you are back in the Admiralty. What I want you and the Prime Minister to know is that I shall at all times welcome it if you would keep me in touch personally with anything you want me to know about.'[31]

It was an extraordinary proposal, for the head of one government to establish correspondence with an ordinary Cabinet member of another government. Churchill obtained the approval of Chamberlain and Lord Halifax, the Foreign Secretary, before responding. Roosevelt and Churchill would eventually exchange some 1,688 messages of various kinds during the war, in addition to a number of telephone conversations.

The British were inclined to believe the most ridiculous rumours about Ireland. 'Frequent reports coming about submarine bases on the west coast of Éire,' Guy Liddell noted in his operational diary on 22 September 1939. Such reports fuelled Churchill's suspicions.[32] Two days later, on 24 September, Churchill outlined his views in a note to the Deputy Chief of Naval Staff headed, 'General Principles for the Admiralty Attitude towards Southern Ireland':

> There seems to be a good deal of evidence, or at any rate suspicion, that u-boats were being succoured from West of Ireland ports by the malignant section with whom de Valera dare not interfere. If the u-boat campaign became more dangerous we should coerce Southern Ireland both about coast watching and the use of Berehaven, etc.[33]

In theory, de Valera's promise to radio reports of u-boat sightings to Dublin seemed good, but at the outset none of the eighty-two lookout posts scattered around the coast had any telephone. Somebody had to cycle or walk anything up to 12 miles to the nearest Garda station to telephone word of the sighting, so that that word could be radioed on to Dublin. Nevertheless the British were allowed to take steps of their own, and base a spotter aircraft at Foynes, County Limerick. Officially it was testing equipment, but actually it was scouring the Irish coast looking for u-boats lurking in prominent and obscure Irish bays and harbours. It never found any.[34]

Chapter 3 ∾

CHURCHILL'S DANGEROUS DESIGNS

On 3 October, when he officially took up his post as British Representative to Ireland, Maffey met de Valera for two hours. 'I again explained to him the dangers which lay ahead for him unless our Admiralty were really satisfied through direct contact with his organization.' Shortly after this meeting, Walshe of the Department of External Affairs 'phoned urgently about a U-boat in Dingle Bay'.[1]

At 5.30 p.m. on the evening of 4 October 1939, residents of Ventry watched in amazement as a U-boat entered the same harbour where an RAF aircraft had put down a fortnight earlier. The *U-35* dropped off twenty-eight men—survivors from a Greek freighter, *Diamantis*, which the U-boat had sunk off the south-west coast of England two days earlier. One of the Greek lifeboats overturned in the rough seas. The Germans rescued the men and the U-boat commander, *Kapitaenleutnant* Werner Lott, invited those in a second lifeboat to board the submarine. They were kept under guard, but treated very kindly. The Germans offered them their beds and told them to make themselves comfortable.

'During the 36 hours we were on the submarine we had our meals as regularly as the crew, and they were quite good meals,' Paderas Panagos, the master of the *Diamantis*, told reporters.[2]

'When the Greek sailors said good-bye to me on the conning tower, they went on their knees and kissed my wedding ring as if I was a bishop,' Lott recalled.[3]

'We owe our lives to you,' the sailors told Lott. 'You have treated us very nicely.'

While the U-boat was in the harbour about thirty local people gathered on the shore. Séamus Fenton, a local boy, was amazed at the attitude of the Greeks towards the Germans who had sunk their ship. 'German skipper, goot man,' they kept saying.[4]

The incident increased Churchill's alarm. The war was not even two weeks old when he told the War Cabinet a fanciful story about the crew of a u-boat supposedly going ashore in Ireland. He said they were found in possession of Irish cigarettes after their submarine was sunk.[5]

The U-35 incident received 'a good deal' of publicity in Canada, according to the Irish High Commissioner, and the story made the cover of *Life* magazine in the United States.[6] Ireland was in the international news again a couple of days later after *Grossadmiral* Eric Reader, the head of the German Navy, warned the us Naval Attaché in Berlin that a 'very reliable' source in neutral Ireland had warned that the American ship *Iroquois* was going to be sunk in the Atlantic by the British in an attempt to blame Germany and thereby inflame American opinion and bring the United States into the war.[7] The *Iroquois* was already about 1,000 miles west of Ireland, with 566 Americans on board. Churchill telephoned Roosevelt on 5 October to suggest the main threat to the ship would be if a time-bomb had been planted on the vessel during a stopover in Cobh two days earlier.

'We think this not impossible,' he explained.[8] He suggested Roosevelt should publish the full facts without delay, especially his source for the information. The ship was met in the Atlantic on 8 October by a us coastguard cutter and two naval destroyers, which escorted it safely into New York harbour three days later. (The *Iroquois* was afterwards converted into a hospital ship and served in the Pacific under the name of *Solace*.)

When the U-35 returned to Germany in mid-October, the crew was celebrated on the cover of *Die Wehrmacht*. Admiral Karl Donitz, the head of the German u-boat service, greeted the submarine and Lott was decorated with the Iron Cross, although Donitz privately admonished him for endangering the lives of his men. The U-35 was sunk in the North Sea on its next tour of duty, on the morning of 29 November 1939. Badly damaged by depth charges, the vessel surfaced involuntarily and Lott ordered his men to abandon ship. Much to his surprise, the British stopped in the water and picked up all thirty-one members of the crew. They were imprisoned for a time in the Tower of London, where Earl Louis Mountbatten, the rear admiral in charge of the British flotilla that sank the U-35, visited Lott, who thanked him for rescuing his crew and treating them so honourably.

'That is how life is,' Mountbatten replied. 'You were extraordinary picking up the Greeks.'[9]

The extensive publicity surrounding the U-35 embarrassed the Dublin government because it gave credence to wild rumours about u-boat activity off the Irish coast. Even MI5 seemed to believe some of the stories. 'Éire's neutrality is rapidly becoming a farce,' Guy Liddell noted in the MI5 diary on 12 October. 'German sub sailed into Dingle for repairs.'[10]

Churchill, who was not only ready but apparently eager to believe such stories, posed the biggest danger to Irish neutrality because he was establishing a growing influence within the British Cabinet. He was also serving as the main link between Cabinet and the White House, because Roosevelt had become particularly wary of his Ambassador to Britain, Joe Kennedy. On the morning of 3 September 1939 Kennedy telephoned Roosevelt at 4.00 a.m. (Washington time), before Chamberlain delivered his famous broadcast. The Prime Minister had shown him the text of the speech, and Kennedy was deeply moved. 'Everything that I have worked for, everything that I have hoped for, everything that I have believed in during my public life has crashed in ruins,' Chamberlain planned to say. This resonated with Kennedy. 'It is the end of the world, the end of everything,' he told Roosevelt on the telephone.[11]

'There are signs of decay, if not decadence, here, both in men and institutions,' Kennedy wrote to Roosevelt from Britain at the end of the first month of the conflict. 'Democracy as we now conceive it in the United States will not exist in France and England after the war, regardless of which side wins or loses.'[12] He feared the Allies and the Axis would wear themselves out, and the communists would be the ultimate victors. Kennedy seemed to share Chamberlain's outlook, and it was significant that Roosevelt suggested his ambassador should 'put some iron up Chamberlain's backside'.[13]

Shortly before the war broke out, Kennedy telegraphed the State Department that the British Ambassador in Berlin had reported that Hitler would 'make a deal with England that would guarantee the British Empire forever' and that he 'would go back to peaceful pursuits and become an artist, which was what he wanted to be'.[14] Roosevelt just laughed; after the way Hitler violated the Munich Agreement, one would have to be very gullible to believe him. Even after the war began, Kennedy still hoped the President could intervene to halt the conflict. 'I believe that it is entirely conceivable that the President can get himself in a spot where he can save the world,' Kennedy wrote to the State Department on 11 September.[15] In the following days he floated ideas as to how Roosevelt could mediate to end the conflict, including a suggestion that the President behave like a 'combination of Jack Dempsey and the Holy Ghost'.[16] Roosevelt told Jim Farley it was 'the silliest message' he ever received.[17]

From the Irish perspective, Churchill's judgment was just as flawed in relation to Ireland. For instance, Churchill told the British Cabinet that Irish ports were indispensable to Britain's security, and he produced a report by the Chief of Naval Staff concluding it was 'of vital importance' that Ireland's 'waters shall be available for the use of the Navy which protects Irish as well as British trade and soil'.[18] His pressure on Admiral John Godfrey, the head of

Naval Intelligence, to report on possible German submarine activity in Irish waters prompted the admiral to have the submarine *H33* begin patrolling the south and west coasts of Ireland on 10 October. A converted British Navy trawler escorted the submarine. An RAF plane observed a U-boat in Donegal Bay on 18 October and another U-boat was sighted off Valentia Island, County Kerry, two days later, but *H33* and the trawler saw no sign of any submarine activity during their nine-day sweep of Irish harbours on the west coast.

On 14 October the Royal Navy suffered a grievous setback when a German U-boat penetrated the defences at Scapa Flow in the Orkney Islands, off north-east Scotland, and sank the battleship *Royal Oak* at anchor, with the loss of 833 sailors. Irish ports would have provided no protection for Scapa Flow, but Churchill fulminated over the denial of Berehaven and Lough Swilly. 'The time has come to make it clear to the Irish Government that we must have the use of these harbours and intended in any case to use them,' he insisted.[19] The War Cabinet decided Eden should advise on the best way to approach de Valera, and Churchill should formulate the reasons for such an approach. In drawing up those reasons, Churchill admitted he had 'perhaps rather overstated' the need for Irish anchorages, but he urged Eden to 'do everything in his power to persuade de Valera to meet us over the question of Berehaven as soon as possible'.[20]

While the agreement handing over the ports in 1938 had been unconditional, Maffey was instructed to say the British had 'always felt' that 'emergency circumstances might arise which rendered it imperative, in the interest of both countries, that such facilities should be accorded. These circumstances have now arisen.'[21] Maffey was to ask de Valera for the use of Berehaven, but there were divided opinions within the British government.

Dominions Secretary Anthony Eden was already sceptical about 'our woolly plans'. He warned Foreign Secretary Lord Halifax that de Valera could not hand over any ports, and Britain was not in a position to seize them. 'I fear that it has become every day clearer that it is scarcely possible for 'Dev' to square neutrality with the grant of the facilities for which the Admiralty ask,' Eden wrote. 'At least 80% of the Irish people favour neutrality. Altogether a pretty problem.'[22]

During a 90-minute meeting on 21 October, de Valera refused Maffey's request for Berehaven. 'He maintained that there could have been no mental reservations on our side justifying any belief that Éire would adopt any particular course in the event of a world conflict,' Maffey reported. 'I said that nevertheless such mental reservations had existed, and that the path of generosity had been followed as an act of faith and in the belief that in the hour of need the hand of friendship would be extended.'[23]

'If we had paved the way to Irish unity, Ireland today might—only "might" have been able to cooperate with us,' the Taoiseach continued, according to Maffey. 'He would greatly regret a German victory. His sympathies were with the Allies, but if there was on the whole, perhaps, a vague majority sentiment in favour of the Allies, any encroachment upon an Irish interest would create a swift swing over of opinion. Many people in Ireland were ready enough to acclaim a British defeat at any price, though that view might be based on ignorance. It had its roots in history.'

'His policy has been quite consistent,' Maffey wrote. 'His goal had been to maintain neutrality and to help us within the limits of that neutrality to the full extent possible. The measures arranged with me in regard to information and liaison were all evidence of this, and of the fact that he was being helpful, perhaps beyond the strict definition of neutrality.'[24]

'England has a moral position today,' de Valera said. 'Hitler might have his early successes, but the moral position would tell.' Seizing Irish ports would, however, shake that 'position of moral strength'.

'Not if help were voluntarily conceded,' Maffey argued.

'No, but that would stir up trouble which would quickly compromise your moral position,' the Taoiseach insisted.

From the outset the Irish cooperated in forwarding weather information. The British had taken responsibility for collecting weather data in Ireland until 1936, when the Irish meteorological service was established under British supervision. Various British and European meteorologists staffed it, until the first Irishman was recruited in 1939. Throughout the war the Irish regularly forwarded weather reports to the British. These were encrypted from 1941.

The Irish had further demonstrated the benevolence of their neutrality by raising no objection to handing over seven Irish-registered oil tankers to the British registry in September 1939, and Dublin agreed to a British request not to charter neutral ships except through Britain. In this way Anglo-Irish competition for neutral shipping could be eliminated in order to keep chartering rates down. No efforts were made to prevent Irish people from going to Britain to volunteer for British forces or to work in factories. In fact, the de Valera government, which was confronted with chronic unemployment at home, actually encouraged this emigration by ordering that the British Ministry of Labour's *National Clearing House Gazette* be displayed at employment exchanges throughout Ireland.

Maffey warned that London should not be blinded by de Valera's refusal to hand over Berehaven because there was a bright side to his policy, as shown by:

(a) The instant reporting of the u-boat in Dingle Bay.
(b) Arrangement for signalling to us of presence and whereabouts of enemy submarines.
(c) Acceptance of a naval attaché with facilities for travelling and checking up the efficiency of Eire coastal watch and war service.
(d) Holding up, at my request, a series of emergency orders implementing neutrality in detail.
(e) Retention of Admiralty tug at Cobh.
(f) Acceptance of the fact, whatever the regulations may be, our surface craft will pursue and attack hostile submarines in the territorial waters of Éire.
(g) Exclusion from instructions to coastal organisations of any mention of aircraft. Today our aircraft are flying over the headlands of Éire, and even inland, and nothing is being said.[25]

Next day, Walshe informed Maffey that the British could station a tug at Berehaven for rescue purposes, and he added that they could ask for facilities for a further tug later on. 'It is quite understood and agreed that the tug or tugs will carry a gun,' Maffey explained. 'I hope this facility may be of use to the Admiralty. I was not authorised to make the suggestion but it seemed to me to be the moment to try to get something.'[26]

As Maffey was due to go to London to report on his meeting, de Valera sent him 'a message asking me to assure Mr Chamberlain of his genuine friendship, but to tell him that he could not grant what was impossible'.[27] De Valera considered Chamberlain a truly great statesman and was convinced posterity would restore his reputation. In the lead-up to the war the Taoiseach considered the Polish corridor an incongruity and felt that Czechoslovakia would easily have justified adjustment.

> In the United States the Allies' cause would never have found the support it did unless Chamberlain had first exhausted all peaceful methods, nor would the people of England have been united back of the war the way they are now. It is true that in the light of wisdom Hitler's moves in Poland and Czechoslovakia were but a part of bigger schemes.

However, this only became apparent later, when Hitler invaded other countries. Chamberlain would never have had the same moral position if he had gone to war at the time of the Munich crisis. On the whole, the Taoiseach believed Chamberlain's 'statesmanship was far-sighted'.[28]

While de Valera did not publicise his Allied bias, this should have been obvious to Irish people from the attitude of the *Irish Press* newspaper, which he essentially controlled. During the early weeks of the war editorials in the *Irish Press* commended the Poles for fighting gallantly. Following the partitioning of Poland by Germany and the Soviet Union, the *Irish Press* remarked that 'to all intents and purposes, Russia and Germany are now in the closest alliance'.[29] Yet in the following weeks the newspaper was blisteringly critical of the Russian communists, especially following the Soviet invasion of Finland.

Foreign Secretary Halifax obviously agreed with Anthony Eden in relation to Ireland. Halifax told the British Cabinet on 22 October, 'Éire is to be regarded as a neutral state'.[30] But Churchill complained afterwards that the neutrality proclaimed by de Valera was in no way similar to the declarations of neutrality by Holland or Switzerland. 'What is the international judicial status of Southern Ireland?' Churchill asked. 'It is not a Dominion. They themselves repudiate the idea. It is certainly under the Crown. Nothing has been defined. Legally I believe they are "At war but skulking"'.[31]

The British War Cabinet discussed the issue of Irish ports at some length on 24 October. Churchill argued that Britain 'should challenge the constitutional position of Éire's neutrality'. Unlike the dominions, which were thousands of miles away, 'Éire was an integral part of the British Isles', he argued. As the submarine menace grew, he contended Britain would have to 'insist' on the use of Irish harbours. At the time, he said, Éire 'was having the best of both worlds' in that it had the advantages of being considered a British dominion without assuming the responsibilities. It should therefore be brought home to the Irish government what they 'stood to lose in being declared a foreign power'.[32]

Three courses were open to the British, according to Eden: they could seek further discussions with de Valera, which he thought pointless; they could accept de Valera's attitude and work on him to get further minor concessions; or they could seize the harbours they desired. If Britain seized the ports, Eden 'did not think that de Valera would oppose us with military force, but he would indict us before the world and rally his people against us. There would be serious repercussions in the United States and in the Dominions, and the passive support which we now receive from great numbers of Irish people would be alienated. In addition, Éire might grant facilities to the enemy.'[33]

Churchill had made a 'powerful case' about the Irish ports, according to Chamberlain, but if Britain seized them, it 'would have most unfortunate repercussions in the United States and in India, where it would be hailed as a highhanded and unwarranted action'.[34] Even Churchill appreciated the danger of antagonising American opinion, especially while the Roosevelt administration was faced with strong opposition to its efforts to repeal neutrality legislation, which prohibited any arms trading with belligerents.

'No doubt,' Churchill acknowledged, 'it would be advisable to postpone action until the United States Neutrality Act had been repealed; but we should then, having set out the judicial position and made clear to the world that we are not committing a violation of neutrality, insist on the use of the harbours.' He suggested the Cabinet 'should take stock of the weapons of coercion'. In particular, he wished to know 'the consequences to Ireland as regards trade, employment and so forth of her being declared a foreign country'.[35]

The Cabinet decided that Eden should 'take every opportunity of bringing home to the Dominions that the use of ports in Éire by the Royal Navy was essential for the security of the Empire, and that the present attitude adopted by Éire in the matter was intolerable'. Meanwhile the Lord Chancellor and Law Officers of the Crown were to 'prepare a memorandum setting out the legal and constitutional issues involved in the termination of Éire's membership of the British Commonwealth'. Eden was also to prepare 'a memorandum on the financial, economic and political considerations involved in the termination of Éire's membership of the British Commonwealth'.[36]

As the Dominions Secretary was drawing up the memorandum, Churchill wrote wondering if Eden was 'fully conscious of the grave wrong that has been done to us and to our vital interests and of the urgent need to repair it. If I were to let the public know the facts about how we are being hampered, there would be a storm of wrath against de Valera and his adherents, not only in Great Britain but in Southern Ireland, as have never been seen. The British nation has a right to know who are the enemies who are hampering our efforts to feed them.'[37]

Whatever about the likely attitude of the British people, Churchill was obviously deluded about Irish opinion. 'There is no gainsaying Mr de Valera's view that any tampering with the neutrality of the ports would raise a storm here, the consequences of which are beyond computation, and which would certainly bring him down. There is a general consensus of opinion as to that,' Maffey wrote the same day. 'It is remarkable how even the 'pro-British' group, men who have fought for the Crown and are anxious to be called up again, men whose sons are at the front to-day, loyalists in the old sense of the word, agree generally in supporting the neutrality of Éire. They see no possible practical alternative.'[38]

De Valera was being assailed at home by 'the die-harders and the Anglo element', John Cudahy wrote to Roosevelt on 27 October. 'The one accuse him of being in the vest-pocket of England, and the Anglos are contemptuous of Irish neutrality believing that this island is still part of the United Kingdom.' The British posed the main external danger to Ireland at the time, according to the American Minister. 'You as a naval man will readily appreciate this,' he wrote to Roosevelt, 'there is a real danger in the importance of Berehaven and Bantry Bay in the plans of the Admiralty. At present British destroyers must operate from Pembroke and Plymouth 200 and 300 miles further than these Irish ports. And as you know so well the most frequented approach to England is by this south-west coast of Ireland.'[39]

There was a danger Churchill might insist on seizing Bantry or Berehaven as the war intensified. 'This would be a great mistake,' Cudahy warned the President, 'for if any attempt was made by the British to occupy any part of the Irish Coast you would see the same hostility towards England that you personally witnessed here during the last war.'

Even Eden, one of Churchill's strongest backers, was disillusioned with Winston's attitude towards Ireland. 'De Valera is doing all he can for us and it would be madness to drive him further and start up all the trouble again,' Eden warned. 'And what would the USA say? Apart from that, Éire even now is our best recruiting ground.'[40]

Later it would become apparent that Churchill grossly exaggerated the importance of the Irish ports and also failed to appreciate the true implications of de Valera's policy. 'I did not succeed in getting all that I wanted from my efforts to improve relations with Éire,' Chamberlain wrote to Maffey shortly before his death, 'but like most of my failures it left something solid behind it.'[41]

'From the very first and through our darkest days,' Maffey later explained, 'Mr de Valera spoke with deep respect of Mr Chamberlain, and with well-informed understanding and approval of the course he had followed.' Chamberlain had done all he could to avoid the war and therefore deserved moral support. 'I have never found any reason to revise that opinion I formed in my vantage-point in Dublin that Neville Chamberlain laid the moral foundations on which our country triumphed and without which we might have gone under,' Maffey concluded.[42]

The IRA was anxious to strike at Britain, but the Fianna Fáil government rounded up eighty-two of its more active members. Fifteen were brought before the courts and jailed, while the other sixty-seven were interned without trial. A strict press censorship was introduced under the direction of Frank Aiken, Minister for Co-ordination of Defensive Measures, to bolster support for neutrality and to prevent people from trying to drag Ireland into the war on one side or the other. The IRA refused to submit copies of its clandestine, mimeographed *War News* to the censor. On 28 October 1939 the first issue of a sporadic run of *War News* appealed to the Irish people:

England's Difficulty—Ireland's Opportunity has ever been the watchword of the Gael. British cities and ports are now beleaguered by Germany's

Aeroplanes and Submarines. Now is the time for Irishmen to take up arms and strike a blow for our Ulster people. By destroying the Orange Ascendancy, by expelling the British Army, by abolishing the Border, *we shall cut away the cancer that is gnawing at the heart of Ireland.*[43]

Jack Neela, who organised the publication of *War News*, got his hands on a radio-transmitter smuggled from the United States. On 29 October the IRA made contact with the German military intelligence organisation, Abwehr II, with a request for arms. In the following days British Intelligence received information 'from a source with whom we are not normally in touch' that the IRA had set up a training camp in Killiney, near Dublin, under the direction of Peter O'Flaherty. 'Definite plans are being laid for the launch of an armed attack on Northern Ireland some time between Christmas 1939 and April 1940', according to the information. 'Now that Britain is engaged in a major European War, it is considered that the North could be conquered in about six weeks' time.'[44]

'Every indication points to the fact of the government having the IRA well under control,' Maffey wrote in dismissing the report. 'Peter O'Flaherty is an ex-student of Trinity and merely a joke. Germany is extremely anxious to remain on good terms with Éire, and it would not be good policy for them to assist any subversive movement in this country.'[45] O'Flaherty was already in custody, having been arrested on 9 September and sentenced to eighteen months in jail.

The German minister was urging Berlin to avoid involvement with the IRA. 'In my opinion complete restraint continued to be advisable for us,' Hempel telegraphed Berlin in mid-November. 'In view of the wide-spread aversion to present-day Germany, especially for religious reasons, this could rob the IRA of all chances of future success. England would be given a pretext for intervening' in Ireland.[46] In a further telegram at the end of the month, Hempel suggested Germany should allow Britain to violate Irish neutrality first.

While others appreciated the secret Irish cooperation, Churchill remained highly critical. On 21 November he presented Cabinet colleagues with a memorandum drawn up by Admiral Godfrey, depicting Éire as 'a centre for enemy espionage' that was 'much affected by enemy penetration' due to the German diplomatic presence. He also noted it was 'a base of U-boats', though the memorandum acknowledged that the term 'base' was being 'used loosely' because there was 'no evidence proving the existence of refuelling base, [but] there was evidence to show that U-boats were at least using Eire territorial waters for the purposes of occasional rest, and quite possibly were also landing crews for purposes of relaxation and obtaining fresh provisions.'[47]

The report ridiculed the Irish coast-watching cooperation on the grounds that a number of U-boat sightings had not been reported. U-boat sightings by an Irish aircraft had been radioed to Dublin *en clair* on four different days, the report acknowledged, but other than those, 'no reports whatever have reached this country through the Eire coast-watching organisation, excepting the possible case of the U-boat which landed the Diamantis crew in Dingle Bay'. Maffey was quite positive about having been informed immediately, but Churchill's staff was not impressed. 'This report could hardly have failed to reach us as it was given wide and immediate publicity in the press.'[48]

Churchill wished to be authorised to have Secret Intelligence Service (MI6) establish an espionage network in Ireland. But Eden contended they should wait until after Captain Alexander Boyd Greig, the newly appointed British Naval Attaché, had a chance to evaluate the Irish coast-watching facilities. With the cooperation of the Irish authorities, Boyd Greig had recently begun a tour of inspection. Eden noted that other U-boat sightings had, in fact, been reported by the Irish, 'but owing to some misunderstanding about the wavelength, these had not been received by the Admiralty'.[49]

Leslie Hoare-Belisha, the Secretary of State for War, noted that there were excellent relations between MI5 and G2, and 'it would be quite impossible' for MI6 'to obtain the information now being received by MI5 from Colonel Archer, who had the whole machinery of the Eire Government at his disposal'. Although Churchill 'did not consider that there was much to be gained by waiting for the report of the Naval Attaché', he was overruled initially.[50] A fortnight earlier the Irish had agreed to the re-routing of a telegraph cable through London that had previously come directly to Ireland from the Continent.[51] Nevertheless MI6 did set up secret operations in Ireland in the final weeks of 1939.[52]

In November the submarine *H43* took over the task of patrolling the west coast of Ireland with the armed trawler, *Tamura*, under Lieutenant Commander W.R. Fell, who was described by Admiral Godfrey as 'not only adventurous but also credulous'. At one stage he went ashore chasing a suspected spy and got himself arrested by the Irish police, but they released him the following day.[53] In three months the *H33*, *H43* and the *Tamura* failed to detect any German submarine in Irish waters. They repeatedly scoured Irish coastal waters, from Cork to Donegal. Robert Fisk concluded the futile patrols 'were not only steering illegally through the neutral waters of Éire but were also navigating the wider oceans of Churchill's own vivid imagination'.[54]

The Dublin government suffered a serious setback in early December, when the High Court ruled that the law under which an internee was being held was unconstitutional and directed that the internee be released. The State attempted to appeal that decision, but the Supreme Court held there could be no appeal from the granting of an order of *habeas corpus*. The Government therefore felt compelled to release all of the Republican internees. Many had been on hunger strike for several weeks, and this appeared a victory for them.[55] On 23 December the IRA pulled off another coup with a raid on the Army's Magazine Fort, but it soon proved to be a pyrrhic victory. The government moved swiftly to plug the loophole in the emergency legislation, while most of the stolen material was quickly recovered, along with a considerable amount of the IRA's previous arsenal.

Chapter 4

IRISH-AMERICANS, FDR AND THE EUROPEAN WAR

T he Irish-American influence on United States politics played a vital role in shaping both British and American policy towards Ireland, as well as de Valera's policy in relation to the war. He relied on the disruptive potential of Irish-Americans to keep the British at bay.

Although Irish-Americans comprised only about 15 per cent of the population of the United States, their political importance far outweighed their numerical strength because of their concentration in the most populous states and their tendency to support Democratic candidates. This made them a potent force within the Democratic Party. They had begun to assimilate into American society, but remained bonded by a sense of being discriminated against, in that Roman Catholics were still second-class citizens because none had ever been elected President. Governor Alfred E. Smith of New York, who was of German and Irish extraction, was the first Catholic to be nominated by a major party, but was heavily defeated by Herbert Hoover in the 1928 election. This still rankled and prompted a sense that solidarity was necessary for Catholics to get their fair share in Protestant America.

Irish-Americans controlled the Democratic Party's political machines in some of the larger cities, like New York, Philadelphia, Boston, Chicago and St Louis. In addition, they filled many of the influential positions within the Roman Catholic Church in the United States. Two of the country's three cardinals—William Cardinal O'Connell of Boston and Denis Cardinal Dougherty of Philadelphia—were sons of Irish immigrants, and each adopted a rather jaundiced view of Roosevelt's foreign policy. The other cardinal, George Mundelein of Chicago, had American parents of German extraction and tended to support Roosevelt, especially against the ranting of Father Charles E. Coughlin, the radio priest who is remembered as the 'father of hate radio'.[1] But Mundelein died in October 1939. The great majority of the archbishops and bishops were of Irish extraction; hence the Irish-American influence extended to millions of Americans of other than Irish ancestry.

Irish-Americans deserted the Democratic Party in significant numbers in the presidential election of 1920, possibly in reaction to President Woodrow Wilson's lack of sympathy for the Irish cause. Although their defection was only one of a number of reasons why the Democrats lost the White House in that election, it was a warning that the Irish-American vote could not be taken for granted. One man who undoubtedly learned that hard lesson in 1920 was the party's vice-presidential nominee, Franklin D. Roosevelt.

By 1932, when Roosevelt ran for President, the Irish-Americans were solidly back in the Democratic fold. Al Smith's nomination as the party's Presidential candidate in 1928 had helped to re-entrench Irish-Americans within the party, with the result that they voted almost en masse for Roosevelt in 1932 and overwhelmingly for him again in 1936, even though Al Smith campaigned for the Republican Party's candidate that year.

The rift between Roosevelt and Smith in 1936 was over domestic issues. Foreign policy was only of secondary concern to the American people, who were still struggling to extricate the country from the Great Depression. Isolationism thrived in the United States during those years, especially after Congressional hearings, held under the chairmanship of Senator Gerald Nye, concluded that World War I had resulted from the imperial ambitions of the European antagonists. The United States had supposedly become involved due to the machinations of American munitions manufacturers, who—having extended enormous credits to the Allies—pushed America into the war to protect their investments when it appeared the Allies might lose. Aided by a great deal of insidious Allied propaganda, the businessmen supposedly managed to convince the American people that the Allies were fighting a war to end all wars for the preservation of democracy and the rights of small nations.

Although the Ney Committee's findings were much too simplistic, they were widely accepted by Americans at the time. Consequently, when the spectre of another war began to cast a shadow over Europe, there were widespread calls for legislation to ensure the United States would remain neutral, thereby preventing a repetition of the previous disaster. Congress passed neutrality laws banning the export of munitions and credit or loans to belligerent countries. The President was also authorised to forbid Americans to travel on ships of belligerent countries.

While this legislation reflected the public mood of the United States before the war, the vast majority sympathised strongly with the Allies by the outbreak of hostilities. As a result, Roosevelt asked Congress to repeal neutrality legislation prohibiting the sale of armaments to belligerents because those measures favoured the Germans, as they did not have the capability to transport equipment from the United States. The Allies, on the other hand, had the ability, but the munitions embargo prevented them from making full use of their naval superiority.

Both of Roosevelt's most prominent Irish-American diplomats—Joe Kennedy and John Cudahy—were determined to keep America out of the war, but each favoured repeal of the Neutrality Laws. 'Those of us who believed in the arms embargo realise in experience that we were wrong,' Cudahy wrote to Roosevelt.[2] But the President's repeal proposals ran into a storm of isolationist criticism, much of which emanated from Irish-American circles.

Senator David I. Walsh came out strongly against the President's plans. Born in Massachusetts in 1872, Walsh was still in his thirties when he became the first Roman Catholic Irish-American to be elected Governor of the state in 1914. Four years later he became the first Irish-American Catholic to be elected to the United States Senate from Massachusetts. He was the main speaker to welcome Eamon de Valera to Fenway Park on 29 June 1919, when some 50,000 people turned out to see him at the beginning of his famous American tour. Walsh was one of the Senate Democrats who opposed the Versailles Treaty and helped to undermine Woodrow Wilson's plans for the League of Nations. By 1939 Walsh's 'manner and appearance established him as nearly a caricature of the Irish pol'.[3] He dressed in bright-coloured, striped silk shirts, with his stomach protruding over his belt and double chin bulging over his stiff collar. As chairman of the Senate Naval Affairs committee, he denounced Roosevelt's repeal proposals in an address broadcast on the National Broadcasting Company (NBC) network.

'If it is real neutrality to bar our ships, forbid loans, and keep our citizens from war zones, in simple logic and plain common sense, what more effective and practical neutrality could we pursue than refrain from trading with any of the belligerents?' he asked. 'To my mind, it is unthinkable that we can escape involvement in the European war and at the same time advocate intervention. It is real intervention to threaten before or during the war to sell death-dealing instruments to one of the belligerents.'[4]

The ethnic Irish-American press unanimously opposed the repeal proposals. The *Irish World* (New York), one of the more moderate Irish-American newspapers, simply advocated that Americans avoid any involvement in the war because it was 'neither the war to end war, nor is it a struggle to uphold democracy. It does not concern us in any way, and the sooner it is over, the better'.[5] The more radical *Gaelic-American* warned that repeal would be similar to the mistake the United States made during World War I when it sympathised with the Allies, with disastrous consequences. 'It is to aid the empires that framed the Versailles crime', the editor asserted, 'that

President Roosevelt had asked [for] the elimination of the Arms and Ammunition provision of the Neutrality Act.'6 The San Francisco *Leader* went further in calling on its readers to reject Roosevelt's request in order 'to save our country from entanglement in this mess, and to take advantage of every opportunity offered by the difficulties of England to secure the freedom of Ireland'.7

The Irish-American newspapers generally ignored those supporting repeal, while giving prominence to the behaviour of those opposing the President, such as Nevada Senator Patrick A. McCarran's denunciation of repeal during an address to the Keep America Out of War Committee in New York, or Senator David I. Walsh's letter to every priest in the United States asking for suggestions on ways of opposing repeal. The ethnic press also gave full coverage to Father Charles E. Coughlin, founder of the National Union for Social Justice, which had its own newspaper, *Social Justice*. His weekly radio address was broadcast over up to forty-eight radio stations each Sunday afternoon. It was estimated that he had as many as forty million listeners. He commanded more attention than any American Catholic before him, as he had a following among other religions, including racist elements like the Ku Klux Klan, which had traditionally been anti-Catholic as well as racist.

The son of third-generation Irish immigrants, Coughlin was born and reared in Ontario, Canada. After his ordination to the priesthood he began ministering across the St Lawrence River in the Detroit area. He was an early supporter of Roosevelt's New Deal, but quickly became disillusioned. In May 1934 he began talks with Senator Huey Long of Louisiana to set up the Union Party to oppose Roosevelt's bid for re-election. Long was to be the candidate, but he was assassinated in September 1935. Coughlin then essentially chose Senator William Lemke of North Dakota as the Union Party standard-bearer in 1936, along with a dissident Democrat, Thomas C. O'Brien, a labour lawyer from Boston, as his running mate.

As the National Union for Social Justice claimed six million members, the Union Party seemed to have real political clout. In campaigning vigorously for Lemke, Coughlin denounced Roosevelt as a communist, a liar and a double-crosser. 'We are at the crossroad,' Coughlin said. 'One road leads toward fascism, the other toward Communism. I take the road to fascism.'8

'To Catholics, and especially to the Irish, a priest is a figure of more than ordinary dignity; he is a traditional source of authority and wisdom,' William V. Shannon, a future us Ambassador to Ireland, noted in his book *The American Irish*. A priest who evoked religious imagery to voice radical, rebellious sentiments in a dignified manner might have had a receptive audience. 'But Father Coughlin literally tore off his Roman collar, harangued audiences in an open-neck, sweat-stained shirt, screamed invective and abuse,

[and] threatened to beat up a reporter,' Shannon wrote. 'When he abandoned his dignity and priestly manner, Father Coughlin lowered himself in the eyes of many to just another cheap, shouting politician.'[9]

Coughlin, who predicted that Lemke would outpoll the Republican candidate, said he would quit broadcasting if his candidate did not get at least nine million votes, but Lemke failed to get even one million. With 892,378 votes, he finished well behind Alf Landon's 16,681,862, while Roosevelt swept forty-six of the forty-eight states with 27,752,648 votes.

Popular radio was still in its early years, and Coughlin and others obviously had an exaggerated sense of its influence. The election result was crushing evidence of Coughlin's poor political judgment. His confidence was clearly dented. 'For a time, he drifted aimlessly, becoming just another anti-administration voice,' Shannon wrote.[10] In the autumn of 1938, as the anti-Semitic virulence was reaching a crescendo in Germany, Coughlin became particularly anti-Semitic in his broadcasts. On 23 May 1938 his magazine, *Social Justice*, called for the establishment of an organisation to unite believers. This led to the formation of the Christian Front, a loose confederation of about half-a-dozen anti-Semitic and Fascist groups in about a dozen cities. It was especially strong in New York, Boston, Philadelphia, Pittsburg, Detroit, Minneapolis and St Louis.

Ostensibly órganised to combat the threat of communism, the Christian Front denounced Jews, labour leaders, liberals and New Dealers as communists. By 1939 the organisation had some 200,000 members, many of whom were associated with the German-American Bund, which was drilling secretly with military equipment and engaging in violent anti-Semitic agitation. Coughlin essentially encouraged this anti-Semitism. 'Must the entire world go to war for 600,000 Jews in Germany who are neither American, nor French, nor English citizens, but citizens of Germany?' he asked in January 1939. 'The average Jew, the kind we admire and respect, has been placed in jeopardy by his guilty leaders. He pays for their Godlessness, their persecution of Christians, their attempts to poison the whole world with Communism,' Coughlin added that August.[11]

His friend, Ambassador Joseph P. Kennedy, was expressing similar sentiments in London. 'Individual Jews are all right,' Kennedy told Harvey Klemmer of his embassy staff, 'but as a race they stink. They spoil everything they touch. Look what they did to the movies.'[12] According to a public opinion poll, 61 per cent of Americans preferred Fascism to communism, but 67 per cent of American Jewish people preferred communism.

The Christian Front was especially strong in Brooklyn, where about 90 per cent of its members were of Irish Catholic extraction. John F. Cassidy was the recognised leader and became notorious as one of the movement founders.

He took a leading part in a number of initiatives, including the drawing up of the Christian Index, which sought to promote Christian-owned businesses and thus boycott Jewish businesses. He graduated from St John's Law School in 1933 and passed the Bar examination at his sixth attempt in 1938, but because of his involvement in the Christian Front, he was not actually called to the Bar until more than half-a-century later.

The Christian Front advocated hiring Christians only and emblazoned on its material: 'Think Christian! Act Christian! And Buy Christian!' Priding itself on its Christian ethos, it proclaimed its aims were 'To fight Communism, Atheism, and all other un-American Ideas'. It was so anti-communist that it effectively became pro-Fascist. Walter Winchell, the famous broadcaster, dubbed Cassidy 'the Führer of Flatbush'.[13] Cassidy organised large public meetings that were addressed by Father Coughlin over the public address on a telephone link.

The Christian Front was slow to get off the ground in Boston because Cardinal O'Connell was known to be very cool towards Coughlin. Francis P. Moran, a staunch supporter of Coughlin, set up the Committee for Constitutional Rights, which had essentially the same aims as the Christian Front. Moran gradually began to show his hand. On 8 September 1939 he organised a meeting at the Boston Arena, which was packed with some 6,000 people. He introduced Jack Cassidy to the meeting as National Director of the Christian Front. 'This is not a Christian Front meeting,' Moran told the gathering. 'But, if you are interested in the Christian Front, as I am, come to Room 204 at the Copley Plaza.'[14]

Thereafter Moran became more open in his support of Coughlin and the Christian Front, and he shared platforms with Cassidy and the Brooklyn priest Edward Lodge Curran. The balding, florid-faced priest was trained as a civil lawyer and was a spellbinding orator, with a penchant for picturesque invective. A popular speaker at anti-communist and pro-isolationist rallies, he became known as the 'Father Coughlin of the East'.[15] Boston, with its large Irish-American population, became one of the strongholds of the Christian Front, whose ultra-radical cliques spawned a number of other organisations, such as the Christian Mobilizers. Its advisory board included people with distinct Irish names, such as Thomas Monaghan, Joseph McDonagh, James Downey and Edmund Burke. A popular speaker at rallies of the Christian Mobilizers, which became closely allied with the German-American Bund, was another priest with an Irish background, Father Edward F. Brophy.

Following the outbreak of war in Europe, the Brooklyn *Tablet* supported Coughlin and called on readers to write or telegram their Congressional representatives to oppose Roosevelt's efforts to repeal the neutrality legislation. 'No cash or carry, no foreign entanglement, and no blood business,' the *Tablet* proclaimed.[16]

In the first issue of *Social Justice* following the outbreak of hostilities in Europe, Coughlin predicted that 'the National Socialists of America, organised under that or some other name, eventually will take control of the Government on this Continent.' In effect, he was saying that American Nazis were going to take over the whole of North America, and he went on to forecast 'the end of Democracy in America'.[17]

Father Curran denounced Alfred E. Smith for supporting the repeal of the neutrality laws in a radio address. Even though Smith had opposed Roosevelt in 1936, he supported the President's call for repeal as the best way of keeping the country out of the war.[18] 'This was not time for Mr. Smith to arise and defend the President's policy,' Curran argued that same evening. Since Smith had been introduced as 'a prominent Catholic layman', Curran contended that Smith's name was being used 'to drown out the voice of Fr. Coughlin'.[19]

Smith was only one of many Catholics with strong Irish connections to support repeal. Monsignor John A. Ryan, a recently retired professor of political science and moral theology at the Catholic University of America, was used by some of the same radio stations to provide a balance to Coughlin. During the 1936 presidential campaign, when Coughlin was vociferously opposing Roosevelt's re-election, Ryan attracted national attention with a radio broadcast repudiating Coughlin and urging voters to support the President and the New Deal. Ryan, the Minnesota-born son of Irish immigrants, had become so friendly with Roosevelt that he was nicknamed the 'Right Reverend New Dealer'.[20] In 1937, at the invitation of Roosevelt, the Monsignor became the first Catholic priest to deliver the invocation at a presidential inauguration. He subsequently supported Roosevelt's foreign policy. 'The person who asserts that we should be impartial and indifferent with regard to the conflict between the Hitler government and the Allies repudiates not only Christ's gospel of brotherly love, but the principles of national morality,' Monsignor Ryan warned his audience in October 1939. 'In the present crisis our country is morally obliged to do all that it can reasonably do to defeat Hitler and Hitlerism.'[21]

Two Gallup polls published that month found that 95 per cent of all-Americans and 96 per cent of Americans whose fathers were born in Ireland favoured staying out of the European war, while 61 per cent of Americans whose fathers were born in Ireland favoured repeal of the neutrality laws, which was marginally higher than the 60 per cent among Americans whose fathers were born in the United States.[22] The *Gaelic American* denounced that poll as unbelievable, because the United Irish Societies of New York could not find one of its members supporting the repeal provisions. Certainly anyone reading only the ethnic press and the various resolutions of the different

Irish-American organisations could hardly have avoided the conclusion that the vast majority of Irish-Americans were opposed to furnishing any kind of assistance to the Allies.

One is immediately confronted with the problem of determining who the Irish-Americans were. Generally speaking, all were Americans of Roman Catholic Irish decent, but not all were imbued with Irish-American nationalism, nor had all retained their Roman Catholic heritage. Many of those whose forbears had moved to states with few Roman Catholic priests had adopted Protestant religions, and many had simply assimilated into American society, especially in the 1920s and 1930s. During those years American interest in Irish affairs was low because Irish-Americans were preoccupied with their own problems. They had begun the move to suburban America, where they were forming loyalties and attachments to their new neighbourhoods, to their various economic groups and to their professions. Irish-American nationalism was therefore weakening even before World War II.

This nationalism was found mainly in areas where Irish-Americans still congregated in closely knit communities, especially in the large urban centres of north-eastern states like Massachusetts, Connecticut, Rhode Island, New York, New Jersey and Pennsylvania, or in mid-western states like Illinois and Michigan, or further west in California. So-called professional Irish-Americans, who controlled the ethnic newspapers circulating within those communities, had a virtual monopoly on ethnic news coverage. Hence the strength of isolationist sentiment among Irish-Americans tended to be distorted. Roosevelt asked aides on 20 October 1939 whether some of those Irish-American congressmen could be won over if they were shown the letter he had received from de Valera thanking him for his intervention in the talks leading to the return of the Treaty ports. While it was most unlikely that de Valera's attitude would have influenced those Congressmen, the fact that Roosevelt suggested the idea was indicative of a rather inflated view of de Valera's influence in America. Over 60 per cent of Congressmen with Irish surnames actually voted for the repeal measures.

That so many favoured repeal of the embargo in 1939 was not indicative of interventionist sentiment. Many people, such as Al Smith, Joe Kennedy and John Cudahy, believed repeal was the best way of keeping America out of the conflict, because the President had astutely included a provision in his bill forbidding American ships to travel in waters in a zone extending around belligerent countries and including such neutrals as Belgium, Holland and Ireland. Thus, it was argued, the Bill reduced the danger of American opinion being inflamed either by a deliberate or accidental sinking of an American ship.

Coughlin and the Christian Front were losing the battle for public opinion. The drop in financial contributions to his Radio League and his church were indications of his waning influence. In 1938 he received $574,416, but this declined to $102,254 in 1939. Yet he still seemed to be a force to be reckoned with.

In view of the radio priest's following, Roosevelt was particularly worried about the opposition of Roman Catholics, especially people like Coughlin's friend Joe Kennedy. It was Kennedy who brought Coughlin to Roosevelt's home, in an effort to patch up their differences, on 10 September 1935—the day Huey Long died. Kennedy demonstrated his contacts among influential Catholics by organising the first meeting between a Vatican official and an American President. Just two days after the president's re-election in 1936, Kennedy had brought the Vatican Secretary of State, Cardinal Eugenio Pacelli, to Roosevelt's home in Hyde Park, New York. Pacelli had become Pope Pius XII in March 1939.

While Irish-American church figures may have shared a desire to avoid war, they were far from united. Cardinal O'Connell had been highly critical of Coughlin behind the scenes from as early as April 1932, when he denounced 'hysterical addresses' by priests talking 'nonsense'.[23] The cardinal further denounced the radical ideas of Coughlin in 1933 and 1934, only to receive a flood of protest mail from Boston Catholics. After that he became guarded in his criticism of the radio priest. Cardinal Dennis Dougherty of Philadelphia, both of whose parents came from County Mayo, was also an early critic of Coughlin over his initial enthusiasm for the New Deal. He even suggested Coughlin relied on Jewish support. By 1939 such criticism seemed utterly absurd.

Cardinal Dougherty greeted and shook hands with Hiram W. Evans, the Imperial Wizard of the Ku Klux Klan, at the dedication of the new Cathedral of Christ the King in Atlanta on 18 January 1939. The Solemn Pontifical Mass on that occasion was celebrated by Archbishop James Michael Curley of Baltimore, who was born and reared in Ireland and who had returned to celebrate High Mass at the Phoenix Park, Dublin—at which John McCormack famously sang *Panis Angelicus*—during the Eucharistic Congress of 1932. After the Atlanta ceremony, elements of the Christian Front began forging ties with the Ku Klux Klan, which had hitherto been notoriously anti-Catholic as well as anti-black.

Alive to the danger of alienating the Catholic vote, Roosevelt was deft at playing off the ambitions of Irish-Americans and others against each other. When Postmaster General James A. Farley announced his intention of contesting the Democratic Party's primary election in Massachusetts, Roosevelt privately denounced Farley's actions as an affront to Kennedy by going into his backyard. The President encouraged Kennedy to stand against

Farley in the primary. It was still little over a decade since Al Smith's landslide defeat had been widely attributed to his Roman Catholicism, so Kennedy hesitated. 'There are many reasons that militated against my candidacy for that office, including my Catholic faith,' Kennedy later explained. 'The time was not propitious.'[24] During a visit to Washington in December 1939, Kennedy publicly endorsed Roosevelt to run for an unprecedented third term.

The problems facing the American people were already so great that 'they should be handled by a man it won't take two years to educate,' Kennedy told reporters. 'War at this time would bring to this country chaos beyond anybody's dream. This, in my opinion, overshadows any possible objection to a third term.'[25]

Kennedy actually brought a request from the British, who were seeking secret American approval for the mining of Norwegian waters, which would be a violation of Norway's neutrality. When Roosevelt had no objection, Churchill began thinking again in terms of acting against Irish neutrality. 'As we are now contemplating action which would infringe the neutrality of both Norway and Sweden,' Churchill wrote, 'consideration might be given at the same time to the question of occupying Berehaven.' He insisted that the port would be 'of the greatest value' for anti-submarine operations.[26] The British had no fear of the resistance of the Irish at home, but they dared not move because of the likely repercussions among Irish-Americans, who seemed to pose a real political threat to the White House and thus to Britain's American support.

Relations between Kennedy and Roosevelt were by then riddled with duplicity. Kennedy feared the President was scheming with Churchill to drag the United States into the war. Roosevelt tried to allay those fears by expressing his own suspicions of Churchill. 'I have always disliked him since the time I went to England in 1918. He acted like a stinker at a dinner I attended, lording it all over us,' the President explained. 'I'm giving him attention now because there is a strong possibility that he will become the prime minister and I want to get my hand in now.'[27]

Kennedy was offended by the developing correspondence between Churchill and Roosevelt, not only because he was being by-passed as ambassador but also because he distrusted Churchill. 'Maybe I do him an injustice,' Kennedy reported after he and his wife, Rose, were invited to Churchill's Chartwell home, 'but I don't trust him. He always impressed me that he was willing to blow up the American Embassy and say it was the Germans if it would get the United States in.'[28]

The ambassador's relationship with Roosevelt was strained even before the outbreak of hostilities because Kennedy had been intriguing with the media, and some of his indiscretions were major. He had been scheming with the

Washington correspondent of the *New York Times*, Arthur Krock, who reported that Kennedy was on the verge of resigning because he was so disillusioned with the President. Kennedy was reluctant to return to London after his visit to Washington in December 1939, but he feared that quitting the British post in the midst of the crisis could damage his political ambitions, especially when Roosevelt was contending his presence in Britain was vital. It was not that the President really wanted him in London; he just wished to keep him out of the country because he was afraid of the damage Kennedy might do in the United States.

The dangerous potential of the radical Catholic elements was sensationalised on 13 January 1940, when the Federal Bureau of Investigation (FBI) arrested eighteen members of the Christian Front. FBI Director J. Edgar Hoover went to New York for a press conference, at which he accused the men of conspiring to overthrow the government of the United States. He said they were planning 'to knock off about a dozen Congressmen' who had supported repeal of the neutrality laws. In addition, they were accused of planning to bomb the premises of the Jewish *Daily Forward* and the communist *Daily Worker*, the Cameo Theatre on West 42nd Street, which showed Soviet-made films, as well as bridges, power plants, telephone and telegraph networks, docks, railway terminals, the General Post Office, along with the Federal Reserve Bank in order to get hold of the gold in New York City.[29]

'Plans were discussed', according to Hoover, 'for the wholesale sabotage and blowing up of all these institutions so that a dictatorship could be set up here, similar to the Hitler dictatorship in Germany, seizing the reins of government in this country as Hitler did in Germany. Their scheme was to spread a reign of terrorism so that the authorities could become thoroughly demoralised.'[30]

Those arrested hailed Father Coughlin as their leader. Hoover named Jack Cassidy as the leader of the group. Nearly all were Catholics and half of them had Irish names, like Michael J. Bierne, a native of Raheela, County Roscommon, and County Cork-born Andrew Buckley, along with Leroy Keegan, George Kelly, Frank M. Malone, Alfred J. Quinlan, Edward Walsh and John M. Ryan. In the course of the arrests some bomb-making equipment was found, along with seventeen rifles and some machine-gun ammunition. This was hardly the kind of arsenal that would be required to overthrow the government of the United States, or do the kind of damage they were supposedly planning.

Ryan was promptly released, but the other seventeen were arraigned as Hoover ensured the arrests were further sensationalised. 'You wouldn't believe the show he staged!' Cassidy recalled years later. 'One by one, we were led out of the Federal detention headquarters into a car. There were three agents in each car and a motorcycle in front. Multiply that by seventeen defendants! The whole motorcade screaming through downtown Manhattan. And above us, on the West Side Highway, they had a truck full of special agents with machine guns pointing at us.'[31] The trial, which began in the spring, extended over three months before Cassidy and nine others were acquitted. The jury was unable to reach a verdict in the other cases, and all were eventually acquitted.

Chapter 5

DIPLOMATIC CHANGES IN DUBLIN

John Cudahy was the grandson of Irish immigrants who fled to the United States in the immediate wake of the Great Famine. His father left Ireland as an infant and grew up to become fabulously wealthy in the meatpacking industry in Milwaukee and Chicago. John dabbled in state politics and ran unsuccessfully as a Democrat for Governor of Wisconsin in 1916. He served with the American Expeditionary Force in Europe during World War I and was later part of the American force sent to Archangel to help the White Russians in their struggle against the Bolsheviks.

If he was fired by the idealism that President Woodrow Wilson inspired in undertaking such ventures, Cudahy's eyes were opened in Archangel. He wrote a highly critical book on that futile venture. Now he was convinced America needed realism rather than the kind of adventurous idealism that he had witnessed during his early manhood.

After a term as Ambassador to Poland, Cudahy was transferred to Dublin at his own request. He fancied himself as a statesman and was initially critical of appeasement. He thought the policy 'may be fatal in encouraging the dangerous adventures of both Mussolini and Hitler'.[1]

'Your analysis', Roosevelt wrote, 'is the best I have seen. If a Chief of Police makes a deal with the leading gangsters and the deal results in no more hold ups, that Chief of Police will be called a great man—but if the gangsters do not live up to their word the Chief of Police will go to jail. Some people are, I think, taking very long chances—don't you?'[2]

Cudahy got that right, and his advice in relation to Roosevelt's intervention in the Anglo-Irish talks turned out to be particularly perceptive. On other matters, however, his judgment was not nearly as sound. Back in 1933 when first appointed as ambassador to Poland, for instance, he had suggested there was no cause for alarm about the paramilitary organisations being formed in Germany. He compared the notorious ss to the Order of the

Elks, a service organisation in the United States, and described them as a peculiar manifestation of the national spirit of the Germans, who liked to put on uniforms and let off steam, marching around to martial music. Roosevelt pointedly noted, however, that when 'Germans put on uniforms and marched around to martial music, they often marched across someone's borders'.[3]

In the following years the Germans marched into the Rhineland, in violation of the Versailles Treaty, while Britain and France looked on. They stood by again in March 1938 when Germany seized Austria. 'The basic thing about Austria is that now there is no balance on the continent,' Cudahy wrote to Roosevelt in April 1938. 'It is like a structure of which the keystone has been taken away. Nothing can now be predicted for the post-war status quo is irretrievably lost.' There was no knowing where Hitler would strike next. 'I think Chamberlain's is the most weak, vacillating, humiliating policy England has ever presented,' he added. 'That is the tragedy. There is no leadership to oppose the dictators.'[4]

Although blisteringly critical of Chamberlain's appeasement, Cudahy did not appear very brave the following month when his niece, Jane Dahlman, married Harold Ickes, Roosevelt's Secretary of the Interior. They got married in Dublin, away from the glare of publicity. Ickes traveled under an assumed name and arrived in Ireland unannounced, but his marriage still attracted international attention. The sixty-four-old Ickes was more than twice the age of his twenty-five-year-old bride. Cudahy tried to persuade her not to marry Ickes, who found that understandable, but then he refused to attend the wedding at the Presbyterian Church on Adelaide Road because, he said, this would put him in an embarrassing position as a Roman Catholic and the US Minister to a Catholic country.

'Of course I scoffed at this as the flimsiest kind of an alibi,' Ickes noted. 'It is no concern of the Irish Free State where I was to be married.'[5]

During the initial months of the war Cudahy showed little interest in Irish affairs. He was faced with helping the thousands of Americans clamouring to get back to the United States. 'There are, as far as we know, in France, England and Ireland, about fifteen thousand Americans anxious to get out,' Cudahy wrote to Roosevelt. 'I believe we shall have almost all of them on their way home by the first week in October. From the present outlook we will have all Americans started home within another three or four weeks, and then I will be among the unemployed.'[6]

His wished to be transferred to someplace closer to the action, but Roosevelt could hardly have been impressed with some of Cudahy's early observations on the war. For instance, he warned that Germany would be offended by suggestions that a U-boat had sunk the liner *Athenia*. He advocated that similar diplomatic notes be sent to all the belligerents in protest against the sinking of the *Athenia*. 'There never was any evidence that the Athenia was sunk by a German submarine,' Cudahy argued. 'If we protested to Germany alone and ignored the other warring nations we would be protesting upon presumption, not on proof. In this way we made a record in the last war from which we could not recede, as you know so well.'[7]

'The State Department feels that you ought to stay in Dublin,' Roosevelt wrote to Cudahy on 17 October 1939.[8] He received the letter, but did not seem to get the message.

'Everything here in order for me to visit France and Germany except permission,' Cudahy wrote on 28 October. 'I wish you would let me go. I am dying of slow rust and rot here.'[9]

In the following days he began beseeching others to intervene with the President on his behalf. He asked the President's private secretary, Marguerite 'Missy' Le Hand, for help. 'There is little to do and absolutely no pressure,' he wrote. 'I am slowly passing out through disintegration and disillusion.'[10] 'I want to go on the Continent,' he added. 'I know I could do this usefully but nobody falls in with my suggestion. If you hear of me falling into the Liffey by mistake, you will understand everything.'[11] Cudahy also mentioned to R. Walton Moore, Counselor of the State Department, that he had asked Joe Kennedy to make representations on his behalf during his visit to Washington in December 1939. He asked him 'to revive the legend of the Forgotten Man in the direction of one marooned on this Island'.[12]

It looked like Cudahy was stuck in Ireland and that whatever influence he was going to have on the course of the war would have to be exercised from Dublin. In early December he tried to persuade de Valera to undertake a peace initiative by going to an emergency session of the Assembly of the League of Nations, which was convened to discuss the Soviet Union's invasion of Finland. De Valera had been elected President of the last Assembly during the Munich crisis, and Cudahy argued that he would be re-elected and could then speak at Geneva from a platform that would command world attention. 'I told him what a wonderful opportunity he had for leadership at this time if he voiced the moral issue involved in the invasion of Finland.'[13]

'No,' de Valera replied. 'People would say "that fellow is talking too much!"'

'Nothing could be gained by talk, he said,' according to Cudahy. 'There had already been too much talk; what was required if the civilization of Europe was to be saved was action.'[14]

'The only country which could speak with any effectiveness was now the United States, and it would do no good for us if we did not follow words with actions,' de Valera continued, according to Cudahy. 'The only language which had persuasion these days, he said, was "Tanks, Bombs, and Machine Guns".'[15]

De Valera had clearly lost faith in the League of Nations. 'He spoke very bitterly and cynically of the League, describing it as "debris", according to Cudahy. The League had been seriously damaged by Japan's open flaunting of its authority by invading Manchuria, and this was compounded by the Italian invasion of Ethiopia. 'He had taken a clear-cut position in opposing Italy, for never was the issue in international conduct more clear,' de Valera explained. But the League failed dismally when it came to sanctions. He blamed the French Foreign Minister Pierre Laval for coming to a secret understanding with Mussolini. 'And so again,' de Valera added, 'the League was brought into disrepute and, as in the case of Japan, was shown up to be feebly ineffectual in the face of unlawful, arrogant force.' The same thing would happen again if sanctions were used, he believed. It was necessary to act, but Ireland could not act effectively, so there was no use in talking.

'I told him just as earnestly as I could what a great opportunity was given him to strike out and say that morality among nations did count and was still a power to be reckoned with,' Cudahy contended.

If he talked about the Finns at the League of Nations, de Valera told Cudahy, he would also have to mention Poland, Slovakia and the other invaded countries. Germany might take offence and this could lead to Ireland's involvement in the war, which he was determined to avoid. Moreover, he did not believe that any representatives of any consequence would be at the Assembly. 'He is only sending a civil servant to Geneva, and is sure the meeting of the League will be a fizzle.'

'I talked to him at great length in an attempt to point out the opportunity he had for a genuine peace effort at this time, but he could not see it that way,' Cudahy added.

'There is no use in an oration at this time,' de Valera replied. 'We must have proposals for a general settlement of Europe. What would you do; what proposals have you to make?' With his voice shaking with agitation, de Valera added he felt 'like a man behind a glass wall witnessing the destruction of everything he held dear, but absolutely paralyzed and impotent to take action to avert universal destructions'.[16]

De Valera called for an international conference in a Christmas radio address to the United States, broadcast over the CBS network:

The last great war should have taught us that wars can end and leave unsolved the fundamental difficulties from which they spring. The conference which comes at the end of a war takes place in an atmosphere which precludes justice. It is an atmosphere of fury and resentment, of hate and fear, whereas the conference that is needed is a conference of equals where each side's difficulties are appreciated, where the stability of the selected tribunal could be maintained after being established, and the abiding good of all people concerned are kept ever in the foreground as the proper purpose of the conference and not the spoliation and disablement of the defeated.[17]

Cudahy got his wish to go the Continent in early January 1940, in the wake of a crisis after a German aircraft crashed in Belgium and was found to be carrying plans for a German invasion of the country. Cudahy left Dublin in a great hurry. 'I took my leave very precipitously,' he wrote to a friend a couple of weeks later. 'Only six hours elapsed from the time my instruction came until I was on my way across the Irish Sea. I had two hours in London, flew to Paris, and, because aviation was suspended across the Belgian frontier, had to take an evening train arriving in Brussels the next morning at about two.'[18]

'When I took my abrupt leave of de Valera,' Cudahy wrote to President Roosevelt, 'he told me very frankly that he was disappointed that another Minister had not been designated for Ireland.'[19]

'By your own definition,' de Valera said, 'Ireland is in the combat zone. These are trying times and we should have an American Minister in Dublin.'[20] The Taoiseach asked Cudahy to urge Roosevelt to send a Minister at once.

Shortly before Cudahy's departure, Canada appointed a High Commissioner to Ireland. John Hall Kelly arrived in Dublin on 8 March 1940 to take up the new position. He was a sixty-year-old lawyer who had spent a quarter-of-a-century as a Liberal member of the Quebec Legislative Assembly. He was a close associate of Dominique Lévesque, whose son, René, later became famous as the founder of the *Parti Québécois* and Premier of Quebec. Kelly was of Irish extraction and a practising Roman Catholic, which Prime Minister W.L. Mackenzie King thought de Valera would welcome.

The Prime Minister's instructions to Kelly were fairly basic. 'My advice to him was to learn all he could about Ireland and say very little,' Mackenzie King noted in his diary. 'Men seldom lost by what they had not said, and many destroyed their influence by what they had to say. Ireland was a very difficult country just now. Best to tell them that he had come to learn about them from them, not to talk to them. He agreed to this.'[21]

As Kelly had no diplomatic experience, his appointment was seen a political reward for his involvement in provincial affairs. The Toronto *Globe and Mail* criticised the failure to appoint a career diplomat. De Valera indicated he would prefer Kelly be known as 'Canadian Representative to Ireland', but he did not press the matter when Mackenzie King explained that altering the title would cause him problems.[22]

The Secretary of the new Canadian High Commission, Edward J. Garland, was a particularly interesting character. Born in Dublin, the son of a doctor, he was educated at Belvedere College and later at Trinity College before emigrating to Canada and settling in Alberta in 1911. He served in the Canadian Parliament from 1921, until losing his seat in 1935. He was now in his mid-fifties, but his mother was still living in Dublin, so he was essentially returning home.

'When he spoke of his duties in Ireland,' Mackenzie King noted in his diary, 'I stressed the critical situation there and that I would like him to feel that every thing that he did should be in the nature of an effort to keep Ireland, Canada and Britain all together—all part of the British Commonwealth of Nations, realizing that each had complete autonomy; that by keeping together as a galaxy of nations, we were helping our own freedom and that of the world.'[23]

Ireland was as politically important in Canada as in the United States. The Irish-born population in Canada were aging and their numbers were dwindling rapidly. At the time of the last census, in 1931, there were 107,544 people of Irish birth in Canada, but that number would decline by almost 20 per cent by the time of the next census, in 1941. Those listing of Irish ancestry were little over 1.2 million people, but many would have been of Scots-Irish descent, and hence Dublin did not have the same kind of political clout in Canada.[24]

Less than a month later David Gray took up his position as US Minister in Dublin. Gray, who had retired after a varied career, was married to an aunt of President Roosevelt's wife. He met Cudahy on board ship the previous summer, during a transatlantic crossing.

'You have the only job in the gift of the President which I would really like,' Gray told Cudahy at the time.[25]

'Why don't you ask him for it?'

'I cannot ask him for anything for he has been a close personal friend for twenty-five years, and his wife is my wife's niece.'

'That is not a good reason,' Cudahy insisted. 'I will ask him to give you the job because I am getting out very soon.'[26]

Cudahy suggested Gray as a possibly replacement in the hope of speeding up his own transfer. Roosevelt talked to Gray about the Dublin post in November 1939, and he appointed him to replace Cudahy. Born in Buffalo, New York, in 1870, Gray was the son of a newspaper publisher. He graduated from Harvard University before going into the newspaper business as a reporter and editorial writer in Rochester, New York. His first editor was William Purcell, an Irishman. He then worked at the *New York World* under the famous Joseph Pulitzer. After acquiring some experience, he moved to his father's newspaper, the Buffalo *Courier*, and became one of the country's youngest managing editors. But he sold the newspaper when it lost circulation.

In 1899 Gray passed the Bar examination and began a three-year practice as an unsuccessful criminal lawyer. He then abandoned the legal profession and tried his hand at writing short stories. He had a number of sporting stories published in *Century* magazine and received the sure stamp of success by being published in the prestigious *Saturday Evening Post*. He also wrote a number of novels and one play, 'The Best People', which had a successful run in New York, Chicago and London. Gray served with the signal corps of the American Expeditionary Force in France during World War I. Afterwards he returned to writing and spent considerable time travelling. In the summer of 1933 he first visited Ireland and became enthralled with the hunting and fishing opportunities. He returned in June of 1934 and remained until the following May in Castletownshend, County Cork, where he enjoyed the literary scene. He became friendly with Edith Somerville and her collaborator, Violet Martin, of Somerville and Ross fame. Gray subsequently made three further visits to Ireland before returning in April 1940 as United States Minister.

He obviously owed his appointment to his family connections. His wife, Maud, was First Lady Eleanor Roosevelt's mother's youngest sister. Eleanor was reared by her maternal grandmother, however, along with Maud, who was only six years older. As a result their relationship was really more akin to that of sisters than aunt and niece. Indeed, Eleanor later wrote that she always thought of Maud as a sister.

On her father's side Eleanor was a niece of President Theodore Roosevelt, so Gray found that his marriage gave him an easy *entrée* into powerful circles. An outspoken yet affable gentleman with a fund of stories, he was great company and a particular favourite of Franklin Roosevelt's children. In diplomatic terms the Irish post was never considered very important. When Gray asked Secretary of State Cordell Hull if he wished him to do anything in Ireland, Hull told him to have a good time, enjoy himself and keep his eyes open.

Gray believed the United States should provide as much help as possible to the Allies because they were basically fighting for ideals cherished by America. If the Allies were beaten, he was convinced the United States would be dragged into the conflict with the Nazis; therefore he felt it would be silly not to give the British as much help as possible. He thought he could play an important role in Ireland because of the influence that Irish affairs exerted over those Irish-Americans who were imbued with such a deep hatred of Britain that they were bitterly resisting Roosevelt's pro-British policies. In an attempt to mollify their opposition, Gray suggested he be authorised to explore the possibilities of resolving the partition question. If he could arrange a settlement, he was convinced Roosevelt would win over many of his

Irish-American critics. The President liked the idea and authorised Gray to engage in some preliminary talks before going to Dublin. Gray's first call was to the Vatican, where he discussed the Irish problem with Pope Pius XII on 21 March 1940.

'The Irish question had maintained an abnormal and almost continuous pressure on American foreign relations which the great majority of Americans resented, without being able to do anything about it,' Gray told the Pope. The resulting popular resentment was actually fostering a prejudice against Roman Catholic politicians to the extent of provoking 'a situation which made it practically impossible to elect a Catholic to the Presidency'.[27]

'You mean Alfred E. Smith?' the Pope interjected.

'Yes,' Gray said, adding that he had personally voted for Smith and 'was humiliated that he should have been beaten on religious grounds'.

The Pope seemed to know little about the Irish situation. When Gray asked if there were any particular Irish bishop to whom he should turn for advice, the Pope suggested he talk with the Papal Nuncio, whom he described as a very sound and astute man. Gray was trying to learn if the Holy Father would object to an Irish settlement involving a complete separation of Church and state. 'In the key of the studied generalities in which he pitched the interview,' Gray reported, 'I could not ask this directly so I said: The Catholic Bishops I know in America tell me that they do not regret their entire separation from the state, that on the contrary they feel the Church to be stronger and more spiritual as a consequence.'

'*Absolument*,' the Pope replied, going on to explain that he saw the Church as strictly spiritual in nature. The Pope was 'very emphatic about this', Gray noted. He was satisfied this provided the assurance for which he had gone to the Vatican. He was confident 'there would be no objection there' if the issue of complete separation of Church and state in Ireland were referred to the Vatican.[28]

While on the Continent, Gray had discussions about partition with Michael MacWhite and William B. Macauley, the respective Irish Ministers to Italy and the Vatican, and in Paris with Seán Murphy, the Irish Minister to France. Then in London, where he remained for a week, he had discussions with High Commission John Dulanty, as well as a number of leading British politicians. With each of them he was careful to stress that he was interested in partition because of the abnormal outside influence it was exerting upon American politics. This would have been particularly obvious at the time, with de Valera's picture gracing the cover of the latest issue of *Time*.

A settlement would take years, Dulanty told him. The most one could realistically expect in the near future was a joint commission on roads, or an all-Ireland football team, but he encouraged Gray to 'explore away and if you turn up any chance, tell us'.[29]

Gray's discussions included meetings with Winston Churchill and Dominions Secretary Anthony Eden, as well as Information Minister Duff Cooper. He also met prominent civil servants, such as head of the British Broadcasting Corporation (BBC) Harold Nicolson, Euan Wallace of the Treasury and Sir Horace Wilson, Chamberlain's trusted adviser. All seemed to desire an Irish settlement, but they insisted that Northern Ireland could not be coerced.

During two hours with Gray, Churchill 'roared' that he was sick of the Irish. Britain had given them 'a generous settlement' in 1921, but they had immediately violated the agreement and were now 'stabbing England in the back' by denying her the use of Irish ports.[30]

London had failed to understand that what the Irish had been seeking over the years was a generous recognition 'that Irish sovereignty derived from the Irish people and not from the British Crown', Gray argued. Although supposedly only exploring the facts of the situation, Gray was already hoping Dublin would abandon neutrality in return for Irish unity. He was therefore anxious to learn how far the British would go to persuade Belfast to be accommodating. The answer was simple: as far as Churchill was concerned, Britain would not coerce Northern Ireland, and therefore any proposal would be a matter for Craigavon. As Gray set out on the last leg of his journey to Dublin, he was convinced that neither the Vatican nor London would stand in the way of proposals acceptable to Belfast and Dublin.

On arriving in Dublin on 6 April 1940, Gray was promptly brought to Government Buildings for a meeting with de Valera and Joe Walshe. He personally conveyed a message from Roosevelt. 'The President hopes that you will be able to come and visit him this spring,' Gray said. 'He tells me to tell you that his foreign policy is substantially the same as yours.'[31]

Although much of Europe was officially at war, things had been relatively quiet on the western front. The conflict had settled into the so-called 'phoney war' following the fall of Poland. As a result, the Taoiseach was preoccupied with the domestic political situation as there was a good deal of public unrest over the ongoing hunger strikes. Gray offered his services to de Valera. 'If in your view it might be helpful for me to see the hunger strikers and tell them that the President of the US was endeavouring to promote the solution of all political differences by peaceful political means, and that the Pope recently had spoken to me in the same vein I would gladly do so,' he wrote to the Taoiseach next morning, 'if the thing could be kept strictly private as at all costs I must avoid any action capable of being interpreted as meddling with your internal politics.'[32]

The following afternoon Gray had a long private discussion with de Valera.

'He seemed grateful for my offer but said he thought it would be interpreted as weakness on his part,' Gray reported. The IRA would think de Valera had instigated the visit. But if IRA supporters called on Gray, as they undoubtedly would, the Taoiseach asked him to impress on them that he realised the hunger strikers were not bluffing, but neither was he.

This was Gray's first strictly private meeting with de Valera. 'I told him that there was no use my pretending to be personally neutral,' the American Minister wrote. 'I was prepared to be absolutely correct as representing a neutral power but that personally I was so opposed to Hitlerism, the persecution of the Jews, the rape of the small countries in violation of express and newly made pledges, that I considered the success of the Allies desirable.' If Germany won the war, 'she would take our South American trade from us over night', Japan would take over Australia, the Germans would seize South Africa 'and we would be condemned to armed self-defence for generations'.

'Much as we might resent certain practices of Britain,' Gray continued, 'I would rather go on with her than with Hitler.' De Valera agreed with him:

He said he felt much the same way, but that his people could not see that they were in danger until it was upon them, that the IRA had stirred up the anti-British feeling again. I asked him how important numerically he thought the movement was. He said probably not very large numerically, perhaps a couple of thousands of individuals but that they appealed to something 'very deep in the Irish heart'. We talked intimately about Ulster and he gave me a map showing the majority sentiment in each of the six counties. He claims at least two of these counties are overwhelmingly for union [with the South] and are in effect being COERCED. That is his line. The British refuse to coerce Belfast but connive at the coercion of these two counties and elements in the others.

Would the Dublin government be willing to shut down the German Legation and allow the British to use Berehaven in return for Irish unity? Gray asked.

'No,' de Valera replied without hesitation. 'We could never bargain with our neutrality.'[33]

De Valera had no objections to Gray meeting with the Prime Minister of Northern Ireland. 'I would see him myself,' the Taoiseach said, 'but he will not see me.'[34]

In the following days the war on the Continent began to heat up when the British mined Norwegian waters and the Germans invaded Denmark and Norway. The *Irish Press* pointedly mentioned that while the Germans had used Britain's mining of Norwegian waters to justify their invasion of Norway, Britain had not made any move against Denmark, and the Germans had made scarcely any attempt to justify their Danish attack. Although the editorials stopped short of actually denouncing the Germans, no reader could escape the implied criticism of Berlin.

Gray had discussions with several members of the Irish Cabinet, such as Tánaiste (Deputy Prime Minister) Seán T. O'Kelly, Frank Aiken and Seán MacEntee. All gave him the impression of 'being definitely anti-German and pro-Ally'. They had 'no illusion as to where they would be in case Britain goes down'.[35]

That evening one of the hunger strikers died and the others called off the hunger strike. Before morning, another would be dead. 'Had Irish hunger strikers succumbed under British rule, their names would have been enrolled in the muster of martyrs,' the *Toronto Telegram* noted in an editorial. 'The two who have recently died in Irish prisons, however, will probably be remembered only for their folly, and six others who started on a hunger strike have thought better of their plan and are now taking food.'[36] Jack Plunkett and Thomas MacCurtain survived, but the IRA was more estranged than ever from de Valera's government. On 25 April the IRA managed to set off a bomb within Dublin Castle—the nerve centre of security operations against the organisation. The bomb was intended to destroy the communications centre, but was planted in the wrong place. Although comparatively little damage was done, the whole thing was a potent warning of the IRA's ability to strike anywhere in the country.

Chapter 6 ∾

| SPY SCARE

D
avid Gray had de Valera and his wife, Sinéad, to lunch at his Phoenix Park residence on 2 May 1940. It was a very rare occasion for de Valera's wife to accompany him to such a function. They politely asked the Grays afterwards not to invite them to any further social functions. Ultimately this probably did not help relations between de Valera and Gray, as the latter operated extensively through social networking.

Over lunch the Taoiseach explained he had no 'specific or immediate' worries about German intentions, but there were signs of alarm in the British press. The *News Review* reported that de Valera was impotently 'watching intrigues' between the German Minister and the IRA as 'strange men with square heads' were 'striding self-importantly in and out' of the German Legation.[1] The *Daily Mirror* suggested Irish authorities were giving German spies a free hand, but Walshe assured Maffey that there was no question of the Germans having a secret service organisation in Ireland, because the Irish were keeping a close watch on the German Legation. He went on to say the British could station agents in Dublin to keep on eye on the Germans, too, if they wished.

Guy M. Liddell, the head of MI5's counter-intelligence division, was satisfied with the cooperation of G2. He therefore opposed the idea of stationing British agents in Dublin to watch the German diplomats. 'Personally, I think it is quite out of the question to consider posting agents outside the German Legation in Dublin,' Liddell noted in his diary on 26 April 1940. 'This would be insulting to Archer and would inevitably lead to trouble. As regards wireless, we have definite evidence that a station has been broadcasting within 25 miles of Dublin in official German diplomatic code to Nauen.'[2]

Liddell, who had helped Sir Basil Thompson to reorganise the Special Branch at Scotland Yard in 1919, had moved to the counter-intelligence division of MI5 in 1931. He was largely behind the double-cross system, which turned German spies to work as double agents for the British. Historian Hugh

Trevor-Roper celebrated Liddell as 'the man who put intelligence into spying'.[3] Guy Liddell had a particular interest in Ireland because his brother, Cecil, was in charge of MI5's operations there. Cecil Liddell had run the Irish section, unaided, from 1938 until May 1940, when John Stephenson was assigned to assist him. Stevenson, a barrister, was not only the son of Sir Guy Stevenson, who was the assistant prosecutor at the trial of Roger Casement in 1916, but also a nephew of Lord Frederick Cavendish, the Lord Lieutenant who was murdered in the Phoenix Park in 1882.

On 7 May the IRA shot two policemen delivering mail to Maffey. De Valera went on Radio Éireann next day to announce the government had lost patience with the IRA's murders and terrorism. The previous month the IRA had set off the Dublin Castle bomb. If this and the latest attack on the police delivering mail to Maffey were tolerated, the country would become 'easy prey to any invader', he warned.[4] He sent Joe Walshe to London, where he told Guy Liddell that de Valera henceforth desired that all communications should be in cipher, though Walshe realised this would be impractical.

'Walshe was extremely friendly and was very anxious that I should go over to Dublin as soon as it was convenient,' Liddell noted. 'He expressed his willingness to do anything he possibly could to help us in stopping any loopholes.'[5]

The prompt action of the Irish in relation to the attack was fortuitous because it provided reassurance to the British at a critical time. Two days later, on Friday, 10 May, the Germans invaded the Benelux countries.

'Where did Ireland stand?' Maffey asked the Taoiseach that day. 'Why not send an Irish brigade to France?'

'De Valera at once invoked the old bogey of partition,' according to Maffey.

'I cannot understand why Mr Chamberlain does not tell Craigavon to fix up his difficulties with us and come in,' the Taoiseach said. 'That would solve the problem.'

'If the Partition question were solved today, would you automatically be our active Ally?' Maffey asked.

'I feel convinced that that would probably be the consequence,' de Valera replied. He was not prepared to go further. 'He seems incapable of courageous or original thought and now on this world issue and in every matter he lives too much under the threats of the extremists,' Maffey continued. 'Unfortunately he is a physical and mental expression of the most narrow-minded and bigoted section of the country. In all circumstances great difficulties surround the path of the leader there, but de Valera is not a strong man and his many critics know that well.'[6]

De Valera publicly denounced the invasions of Belgium and Holland. 'Today,' he told a Fianna Fáil gathering, 'these two small nations are fighting for their lives, and I think I would be unworthy of this small nation if, on an occasion like this, I did not utter our protest against the cruel wrong which has been done them.'[7] The Germans were claiming to have acted merely to forestall an Allied attack on the Ruhr Valley via the Low Countries. Even though de Valera did not mention the Germans by name, nobody doubted he was criticising them. The German Minister protested, and Freddy Boland was reportedly apologetic at the Department of External Affairs, but he told Hempel to talk to the Taoiseach, who pointed out that he had not mentioned Germany. 'I got the impression that it was considered of great important that no unfavourable view in regard to Irish neutrality should arise,' Hempel noted.[8]

There was some confusion later over whether Dublin actually apologised to the Germans for the speech. Under Secretary of State Ernst Woermann noted in Berlin that Warnock had expressed himself in an 'apologetic manner'. Years later Warnock wrote to Hempel that he remembered Woermann just saying that he did not like the speech. 'At the end of my visit he said to me: "but that is now past!"'[9] Nobody suggested that de Valera actually apologised for denouncing what had happened to Belgium and Holland.

The threat to Irish neutrality seemed to increase within hours when Winston Churchill replaced Neville Chamberlain as British Prime Minister. Churchill, with his erratic temperament, had a dismal record in relation to Ireland. He had been Minister for War during the Black and Tan period, and the dreaded Auxiliaries had been his brainchild. He had supported Field Marshall Sir Henry Wilson, the Chief of Imperial General Staff, who advocated that Crown forces should put up lists on church doors of local people to be shot as authorised reprisals for any members of the security forces killed. It is difficult to imagine a policy that would have antagonised the Irish people more than desecrating the churches in such a barbarous manner. 'It is monstrous that we have 200 murders and no one hung,' Churchill complained.

He advocated the British behave in Ireland like the Bolsheviks were behaving in Russia. 'After a person is caught he could pay the penalty within a week,' he said. 'Look at the tribunals, which the Russian Government has devised. You should get three or four judges whose scope should be universal and they should move quickly over the country and do summary justice.'[10] For six months Churchill clamoured for hangings, but Prime Minister Lloyd George delayed, primarily because of the likely reaction in the United States. The government eventually relented and hanged Kevin Barry, a teenage college student, who had been involved in an attack in which two British soldiers had been killed. The British executed Barry on 1 November 1920, a

Catholic holiday, All Saints' Day. In the process the young man became sanctified as a hero who would be immortalised in a popular ballad as 'another martyr for old Ireland'.[11]

Churchill pressed the government into that execution and de Valera later blamed him for pushing Michael Collins into firing on the Four Courts in June 1922, at the start of the Irish civil war. Thus Churchill's advent to power in 1940 was viewed with a degree of alarm in Dublin, especially as the Irish knew he was bitterly opposed to the handing over of the Treaty ports in 1938, and had clearly been exerting pressure to secure their return since the beginning of the war.

De Valera regretted the fall of Chamberlain, to whom he sent a warm telegram: 'You did more than any former British Statesman to make a true friendship between the people of our two countries possible, and, if the task has not been completed, that is has not been for want of good will on your part.'[12]

Chamberlain remained in the War Cabinet, which turned to him to take charge of talks with de Valera in the coming weeks because of his relationship with him. 'I trust you will consider very seriously the danger of enemy landings from troop-carrying planes,' Chamberlain wrote to the Taoiseach. 'The Germans do not respect neutrality and the rapidity and efficiency of their methods are terrifying.'[13]

Colonel Archer admitted to Guy and Cecil Liddell on 15 May that he could not see how Ireland could resist a German invasion 'for more than a week'. The Irish Army was pathetically armed. 'They had no equipment,' Liddell noted. 'Orders had been placed in this country as much as 18 months ago, but it has not been possible owing to pressure of work for the firms to fulfil them. He mentioned to me quite privately that in some quarters in the Government it was thought that the arms were being intentionally withheld owing to doubt about the use to which they might be put.'

'We raised the question with Archer as to the possibility of some sort of staff talks in preparation for a possible German landing in the interim,' Liddell continued. 'We told him that in our view it was a thing which might happen any day. He said that he was a soldier and that this was more a matter for the politicians.'

There would be general resentment and a certain degree of Irish resistance to a German invasion, but Archer said quite a number of people would adopt the attitude: 'Oh, well, they are here in force, we can't do anything about it.' It was still less than twenty years since the Black and Tans were terrorising Ireland, and many Irish people 'would not mind Great Britain getting a licking'. But even those people were beginning to realise this would not be in Ireland's interest. 'What would happen to us if they did?' such people were beginning to ask, according to Archer.[14]

From the outset of his tenure as Prime Minister, Churchill was worried about the Irish situation. 'We have many reports of possible German parachute or airborne descents in Ireland,' he cabled Roosevelt on 15 May 1940. 'The visit of a United States squadron to Irish ports, which might well be prolonged, would be invaluable.'[15] De Valera was obviously thinking on similar lines because the following day he asked Gray to inquire, confidentially, if Roosevelt 'could proclaim that the United States was vitally interested in the maintenance of status quo in regard to Ireland'.[16]

'What you would like would be an American guarantee of your independence!' Gray noted. 'He admitted that it was but saw that it was out of the question to ask that.'

Gray had already made arrangements to meet Craigavon the following week, so he hoped de Valera might be amenable to some measure of cooperation between Dublin and Belfast in order to make progress on the partition issue. The Taoiseach told him, however, that he had already compromised as much as possible. Gray wrote:

> His suggestion was that Ulster join them in neutrality and in return he would reaffirm publicly their adherence and loyalty to external association with the British Commonwealth ... I asked him if he did not think that the crisis was the time to make progress toward union, that a compromise now might produce results that would otherwise be impossible for years to come assuming the allies won. If they did not win Irish freedom was a vanished dream. He agreed in principle but could devise no line of compromise. I fear the common view of him is true that he is incapable of compromise. He had got out on a limb and he is lonely there but does not know how to get back.[17]

De Valera had no desire to get off the neutrality limb, and the Northern Unionists had no intention of compromising anyway. 'He is frightened by the situation but not prepared to cope with it,' Gray wrote. 'I like him and admire him but he is not the man for war. He went to America while Collins was making the decisions.'

A couple of days later Gray had conversations with Tánaiste Seán T. O'Kelly and de Valera's predecessor, W.T. Cosgrave, who was leader of the Opposition at the time. Both conversations were heartening. 'You can be sure,' he wrote to Roosevelt next day, 'that neither the Government nor Opposition will do anything like stabbing Britain in the back but neither will go farther than a beneficent neutrality unless the Germans attack.'[18]

When Gray went to Belfast on 22 May, he learned that Craigavon had been summoned to London urgently, so the American Minister had to be content with a discussion with Finance Minister Sir John Andrews and Agriculture Minister Sir Basil Brooke, who would each, in turn, succeed Craigavon as Prime Minister of Northern Ireland. Both adamantly opposed any suggestion of a united Ireland.

It was a particularly eventful day, because Gray learned President Roosevelt had rejected de Valera's request for a pronouncement that the United States was interested in Irish neutrality. 'Any such declaration would imply that we are departing from our traditional policies in regard to European affairs, and would inevitably lead to misunderstanding and confusion in the United States and abroad,' the President telegraphed Gray.[19] The problems of the Dublin government were compounded when the Irish police uncovered evidence of collusion between the IRA and Germany.

During a raid on the Dublin home of Stephen Held, police discovered evidence that he had recently returned from Berlin, where he had gone as an emissary of the IRA in April 1940. He had asked the Germans to send a liaison officer to Ireland to discuss cooperation with the IRA and had presented the *Abwehr* with a plan calling for a German invasion of Ireland to coincide with an IRA uprising. The plan—code-named Kathleen—was for the Germans to land in Ulster and announce they were liberating Northern Ireland. They would then invite Irish nationalists to join them. The Germans were suspicious of Held, however, because, despite his German name, he spoke no German. The forty-three-year-old was born and reared in Ireland and had acquired his name from his adopted father, Michael Held, a German businessman who had migrated to Ireland in 1890.

The police found a copy of the Kathleen plan, as well as evidence that Held was harbouring an *Abwehr* spy, Hermann Goertz, who had been dropped by parachute near Ballivor, County Meath, in the early hours of 5 May 1940. He was the second spy that the *Abwehr* sent to Ireland in 1940.

Ernst Weber-Drohl had landed from a U-boat in Killala Bay on the night of 8 February, but he lost his radio when the small boat in which he was heading to shore overturned. He had been to Ireland before as a circus performer, using the name of 'Atlas the Strong'. He had actually fathered two children while living with an Irish woman in Dublin in 1908 and 1909. He had left her and the children to go to America, promising to send for them, but he never did. The children were put in care and their mother died in a mental hospital in 1923. By 1940 Weber-Drohl was in his sixties, and his mission was to establish contact with James O'Donovan of the IRA and make arrangements to supply German arms to the organisation. After making contact with O'Donovan and the IRA, his efforts to contact Germany were hampered by the loss of his transmitter. He was arrested on 24 April and charged with entering the country illegally. He told a sob story about looking for his children, and the court released him. He was kept under surveillance and was eventually interned in August 1942.

Goertz was sent to Ireland to set up contact with the IRA for the *Abwehr*. He was also to try to reconcile the IRA with the Irish authorities, as well as to direct the activities of the IRA against British military targets and to report any matters of military importance. He brought a radio, which was dropped on a separate parachute, but he was never able to find it. Before leaving Germany, Hempel had met Francis Stuart, the Australian-born, English-educated husband of Iseult Gonne, the daughter of Maud Gonne MacBride. Stuart, who was lecturing at the University of Berlin, gave Goertz the address of his wife in Laragh, County Wicklow. Goertz arrived at her home on the morning of 9 May. She was a half-sister of Seán MacBride, a former Chief of Staff of the IRA during the 1930s. The IRA brought Goertz to Dublin and put him up in a number of houses, including Held's home in the Templeogue area. On the night of 22 May he planned to meet Stephen Hayes, the IRA's acting Chief of Staff, but Hayes cancelled the meeting. Held and Goertz went out for a walk. They arrived back to find police at the house, so Goertz hid.

The police found his papers during the raid, along with a radio-transmitter, receiver and a file containing information about Irish airfields, harbours, roads, bridges, landing places and the distribution of Irish defence forces. Held's passport had not only been stamped as he crossed the border from Holland into Germany, but also, even more ominously, in Britain upon his return from the Continent. In May 1918 the British had rounded up de Valera and practically the whole leadership of Sinn Féin for supposed involvement in a so-called German Plot. The evidence then had not been any more compelling, so there was a real danger Churchill might use the Held affair as a pretext for acting against Ireland.

De Valera moved boldly. He invited the two main opposition parties, Fine Gael and Labour, to join with the government in a consultative Defence Conference, to be made up of three representatives from Fianna Fáil, three from Fine Gael and two from the Labour Party. The representatives were: Frank Aiken, Defence Minister Oscar Traynor, and Justice Minister Gerry Boland of Fianna Fáil; Deputy Leader James Dillon of Fine Gael and his colleagues Richard Mulcahy and T.F. O'Higgins; and Labour leader William Norton and his colleague William Davin. The conference was designed as a show of solidarity in order to allow a united Dáil to call on the Irish people to support neutrality. For the first time since the civil war, men with deep personal animosities began to share public platforms in support of the government's defence policies at public meetings and recruiting drives for the Army and Local Defence Forces (LDF)—a kind of reserve or Home Guard.

The government lost no time in notifying the British about the Held affair. Joe Walshe and Colonel Archer went to London, where they met the new Permanent Under Secretary at the Dominions Office, Eric Machtig, and other officials on 23 May to assure them that if Germany invaded, Ireland would fight and would call for British help 'the moment it became necessary'. There would be no question of simply surrendering, as Denmark had done. They agreed to a recent British request to establish a secret liaison between the British and Irish military to prepare joint contingency plans to resist a German invasion. The British moved a Royal Marine brigade to Milford Haven, Wales, in preparation to go to Ireland 'at the shortest possible notice', but the bulk of the British forces would intervene from Northern Ireland.[20]

After the talks in England, Walshe and Archer went to Northern Ireland with a staff officer to meet with General Sir Hubert Huddleston, the General Officer commanding British forces in Northern Ireland. Two of Huddleston's officers then accompanied Walshe and Archer to Dublin next day for talks with Lieutenant General Daniel McKenna, the Chief of Staff of the Irish Army. A combined Anglo-Irish response was agreed in the event of a German invasion. A British signals group was attached to the Irish Army headquarters in Dublin to provide direct communications with the British Army headquarters in Northern Ireland, and the British air attaché was authorised to set up an RAF radio station in Maffey's office.

The British were happy with the staff talks, but feared the Irish might be 'somewhat too confident in their ability to deal with internal subversive activities'.[21] An inter-service committee consisting of Admiral Sir Dudley Pound of the Royal Navy, Marshal Sir Cyril Newall of the Royal Air Force and Lieutenant General Sir Robert H. Haining of the Army informed the British Cabinet on 30 May that 'the Irish Authorities have shown a genuine desire to cooperate'. But this committee still thought Irish neutrality was a handicap to the British war effort. 'Our conclusions are that a neutral Éire assists Germany in general prosecution of the war, and denies us the use of important bases,' they reported.[22]

When the British War Cabinet discussed Ireland that day, even Chamberlain betrayed alarm, contending that the IRA had become 'almost strong enough to over-run the weak Éire forces'. Britain should therefore be 'ready to send forces to southern Ireland', he suggested. [23] Contingency plans had already been drawn up.

From Dublin that same day Gray was fatuously suggesting to President Roosevelt that de Valera might be toppled by his own representatives on the Defence Conference in conjunction with opposition members. After meeting with James Dillon, the deputy leader of Fine Gael, Gray reported that Dillon 'is for throwing in with Britain at once as the lesser of two dangers'. If de

Valera held back, Gray suggested the opposition might win over some of his representatives and 'take over for the duration of hostilities as they did in the Black and Tan times and later in the civil war. He lacks the quick decision for emergency.'[24] The American Minister was relying on a very superficial knowledge of Irish history and allowing his own desires to get the better of his judgment. The Defence Conference was merely a consultative body, with no executive function.

In the same letter to Roosevelt, Gray also mentioned that there was a danger the British would seize Irish territory. 'The most important thing, however, of which I dare not write except most confidentially, is the possibility of events shaping so that the British would have to occupy Berehaven to combat the submarine menace when it starts up again.'[25]

Churchill was not as anxious as some of his colleagues. He showed no concern when General Hastings Ismay warned on 29 May that 'secret sources' had indicated the Germans had 'detailed plans with the IRA and that everything is now ready for an immediate descent upon the country'.[26] A German attack on Ireland would have 'various advantages for us', Churchill replied. The British would have the advantage in confronting the Luftwaffe over Ireland, and they would then be able to take Berehaven for their own use. 'We should have split the Sinn Féiners effectively and should have the greater part of the population on our side for the first time in history,' he added.[27]

Greatly embarrassed by the Held affair, Hempel recommended that any mention of Northern Ireland on German radio should 'be considerably toned down' or postponed for the time being. He was under no illusions about de Valera's attitude.[28] On the same day that Walshe went to London, Hempel warned Berlin that de Valera would 'maintain the line of friendly understanding with England as far as it is at all possible, on account of geographical and economic dependence, which will continue even in the event of England's defeat, as well as his democratic principles, even in the face of the threatening danger of Ireland becoming involved in the war'.[29]

The manner in which de Valera confronted the challenge unfolded in the following weeks. His policy was to present a united front at home to convince the belligerents that Ireland would use all its resources to resist invasion by anyone. He sought assurances from the British and German governments that they would respect Irish neutrality, but both initially refused. He therefore tried to play them off against each other by making it clear that if Germany invaded, he would enlist British help, and that if Britain invaded, he would call for German assistance. The British and Germans were already fighting each other, so this threat was not a deterrent. He needed to convince each side it had more to lose than gain by violating Irish neutrality.

With Churchill fulminating over the denial of Irish bases, it was easier to convince the Germans that Irish neutrality was in their interest. Walshe told the Italian Minister that his confidence in the Germans had been so shaken by the discovery of the *Abwehr* spy that some guarantee was needed in order to withstand mounting British pressure. He was basically using the Italian Minister to pass on a veiled threat that concessions would be made to the British unless the Germans gave an assurance to respect Irish neutrality.

In private conversations with German representatives, Irish officials naturally sought to depict Irish policy in as favourable a light as possible towards Germany. For the most part, de Valera kept his contacts with Axis representatives to a minimum, usually leaving discussions with Hempel to either Walshe or Frederick H. Boland, the Assistant Secretary of the Department of External Affairs, or the Irish fobbed off Hempel by suggesting that matters be taken up with William Warnock, the Irish *chargé d'affaires* in Berlin.

Although acting in a senior capacity, Warnock was only a junior official. He took over on 1 August 1939 after the recall of Charles Bewley, who had become bitterly anti-Semitic and was critical of de Valera's lack of sympathy with the Fascists. Rather than return to Dublin, Bewley quit the service in virtual disgrace and went into retirement on the Continent. The war began before Eoin McKiernan could replace him. Once Britain went to war with Germany, de Valera decided not to ask the British King to provide a letter of credence for McKiernan. Warnock, the Secretary of the Legation, therefore remained as *chargé d'affaires* until late 1943. As a relatively junior official, he had little scope for personal initiative, and it was easy to exploit his difficulties in communicating with the Department of External Affairs as a means of frustrating German initiatives. At times, however, especially in the latter half of 1940 and the first half of 1941, when the Nazis appeared almost invincible, Walshe, Boland and Warnock may have gone a bit further in depicting themselves as favourably disposed towards Germany than they might later, in hindsight, have thought prudent.

On 21 May 1940, for instance, the Director of the Political Department of the German Foreign Ministry reported that Warnock had told him that Ireland had 'struck too early' against England during World War I and should not make the same mistake again.[30] Warnock did not actually say that Ireland intended to exploit Britain's difficulties, but he obviously hoped the Germans would infer this from his remarks. As German forces were rolling over France, Hempel reported, 'Walshe expressed great admiration for the German achievements.' He gave the distinct impression of being more afraid of Britain than Germany by suggesting that 'fears of England occupied first place'.[31] This was essentially accurate, as de Valera later admitted he was more afraid of the British at the time. 'The least of the government's worries then during the period was the danger of attack from the continent,' he explained in 1950. His fears were exacerbated by the attitude of the British. 'I tried to get from them an assurance that there would not be an attack by them upon this country,' he said. 'But I did not get that assurance. There was always a reservation.'[32]

Both Walshe and Boland pretended to suspect that Stephen Held might have been a British *agent provocateur*. Since Hitler had recently told an American reporter that Germany had no intention of dismantling the British Empire, Walshe expressed the hope to Hempel that Hitler would not abandon Ireland to the wrath of the British after the war.

The Germans did not wish to drive the Irish into the arms of the British, so Berlin instructed Hempel to tell the Irish that Goertz's mission was 'aimed exclusively against England' and 'activity of any sort against the Irish government was expressly forbidden'. Some Irish people had proposed 'subversive plans against the Irish government' to Goertz, but he had 'always' rejected them, according to Berlin.[33] The German Foreign Office noted Hitler was anxious to facilitate the Irish in some way in relation to the blockade of the British Isles. 'The Führer wishes,' the Foreign Office explained on 6 June, 'to make an exception in some form for Ireland, as otherwise Ireland, instead of being separated from England, will be forced into her arms.'[34]

Nevertheless the Germans pointedly refused to declare at that time that they would not invade Ireland. 'Such a declaration was impossible in the present circumstances,' Hempel said.[35] He told Walshe, however, that he felt sure Germany did not intend to attack Ireland. 'But he could not ask his Government—as I had suggested—to make a statement saying they would not make use of Irish territory in their attack on England,' Walshe noted. 'That would be tantamount to a partial revealing of their plans to the enemy.'[36]

Chapter 7 ⌇

| RESTRAINING CHURCHILL

De Valera kept Churchill at bay by threatening to appeal to American public opinion and by enlisting the help of the Irish-American community to condemn any British violation of Ireland's neutrality. The government also sought to bolster the country's defences in a number of ways. Internment of IRA suspects was stepped up dramatically and a concentration camp opened at the Curragh.

'When great powers are locked in mortal combat the rights of small nations are as naught to them,' de Valera warned in an address on Radio Éireann on 1 June 1940. 'The only thing that counts is how one may secure an advantage over the other, and, if the violation of our territory promises such an advantage, then our territory will be violated, our country will be made a cockpit, our homes will be levelled and our people slaughtered.' The greatest danger was 'internal division', he added, 'for assuredly in this hour if we do not in our several sections hang together we shall indeed hang separately'.[1]

The American Minister saw the Irish difficulties as his chance to acquire influence in Dublin by securing much-needed equipment for the Irish Army. He urged the State Department to do what it could to comply with Irish requests to purchase twenty-five fighter planes, seventeen armoured cars, 1,000 rifles, ammunition and other items, including four destroyers. 'No time for economy,' he telegraphed the State Department on 4 June. He pressed Roosevelt and the State Department to supply equipment as soon as possible. He only balked at a request for the destroyers. 'The Irish government has no more use for one destroyer than I have for a white elephant,' Gray wrote. 'To defend this coast with a navy would require, in the opinion of experts, a fleet of submarines and fast torpedo boats, entirely beyond the means of the nation.'[2]

Secretary of State Hull asked Joe Kennedy to find out if the British had any objections to the United States supplying arms to the Irish. 'Provided it does not impede or postpone delivery of any similar material ordered by the British government,' London had no objection, according to Kennedy.[3] This effectively scuttled the whole thing because the British were already looking for so much.

Churchill again pressed for the US Navy to visit Ireland. 'An American squadron at Berehaven would do no end of good I am sure,' he wrote to Roosevelt on 13 June 1940. But the President turned down the request.[4]

Gray persisted in believing the Irish could be persuaded to abandon neutrality in return for a deal on partition and better equipment for the Irish Army. He was trying desperately to avert a British violation of Irish neutrality, because of its likely impact on American public opinion. If it became necessary to seize Irish bases, he warned Information Minister Duff Cooper, the British should announce the action was being taken to ensure the continued delivery of vital supplies to Ireland, or say that de Valera had made 'a gentleman's agreement' with Chamberlain at the time the ports were handed over in 1938, guaranteeing Britain use of bases in case of an emergency.[5] Either of these pronouncements might deceive some people, but Gray realised it would be best if Dublin gave up the facilities voluntarily in order to make progress towards ending partition. He therefore arranged a meeting with Craigavon for 7 June 1940 at Government House in Hillsborough.

Foreign Secretary Lord Halifax and former Prime Ministers Neville Chamberlain and Stanley Baldwin were already having second thoughts about partition. On 27 May the War Cabinet invited Chamberlain and the new Dominions Secretary Lord Caldecote (formerly Sir Thomas Inskip) to prepare 'an immediate approach to de Valera in order to bring home to him the danger facing Éire, and the need, in order to combat it, for early and full cooperation with this country'. It was also decided to 'invite Lord Craigavon to agree that the Government of Northern Ireland should take part in an All-Ireland Council during the period of the present emergency'.[6]

Chamberlain met with Craigavon on 5 June and appealed to him to consider what conciliatory gestures the people of Northern Ireland would be willing to make. Maffey told Gray that Craigavon had been called to London, where he was supposedly given 'merry hell' and told to 'end partition on the best terms he could'.[7] As a result, Gray expected Craigavon to be more accommodating than Andrews or Brooke had been, but he was to be disappointed.

'I never would have known that he had been crushed by the Downing Street steam roller,' Gray reported. He described Craigavon as 'a red faced hard bitter fellow of 71 with fishy grey blue eyes set at an angle. He has a pleasant smile for a face cut out of granite rock. However I liked him from the start and we got along fine.'[8]

'I became satisfied that he intended to do nothing or learn nothing,' Gray also wrote. 'He was a perfect Bourbon but very pleasant.'[9]

Although Craigavon seemed pleasantly surprised to hear de Valera had been making serious preparations to prevent Germany from using Ireland as a back-door to Britain, he was still unwilling to consider any political concessions to Dublin. What would happen if the Nazis invaded Northern Ireland and proclaimed they were liberating the area? Gray asked.

'Oh, we'll take care of them,' Craigavon replied.[10]

When Gray suggested the whole island establish a united defence front, Craigavon said it was a good idea, but it was a matter for the General Staff in London. 'He absolutely refused to take any step that would recognise the South in any way that differentiated Ulster from Britain,' according to Gray.[11]

De Valera had been highlighting his own government's weakness by insisting that Irish people were so divided, he had to remain neutral. As a result the British became susceptible to outrageous rumours of weakness on the part of the Dublin government. MI6 agents—who were drawn mostly from former servicemen or Anglo-Irish loyalists—generated absurd rumours, and people who should have known better credulously accepted these alarmist reports.

'A submarine base is said to exist near the mouth of the Doonbeg river in south west Clare,' Guy Liddell noted earlier in his MI5 diary on the basis of MI6 information. 'A submarine comes in 3 times a week and is camouflaged with a canvas screen.'[12] Desmond Morton—who, as an opponent of British appeasement, had provided Churchill with important intelligence on German rearmament in the 1930s and had been appointed a Personal Assistant when Churchill became Prime Minister—warned that the Nazis already had their *Gauleiter*s functioning in Éire, and that Seán Russell had formed a shadow cabinet and was ready to play the role in Dublin that Vidkun Quisling had played for the Nazis in Oslo following the German invasion of Norway. Russell was not even in Ireland at the time.

Morton supported his views with an alarmist intelligence report from Sir Charles Tegart, a graduate of Trinity College Dublin whom Lloyd George had sent to Dublin Castle to serve as chief assistant to Ormonde Winter, the head of British intelligence operations in Ireland during the Black and Tan period. Tegart got squeezed out in the bureaucratic intrigue and went on to become British police chief in Bombay, India. He retained contacts at Trinity College and was awarded an honorary doctorate in 1933. He made a number of trips to Ireland for MI6 and he credulously reported that German submarines were calling regularly to isolated spots around Ireland. 'Local Irishmen accept the visits of U-boats with as common place an air as they accept the sun rise on a fine day,' reported Tegart. He added that 2,000 Germans had already landed in Ireland, 'many ostensibly studying folklore'. This report, which was submitted to the British Cabinet, noted the Germans were buying up interests on the south and west coasts of Ireland, rooting up hedges and levelling suitable fields for landing grounds. Tegart's report was largely hysterical nonsense. It was a measure of the hysteria gripping Britain about Nazi intrigue in Ireland that, even though Chamberlain realised there was no back-up data, he still chose to believe that 'the general picture presented is a true one'.[13]

As the Allied position crumbled on the Continent, Gray looked on in frustration. The British had been lucky to escape at Dunkirk, but the French were left prostrate in front of the advancing German forces. Then on 10 June 1940 Italy entered the war on the side of Germany. Gray learned of the Italian move from the BBC. 'We heard Duff Cooper announce Mussolini's entrance into the war in a speech that is probably the bitterest speech ever made over the radio,' Gray wrote to Roosevelt. 'I don't suppose there ever was quite such a son of a bitch. I shall wait up to hear you at twelve fifteen.'[14] The President used his speech to inform the American people of his plan to aid the Allies more directly. 'The whole of our sympathies lies with those nations that are giving their life blood in combat against these forces,' Roosevelt announced that night. The United States was therefore going to 'extend to the opponents of force the material resources of this nation'.[15]

In the early hours of the following morning the *SS Washington*—an American passenger liner with 1,020 passengers bound for Galway, from Lisbon, en route to the United States—was stopped by a U-boat, which gave those aboard the *Washington* 10 minutes to abandon ship. The ship signalled frantically with a blinker that she was an American vessel. The U-boat then invited her to go on her way. Gray was told the *Washington* had actually been torpedoed, but she arrived safely in Galway and took on an additional 852 American passengers, before setting out on 15 June for New York, where she was greeted with much fanfare six days later.

The whole thing was a sidelight on the war for the Irish, but it was a reminder for Americans of how public opinion in the United States had been inflamed against Germany prior to America's entry into World War I. Gray threw diplomatic caution to the wind in an effort to help the British. He went out on a limb by calling on colleagues of both de Valera and Craigavon to use their influence to get the two leaders to compromise with one another. He urged Joe Walshe, on 12 June, to put pressure on the Taoiseach. 'Dev is sure not to compromise,' he said, and they should therefore 'put pressure on him from within his own party'.[16] Gray's behaviour was not only extraordinarily indiscreet, but also patently inept.

Walshe was a civil servant with the typical attitude of his profession. He loyally served the government and implemented its policy regardless of his own personal views. He had never been a member of Fianna Fáil. In fact, he had supported the opposite side in the civil war of 1922–3 and would therefore have had very little influence within Fianna Fáil. De Valera was actually resisting the anti-British overtures of some of his more radical Republican supporters from the past. 'You are deceiving the Irish people,' warned Mary MacSwiney, a sister of Terence MacSwiney, the Lord Mayor of Cork who died on a famous hunger strike in 1920. 'You are calling for unity and will not do the only thing which will bring unity. Was there ever a period in which England's difficulty was more surely Ireland's opportunity than now?' she asked. 'You could unite the country for the Republic. You still have the chance to do that. Failure to do so, here and now, will write you down in time to come as the greatest failure Irish history has ever known. The pity of it! If you bring a new civil war on this country, and you are going the right way to do just that, you will deserve a fate worse than Castlereagh's.'[17]

'What terrifies me,' de Valera told Gray, 'was the danger the Germans would invade County Donegal and announce that they had come to liberate Northern Ireland. 'If I was the Germans, I would land at these points and proclaim myself a liberator,' he explained as he pointed out a couple of spots on Donegal Bay on a map. 'If they should do that, what I could do I do not know.'[18] He was obviously afraid the Germans would try to implement the IRA's Plan Kathleen.

Early on the morning of 13 June the Germans landed another spy in Ireland, this time by submarine. Walter Simon (58) was landed near Dingle. He was seen burying his radio. He had been interned in Australia for the duration of World War 1 and had been caught spying in Britain in 1937 and spent six months in jail. He was sent to Ireland to prepare for Operation Sea Lion, the planned German invasion of Britain. He was supposed to observe the movement of British naval vessels in Northern Ireland and was instructed to have no contact with the IRA. He could not have been landed much further from Northern Ireland. Seeing a railroad track, he asked some workmen what time the next train was due, only to be told the last passenger train had run fourteen years earlier. He went into Dingle and took a bus to Tralee, but by then the alarm had been raised and all the local defence units were scouring the countryside.

Simon planned to take a train to Dublin, but two local detectives, James Colley and Bill Walshe, noticed sand on his shoes and became suspicious. They engaged him in conversation and accompanied him on the journey to Dublin. They notified Gardaí in Dublin, and Simon was duly arrested when he arrived there. He gave a false name, but his true identity was uncovered when his fingerprints were checked with the British. He was sentenced to three years in jail for illegal entry and was interned for the duration of the war.

Churchill tried to enlist the diplomatic influence of friendly governments to appeal to the Dublin government to allow Britain to use Irish bases. South

African Premier Jan C. Smuts, who thought appealing to de Valera would be a waste of time, advised Britain to seize the Irish bases forthwith, but Churchill rejected this because of likely American repercussions. 'Although as a last resort we should not hesitate to secure the ports by force,' Churchill said, 'it would be unwise at this moment to take any action that might compromise our position with the United States of America, in view of the present delicate developments.'[19]

Vincent Massey, the Canadian High Commissioner in London, advised his government to appeal to both de Valera and Craigavon. Every effort was being made to impress the gravity of the situation on both de Valera and Craigavon, but neither seemed likely to come to London. 'Should German forces succeed in landing on Irish soil and gaining a foothold there, they could easily establish air bases from which they could gravely threaten western ports of Great Britain,' Massey wrote. 'It is profoundly to be hoped that before it is too late both will realise that presence of Nazi *Gauleiter* in Ireland would extinguish the ideal for which both Ulster and Éire stand.'[20]

Oscar Skelton, the longtime Under Secretary of State for External Affairs, agreed with Massey. 'Again English Tories are paying for their sins in not having met the Irish situation long ago and in obstinacy of Craigavon today,' Prime Minister Mackenzie King noted in his diary.[21] He had been worried about the possibility of German invasion of Ireland for the past couple of weeks. When he talked to the Catholic Archbishop Arthur A. Sinnott of Winnipeg, the archbishop 'seemed to regard it as a great joke that de Valera might have to defend Ireland against the Germans', but Mackenzie King thought it was 'a tragedy that a settlement was not made with the Irish years ago'.[22]

'Conquest of Ireland by the Germans is the next possible appalling possibility,' the Canadian Prime Minister observed. 'Another would-be neutral nation will be pierced at its heart in consequence of its neutrality. The world is learning that with moral issues there is no such thing as neutrality.'[23] He approved the similar telegrams drafted by Skelton to de Valera and Craigavon. 'I venture to assure you of the deep and friendly concern of the people of Canada for what the unbounded ambitions of Nazi leaders may shortly hold for the people of Ireland as for all other free peoples,' Mackenzie King explained. 'There is little doubt that their forces will be directed against Ireland, because of its tempting value as a prize in itself and as a base for immediate operations against Great Britain.'[24]

'If that attack succeeds,' he continued, 'it will mean that the individual liberties, the national aspirations, and the deep loyalties of all Irishmen, whatever differences may have divided them in the past, will be in equal and deadly jeopardy. The people of Canada who owe so great a debt to the men and women of Ireland, north and south alike who have shared in the building of our country, would feel that fate their own.' He therefore urged the two to meet each other and work out a 'basis upon which united and effective resistance could be offered in the event of invasion or attack'.[25]

Craigavon would have nothing to do with this. 'Any question of rendering assistance to Mr De Valera to guard against enemy invasion is one for His Majesty's Government in United Kingdom in consultation with Mr de Valera,' Craigavon replied to Mackenzie King's telegram.[26] De Valera, on the other hand, did not even acknowledge the Canadian Prime Minister's telegram until the following September.[27]

While efforts to get the Dublin government to join openly in the defence of Britain were making little headway, the British ordered that plans be drawn up for the occupation of the Shannon estuary, Cobh and Berehaven.[28] Chamberlain and Dominion Secretary Caldecote had failed to get Craigavon to make a gesture towards Irish unity, and de Valera refused to come to London for talks, fearing such a move could lead to complications at home. Chamberlain would be too easily recognised in Ireland, so the War Cabinet instead sent Health Minister Malcolm MacDonald to Dublin, in an attempt to convince de Valera to abandon neutrality and to 'invite British troops' in to help defend the island.

The British aim was to entice de Valera by proposing the establishment of 'a Council for the defence of all Ireland' that would organise the island's defences against a German invasion. 'It would be too late to do anything after the invasion had started, when bridges would be blown up to impede troop movements, and de Valera himself probably shot,' Chamberlain argued. 'The whole thing might be over in a matter of hours.' If de Valera agreed, the British Cabinet authorised MacDonald to discuss the issue with Craigavon.[29]

MacDonald had a three-and-a-half-hour meeting with de Valera on the evening of 17 June 1940. 'His mind is still set in the same hard, confined mould as of yore,' MacDonald reported. 'But in another way he appeared to have changed. He made no long speeches; the whole procedure was much more in the nature of a sustained conversation between two people than used sometimes to be the case. He seemed depressed and tired, and I felt that he had neither the mental nor the physical vigour that he possessed two years ago.'[30] As Ireland was too weak to defend herself against a German attack, MacDonald suggested de Valera abandon neutrality immediately and join with Britain. 'From this moment onwards cooperation could be complete and we could put whatever naval and military forces were required at his disposal,' MacDonald argued. 'We did not give this advice simply because it would help us; indeed, we gave it principally in the interests of Éire itself.'[31]

If partition had been ended before the war, de Valera said he might be in a position to invite the British in, but the way things stood, he could not agree to a defence arrangement with Northern Ireland because this would be a violation of neutrality. From a purely democratic perspective, he had no option but to remain neutral. 'The whole force of public opinion was against any abandonment of neutrality,' he insisted. Irish people did not understand the real Nazi menace because they knew little of what the Germans were doing on the Continent, and their ignorance was bolstered by a strong historical prejudice against Britain that would 'take a long time to remove'.[32] It was less than twenty years since Churchill had been instrumental in imposing a reign of terror in Ireland. The dreaded Auxiliaries, an elite corps of officers who served as part of the Black and Tans, were his brainchild as Minister for War. They were responsible for probably the most infamous incident of the whole conflict, on the afternoon of Bloody Sunday, 21 November 1920. The Auxiliaries fired indiscriminately on the crowd of spectators at a football game in Croke Park, Dublin, killing fourteen spectators and one of the players on the field. The action had been a reprisal for the killing by the IRA of twelve undercover British agents and two Auxiliaries in the city that morning. Less than twenty years later many Irish people felt it would do the British some good to suffer some of their own medicine for a change. But this did not mean the majority of the Irish people hoped the Nazis would win the war.

While people on extremes of both the left and right of the Irish political spectrum—Republicans and Blueshirts—believed Germany would liberate Northern Ireland, their views were representative of a distinct minority. People like Dan Breen and Tom McEllistrim, who had been responsible for some of the earliest incidents of the war of independence, advocated an alliance with Germany, but the vast majority of Irish people hoped Britain would ultimately win the war. According to Gray, the real Irish attitude was epitomised by the farmer who said, 'I'd like to see England NEARLY bate.'[33]

De Valera laughed when Gray told him the story. 'That's it,' he said. 'NEARLY. But that has never been my idea. As soon as I was confident that they were going to let us alone I have wanted a very strong England.'[34] But he was in no position to invite British forces into Ireland. If Germany attacked, he said, 'his men would fight magnificently', according to MacDonald. 'The Germans would not find things easy, for the Irish were very skilful at guerrilla warfare; they were very good hedge fighters and would fight the invader from hedge to hedge.'[35] De Valera seemed to be talking in the absurd terms of the Irish people resisting by hiding behind hedges when they would have little more than rocks to throw at advancing Germans.

The Taoiseach believed 'he was carrying out a completely realistic policy and regarded determination to resist any attacker to the uttermost as the only possibility to reduce the danger,' according to the German Minister. 'In an English invasion we would fight with Irishmen against the English,' Hempel wrote. 'In a German invasion the English would fight along with the Irish.'

Freddy Boland told Hempel that British pressure was being exerted against neutrality with the 'bait' of concessions on Northern Ireland being offered, but he said de Valera had rejected all advances 'most vehemently'.[36] De Valera, for his part, made it clear to the German Minister the same day that he was only looking for a peaceful solution to the partition issue. 'With regard to the solution of the Northern Irish question he must, in view of the English-Irish power relationship, adhere to a peaceful solution, as only so could a permanent and tenable position be reached.'[37]

Some in London had growing reservations about giving Craigavon an effective veto, especially if the alternative was British seizure of Irish facilities. Ambassador Kennedy warned the State Department on 18 June that the British were considering action over Ireland very soon.

'What Maffey is chiefly concerned about,' Gray wrote to Roosevelt, 'is the possibility of submarine war making the need of a protected port essential in Southern Ireland. I warned him again against forcible action on the score of its effect upon American opinion and the opportunity it would give enemies of Britain to score.'[38] In the circumstances, the idea of offering to end partition in return for Irish cooperation gained momentum in London. Labour Minister Ernest Bevin urged Churchill to enlist Roosevelt's support for the joint Defence Council, 'on the basis of a united Ireland at the end of hostilities'.[39]

'I certainly sh'd welcome any approach to Irish unity,' Churchill noted at the end of Bevin's letter, 'but I have 40 years experience of its difficulties. I c'd never be a party to the coercion of Ulster to join the Southern counties; but I am in favour of their being persuaded. The key to this is de Valera showing loyalty to the Crown and Empire.'[40] If the Germans invaded Ireland from the air, Churchill told a secret session of parliament on 20 June, 'Germany would fight in Ireland under great disadvantages' because her troops would have to fight without much heavy artillery. Hence he would 'much rather they break Irish neutrality than we.'[41]

Once the French ports were in German hands, the value of the Irish ports to the British diminished, though some of the British naval authorities did not realise this for some time. Admiral Tom Phillips, the Vice Chief of Naval Staff, thought the use of southern Irish ports had become more vital to protect British shipping. Hence plans were prepared to seize the bases. Even Chamberlain concluded the ports should be seized, if necessary. He felt, however, that every effort should first be made to win over de Valera, going so far as offering to end partition. He said Craigavon 'would have to be told that the interests of Northern Ireland could not be allowed to stand against the vital interests of the British Empire.'[42]

The Cabinet sent MacDonald back to Dublin to determine whether de Valera would be willing to hand over the ports in return 'for a declaration stating His Majesty's Government were, in principle, in favour of the establishment of a United Ireland'.[43] Even at this stage, however, Chamberlain feared it was too late to change the 'unshakable obstinacy' of de Valera. 'I am still at him,' the former Prime Minister wrote to his sister next day, 'but fear he won't be moved till the Germans are in Dublin.'[44]

'Obviously we could not likely undertake the conduct of another war in Ireland at the present time,' Dominion Secretary Caldecote wrote. 'It may be that circumstances will arise in which no other course is open to us, and that we may have to choose what, at the time, appears to be the lesser of two evils. But anyone who remembers the extraordinary difficulties experienced in military operations in 1920 and 1921 and who considers the extremely bad effect on relations with the United States which such a step would have, must necessarily hesitate before recommending that such an extreme step should be taken.'[45]

De Valera asked Gray about the significance of Roosevelt appointing two prominent members of the Republican Party to his Cabinet: Henry L. Stimson as Secretary of War, and Frank Knox as Secretary of the Navy. Both men were outspoken interventionists. Stimson had served in the same post as early as 1911, under President William H. Taft, and had distinguished himself as Secretary of State in the administration of Herbert Hoover, while Knox was vice-presidential nominee on the Republican ticket defeated by Roosevelt in 1936.

'Our position was that of being morally at war with Germany now,' Gray explained. 'Neither Stimson nor Knox could have taken this step except after consultation with other Republican leaders,' he continued. 'Personally I could only regard it as a step toward more active assistance to the Allied cause in the interest of American defence.'[46]

In the light of these changes de Valera was obviously hoping there might yet be a possibility of getting an American guarantee for Irish neutrality. 'He asked me whether if Ulster joined the South in neutrality the United States could not guarantee that combined neutrality,' Gray reported. 'I told him that the Secretary of State's reply to his inquiry as to the possibility of guaranteeing Éire's status quo would in my opinion be the answer to a new inquiry, namely that it was impossible.'[47]

'I told him I thought he was doing everything he could do and doing it very well and asked him if any word had come from Craigavon. He said no,'

Gray wrote. 'If I were you I would sit tight and wait for it,' Gray said, 'but when it comes I think you would do well to make compromises and meet them more than half way.'

'There is only one solution of this thing and that is for the North to join us in our neutrality until we are invaded,' de Valera replied. 'We could be more useful that way.'

'That was absolutely out of the question,' Gray insisted. 'Britain must control the narrows on both sides and have access to the ports.' If England were defeated, Germany would occupy Ireland in order to control the Atlantic.

'If America came in, it would alter our situation over night,' de Valera said, 'but as it is I can't throw in with Britain now. We have no arms.' He could not ask the nation 'to face an enemy in coats of mail, even if I were sure the people would follow me'.

'Perhaps if you throw in now, England would share her arms with you,' Gray contended.

'Why doesn't she do it now?' de Valera asked. 'They ought to let us have anti-tank guns for one thing,' he added. 'A few tanks, if landed Wicklow way or on the West, could roam about Ireland unmolested except by landmines and it would only be chance that we could mine the right roads.'[48]

Chapter 8 ∾

| A LAST DESPERATE EFFORT

'I have been telegraphing frantically to you for rifles for the volunteers the past few days first because they are needed here and second because the time may come soon when the most useful thing I can do for you is strongly to urge compromise with Ulster on Mr. de Valera and I want to be thought of as helpful to them and well disposed,' Gray wrote to Roosevelt on 19 June 1940. 'The Government needs the rifles even more to establish confidence in its power to obtain them than for actual defence.'[1]

In messages to the State Department, Gray stressed the importance of helping Dublin get arms in order to bolster American influence on de Valera as the Ulster situation was coming to a crunch point. 'If he balks at a reasonable compromise which will save Ulster's face,' Gray wrote to Roosevelt, 'we'll have to tell him that American opinion will not stand for it.'[2]

Would the Dublin government agree to a 'joint Defence Council' with Northern Ireland in which the Six Counties would remain a belligerent while the rest of the island would stay neutral, but allow the British to use Irish bases, if there was 'a declaration of a United Ireland'? MacDonald asked de Valera on 22 June. The Taoiseach again insisted the best way of ensuring the Germans did not get hold of Ireland was for Northern Ireland to withdraw from the war and agree to Irish unity, and then have Britain and the United States guarantee Irish neutrality. MacDonald dismissed this as 'entirely impracticable'.[3]

De Valera was really evading the issue. MacDonald wanted to know would the Irish government abandon neutrality and join the Allies if Britain declared a united Ireland in principle, with the practical details of this union to be worked out later?

'If there were not only a declaration of a United Ireland in principle, but also agreement upon its constitution, then the Government of Éire might agree to enter the war at once,' de Valera replied. 'But the constitution of a United Ireland would have to be fixed first.'[4]

The British government would need more than just a 'might' to go on,

MacDonald said. But de Valera candidly explained that there was 'a very big question mark after the "might"'. Even if he supported the idea himself, he said he was not sure it would pass because some of his colleagues would undoubtedly be opposed to abandoning neutrality. The Irish people 'were really almost completely unprepared for war', he said. The army was not properly equipped to resist tanks or mechanised troops, and Dublin was practically undefended. 'There were not even any air-raid shelters in the city and the people had no gas masks,' de Valera continued. 'They would be mercilessly exposed to the horrors of modern war, and he and his colleagues could not have it on their consciences that in this state of affairs they had taken the initiative in an action which so exposed them.' If the British had offered to end partition a few months earlier, Maffey was convinced de Valera would have jumped into the war. Indeed, he still thought such an offer might yet sway the Irish Cabinet.[5]

'I suggest that we test this,' Chamberlain said when the British Cabinet considered the latest report on 25 June. He advocated making a formal offer to end partition in return for Irish cooperation. The Cabinet agreed, but Churchill stitched into the record the suggestion that this would ultimately be conditional on Northern Ireland's acceptance. After a short discussion the Cabinet 'agreed that, while the proposed communication did not go beyond asking Mr. de Valera what his attitude would be to the plan suggested, it was liable to be represented as an offer'. Therefore Chamberlain was asked 'to write to Lord Craigavon informally, indicating to him in broad outline of the communication being made to Mr. de Valera'.[6]

Eric Machtig of the Dominions Office explained to Maffey, 'While we have always agreed with you in thinking that a Union of North and South with the consent of both parties was an ideal to be aimed at, it was not until the last phase of the war that we were prepared to face the risk of exercising sufficient pressure to afford a chance of this being achieved.'[7] As a politician, however, Churchill was not about to make such an offer without some reservations, especially when even Chamberlain thought there was little likelihood of success. Ambassador Kennedy warned Washington that Chamberlain believed the initiative would be rejected because 'the Irish unquestionably believe that Britain is going to get licked'.[8]

The British offer was incorporated in a six-point memorandum that MacDonald handed to de Valera the next day, 26 June 1940. The Taoiseach was having great difficulty reading it because his eyesight was failing, so MacDonald read it to him:

(i) A declaration to be issued by the United Kingdom Government forthwith accepting the principle of a United Ireland.

(ii) A joint body including representatives of the Government of Éire and the Government of Northern Ireland to be set up at once to work out the constitutional and other practical details of the Union of Ireland. The United Kingdom Government to give such assistance towards the work of this body as might be desired.

(iii) A joint Defence Council representative of Éire and Northern Ireland to be set up immediately.

(iv) Éire to enter the war on the side of the United Kingdom and her allies forthwith, and, for the purposes of the Defence of Éire, the Government of Éire to invite British naval vessels to have the use of ports in Éire and British troops and aeroplanes to cooperate with the Éire forces and to be stationed in such positions in Éire as may be agreed between the two Governments.

(v) The Government of Éire to intern all German and Italian aliens in the country and to take any further steps necessary to suppress Fifth Column activities.

(vi) The United Kingdom Government to provide military equipment at once to the Government of Éire.[9]

There followed an elaborate list of armaments that the British were prepared to hand over immediately, including sixteen anti-aircraft guns, twelve anti-tank guns, eighty anti-tank rifles, 175 Brenguns, 650 pistols, twenty-four searchlights and 10,000 steel helmets. [10]

In 1914 the British parliament had passed Home Rule for the whole island of Ireland, but its implementation was suspended until after the war. The great majority of Irish people were later shamefully betrayed when, instead of Home Rule, they got the Black and Tans, repression and partition. They had also deceived the Irish delegation with the Boundary Commission in the 1921 Treaty, which was supposed to transfer the contiguous nationalist areas of Northern Ireland to the Irish Free State. Now the British were paying for their duplicity. The offer was so vague that it really amounted to no more than 'a pious hope', in de Valera's view.[11]

'Will you come into the war if we create a united Ireland straight away?' MacDonald asked.[12]

'If we have a united Ireland,' de Valera replied, 'it will be neutral for at least twenty-four hours. We will then call a meeting of our assembly and it will decide if we—as an independent nation—will come into the war.'[13]

Next morning, de Valera's Cabinet rejected the proposals. France had already fallen and Britain seemed on the verge of defeat, with the result that joining the British seemed a preposterous proposition, especially when it was inconceivable that Irish help would make the difference between victory and defeat. Most of the Irish Cabinet sympathised with the British against the Nazis, but some—Frank Aiken and P.J. Little—were convinced Germany would win the war and were therefore anxious to curry favour with the Germans. Those two were so nervous, according to Seán MacEntee, that they gave the impression at Cabinet meetings that Hempel might be looking over their shoulders.

De Valera, Lemass and Aiken met with MacDonald that afternoon. 'Aiken did most of the talking on their side and was even more persistent than de Valera himself had been in urging that the proper solution is a United Ireland which is neutral,' MacDonald reported. 'Lemass seemed to be prepared to discuss our plan in a more reasonable way, but his contributions to [the] discussion were usually cut short by fresh uncompromising interventions from one or other of his colleagues.' They thought the British offer did not provide an assurance of Irish unity.

'I got the impression that de Valera had not passed on to his colleagues the assurance I gave him yesterday that declaration of a United Ireland would settle the issue once and for all, and that there would be no going back on that, for he said that one of the principal reasons why his Cabinet regarded the plan as unacceptable was that they believed a United Ireland would not materialise from it,' MacDonald noted. 'I repeated my assurances categorically to all three ministers and told them that if they rejected [the] plan on this ground it was a false point. I think Lemass, and even Aiken were impressed.'

MacDonald felt it would strengthen the offer if the document was amended 'to give a specific assurance' on the unity issue. Lemass seemed impressed when MacDonald said, 'We would be sufficiently content if Éire did not positively enter war, but remained neutral and invited our ships into her ports and our troops and aeroplanes into her territory as an additional defence against violation of that neutrality.' In other words, Dublin could put the onus on the Germans of declaring war on Ireland. MacDonald had little hope that the proposed amendments would make any real difference. 'I am definitely of opinion that the cabinet here will reject our plan,' he reported. 'I feel their attitude would be different if they had not an impression that we are going to lose the war, and that it would be a mistake for them now to throw in their lot with us.'[14]

'The de Valera people are afraid we are going to lose, and don't want to be involved with us,' Chamberlain noted in his diary.[15] Thus it became easy for London to reassure Craigavon when he voiced alarms about 'sinister evidence that something serious is afoot'.

Senator Frank MacDermot, who was acting as Irish correspondent for *The Observer*, the British Sunday newspaper, had approached Craigavon for his views on the rumoured talks in Dublin. 'I will be no party, directly or indirectly, to any change in the constitution conferred upon Northern Ireland, which assures us of full partnership in the United Kingdom and British Empire,' Craigavon told *The Observer*. 'Nevertheless in the interest of both north and south I am prepared to enter into closest cooperation with Mr de Valera on matters of defence provided he takes his stand, as we are doing, on the side of Britain and the Empire, clears out the German and Italian representatives from Éire and undertakes not to raise any issue of a constitutional nature.'[16]

The British were playing a double game. When Craigavon complained that negotiations were being carried on behind his back, Chamberlain told the War Cabinet on 28 June that 'such an accusation was, of course, entirely unjustified. All that the Government had done was to enquire what would be the attitude of the Government of Éire towards a certain plan. It had throughout been made clear that it would be necessary to obtain the assent thereto of the Government of Northern Ireland.'[17] MacDonald's own reports made patently clear that the offer he brought was essentially to hand over Northern Ireland in return for the use of Irish bases. Maffey led Gray to believe the British were offering to end partition 'lock, stock, and barrel'.[18]

Some months later, after MacDonald was appointed High Commissioner to Canada, Mackenzie King noted in his diary that MacDonald told him of being authorised

> to tell de Valera that the British Government were prepared to concede at once the principle of Home Rule for the whole of Ireland; to make an open declaration on the matter; to appoint a constituent assembly or some other suitable body to draft a Constitution, and to see that all headway possible was made in bringing it into being, if de Valera would agree to join in with Northern Ireland for its support of the war. Malcolm added confidentially, that the government were prepared to compel Northern Ireland to meet Éire in the matter. They had reason to believe they could get that cooperation. De Valera said he would accept the proposal, but only on condition that Ireland could remain neutral, which of course was what the proposal was meant to get over. Malcolm thought it was a great opportunity lost by de Valera. He said that the two men who have the least appreciation that a great war was being fought were de Valera and Craigavon; that both were rigid and inflexible on maintaining their own positions and seemed not to be able to get beyond their previous positions on these matters.[19]

'We believed that if we were foolish enough to accept that invitation,' de Valera told the Dáil some years later, 'we would have been cheated in the end.'[20] As

Sir Basil Brooke, the future Prime Minister of Northern Ireland, later wrote to Gray, 'De Valera knew, of course, that Britain was not in a position to hand us over.'[21]

Was the offer made without the authority of Churchill, or was Churchill just pretending it was always dependent on the eventual approval of Stormont? Only weeks earlier Churchill had put forward a plan for a political union between France and Britain in a vain attempt to keep the French in the war. If de Valera had been interested, there is little doubt that Churchill might well have been prepared to put pressure on Belfast, but just how far he would have gone must remain a matter of conjecture.

After the Dublin government turned down the offer of unity, it was easy for the British to say it was contingent on Craigavon's approval. 'The whole plan depends on our obtaining the assent of Northern Ireland,' Chamberlain wrote to de Valera on 29 June. 'I cannot, of course, give a guarantee that Northern Ireland will assent, but if the plan is accepted by Éire we should do our best to persuade Northern Ireland to accept it also in the interests of the security of the whole island.'[22]

On 2 July de Valera informed Richard Mulcahy of Fine Gael about the British proposals. Mulcahy responded that Fine Gael would support the offer, if the government 'decided that as a united Ireland it would go to war'.[23] The Taoiseach explained the proposals were too vague. Privately, Mulcahy suspected that even with Cosgrave's support, de Valera would be unable to carry the Dáil on the British terms. In Mulcahy's opinion, more than half of Fianna Fáil, one third of Fine Gael and the whole Labour Party would oppose the offer.

'If the Government in changing circumstances feel it necessary to depart from the policy of neutrality in which they have had our support up to the present,' Cosgrave assured the Taoiseach, 'my colleagues and I would be prepared to give them our fullest support in such a change of policy.'[24]

'The assumption that hostile invasion need be feared from one side only is one which cannot in all circumstances be relied upon,' de Valera told Cosgrave. 'As long as we are neutral, there is a possibility that the danger of attack may be averted; whilst if we invite military assistance from one side, immediate attack by the other, with all its consequences, will be almost inevitable.'[25] The Fine Gael leader emphasised that he was not trying to suggest the policy should be changed, but merely indicating his party's view 'if the Government thinks it necessary to take such a decision'.[26]

James Dillon, the only member of the Dáil to advocate abandoning neutrality during the war, agreed with Mulcahy's assessment. 'If de Valera tried to carry the country for abandoning neutrality on the strength of the present British promises,' Dillon told Gray, 'he would be beaten.'[27]

De Valera formally rejected the proposals in a letter to Chamberlain on 5 July. 'The plan would involve our entry into the war. That is a course for which we could not accept responsibility,' he wrote. 'Our people would be quite unprepared for it, and Dáil Éireann would certainly reject it.' The whole thing was too vague because 'it gives no guarantee that in the end we would have a united Ireland', unless the Unionists were given concessions which would be 'opposed to the sentiments and aspirations of the great majority of the Irish people'.[28]

'Our present Constitution represents the limit to which we believe our people are prepared to go to meet the sentiments of the Northern Unionists,' de Valera added, 'but, on the plan proposed, Lord Craigavon and his colleagues could at any stage render the whole project nugatory and prevent the desired unification by demanding concessions to which the majority of the people could not agree. By such methods unity was prevented in the past, and it is obvious that under the plan outlined they could be used again.'[29]

'Get this into your head, MacDermot,' Aiken told Senator Frank MacDermot privately, 'there are no terms on which we would abandon neutrality.'[30]

'The real basic fact is that it is not partition which stands in the way at this moment but the fear of Dev and his friends that we shall be beaten,' Chamberlain concluded. 'They don't want to be on the losing side and if that is unheroic one can only say that it is very much the attitude of the world from the USA to Rumania and from Japan to Ireland.'[31]

Even Gray suspected the British would have been unable to compel Northern Ireland to agree to Irish unity. 'Éire, from the point of view of her own interest in view of existing circumstances, could have done nothing else than refuse the bargain,' he reported. 'In a long view it is better for Anglo-Irish relations that the proposals should have been rejected than that they should have been accepted and Britain had failed to force Ulster into a united Ireland.'[32]

'In the present circumstances acceptance had been impossible,' de Valera later told Maffey. 'It would have meant civil war.'[33]

The first half of July 1940 was probably the most anxious period of the whole war for the Dublin government. The British were hysterical about the danger of Irish fifth columnists and German agents in Ireland, and Hitler was fuelling their paranoia by deliberately trying to deceive the British into thinking Germany was about to invade Ireland. On 28 June Hitler ordered 'all available information media' to indicate a German invasion of Ireland was imminent.[34] The Swiss correspondent of the London *Daily Express* reported, for instance, that the Germans were complaining that Ireland was not observing neutrality. 'Sooner or later,' German newspapers reportedly warned, 'Germany may have to act in consequence as in the case of other small European neutrals.'[35] Reuters news agency reported on 7 July that Hitler and Count Ciano, the Italian Foreign Minister, discussed plans for an offensive against Britain, and that the Rome correspondent of *Basler Nachrichten* reportedly said Ireland would be the first object of any attack on the British Isles.[36]

Only weeks earlier Hempel had refused to give an assurance that Germany would respect Irish neutrality, but now—fearing that de Valera might be going over to the British—he considered it necessary to reassure him and thus bolster the efforts of Walshe and Boland to keep Ireland neutral. As Hempel explained: 'I have had since the beginning of the war, and now to an even greater degree, the impression that the Irish Government is extremely concerned to do everything possible to maintain strict neutrality in spite of the recognised difficulties and that particularly Walshe and Boland are exercising a strong influence on de Valera in this direction.'[37]

German propaganda was, of course, exacerbating fears of a pre-emptive British assault, but Churchill had too many other concerns to be that anxious about a German invasion of Ireland. 'It is not likely that a naval invasion will be effected there,' he wrote on 30 June. He was confident an airborne invasion could be repelled because the Germans would not be able to 'carry much artillery'. Therefore, he concluded, 'nothing that can happen in Ireland can be immediately decisive.'[38]

Irish fears were intensified on 4 July, however, when Churchill referred to the German threat to Ireland during a speech justifying the British attack on the French fleet at Oran and Mers-el-Kebhir hours earlier. Having authorised the attack on ships of France, his recent ally, in order to ensure they did not fall into German hands, there could be no doubt he would endorse drastic action to prevent the Germans getting hold of Irish bases. 'We are making every preparation in our power to repel the assaults of the enemy whether they be directed upon Great Britain or upon Ireland—which all Irishmen, without distinction of creed or party, should realise is in imminent danger,' Churchill told Parliament.[39] Next day he told his cabinet he intended to inform Roosevelt 'that it might be necessary for us, in the near future, and in order to forestall German action, to make a change in our policy towards Éire'.[40] The same day the War Cabinet had a memorandum from the Dominions Secretary, stating that Joe Walshe had secretly assured the British that Dublin 'would turn a blind eye to any action' by British aircraft or vessels investigating suspicious activity in Irish territorial waters or airspace, 'provided our activities were conducted in such a way as not to excite comment'.[41]

Around this time Lieutenant-General Bernard Montgomery noted in his memoirs that he was ordered 'to prepare plans for the seizure of Cork and

Queenstown in Southern Ireland, so that the harbour could be used as a naval base for anti-submarine war in the Atlantic'.[42] De Valera read the ominous signs and his government issued a statement that it was 'resolved to maintain and defend the country's neutrality in all circumstances'.[43] He and Aiken turned to the United States to enlist the support of American public opinion.

During a radio interview, Aiken told Denis Johnson of the American NBC network that Ireland had been scrupulous in observing its neutrality and in an effort not to provoke any of the belligerents had 'avoided doing a lot of things the law permits neutrals to do'. If Ireland were attacked, he said, she would call for help. He dismissed rumours of an internal threat being posed by foreigners. 'The total number of aliens in the country is 2,610,' he said. 'Of these, a couple of weeks ago, almost exactly half were American citizens.' The others came from thirty-four countries; 326 were Germans and about half of those were refugees who had fled the Nazi regime. 'You know how the old Irish saying goes, "God likes a little help," and we are going to try to give Him all the help we can,' Aiken insisted.[44]

De Valera stressed the same theme in an interview with Harold Denny of the *New York Times*. 'We do not have the slightest intention of abandoning our neutrality. We intend to resist any attack, from any quarter whatever,' he said. 'And whoever comes first will be our enemy.'[45]

When addressing an American audience, there was a real danger his words would be interpreted as a veiled attack on the British, so he was quite positive in his remarks about Britain. 'We have got on very well with Britain,' he said. 'All questions between us have been amicably settled except the most important one of all—partition.' While there was still a great deal of Irish bitterness against Britain, he said this did not translate into support for the Nazis. 'Probably few are actually pro-German,' de Valera explained, 'for many Irishmen realise that the Irish with their passion for individualism are the last people in the world who could endure fascist rule.'[46] The interview was an attempt to build up a kind of common identity with the individualism of Americans and remind them that the Irish people shared their desire to avoid involvement in the war. Any British violation of Irish neutrality would make Churchill look little better than Hitler and would probably damage the popular support the Roosevelt administration needed to provide effective aid to Britain.

Both sides in the war were distorting the Irish situation for their own purposes. Although Hitler had ordered the media to indicate that Germany was about to invade Ireland, Hempel told Walshe the Foreign Ministry instructed him to say that such stories 'were pure invention' because 'no such statements had appeared in the German press'. Walshe's response to the German threat was essentially the same as to the British one—to enlist the protection of American public opinion. 'I took the opportunity to urge upon him once more how disastrous it would be for Germany's relations with the United States if his Government acted against his (Hempel's) advice and that of his Foreign Office.'[47]

Churchill, who was particularly anxious to get some American destroyers, was putting the finishing touches to a message to Roosevelt warning that the Irish situation had deteriorated. He sent a copy of the proposed telegram to Halifax, who showed it to Joe Kennedy on 5 July. Unless the British got the destroyers they were seeking, it would not be possible to defend the Channel against Hitler, with the result that the Americans would bear a 'grievous responsibility', Churchill intended to telegraph Roosevelt. 'De Valera and his Party are reconciling themselves to throwing in their lot with the Germans, whom they think are bound to win,' Churchill wrote. 'They are in imminent danger of being invaded by Germany from the air, or possibly from the sea, if we cannot stop the latter. They are quite unprepared. In these circumstances it may be necessary for us to forestall German action by a descent on certain ports, and I think it right to let you know this, even though you might feel unable to make any comment on it.'[48]

Both Halifax and Kennedy thought the message was too pessimistic, so Halifax persuaded Churchill not to send it. But Kennedy warned Washington anyway that the Prime Minister was despondent and seemed to fear that 'de Valera and his crowd' were going over to the Germans.[49]

On 8 July Secretary of State Cordell Hull warned Lord Lothian, the British ambassador, against any attack on Ireland. Lothian responded with an assurance that no such venture would be undertaken unless the Germans attacked first. The British were never prepared to give Dublin the same assurance, however, which only heightened the anxiety of the Irish government, especially after the British attacked the French fleet at Oran.

'Who would have guessed three months ago that the British would attack the French fleet?' de Valera asked Maffey.[50]

De Valera was again more worried about the British than about the Germans. A German invasion was 'the least of the government's worries', he later admitted. Hempel had been authorised, on 11 July, to provide an assurance to the Dublin government. 'As long as Ireland conducts herself in a neutral fashion,' Foreign Minister von Ribbentrop telegraphed Hempel, 'it can be counted on with absolute certainty that Germany will respect her neutrality unconditionally.'[51] De Valera might not have placed much faith in the German promise, but it was more than the British ever offered, even though he repeatedly sought a similar guarantee from them. 'I did not get that assurance,' he later told the Dáil. 'There was always a reservation.'[52]

After the fall of France, transatlantic shipping bound for Britain began to sail around Northern Ireland because the route via the south of Ireland was too vulnerable to attack from German aircraft in France and submarines in the Bay of Biscay. Churchill was much more concerned with the need for American aircraft and destroyers. Hitherto, American assistance had amounted to what the British could purchase in the private sector, but this was no longer adequate if Britain were to survive.

Roosevelt wished to provide more help, but he had to move cautiously. After being re-elected in 1936 with the greatest majority in American history, he had got into a political confrontation with the US Supreme Court and clearly lost, but had learned a lesson. Now he moved cautiously in relation to the war because American opinion was strongly opposed to direct involvement. Only 7 per cent of the American electorate would support immediate intervention, according to a public opinion poll, and only 19 per cent would favour such a move if it appeared the Allies would otherwise be defeated. It was an election year and the President had to be extremely careful not to fuel speculation about any secret commitment to join the Allies.

Instead of destroyers, the President initially promised to supply other equipment, including some twenty torpedo boats that were under construction at the time. On learning of Roosevelt's intention, however, Senator David I. Walsh promptly blocked the deal by using his influence as chairman of the Senate Naval Affairs Committee. Congress passed the Walsh Amendment, prohibiting the transfer of any military equipment to any foreign country, unless the American Chiefs of Staff were willing to certify that the material was 'not essential to the defence of the United States'.[53] This was a powerful example of the political clout of one Irish-American. Walsh undermined the transfer of the torpedo boats, and his legislation proved a stumbling block in the following weeks when Roosevelt sought to comply with Churchill's desperate pleas for destroyers.

Chapter 9 ∾

| 'IN IMMINENT DANGER'

Irish authorities became particularly uneasy about British propaganda, especially ludicrous stories about massive spy centres in the German and Italian Legations in Dublin, or U-boat bases on the west coast. The crew of a U-boat reportedly drank a toast to the fall of John Bull in a Dingle pub, according to W.F. Hartin, the naval correspondent of the *Daily Mail*. British newspapers were inclined to give credence to the most ridiculous rumours of German activities off the Kerry coast.[1]

The Irish censor blocked reports to the *Daily Mail* about stories of fraternisation with U-boat crews that 'would make any Briton's hair stand on end'.[2] There was a report that a U-boat called regularly at a jetty on one of the offshore islands to purchase fresh eggs and vegetables. 'Come on, Maggie,' the submarine commander supposedly used to shout, 'hurry up with those cabbages.'[3] The journalist who wrote that was possibly paying for the drink in some local pub, and the more he bought, the more exotic the stories became. Indeed, it would later be suggested that most of the German subs were seen in pubs.[4]

Helen Kirkpatrick of the *Chicago Daily News* annoyed the Irish with some of her reports. David Gray gave her 'lots of stories of things that were going on', she later recalled. He told her, 'German submarines were surfacing in bays on the west coast of Ireland. There were lots of wild, uninhabited places and they were surfacing there to recharge their batteries; and that the Germans had a wireless station which they used to get news to Germany—picking up information and intelligence on what happened in Britain.' She reported from Belfast on 12 June that the staff of the German Legation had been greatly increased since the start of the war, and that it was a channel through which Germany was getting much information about England.

I got into great trouble with having written those stories when I got back to London, because the Irish censorship probably wouldn't have let them through. De Valera denounced me and said it was absolutely untrue—the

Germans were not doing the things that I had alleged they did. His protest, through the Irish Minister in Washington, appeared next to a piece of mine on the front page of the *Daily News* with a note from the editor saying that they had received this protest from the Irish and that they nevertheless accepted my account over the Irish account.[5]

Gray telephoned her to come back. This was an era in which the telephone was notoriously open, and Gray was certainly not endearing himself by his behaviour. 'You know, if you get thrown from a horse, climb right back on,' he said. 'Come on over.'

'Well, I think I'm *persona non grata*,' Kirkpatrick replied.

'Never mind,' Gray said. 'Come over and stay with us.' Visiting Dublin and staying with the Grays then became something of a habit for her.[6]

Amid the rumours of supposed German activities, there was the actual behaviour of German agents. Willi Preetz began operating as a German spy in Dublin. He had already come to the attention of the Irish authorities as a German national the previous November. He claimed he had arrived in Ireland before the war began, and his Irish in-laws backed up his story. After joining the Nazi Party in 1933, Preetz spent much of his time outside Germany as a ship's steward. During his travels he met Sally Reynolds from Tuam, County Galway, and they were married in 1935. She was living with his family in Bremen at the start of the war. He slipped out of Ireland as a stowaway in December 1939 and made it back to Germany, where the *Abwehr* recruited him. He returned to Ireland by submarine and landed on the Dingle Peninsula on the night of 25 June 1940. He buried his radio transmitter and made it to Dublin, where he got a place on Parkgate Street, near the headquarters of G2. He recovered his transmitter on 3 July, but was apparently too busy enjoying life to be an effective spy.

His partying caused problems with his neighbours and his in-laws, especially after he got a teenage girl into what was euphemistically called 'trouble'. He managed to send some messages with weather information. He had no meteorological instruments, so he passed on barometric readings and temperatures that he observed on instruments in shop windows. One message to him on 19 August 1940 requested information about shipping traffic between England and Ireland as well as troop movements, but his intercepted reply suggested he was either unwilling or unable to get the necessary information. He was arrested on 26 August and spent the rest of the war years in custody.

Preetz had provided the Germans with no useful information, but he was one of the more successful of the incompetent spies that they sent to Ireland. He, unlike almost all the others, managed to remain at large for more than a matter of hours. On 8 July three further agents—Henry Obed from India, along with Dieter Gartner and Herbert Tributh, both from what had been German South West Africa—were dropped off from a yacht near Skibbereen in West Cork. Gartner and Tributh were of German extraction and the dark-skinned Obed was sent as their translator. Many people in that part of Ireland would never have even seen a dark-skinned person in the flesh before, so Obed would have stood out, and all the more so when he arrived dressed in bright Indian silks and a straw hat. The three agents were trying to use Ireland as a back-door to England, where they planned to engage in a campaign of sabotage. They managed to get a lift in a lorry to Drimoleague and from there took a bus to Cork City. But a Garda, who observed them, questioned the lorry driver and notified the Gardaí in Cork City. The three were arrested as they got off the bus. The local police rather inelegantly informed Dublin: 'Two whites and a nigger have appeared from nowhere.'[7] They were carrying eight incendiary bombs, along with other explosive paraphernalia.

The first half of July 1940 was a period of great tension in Ireland. Maffey informed Walshe on 14 July that the Germans were planning to invade Ireland the following day, and that they had been about to invade ten days earlier. These warnings may have been the result of the deliberate deception ordered by Hitler, but Maffey realised the Irish had become deeply suspicious of the British. 'During the last three weeks opinion here has swung steadily over to the view that we are now the probable aggressors,' he reported. Even Irish friends of Britain shared this view. 'There is an immense volume of pro-British feeling in this country,' he explained. 'If we do not mishandle the situation that feeling will grow. It has waxed with our misfortunes. It waxed with our determined action against the French fleet but it will wilt at once if we tread on the sensibilities of Éire.'[8]

Irish fears about British intentions had been inflamed on 12 July when a British spy was arrested collecting information to be used by British forces in Ireland. Major Edward Reed Byass, who was serving with the British Army in Northern Ireland, was caught with information indicating he was engaged in military reconnaissance while supposedly on a golfing and motoring holiday with his wife in Ireland. The Irish had already shown their facilities to the British, so they were at a loss to explain his spying.

If such activities continued, Walshe warned Maffey, the Dublin government might feel compelled to demand his recall. Tegart was exposed after he approached some Fianna Fáil ministers. Maffey was decidedly embarrassed by Tegart's distorted reports and the Byass fiasco. 'He seemed to be genuinely horrified at the espionage episode, and he did not express any desire for the early release of the officer concerned,' Walshe informed de Valera. 'It may be significant that Maffey asked me not to tell his military aides about this matter.'

'Maffey turned to me quite earnestly and said that he was in a real difficulty about these "agents",' Walshe added. Maffey suggested Dulanty should tell the Dominions Office to 'send Tegart or any other "agent" here in future, that they were doing nothing but harm, etc. He begged me not to mention his name in this connection as he felt his position would not allow him to object to such missions. I was naturally amazed at this sudden complete avowal of the truth. It quite clearly arose from his conviction, however belated, that a very grave error of judgment had been made.'[9]

After receiving instructions from the Dominions Office, Maffey formally apologised next day and said London had nothing to do with the Byass mission. The major had been sent by his superiors in Northern Ireland to gather information in case British forces were invited to assist the Irish Army. 'These instructions were given without our knowledge or consent and instructions are being issued to General Officer Commanding British Troops in Northern Ireland that nothing of this kind is to occur again without prior consultation with Éire authorities,' Maffey noted, reading out the passage from his instructions from London. 'We hope the Éire Government will be prepared to accept our apology for what had occurred and release Byass forthwith.'[10]

'This had a tremendous effect and I felt the whole atmosphere changed,' Maffey noted. De Valera pressed for a few anti-tank guns, a few fighters and a few anti-aircraft guns.

'Why will you not trust us?' de Valera asked. 'If you think we might attack the North I say with all emphasis we will never do that. No solution can come there by force. There we must now wait and let the solution come with time and patience. If you think the IRA will get the arms, I can assure you that we have no fifth-column today. There is no danger in that quarter.'[11]

The British had offered to supply arms as part of the proposals brought by Malcolm MacDonald, so the weapons were obviously available. 'Give us help with arms and we will fight the Germans as only Irishmen in their own country can fight,' de Valera said. 'There is no doubt on which side my sympathies lie. Nowadays some people joke about my becoming pro-British. The cause I am urging on you is in the best interest of my own country and that is what matters most to me.'[12]

Relations between London and Dublin had become particularly tense, and de Valera was determined not to give either side an excuse for attacking. 'The best hope of preserving the country from invasion and its consequences lies in maintaining our neutrality, and giving no pretext to either side for violating our territory,' de Valera wrote to W.T. Cosgrave.[13] The Germans and the British had ratcheted up the tension by their behaviour.

'Of course, there were other more subtle causes all combining to give the impression that we were almost eager for the Germans to come in so that we could get in ourselves,' Maffey noted. De Valera had authorised the secret co-operation with the British, but exaggerated rumours were circulating. 'Talk of a military 'pact' had been published and had done great harm,' Maffey warned the Dominions Office.[14]

MI5 was continuing with what was essentially a watching brief. Some British agents were arrested temporarily, such as Major Byass, a Captain Higgins, who was apprehended acting suspiciously in Killarney, and Lieutenant Commander Fell of the Naval Intelligence Division. Once it was realised that they were working for the British, all were let go without being charged. There was no interference with most of the MI6 people. In June, Captain Charles S. Collinson of MI6 was put in charge of the new British Travel Permit Office in Dublin. He recruited Albert Podesta, local manager of Stubbs Gazette, the credit control agency. Podesta, a Cork Protestant who had fought in World War I, was able to use his work as an ideal cover for travelling about the country, investigating people suspected of Nazi sympathies. He also recruited others to help. One of those was another Stubbs employee named Moore, who was secretly reporting to G2. There was no suggestion that these people working for MI6 were seeking to suborn Irish officials or impede Irish policy; they were monitoring foreign activities of suspected Fascist sympathisers and the Axis legations. While the Irish promptly jailed German spies, they were content merely to keep these British spies under surveillance.[15]

De Valera 'begged' Maffey to ensure the Anglo-Irish military liaison 'should be kept as secret as possible'. If the Germans found out, they might retaliate, but if the Irish people learned, it would weaken support for the country's supposed neutrality as an expression of Irish independence. 'If we wish to get into a happier relationship', Maffey advised the Dominions Office, then a concession of arms 'would achieve wonders'.[16]

'The impression which has now developed in Éire is that our policy is to get Éire into the war on our side and that, failing that, we are prepared to occupy the territory of Éire by force,' Viscount Caldecote, the Dominions Secretary, warned the British Cabinet on 18 July. 'This feeling inevitably increases the difficulty of securing the help of the Government of Éire in making such preparations, as are possible while Éire is neutral, against a German invasion.'[17]

'Unless we are prepared to take the drastic step of seizing their territory by force with the certainty of armed opposition on their part and all the incalculable consequences which that would involve, the right course is to try to restore the better atmosphere which had been gradually brought about,' Caldecote argued. 'In particular, we might even jeopardise the secret understanding with them that in the event of serious invasion they will resist the enemy and call upon us for aid.' They could improve the situation in three ways. First, they should clamp down on press comments, and he noted the Minister for Information had already called for a softening. Second, he agreed with Maffey that Britain should announce 'that we have no intention of sending our forces into Éire without a request from the Government of Éire'. Churchill could provide that assurance in response to a question in the House of Commons. Third, Britain should supply some of the requested weapons to the Irish in order to boost Irish resolve and ensure Irish resistance would be as effective as possible.[18]

The Cabinet decided to clamp down on the press campaign and to prepare a list of equipment, on a more limited scale than previously offered. Instead of the sixteen anti-aircraft guns initially offered, eight were now supplied, along with some anti-tank rifles, Brenguns, pistols and twenty-four searchlights. But at Churchill's insistence there was to be no assurance that Britain would not invade Ireland.

Caldecote informed Dulanty that Minister for Information Duff Cooper had told the lobby correspondents to let up on Ireland and the press generally were being asked to do likewise. W.P. Crozier, editor of the *Manchester Guardian*, later told Dulanty that the press had indeed been told to ease off Ireland.[19]

Virginia Cowles of the North American Newspaper Alliance had already reported from Belfast that the German Legation had a staff of 100 people in Dublin, but with the change of attitude in London, this gross exaggeration was refuted. 'Actually it has no more than half a dozen men with two or three women typists,' *The Times* noted. 'Its behaviour has been uniformly correct and the stories as a vast centre of espionage without foundation.'[20] According to the *New York Times* next day, the Legation staff consisted of the Minister, the secretary, the press attaché, two clerks and a maid, with a consul in Limerick, while the Italian Legation comprised a Minister, secretary, three clerks and consuls in Cork and Limerick. The United States Legation, on the other hand, had a staff of nine, in addition to consuls in Cork and Galway, while the British Legation had thirteen people, including military, naval and air attachés.

Since all the messages from London to the United States were passing through the British censor, Dublin concluded that the Ministry of Information had been behind what amounted to a deliberate campaign of misinformation. 'The extent to which we blame the British for matters appearing in American papers is limited by our precise knowledge as to the source and as to the failure of the Ministry of Information to keep a guiding hand on those journalists in London whose superficial knowledge of international affairs leads them to the grossest errors concerning this country,' Walshe told Gray.[21]

The Department of External Affairs instructed Robert Brennan to try to counter this propaganda in the United States. 'Could you inspire all Irish papers to launch campaign against pro-British American journalists who are misleading American public about Ireland and preparing opinion for a British invasion of Ireland,' Walshe instructed. [22]

'Outside a few informed Irish,' Brennan explained in reply, 'everyone here from the highest administration to man in the street considers that we are foolish not to invite British aid and that England shows great forbearance in not securing weak flank by reoccupation: all arguments to contrary such as you use received with a shrug.'

Hempel had already reported that the Irish Minister to the United States had been instructed 'to make contacts with Senators of Irish origin who are friendly to Germany, in order to take steps against agitation against Irish neutrality'. Hempel was probably right in believing a British attack on Ireland was 'being discouraged principally by respect for public opinion in the United States'. Germany could also make use of Irish-Americans, Walshe told him. 'If the Irish element in the United States is properly used, it could constitute a powerful influence in our favour, likewise the Irish-American press,' Walshe said, but he went on to warn 'that if any German participation became known outside, it would easily lead to an undesirable effect in the opposite direction'.[23]

Walshe was obviously trying to ingratiate himself with the German Minister, who realised the Irish authorities had to avoid any appearance of conniving with the Germans 'because of well-justified anxiety about a possible unfavourable British reaction against Ireland'. Yet, Hempel added, 'From various indications in talks with Walshe and Boland I assumed that the Irish Government may be placing hope in future German interest in the maintenance and completion of entirely independent United Irish State. They express this in rather negative fashion by saying that they hope that in a future peace settlement we will not sacrifice Ireland to England, or they speak of negotiation which the Irish Government will have to carry on with us there.'[24]

At the time it seemed like Germany was going to win the war. 'From all our sources of information,' Walshe telegraphed Seán Murphy, the Irish Minister in Vichy, 'belief is general, even in countries friendly to England such as America and Portugal, that Britain has lost the war and at the very most could only achieve a stalemate which might leave her part of her Empire, but it is recognised everywhere that she has no hope of regaining her influence in Europe.'[25] Gray reported that Walshe told him that 'he did not see how it was possible for Germany to be beaten by England and that consequently Ireland had to envisage the possibility of a German victory'. Wondering if he was actually hoping for a German victory in the belief Hitler would end partition, Gray asked about a preposterous suggestion that Germany had promised the IRA to unite the thirty-two counties of Ireland and include two English shires for good measure.

'I don't think I believe that,' Walshe replied. 'But,' he added with a laugh, 'on the basis of Irish majority we ought to have Liverpool.'[26]

When the Irish tried to buy 20,000 American rifles, Roosevelt directed that a lot of 80,000 Lee-Enfield rifles should be sold to Canada, even though it was more than Ottawa had requested. The Irish were then told to talk to the Canadians, who duly sold the 20,000 rifles to them. This was Roosevelt's way of impressing on the Irish that they were dependent on the Allies for protection.[27] 'Those dear people you are with must realise that in the end they will have to fish or cut bait,' Roosevelt wrote to Gray on the day he authorised the rifles for Canada.[28]

The *Abwehr* tried to send two more men to Ireland in August 1940, but this turned into another fiasco. Seán Russell had made it from the United States to Germany via Italy in May 1940 and Germans secured the release of Frank Ryan from a Spanish jail, where he had been languishing since the civil war. The Germans sent Ryan and Russell to Ireland on a U-boat, but Russell became seriously ill and died about 100 miles off Galway, on 14 August. Ryan had no idea what was expected of him, so he returned to Germany on the submarine.

De Valera's internal difficulties increased in the latter half of August. The IRA killed two more policemen on 16 August. Patrick McGrath and Thomas Green (alias Francis Harte) were arrested, summarily tried by a military court, and sentenced to death. In July the death sentence of Thomas MacCurtain for murdering a policeman had been commuted. De Valera concluded that the leniency shown by the state on that occasion had merely earned the contempt of the IRA.

Gray was asked to intervene on behalf of the condemned men, but he had essentially no sympathy with them. 'It is generally believed', he wrote, 'the Government must abdicate if it does not go through with the executions as these murders came on the heels of the commutation of McCurtain who also shot a policeman.'[29] The two were executed on 6 September.

While all of that was going on a German bomber crashed into Mount Brandon, in County Kerry, on 20 August. The five-man crew had a near-miraculous escape. Later that week the Irish were confronted with their first war casualties when a German aircraft bombed a creamery in Campile, County Wexford, in mid-afternoon, killing three workers.

Witnesses identified the German plane, which dropped five bombs, one of which hit the creamery, killing three young women in the canteen, only minutes after some forty employees had finished their dinner. One of the bombs failed to explode, and it was identified as being German. 'The boob must have thought he was in Pembroke instead of the south of Éire,' Gray wrote.[30] The government issued a statement that the *chargé d'affaires* in Berlin had been instructed to protest and claim full reparations.[31]

The Department of External Affairs informed Warnock that Irish public opinion considered the bombing 'an unfortunate mistake', but the British and American press tried to make it out as more sinister. As result Dublin suggested it would be in Germany's interest, as much as Ireland's, to admit the error as early as possible, express regret and acknowledge a willingness to pay compensation.[32] The German Foreign Ministry promptly complied.[33]

Six German airmen who came down on Mount Brandon when their plane crashed on 20 August were held in Cork for some days while an internment camp was constructed. The camp, known as K Lines, was located some 30 miles from Dublin on the Curragh, a 12-square-mile plain, which contained a horseracing track, where the country's classics were run annually. During the Crimean War a small military instruction camp was built on the plain to serve the military in the nearby garrison towns of Kildare and Newbridge, each of which was about 3 miles away. The new camp expanded rapidly. After Irish independence in 1922, the Irish Army took over the Curragh, which housed 227 officers and 5,340 men, with married quarters for eighty-six families. By Irish standards the camp was a fairly large town, with the various conveniences normally associated with towns. Being a military camp it had the advantage of having some of the country's best sporting facilities.

When the German Minister visited K Lines on 2 September, he found the airmen uneasy about the tight security. They complained of being treated like prisoners-of-war. In the strict sense they were not prisoners, but guests of the Irish state, which was merely obligated to ensure that they took no further part in the war. Hempel asked for a relaxation of the prison-like procedures.

This issue took on urgency with the internment of the first British airman on 29 September. Pilot Officer Paul Mayhew was the son of a prominent British businessman. Freddy Boland of the Department of External Affairs warned the Army that the internment of the British airman was going to 'give rise to questions in some ways more difficult than we have to face with the present six men'. The guards would be obliged not to show any favouritism, so he thought it advisable to anticipate and make concessions to the Germans immediately rather than be compelled to make them later, under British pressure.

'What we must be sure of', Boland wrote, 'is that we do not withhold reasonable and usual amenities which it might later be deemed to be expedient to grant to military internees of another nationality to obviate, for example, attacks in the British press.'[34] He suggested the internees should be as content as possible with their lot in order 'to minimise their anxiety and quite natural desire to escape from our custody'.[35] The German requests were reasonable, so he saw no grounds for denying the men a radio, newspapers or magazines. 'None of the points are very serious,' Boland explained. Hempel, whom he described as 'a difficult character', had put forward the suggestions 'in a reasonable conciliatory way'.

The German Minister and the Counsellor at the Legation, Henning Thomsen, engaged in a kind of 'good cop, bad cop' routine. Hempel played the role of the diplomat, while Thomsen acted like a strutting Nazi. As a result the Irish concluded the Minister was in the difficult position, always having to mind his back. Thomsen was an ss officer in his mid-thirties, and the Irish thought he was the Gestapo's man, sent to keep an eye on Hempel. He acted as the Legation's intelligence officer and consorted with a variety of pro-German Irish people, whom Hempel avoided out of a sense of diplomatic decorum.

Thus the Irish were acutely conscious that Hempel might be compelled to be awkward when it came to the treatment of German internees. 'Within the limits of this general obligation to ensure the safe custody of the men,' Boland argued, 'our view is that once their safe custody is assured the men should be granted every facility and amenity calculated to soften their captivity and relieve their monotony. There is no point whatever in our view in refusing them any amenity that does not detract from the measures taken for their safe custody.'[36]

Thomsen presented the internees with a radio, and the Irish Army relaxed the inspections at the camp. Officers were given an allowance of £3 per week and the others £2 per week, as well as £5 each to purchase civilian clothes. This money, along with the cost of their food and medical expenses, was to be recouped from the German government.

Maffey used his influence to get permission for Mayhew to enrol for correspondence courses at Trinity College Dublin. He was given facilities to borrow books by mail from the college's world-famous library and these helped to relieve the monotony of his internment. As a result he was quite satisfied with his treatment. 'I have at least ample time for the "highest activity of the human soul, philosophic speculation",' he wrote to his brother, Christopher, who later became Defence Secretary in Harold Wilson's government in the 1960s. 'Life might be very considerably worse; I'm very comfortable. I'm doing lots of work (many thanks for those books), and I listen to hours of good music on the wireless. In the last hours I've heard

Beethoven's 4th Piano Concerto, which I love, and a good programme of Bach chorals, very well sung, from Germany.'[37]

The internees were allowed out to exercise in the afternoons, and they had the run of some of the country's most modern recreational facilities—a gymnasium, indoor swimming pool, together with squash, handball and tennis courts, as well as a golf course and playing fields for various outdoor sports. They were allowed out of their barbed-wire compound provided they signed a parole promising to return by a specified time and not to 'take part in any activity connected with the war or prejudicial to the interests of the Irish State'.[38]

Mayhew availed of parole most afternoons to play golf. He usually played with retired officers from the British Army living in the vicinity, or with serving Irish officers. 'I expect to be British Amateur golf champion in 1944,' he remarked facetiously in a letter to his father.[39]

The war appeared to be coming closer. The Canadian High Commissioner reported in early October that people in Wexford witnessed an air battle involving six British and eight German aircraft.[40] The *Sunday Express* reported on its front page that U-boats were stopping in Éire for petrol, and James Little, an Independent Unionist Member of Parliament, complained that the Irish government was winking at this, but U-boats used heavy diesel oil, not petrol. 'The idea that heavy oil could be conveyed in large quantities to submarines, which are distinctive warships without anyone knowing about it is grotesque,'[41] Lord Strabolgi remarked. The government admitted that there was no evidence of submarines being refuelled in Ireland. 'So far as I am aware there is no foundation to these allegations,' Information Minister Duff Cooper admitted.[42]

Chapter 10 ∾

IRISH-AMERICANS AND
THE THIRD TERM

J oe Kennedy was decidedly uneasy in London, because he suspected
Roosevelt was scheming to involve the United States in the war. The
ambassador resented emissaries being sent to evaluate conditions in
Britain, such as Under Secretary of State Sumner Welles and William J.
Donovan. Kennedy viewed them as infringing on his turf and essentially
questioning his competence as ambassador. Accompanying Welles on a visit
to the Foreign Office, Kennedy betrayed his exasperation. 'For Christ's sakes,'
he snapped at a British diplomat, 'stop trying to make this a holy war, because
no one will believe you; you're fighting for your own life as an Empire, and
that's good enough.'[1]

As a result of such outbursts and his monumental indiscretions, the British
kept a close watch on Kennedy, but they were even more worried by the
behaviour of Tyler Kent, a code clerk at the embassy. Kennedy had Kent copy
some of the correspondence between Roosevelt and Churchill. Kent used to
slip in an extra carbon to make a personal copy. He allowed Anna Wolkoff, a
Russian *émigrée* and suspected Nazi spy who was already under MI5
surveillance, to copy some of the letters. She passed on the information to the
Italian naval attaché, who in turn forwarded it on the Germans.

Within a fortnight of Churchill becoming Prime Minister, Kent's flat was
raided and 1,929 classified documents were found, including some of the
Roosevelt–Churchill correspondence. Kent was arrested for violating the
British Official Secrets Act. The United States waived his diplomatic
immunity and he was held incommunicado before his case was heard *in
camera* at the Old Bailey in London in late October 1940.

Members of the Democratic Party were causing pressing problems for
President Roosevelt during the 1940 campaign. Serious cracks had already
begun to appear in his Irish-American support. Al Smith announced his
support for Wendell Willkie, even before Willkie secured the Republican

Party's nomination for President. James A. Farley, who had managed both of Roosevelt's previous presidential campaigns, broke with him because he was running for an unprecedented third term. Farley ran against Roosevelt for the nomination at the Democratic Party's national convention. As an astute politician, he knew he had little hope of defeating Roosevelt, but his gesture was indicative of the intensity of his feelings. The President wished to have a Catholic campaign manager, according to *Time* magazine. He played on Kennedy's ego by pretending he would like him to take charge of his campaign. 'I wanted to ring you up about the situation that has arisen here so that you could get the dope straight from me and not from somebody else,' Roosevelt telephoned Kennedy on 1 August 1940. 'The sub-committee of the Democratic Committee desire you to come home and run the Democratic campaign this year, but the State Department is very much against your leaving England.'[2] Roosevelt turned instead to another Irish-American, Edward J. Flynn, the political boss of the Bronx and the most influential Democratic machine leader in the country.

Roosevelt's two main Irish-American diplomats burst into the news during the following weeks. After the closure of the American embassy in Brussels in July 1940, John Cudahy visited Berlin, Rome and London. On 6 August he caused a sensation in Britain with a press conference at the American embassy, where he seemed to suggest that the German invasion of Belgium was not so bad. 'I have not heard one authentic story of an atrocity in Belgium since the Germans went in,' Cudahy said. 'Everywhere I asked the people if they had been ill-treated. All said no, no pillaging, no shooting of civilians. I was a soldier in the last war, and I think these Germans behaved better than United States soldiers would have done.'[3]

Cudahy also disputed Churchill's charge that King Leopold III of the Belgians had surrendered without giving proper notice to the Allies. 'The Allies were informed and fully informed of his decision no fewer than three days before,' Cudahy said. He went on to suggest the British should relax their blockade of the Continent, so the United States could feed the people of Belgium. 'Their situation is very, very serious,' he said. Even with severe rationing, existing supplies would only last until September or early October at the latest. 'If you gentlemen think the Continent is a howling hell now, what do you think it will be this winter?' Cudahy asked the assembled press.[4]

Kennedy became distinctly agitated as Cudahy was speaking. At one point the ambassador slammed a window, a patent hint that Cudahy should shut up. Then he slammed it again violently. But Cudahy refused to take the hint, so Kennedy terminated the press conference and had the reporters promptly ushered out of the embassy. This was followed next day by a firestorm of criticism in the British press.

'Who does Mr Cudahy think invaded Belgium—Britain?' one commentator asked. The *Daily Express* reported that newsmen at the conference had heckled the former Ambassador to Belgium. 'It is generally felt that on the grounds of taste alone, it is hardly for a foreign diplomat, ostensibly in England on a private visit, to praise openly the German conduct of their invasion of an innocent neutral and by implication make it appear that Britain was responsible for the famine in Belgium,' the *News Chronicle* observed.[5]

'It is elementary that no statement on policy may be made by anyone in the diplomatic service without first clearing it through the State Department,' Harold Ickes noted in his diary. 'We certainly demonstrated to the world that this is a land of talking diplomats.'[6] Sumner Welles, who was the acting Secretary of State in Hull's temporary absence, disavowed Cudahy's views on the grounds that they were 'unauthorised and had never been submitted to the State Department'. Welles announced that Cudahy had been summoned home to explain himself, and Kennedy was asked to supply an accurate text of Cudahy's remarks. The implications seemed clear that Cudahy was been recalled in disgrace. 'Proceed immediately to Washington,' Cudahy was ordered by the State Department. 'Since you travelled from Lisbon to London without authorization from the Department the transportation and per diem for that portion of your trip are not payable by the Government.'[7]

'I am going home to be crucified, but the truth must be told,' Cudahy told reporters before leaving London en route to Portugal for a flight to New York.[8]

On the strength of Cudahy's remarks, the New York *Daily News*, which boasted the largest circulation of any newspaper in the United States, started a campaign to help the Belgians.[9] During World War I Herbert Hoover came to national and international prominence by taking charge of food relief for the Belgians. His fame eventually propelled him to the White House in 1929, but his presidency was marred by the onset of the Great Depression, and he lost out to Franklin D. Roosevelt in 1932. On 26 June 1940 Hoover warned in Philadelphia that Europe was faced with the 'spectre of the most dangerous famine in history'.[10] He was anxious to do something to help, as he had done following World War I. In the wake of Cudahy's remarks, he launched what was dubbed the Starving Europe Campaign, which aimed at supplying food to Europe.

When Cudahy arrived in New York by seaplane on 26 August, a crowd of about 500 people greeted him, cheering and clapping. Six policemen had to make way for him through the gathering in the main hall at the seaplane terminal at La Guardia airport. He refused to discuss his remarks in London with the waiting press. 'At this time, I cannot make any statement or answer the questions,' he said. 'I must first report to my superior officers in Washington.' But he did denounce British coverage of his press conference. 'I was violently shocked, absolutely puzzled by reports in several London papers,' he said. 'Only one report approximated what I had said. The stories were so opposed to the facts that I didn't recognise them.' Asked if he was going to resign, he replied, 'I can't say until I have seen my superiors.'[11]

His meeting with Roosevelt next day went well. There was no rebuke. Afterwards Cudahy announced he had come home for a vacation and there never was any hint of his resignation. The President convinced Cudahy that he was determined to stay out of the war, and things went so well between them that Cudahy left the White House not only determined to campaign for Roosevelt's re-election but also harbouring hopes of being promoted to replace Joe Kennedy as ambassador in London.

In an address to the national convention of the Veterans of Foreign Wars, Cudahy stressed that the United States needed to rearm in order to stay out of the war. These remarks bolstered the arguments of Senator Walsh, the Chairman of the Senate Naval Affairs Committee, whose legislation had been frustrating Roosevelt's efforts to aid Britain, because the American Chiefs of Staff were unable to certify that the destroyers Churchill was seeking were 'not essential to the defence of the United States'.[12] The US Navy required the destroyers; therefore Congressional authorisation was required for their transfer. White House officials were convinced Walsh would block such authorisation. 'The chief trouble with him is that he hates England more than he loves the United States,' Roosevelt complained.[13]

During the summer a pro-Allied group of Americans began a propaganda campaign for the transfer of destroyers, arguing that the President should exchange them for bases in British possessions in the Caribbean. This would strengthen American defences, they contended, so the President would not need Congressional approval to exchange the vessels for bases.

William J. Donovan played an active role in all of this. Roosevelt had actually considered appointing him to his Cabinet at the time of the appointments of Stimson and Knox. Donovan's grandfather, Timothy Donovan, was born and reared in Skibbereen, County Cork. He eloped to the United States with a local girl and they settled in Buffalo, New York, where William's father was born. He married the daughter of immigrants from County Monaghan and they lived with his parents, in the house where young William was raised. It was in a staunch Irish-American neighbourhood. There were always Irish immigrants going and coming in the Donovan house, as it was used as a refuge for Irish people being spirited across the border from nearby Canada. William attended Niagara University, which was affiliated with a diocesan seminary. He initially had ambitions of becoming a

Dominican priest, but after three years he decided that he did not have the necessary vocation and transferred to Columbia University, where he studied law and distinguished himself as a quarterback on the university football team.

As a member of the National Guard he served in the New York 69th Brigade, which had been famous during the American Civil War as 'the Fighting Irish'. Donovan served with distinction in the US Army in France during World War I. He was decorated with the Congressional Medal of Honor, America's highest award for gallantry. After the war he established a highly lucrative law practice and dabbled in politics as a Republican. He ran unsuccessfully for Lieutenant Governor of New York in 1922. Two years later he was appointed Assistant Attorney General in the administration of Calvin Coolidge, and became Acting Attorney General for a time in the administration of Herbert Hoover. In 1932 Donovan won the Republican nomination for Governor of New York, but was swamped in the Democratic landslide that brought Franklin D. Roosevelt to the White House. At the instigation of the Secretary of the Navy, Donovan made what was supposed to be a private visit to assess Britain's chances of survival in July 1940. He returned to tell Roosevelt unequivocally that Britain could survive, with proper help.

Donovan warmly endorsed a proposal to circumvent the Walsh Amendment by giving American destroyers to the British in return for British bases in the West Indies. Soon the pros and cons of such an arrangement were being argued publicly. 'The sale of the Navy's ships to a nation at war would be an act of war,' the *Chicago Daily Tribune* thundered. 'If we want to get into war, the destroyers offer as good a way as any of accomplishing the purpose.'[14]

The opposition of the *Chicago Daily Tribune*, with its strong bias towards the Republican Party, was one thing, but the opposition of Senator Walsh, a staunch Democrat, was a different proposition, especially as he had already demonstrated his Congressional influence by killing the transfer of the torpedo boats in June. On 13 August he delivered an impassioned radio address over the CBS network, explaining that he was 'utterly and irrevocably opposed' to the proposed exchange of destroyers for bases. 'The transfer of naval destroyers from our flag to the British flag, no matter by what method or device, makes a mockery of our declared policy of neutrality and non-intervention,' he warned. 'It is an act of belligerency and of war.'[15]

Even though the American people abhorred the conduct of the European dictators, Walsh wrote to Roosevelt the following week, the 'vast majority think practically and realistically that it is too late to endanger American safety by committing ourselves as saviours of surrendered France and Great Britain and can have no other result than war for ourselves'.[16] The deal to hand over fifty destroyers in return for certain bases had already been negotiated with the British by this time. The Attorney General assured Roosevelt the deal did not need Congressional authorisation, because it enhanced the country's defence posture.

Nevertheless Roosevelt was still worried about the public reaction. He wrote to Walsh in an effort to enlist his support. If Hitler wanted to go to war with the United States, he would 'do so on any number of trumped-up charges', the President contended. 'I do hope you will not oppose the deal which, from the point of view of the United States, I regard as being the finest thing for the nation that has been done in your lifetime and mine.'[17]

Gray wrote a short congratulatory note to the White House that seemed to echo the sentiments of Roosevelt's own letter to Walsh. 'The deal . . . seems to me the most important thing that has happened to our nation in my lifetime,' Gray wrote. 'Of course it is far more than what it appears to be on its face. If you can lay the foundations for an Anglo-American control of the world on the principles of Democracy and Justice you will have achieved the most than any man has done since Octavianus. God bless you.'[18]

It soon became apparent that the President had outmanoeuvred his critics. Public opinion strongly supported the deal and also supported the introduction of the first peacetime draft (conscription). Edward R. Burke of Nebraska, whose parents were both Irish-Americans, sponsored the Bill in the Senate, but there was some strong Irish-American opposition. There was a notorious incident in Congress when Martin L. Sweeney of Ohio criticised the draft as a scheme to deliver the United States to Britain.

'I'd rather you would sit somewhere else,' Congressman Beverly Vincent of Kentucky said when Sweeney sat down beside him after speaking. One word borrowed another. 'You are a traitor,' Vincent snapped, adding something that *Time* magazine considered unprintable. Sweeney took a swing at Vincent and missed. But Vincent did not miss. He 'planted a good hard right, smack!' according to *Time*. An elderly Congressional doorman said, 'It was the best blow he had heard in his 50 years in the House.'[19]

Hitler's quick victories had frightened Americans, and they were worried that once he had conquered Europe he would turn to Latin America before eventually waging war on the United States. As a result there was widespread American approval of both the draft and the destroyers-for-bases deal as a means of strengthening the country's defences against possible Nazi encroachment in the hemisphere. Gray was suggesting in Dublin that the Irish-Americans had lost their effectiveness because they were now associated 'in the public mind with Nazis and Fascists'.[20] In Gray's opinion, it was only a matter of time before the United States would be in the war. He wrote a prophetic letter to Roosevelt on 2 October 1940. While the United States might just drift into the war, he predicted it was 'more probable' that Japan would launch a surprise attack on American forces in the Pacific, thereby leaving Washington with no option but to declare war on the Axis powers.[21]

He was obviously thinking on the same lines as Roosevelt. Six days later, following a press conference that was taped, the recorder was still running in the room as the President talked privately. 'This country is ready to pull the trigger if the Japs do anything,' he said. 'The time may be coming when the Germans and Japs do some fool thing that would put us in.'[22]

Hans Thomsen, the German *chargé d'affaires* in Washington, used some Irish-Americans in a surreptitious campaign against Roosevelt. One of his tactics was to distribute 50,000 copies of *Country Squire in the White House*, a book written by the Irish-American economist John T. Flynn, who was a distinguished columnist with the *New Republic* and Scripps-Howard press. He had made a name for himself with his attacks on Wall Street during the 1920s and 1930s. Although an early supporter of Roosevelt, Flynn became disillusioned with the New Deal, which he believed would lead to Fascism. As a member of a three-man advisory council to the Nye Committee, Flynn advocated rigorous restraints on war profits. In *Country Squire in the White House*, he accused Roosevelt of becoming 'the recognised leader of the war party' by engaging in military adventures abroad in order to 'take the minds of the people off' the economic plight of the 11 million unemployed in the United States.[23] Thomsen described Flynn's book as a 'vitriolic attack on President Roosevelt and his administration'. The *New York Times* had described it as more damaging to the President's reputation than anything previously published.[24] The *Chicago Daily Tribune* actually published an extended series of extracts from the book in the days leading up to the election.

Thomsen also used the Irish-American publisher, William Griffin, to publish a captured Polish document purporting to show that Roosevelt intended to lead the United States into the war. The document, dated 7 March 1939, was a report in which the Polish Ambassador to the United States, Count Jerzy Potocki, gave details of a conversation in which the American Ambassador to France had assured him, with Roosevelt's apparent approval, that the White House was prepared to give the Allies 'all-out support in a possible war'. The Germans had released news of the report several months earlier, but Thomsen hoped to inject it into the campaign as an election issue on the weekend before voting, by resurrecting the story as a major news item in the *New York Enquirer*, which would become famous in later decades as the *National Enquirer*. In 1940 it was the only Sunday evening newspaper in New York. The Germans hoped enough people would be influenced to vote for Willkie to help him carry the state, then the most populous in the union. New

York had more electoral votes than the country's twelve smallest states combined. The Germans secretly put up the money to bring out an extra large edition of a quarter of a million copies of the *New York Enquirer* two days before the election, with the bold front-page headline:

ROOSEVELT'S PREPARATIONS FOR AMERICAN ENTRY INTO THE WAR[25]

Although the Germans helped to stir up controversy around the foreign policy issues in the campaign, there was really very little difference between Willkie and the President on such matters. Both men were outspoken proponents of aid for Britain. Yet Willkie sought to attract isolationist support by accusing the President of secretly committing himself to lead the United States into the war on Britain's behalf after the election. These tactics seemed to be paying off as the President's lead in the polls slipped badly.

By mid-October party regulars were inundating the White House with frantic requests for the President to refute Willkie's charges and to assure the American people he would not abandon neutrality, if re-elected. Even though Roosevelt's running mate, Henry Wallace, and Secretary of Labour Frances Perkins shared the platform with him in New York on 27 October, Cudahy got the headlines and dominated the report of the political rally. 'The feeling that the President is trying to get us into the war is being injected into this campaign,' Cudahy told the gathering. There was no truth to this, because Roosevelt was striving for peace. 'Never before in the history of the country have we a man so well equipped, so well trained to take office in a period of crisis,' Cudahy continued to sustained applause. 'This is no time to take chances with our peace and security.'[26]

Less than two weeks before the election there were rumours that Willkie was going to receive some Irish-American help that could prove decisive, as Joe Kennedy returned to the United States, essentially abandoning his post in London, where he had continued to speak indiscreetly. 'His behaviour as ambassador was outrageous,' wrote Henry Luce, the publisher of *Time* and *Life* magazines. 'He was sitting there in the middle of the Blitz phoning me on the open transatlantic phone saying the jig was up for England. You just don't do that kind of thing.' Kennedy had a talent 'for strong opinions and weak judgments', according to *New York Times* columnist James 'Scotty' Reston, who observed that the ambassador 'couldn't keep his mouth shut or his pants on'.[27]

Kennedy's return to the United States led to a flurry of rumours that he intended to endorse Willkie. The ambassador's eldest son, Joe Jr, had earlier campaigned openly for Farley and supported him at the Democratic Party's

National Convention. Maffey told Gray that Ambassador Kennedy was going to denounce Roosevelt, who was understandably uneasy because Kennedy had been privy to much of the secret correspondence with Churchill. 'Joe has always been an appeaser and always will be an appeaser,' the President told Henry Morgenthau. 'He's just a pain in the neck to me.'[28]

The prosecution of Tyler Kent was proceeding *in camera* in London.[29] If news of Kent's arrest or the waiving of his diplomatic immunity got out, it would probably have caused a sensation in the United States. On hearing that Kennedy was returning to the United States, Roosevelt instructed him 'not to make any statement to the press on your way over nor when you arrive in New York until you and I have had a chance to agree upon what should be said. Please come straight through to Washington on your arrival.'[30] The President also asked Senator James F. Byrnes, a friend of Kennedy, to get in touch with the Ambassador to make sure that he made no pronouncements before visiting the White House. Robert Stewart of the British Empire section of the State Department was sent to New York to meet Kennedy's plane with two messages: one was a handwritten invitation for Kennedy and his wife to the White House that night, the other was a telegram from Byrnes.

Kennedy happened to telephone the White House while Roosevelt was having lunch with two Congressional supporters, Sam Rayburn and Lyndon B. Johnson. 'Ah, Joe, it is so good to hear your voice,' the President said on taking the call. 'Come to the White House tonight for a little family dinner. I'm dying to talk to you.' At that point, according to Johnson, Roosevelt made a theatrical gesture of slitting his throat.[31]

Kennedy refused to answer questions from reporters who had come to meet him. 'Nothing to say until I've seen the President,' he explained.

Would he issue a statement?

'After I've seen the President I'll make a statement.'

Did he intend to resign?

'No statement.'

What were his plans?

'I'm going right to the White House—and I'll talk a lot after I'm finished with that.'[32]

He and his wife, Rose, were then rushed by car, with a motorcycle escort, to a plane bound for Washington. The President had invited Rose along because she was susceptible to his flattery and he hoped she could influence her husband to stay in line. Indeed, she began working on him during their flight to Washington. 'The President sent you, a Roman Catholic, as Ambassador to London, which probably no other President would have done,' she said. 'You would write yourself down as an ingrate in the view of many people if you resign now.' Kennedy later said his wife had softened him up for

Roosevelt to disarm him.[33]

The President mollified Kennedy by agreeing with his various complaints. Roosevelt blamed the State Department for fouling things up. After the election he would clean out the State Department and get rid of those officials who had treated Kennedy so badly. Roosevelt knew Kennedy was highly ambitious for his sons and played on this. If Kennedy supported him now, Roosevelt said 'he would support my son Joe for Governor of Massachusetts in 1942', according to Kennedy.[34]

Despite serious reservations, Kennedy was won over. Byrnes said the Democratic National Committee had reserved airtime, and he asked Kennedy to make a radio broadcast endorsing the President. But Kennedy said he would pay for the broadcast himself as his financial contribution to the campaign. By personally paying for airtime, he raised expectations that he was indeed going to make some momentous pronouncement. There was therefore a great air of anticipation as Kennedy began his speech over the CBS network exactly one week before polling day.

'On Sunday, I returned from war-torn Europe to the peaceful shores of our beloved country renewed in my conviction that this country must and will stay out of war,' he said. 'Unfortunately, during this political campaign, there has arisen the charge that the President of the United States is trying to involve this country in the world war. Such a charge is false.'[35]

'My wife and I have given nine hostages to fortune,' Kennedy continued. 'Our children and your children are more important than anything else in the world. The kind of America that they and their children will inherit is of grave concern to us all. In the light of all these considerations, I believe that Franklin D. Roosevelt should be re-elected President of the United States.'[36]

The New York Times and other newspapers published the whole text of the address, which had a tremendous impact. 'As a vote-getting speech, it was probably the most effective of the campaign,' Life magazine noted. 'For more than anything else it allayed fear that Roosevelt would take this country into war.'[37]

The President had by this time already set out on a final campaign tour. In Boston next day he delivered the most celebrated speech of the whole campaign. The ties with Kennedy were greatly stressed. Roosevelt was met at the railroad station by the Ambassador's father-in-law, John 'Honey Fitz' Fitzgerald, a former Mayor of Boston, who was accompanied by his grandson, the future President, John F. Kennedy. In his speech the President spoke in complimentary terms of Ambassador Kennedy and went on to make his famous promise not to involve the United States in the war: 'I have said this before, but I shall say it again and again and again, your boys are not going to be sent into any foreign wars.'[38]

'That hypocritical son of a bitch!' Willkie exclaimed on hearing it. 'This is going to beat me!'[39]

Roosevelt had suddenly managed to turn himself into an anti-war candidate. 'In the last desperate days, Roosevelt made some fearsome concessions to the isolationists,' according to his biographer, James McGregor Burns.[40] He had appeared to commit himself firmly to staying out of the war. Privately he had convinced people like Kennedy and Cudahy to campaign for him as a peace candidate.

An overwhelming majority of American newspapers, 78 per cent, endorsed Willkie, but this was not a reliable guide to public opinion; in 1936 over 60 per cent of the newspapers had endorsed Roosevelt's Republican opponent, who only managed to win in two of the forty-eight states. Although some of the ethnic Irish-American weeklies did not take an editorial stand, their lack of enthusiasm for the President was unmistakable. For several weeks the New York *Gaelic-American* carried a mast across the top of its front page: 'Keep u.s. Out of Foreign War.' In its last issue before the election its main story, directly underneath the mast, was headlined: 'Re-election of Roosevelt Would Undoubtedly Jockey United States into War.'[41] The San Francisco *Leader*, another ethnic Irish-American weekly, warned in an editorial that the continued existence of the United States 'as a republic' depended on the defeat of Roosevelt.[42] Father Coughlin's *Social Justice* called on readers to 'Vote for Willkie to Avert War and Stop Dictatorship'.[43]

The Catholic *Tablet* was scathing in its opposition to Roosevelt as it called for the lifting of the blockade of the Continent in support of former President Hoover's relief campaign. Father Edward Lodge Curran called for Catholic leadership to 'protect this country against propaganda in the press, on the radio and on the silver screen, which is seeking to stampede the United States into the present European carnage on the theory that the present World War is a Holy War'.[44]

The election outcome was much closer than either of Roosevelt's two earlier victories. He carried all the larger cities, with the exception of Cincinnati. He even won the state of New York, in spite of a strong vote for Willkie in areas with heavy concentrations of Irish-Americans. Roosevelt's vote in the Bronx dropped and Willkie got over 100,000 more votes than Alf Landon received in 1936. Willkie actually outpolled Roosevelt in the Queens Borough, increasing the Republican vote by 161,406, while Roosevelt dropped 44,607 votes. But the President still managed to win re-election comfortably.[45]

| CHURCHILL'S OUTBURST

D uring the election campaign in the United States, the danger of a British attack on Ireland seemed to recede, but things suddenly changed as the American people were voting on 5 November 1940. Churchill suddenly gave vent to his frustration at the Irish refusal to surrender the ports.

British forces had just won the Battle of Britain, he told Parliament, but they were facing an even more important battle—the Battle of the Atlantic—under unfavourable conditions. 'The fact that we cannot use the South and West Coasts of Ireland to refuel our flotillas and aircraft and thus protect the trade by which Ireland as well as Great Britain lives', he said, 'is a most heavy and grievous burden and one which should never have been placed on our shoulders, broad though they be.'[1] There was no actual threat in the speech, but it caused uneasiness in Dublin. The German Minister saw the outburst as an indication that 'England was now shedding her fear of unfavourable repercussions in the United States.'[2]

Roosevelt still needed their support in Congress, so Joe Walshe assured Hempel that Britain could still not afford to risk antagonising Irish-Americans. He argued that the importance of Irish bases was being exaggerated and whatever advantages might be gained by seizing Irish bases would be more than offset by unfavourable repercussions in the United States.

Hempel, who was especially uneasy at the reaction of British newspapers, thought Walshe's optimism was possibly an effort 'to play down the matter' in order to ease tension. 'The comments in the British press after the debate in the House of Commons indicate, in my opinion, that at least attempts are being made, or are yet to be expected, to put pressure on Ireland in order to obtain certain concessions,' Hempel warned Berlin.[3]

The press reactions to Churchill's speech troubled de Valera most. He feared it might be the start of a propaganda campaign to justify British seizure of Irish bases, and the attitude of the American Minister could only have compounded matters.

The Irish should allow Britain to use the ports, Gray told Walshe on 7 November. If the United States entered the war, Walshe said Dublin could allow Americans to use them, but not the British because they would never give the ports back. 'I told him,' Gray reported, 'that I thought his government must be prepared for support of Great Britain in the American press in case Churchill, moved by what he considered to be a necessity, announced that he would occupy the ports by force after presenting publicly his brief which would probably include what is reported to be Chamberlain's undocumented understanding at the time he surrendered them, that in case of need the harbours would be available.'[4]

The reference to Chamberlain's understanding was particularly disturbing, as there never been any such understanding, and Walshe had explained this to Gray previously. In fact, he had written to him, quoting Churchill's speech denouncing the Anglo-Irish agreement of 1938 on the grounds that the return of the ports was unconditional. This latest conversation between Walshe and Gray had been so open and free that Walshe was stunned when Gray sent him a detailed memorandum of their exchanges.

'I may have imbibed over-freely of the excellent wines which you gave me at lunch,' Walshe wrote. 'If that is so, I was, of course, capable of saying anything, even the exact contrary of what I would wish to say in my sober moments.' Irish diplomats abroad had often complained Walshe was reluctant to commit himself, especially in writing. 'My dear David, I do not think that an after-lunch conversation of that casual character merited being immortalised in a memorandum,' he wrote.[5] In particular, he refuted the suggestion that there would be little difficulty giving ports to the Americans, if the United States entered the war. 'I do not think I was anything like so definite, but in any case I can make myself clear now.'[6]

There could be no question of handing over or leasing the ports, de Valera told the Dáil on 7 November. 'Any attempt to bring pressure to bear on us by any side', he said, 'could only lead to bloodshed.' As long as his government remained in office, it would defend the country's rights in regard to the ports against any attacker.[7]

Much to de Valera's chagrin, the new British press campaign was echoed in the United States. 'The denial of Irish bases is a serious handicap to Britain,' George Elliott wrote that day in the *New York Herald Tribune*. The article also suggested there were German agents in Ireland, 'where they can, of course, find many ways of aiding the operations of their u-boats and aircraft'. The author concluded, 'American opinion, highly regarded always in Ireland, might be of some service in urging a change of attitude at Dublin.'[8]

Realising that the British were likely to enlist Roosevelt's influence in an attempt to persuade Dublin to give up the ports, the Taoiseach telegraphed

Robert Brennan to give the State Department a copy of his latest speech and to explain that any American attempt would be fruitless. He also sent a telegram to John J. Reilly, president of the American Association for Recognition of the Irish Republic, requesting the association 'and all friends of Ireland to organise and put the Irish case, including partition, clearly before the American public'. It would be an 'inhuman outrage' to force Ireland into the war when the country was virtually defenceless, the Taoiseach explained. The Irish people had the same right as Americans to stay out of the war and were determined to 'defend that right to the utmost'.[9]

Churchill had not actually threatened any action against Ireland. 'The use of naval and air bases in Éire would greatly simplify our problems,' he noted privately, 'but it would be most unwise to coerce Ireland until the danger was mortal.'[10]

Fine Gael thought the Taoiseach had created a crisis for selfish political ends. He had informed the press that he would be making an important address before intimating his intention to the Defence Conference. Even if the government wished to join with the British 'or finesse the ports to them', W.T. Cosgrave warned his colleagues, 'the complete lack of aerial defence for Dublin, etc., would prevent us supporting them—apart altogether from the question of getting the people to support such a line of action.'[11]

The bipartisan approach to defence matters was allowing de Valera to make 'any reckless statement', with Fine Gael appearing to condone it, T.F. O'Higgins complained. He suggested Cosgrave insist the Taoiseach consult the Defence Conference in future before making any important defence pronouncements. Otherwise, O'Higgins warned, members of Fine Gael might just as well merge with Fianna Fáil and accept de Valera as their leader. 'Such a position in practice or in fact,' he added, 'I could not tolerate for one hour.'[12]

Distrust of de Valera within Fine Gael was so intense that when Cosgrave prepared a private complaint to the Taoiseach, Dillon persuaded him to scrap it on the grounds that de Valera would use it as a pretext for dissolving the Defence Conference and accusing the opposition of trying to stab the government in the back in the midst of a crisis. 'If there is to be a breach, we must break with de Valera,' Dillon argued. 'Under no circumstances must we take any action which will give him an excuse for breaking with us.'[13] Fine Gael members of the Defence Conference therefore complained informally, and the Taoiseach promised to consult them in future, if possible.

Although Fine Gael leaders did not share his concern over Churchill's remarks, de Valera was correct in suspecting the British intended to enlist American help in order to secure Irish facilities. On 8 November 1940 Churchill told the War Cabinet of his plans to cable Roosevelt on the following lines:

It will be at least two years before America can give us any effective help since she is only now laying out her armament factories. The question is whether Great Britain can hold out for so long without the Treaty ports. Anything which can be done to get for us the use of the Treaty ports would thus be in defence of American interests.[14]

Before Churchill sent his message, however, Navy Secretary Frank Knox was wondering in Washington whether a systematic campaign among Irish-Americans would encourage de Valera to hand over bases to Britain. When Brennan called at the State Department to deliver the copy of the Taoiseach's speech, Sumner Welles told him the Dublin government was jeopardising its own security by not giving the ports to the British. Ireland's democracy and freedom would be dead if the Nazis won the war, Welles said. While the Roosevelt administration had little sympathy for Irish neutrality, de Valera did find support elsewhere in the United States, especially in the Irish-American press.

'The Irish leader never expressed the sentiments of his race at home and abroad more thoroughly than in the manly, courageous and uncompromising pronouncement,' the San Francisco *Leader* asserted.[15] Charlie Connolly, the Monaghan-born editor and founder of the *Irish Echo* (New York), called on 'all people interested in assisting Ireland in preserving her neutrality' to meet at the Tuxedo Ballroom on 59th Street and Madison Avenue in New York City on Sunday, 24 November.[16]

Connolly was a colourful and obstreperous individual who had difficulty working with groups. He was loud in his denunciations 'and used diatribe without logic or reason', according to the Mayo-born lawyer Paul O'Dwyer. 'He was quick to accuse anyone who disagreed with him of being a "Shoneen" or "Anglophile" and those who came under his condemnation were legion.'[17]

About 2,500 people showed up at the Tuxedo Ballroom, which surprised everyone. An *ad hoc* committee was organised, with Paul O'Dwyer presiding. His brother William, a future Mayor of New York, had gained a high profile as District Attorney in King's County, New York, prosecuting members of Murder Incorporated.

'After I opened the meeting for discussion, it became apparent that more than a majority were made up of German Bundists, Christian Fronters and Christian Mobilizers,' Paul O'Dwyer recalled. 'It would seem that their interest in Ireland was secondary. The articulate ones in the crowd openly expressed the opinion that they were in favour of Germany and against England in the war. I found it necessary to rule that whoever arose to speak would identify himself, not alone by name, but by the association to which he belonged. The first man to conform to the rule was six-foot four inches tall and he called himself Mr Monahan, proclaiming loudly, "I am a soldier of Christ.'"[18]

The proceedings became boisterous, as many were ready to turn the gathering into an anti-British rally. 'This meeting was called for the purpose of counteracting propaganda aimed at forcing Ireland into the war against her will, and discussion will follow on the best way to achieve that end,' O'Dwyer insisted. With things beginning to get out of hand, he called on a priest in the front row to say a few words. 'It might be well for us to have a word from a man of God,' O'Dwyer said in desperation. But instead of exerting a calming influence, the priest only inflamed things by saying he had read in *The New York Times* that the English were scraping the bottom of the barrel. 'May they stay at the bottom of the barrel and may they have the Jews with them,' he exclaimed to thunderous applause.[19] The meeting eventually decided to set up the American Friends of Irish Neutrality (AFIN), to support Irish neutrality, with Paul O'Dwyer as national chairman.

The Taoiseach also received strong support among politicians. Senator Rush D. Holt of Virginia had an editorial from the *New York Enquirer* inserted into the *Congressional Record* accusing Churchill of talking like Hitler and being 'eager to commit the crowning blunder of his career by making an assault on Ireland'.[20] A copy of the editorial, along with a goodwill message signed by eighty senators, 188 members of the House of Representatives and nineteen governors, was also sent to de Valera. Such support was certainly significant, as Roosevelt was in no position to ignore Congressional sentiment.

'As we see it here,' Gray telegraphed Washington on 10 November 1940, 'any attempt by Churchill to negotiate for the ports will be hopeless. He has the choice between seizing them and paying the price in possible bloodshed and certain hostility and doing without.' Even though London could still use economic coercion against the Irish by refusing to allow British ships to supply Éire, Gray warned that de Valera would probably use such pressure to 'his own political advantage'.[21]

Much of de Valera's political power was based 'on his genius for engendering and utilising anti-British sentiment', according to the American Minister, who believed the Taoiseach covered up his political and economic failings by exploiting anti-British sentiment. This was easily excited because the wounds of the Black and Tan period were still causing hurt. Gray wrote that de Valera was

> probably the most adroit politician in Europe and he honestly believes that all he does is for the good of the country. He has the qualities of martyr, fanatic and Machiavelli. No one can outwit him, frighten or brandish him. Remember that he is not pro-German nor personally anti-British but only

pro-de Valera. My view is that he will do business on his own terms or must be overcome by force.[22]

While Gray thought Churchill had made the mistake of trying to frighten de Valera, Robert Brennan was probably nearer the truth in believing the outburst was prompted by distressing news from the Atlantic. Churchill may have been just letting off steam, as he did after the sinking of the *Royal Oak* at Scapa Flow in October 1939. On the afternoon of his latest speech a distress call was picked up from a convoy under attack by a German battleship in the mid-Atlantic.

The British had been unaware that the German battleship *Admiral Scheer* was loose in the Atlantic, so only the *Jervis Bay*, a lightly armed merchant cruiser, was escorting the convoy. As a result there were fears at the Admiralty for the safety of the whole convoy of thirty-eight ships, and those fears were exacerbated some hours later when Berlin radio announced that 'surface units of the German navy operating in the Atlantic have destroyed completely a British convoy in the North Atlantic'.[23] The Germans cited the attack as proof they could strike at British ships a long distance from Britain. 'A new chapter of naval warfare has begun,' the Nazi newspaper *Der Angriff* asserted.[24]

'Normally it is pretty safe to discount the claims of destruction put out from Berlin,' a *New York Times* editorial noted, 'but naval experts are a little hesitant to dismiss so lightly yesterday confident assertion that the North Atlantic raider had "wiped out" a convoy of fifteen to twenty merchant vessels in Mid-Atlantic last Tuesday when distress calls were being picked up by Mackay radio.'[25] The Admiralty refused to comment, but all further sailings were suspended for what transpired to be the longest delay of the war.

The press campaign to spotlight the issue of Irish ports gathered international momentum while the fate of convoy HX84 remained in doubt. The *Economist*, which enjoyed a prestigious international readership, suggested that Britain could cut off supplies to Ireland, but this would cause bitterness, so if Britain were to have the bitterness, 'then she might as well have bitterness and the bases'.[26] The *Observer*, the influential British Sunday newspaper, accused the 'Irish *Führer*' of 'giving, if not positive, at any rate negative, aid to the enemy'.[27] In Canada, the *Montreal Gazette* called on the Taoiseach to give the ports to Britain, while Richard Hanson, leader of the Canadian opposition, depicted de Valera's failure to cooperate as 'a valuable contribution to the Axis powers'.[28]

Hanson called on Mackenzie King to ask de Valera to lease bases to Canada for the duration of the war. The status of the Irish Free State had been defined as similar to Canada's in the Anglo-Irish Treaty and the two countries had cooperated at imperial conferences and at the League of Nations. If bases were given to Britain, de Valera might be accused of bringing back the British, but if he gave the facilities to Canada, there would be no such cry. 'No one can doubt that Canada would fulfil not only the letter but the spirit of the lease and withdraw at the close of the war,' Hanson argued.[29]

Despite German claims, the Admiralty was able to announce that a number of ships in convoy HX84 had escaped. They began straggling into port and continued to arrive for the next twelve days, during which the story of the *Jervis Bay* was flashed around the world. It had engaged the *Admiral Scheer* long enough for the escape of over thirty of the ships in the convoy. The *Jervis Bay*'s Commander, Edward Stephen Fogarty Fegen, whose mother was from County Tipperary, was posthumously awarded the Victoria Cross, Britain's highest award for gallantry.

The significance of Irish ports was being overestimated because British ships patrolling the Atlantic were not short of range. There was a problem for aircraft. If the British had air bases at Foynes and Rineanna, they could have patrolled over 100 miles further south and west than aircraft from Eglington or Lough Erne. The distances were such, however, that it would not have been possible to fly to the rescue of any shipping under attack; it would only have been mere chance for any Irish-based aircraft to aid any ship under attack. While the Irish could thus have provided some extra coverage for the seamen on ships in that comparatively narrow and short corridor in the mid-Atlantic, this would have meant putting Irish civilians the length and breadth of the country in much more jeopardy, because it would have been easier for the Germans to locate and attack any place in Ireland than to find and attack Allied ships on the move in the vast expanse of the mid-Atlantic. For de Valera to jeopardise Irish people under the circumstances would have been both reckless and irresponsible.

Canadian High Commissioner John H. Kelly warned Ottawa that the press campaign was based on the erroneous view that Ireland was anti-British. 'Although Ireland is neutral,' he explained, 'public opinion is certainly not pro-German and sympathy with Britain is constantly increasing. Any anti-Irish campaign can do no good and may prove detrimental.' He therefore suggested, 'The fewer press comments made about the ports, the better.'[30]

'The attitude on the ports is not based on any question of hostility to the United Kingdom,' High Commissioner John J. Hearne argued in Ottawa. 'The attitude to England is increasingly friendly. There is absolutely no pro-Nazi sentiment, though there is an IRA faction which demands that the traditional policy of "England's danger is Ireland opportunity" should be followed by attacking England.'[31] Mackenzie King, who had already ignored Hanson's suggestion that Canada ask for the Irish bases, blocked a radio appeal for Irish bases planned by a group of Irish-Canadians from Winnipeg.

On visiting London, Maffey found officials at the Dominions Office worried over Churchill's outburst. 'They had known nothing beforehand about it, and, of course, the statement was typically Churchillian,' Walshe wrote to de Valera after meeting Maffey on 13 November. 'There was no question of any threat to seize the ports,' Maffey said. Churchill was essentially only letting off steam.[32]

Maffey suggested the Irish should agree to the British appointment of a press attaché to his Legation staff. 'If the Press Attaché was going to help him to keep unfriendly articles out of the British Press as I am sure he would, we should be very glad to see him here,' Walshe replied. The Taoiseach would not have reacted if Churchill's speech had not been followed by other speeches, which led 'our people to believe that there was a serious threat involved', Walshe explained. 'The situation became worse when there was a general press chorus the following day on a still higher pitch, and this spread to the United States.'[33]

De Valera was bitter over the press campaign because Ireland really had no choice. Any town in the country could be bombed from 20 feet. 'He, himself, had always desired a British victory and always maintained the argument that we had done our very best to avert war,' Maffey reported. 'Within the limits of neutrality, as I well knew, he had given every help that it was possible to give.' He seemed to fear that the British had lost a steadying influence on Anglo-Irish affairs with the death of Chamberlain little over a week earlier.

Churchill merely stated 'a bold and obvious fact, the tragic fact that the loss of the Irish ports had gravely handicapped us in our vital connections at sea!', Maffey argued. But de Valera reiterated his belief that the value of the ports was exaggerated, and he warned that Irish public opinion could easily swing into violent anti-British channels. 'I begged him in the light of his talk with me to use his influence to prevent any such retrogression of public opinion here,' Maffey added. 'We had faced difficulties before but with patience we had come through.' The Taoiseach said he could not understand how the British could allow their press to play with fire in such dangerous circumstances.

'I told him that I would bring his anxieties to the notice of His Majesty's Government and in particular direct attention to the danger of threatening good relations between the two countries as a result of press comments on the subject of the ports,' Maffey reported.[34] He probably felt he had to be particularly critical of de Valera in his report to the Dominions Office lest anyone would think he was 'going native' in Ireland. De Valera was a 'complete dictator', Maffey wrote to Machtig. 'It is quite wrong to suppose that de Valera will ever respond to a generous gesture. He is completely ruthless and has achieved great success by never allowing his gaze to be diverted to right or left.

He is the most astute politician and understands exactly what his people will do and what they will not do.'[35]

'Mr de Valera and his extremists will exploit at once all the resources of the old tribal hatred,' Maffey warned Churchill. 'Whatever Mr de Valera may be in Geneva, here, in Ireland, he has never in essentials moved from the track he has consistently followed—the narrow avenue of hate.'[36] Maffey was arguing that London should again dampen the press campaign in Britain's own interest, but with Roosevelt safely back in the White House for another four years, Churchill was unwilling to act.

The Prime Minister wrote to the Dominions Secretary on 22 November 1940, rejecting Maffey's suggestion to soft-pedal the issue of the ports:

I think it would be better to let de Valera stew in his own juice for a while. Nothing could be more harmless or more just than the remarks in the *Economist*. The claim now put forward on behalf of de Valera is that we are not only to be strangled by them, but to suffer our fate without making any complaint.

Sir John Maffey should be made aware of the rising anger in England and Scotland, and especially among the merchant seamen, and he should not be encouraged to think that his only task is to mollify de Valera and make everything, including our ruin, pass off pleasantly. Apart from this, the less we say to de Valera at this juncture the better, and certainly nothing must be said to reassure him.[37]

With the British government unwilling to give any reassurance, the attitude of the Roosevelt administration must have been especially disconcerting for the Irish. On 19 November 1940, Sumner Welles instructed Gray to tell de Valera that Irish freedom and democracy would be dead if Britain did not win the war and that 'the utilisation of Irish ports apparently was imperative to the success of the British Navy under present conditions'. This was the opinion of 'virtually the entire American press and the vast preponderance of public opinion as well', according to Welles.[38]

Before Gray could arrange a meeting, however, de Valera gave another widely publicised interview to an American journalist, emphasising his determination to stay out of the war. He told Wallace Carroll of United Press that giving up the ports would involve Ireland in the war. 'You have seen what has happened to London, notwithstanding its defences,' the Taoiseach said. 'What would happen to Dublin, Cork and other Irish cities relatively unprotected? If we were attacked, we should no doubt have to face these dangers, but no nation can be asked to court them.'[39]

In requesting a meeting with de Valera to carry out his instructions, Gray wrote, 'Nations that are not cooperating with Britain have come to be regarded as not in sympathy with the interests of America.'[40] At the ensuing meeting on 22 November, he adopted a minatory tone. Ireland's survival depended on the British, he said. If the Dublin government did not at least explore the possibility of further cooperation with Britain, then relations between Dublin and Washington might deteriorate.

De Valera replied that he would not discuss leasing as much as an inch of Irish territory to anyone and added, somewhat pointedly, that it was not a war of Ireland's choosing and that it was rather strange that the United States, a neutral power, should deny the right of neutrality to a small country.

'We were not denying any right but that as all right ultimately depended on power he might be relying on the power of American public opinion to support him and that he might fail to receive this support,' Gray replied. 'Americans could be cruel if their interests were affected and Ireland should expect little or no sympathy if the British took the ports.'[41]

'I was not undertaking to defend or justify American opinion, but merely to state its trend and to emphasise the danger to Ireland of counting upon it in the case England attempt to seize the ports for the common protection of the two islands,' Gray later explained in a letter to de Valera.[42] At the time, Gray was arguing that the United States would soon be in the war and Ireland might just as well anticipate that moment by allowing Britain to use the ports. This was not official policy, so Gray did not mention it to the State Department, but he believed it was Roosevelt's aim and he reported fully to the President. He mentioned, for instance, that giving Britain all aid short of war was absurd if that assistance would not be sufficient to defeat Hitler. 'We either ought to cut our losses and declare out *now* or put up what is needed to push Hitler over,' he wrote. 'I am sure that you feel this way about it.'[43]

Following his meeting with the Taoiseach, Gray warned the State Department that it should be cautious in its dealings with de Valera. 'Great care must be taken if any pressure is to be exerted that it gives him no grounds for strengthening his political position,' Gray wrote.[44] He was still anxious to keep the Taoiseach as politically weak as possible so Fine Gael would be able to divide the Dáil, if de Valera sought to resist a British attempt to seize Irish facilities. It later became apparent Fine Gael would not have been prepared to play such a role, but Gray was relying on the mistaken belief that James Dillon, whom he described as 'the real leader of the Opposition', would be unwilling to resist the British. 'If it came to a question of declaring war on England', Gray predicted that Dillon 'would go to the country even if it brought on civil war here'. As a result he suggested to Roosevelt that 'The best chance the British have of getting anywhere with the ports, unless we come in, is to play to this Opposition and try to split the country.'[45]

After a British naval intelligence officer told Gray that the Admiralty had rejected a plan for a surprise attack on Ireland in order to seize the Treaty ports and facilities at Foynes during October, Gray wrote to Roosevelt next day:

> I told him any surprise attack I thought would be a major calamity; that if they felt they had to take this step it should be preceded by an appeal from the Dominions and Colonies with a brief for the British case got up principally for American consumption also giving due notice of the date they were coming in. This would put the matter in the Dáil where the Opposition could have a say. A surprise attack would be dealt with by de Valera and all debate would be quashed. The political advantage of an appeal and due notice I think would outweigh the military advantages of surprise.[46]

There appeared to be no limit to the American Minister's determination to help Britain. Gray was 'very imprudent' and was speaking openly in diplomatic and in pro-British circles in a way that 'may give the impression here that America wants the British to seize our ports', de Valera telegraphed Brennan on 4 December 1940. He instructed Brennan to call at the State Department and re-emphasise the Dublin government's determination to remain neutral.[47] Brennan warned Sumner Welles that efforts to get the Irish to hand over bases would be counter-productive because many Irish-Americans would think the British were just trying to regain their dominion over Ireland. This kind of reaction was already rife in both Massachusetts and Pennsylvania, according to Brennan. Unless stopped, he predicted the press campaign would undermine much of the progress made in Anglo-Irish relations.

Chapter 12 ∾

THE ECONOMIC SCREW

Allied propaganda about Irish neutrality involved essentially four distortions. First, Ireland was depicted as infested with Axis agents; second, the German and Italian Legations in Dublin were reported to have excessively large staffs; third, Ireland was reputed to be affording refuelling facilities to German U-boats; and fourth, the lights of Irish cities were supposedly being used by German pilots to get their bearings on British cities. Although these rumours were authoritatively denied, they persisted throughout the war.

Even though rumours about the size of the German Legation had been refuted during the summer, newspapers like the *Christian Science Monitor*, *New York Herald Tribune*, *Fort Worth Star-Telegram* and *PM Daily* still grossly exaggerated the size of the Legation. In late November Colonel Frederick Palmer of the *Washington Evening Star* reported that Galway was being used as a U-boat base.[1]

Having promised that Irish neutrality would not be used against Britain, de Valera was anxious to scotch these unfounded stories. In an interview with Robert Burnelle of Associated Press on 11 December, he denounced the unsupported rumours of U-boat bases and the size of the German Legation, as well as reports that the Germans could use the lights of Irish cities as beacons for bombing purposes. The lights were cowled in order to prevent a sky glow and the British were apparently satisfied with this, he explained, because they raised no objection.

Churchill delivered 'a little monologue' to the Chiefs of Staff on 3 December 1940 'on the desirability of putting severe economic pressure on Ireland to make her lend us the bases we so badly need'.[2] Later, over lunch with the Dominions Secretary and others, he talked about using economic pressure 'to bring de Valera to his knees in a very short time'.[3] The Prime Minister sent Roosevelt probably his most important message on 8 December. Britain was on the verge of bankruptcy and she could no longer pay cash for war supplies, so he asked the President to devise a plan whereby the United States would give, rather than sell, needed supplies to Britain. If the Americans provided the tools, Churchill wrote, Britain would provide the manpower to defeat Hitler.

Without Irish bases or airfields, he depicted the Royal Navy as being strained to the utmost limit:

> We are so hard pressed at sea that we cannot undertake to carry any longer the 400,000 tons of feeding stuffs and fertilizers which we have hitherto convoyed to Éire through all the attacks of the enemy. We need this tonnage for our own supply and we do not need the food which Éire has been sending us. We must now concentrate on essentials, and the Cabinet propose to let de Valera know that we cannot go on supplying him under present conditions. He will, of course, have plenty of food for his people but they will not have the prosperous trading they are making now. I am sorry about this but we must think of our own self-preservation and use for vital purposes our own tonnage brought in through so many perils. Perhaps this may loosen things up and make them more ready to consider common interests. I should like to know quite privately what your reactions would be if and when we are forced to concentrate our tonnage upon the supply of Great Britain. We also do not feel able in the present circumstances to continue the heavy subsidies we have hitherto been paying to the Irish agricultural producers. You will realise also that our merchant seamen as well as public opinion generally take it much amiss that we should have to carry Irish supplies through air and u-boat attacks and subside them handsomely when de Valera is quite content to sit happy and see us strangled.[4]

Roosevelt was confronted with strong Irish-American opposition at this time, especially from Roman Catholic elements, such as the Coughlinites, and also from the country's two cardinals. On 7 December Cardinal O'Connell denounced the 'exalted hysteria' of the war propagandists who were trying to drag the Americans into the conflict, despite their desire for peace. 'They have taken for granted that the authorities at Washington meant what they said and said what they meant when they promised to keep us out of war,' the cardinal said. Those 'propagandists for war' were not 'real Americans' because they were 'raising their voices in loud accents with the preposterous proposition that America sink her individuality and become a sort of tailend of a foreign empire'.[5]

The country's other cardinal, Denis Dougherty, was also worried about the activities of interventionists. He informed the Irish Minister in Washington that Rossa Downing had been asking Irish-American bishops, on behalf of the Committee to Defend America by Aiding the Allies, to use their influence to persuade de Valera to allow the British to use Irish ports.[6] Although the cardinal described Downing as 'an English emissary', he was American-born and had been active in Irish-American groups during the Irish war of independence. Downing would appear again later as a leading member of an Irish-American group.

The Irish ports were a minor issue compared with the overall perspective of American aid to Britain, but Churchill used the issue in highlighting Britain's need for help. Roosevelt's response to Churchill's latest message for help was to draw up 'lend-lease', in accordance with which the United States would loan Britain necessary war supplies. As this was contrary to the 'cash and carry' legislation passed the previous year, Congressional approval was necessary. The President had to move cautiously. He sent up a trial balloon to test public sentiment. As a British victory would be America's best defence, he told a press conference on 17 December 1940, the United States should therefore 'do everything to help the British Empire defend itself'.[7] He suggested leasing war material to the British. If a neighbour's house were on fire, he said, one would loan the neighbour a garden hose to fight the fire, if only to ensure the conflagration did not spread to one's own house.

Meanwhile the British informed Dublin they were cutting back on petrol supplies to Ireland, in spite of an understanding to maintain the level of such supplies in return for the seven tankers turned over at the start of the war. The Taoiseach realised this was really economic pressure to force him to give up the ports. He promptly sought to bolster Ireland's shipping capacity. He used his annual Christmas address to the United States to ask the Americans to sell Ireland ships to transport food, because Ireland was facing serious shortages as a result of a blockade by the belligerents.

Coming barely a week after Roosevelt hinted at the introduction of lend-lease, administration officials in Washington were annoyed because de Valera's address played into the hands of the President's critics by effectively linking Ireland to the Starving Europe Campaign, which was being waged by former president Hoover, who had recently made a widely publicised speech calling on the British to lift their blockade of the Continent on humanitarian grounds. Since Britain was in control of the seas around Ireland, it seemed de Valera was telling Americans that Britain was blockading Ireland, too. The ancestors of so many Irish-Americans had fled to the United States as a result of the potato famine of almost 100 years earlier, so the talk of Irish deprivation raised emotive fears of another famine. To make matters worse, the version of the speech released by CBS and published in the *New York Times* attributed de Valera with having said 'the overshadowing anxiety' of his government was the 'possibility of incitement which would force our people once more to do battle against Britain and the British'. He seemed to be blaming the British exclusively. In fact, however, he did not mention either Britain or the British by name, but it was some days before CBS corrected the misquotation and explained the error was due to atmospheric conditions.[8]

Roosevelt responded to this by essentially ridiculing Irish neutrality during a radio address of his own on 29 December 1940. What would happen if Britain were defeated? 'Could Ireland hold out?' he asked. 'Would Irish freedom be permitted as an amazing pet exception in an unfree world?'[9]

De Valera's broadcast 'appeared to be an attempt to put the pressure of the Irish-American vote on the government', Gray complained. Conveniently oblivious to his own blatant attempts to influence Irish officials, Gray protested that the Taoiseach would resent it if the United States went over his head in Ireland. 'It was not so much the fact of Irish neutrality as the attitude of Irish opinion reported by American newspapers correspondents which aroused regret in the United States,' he explained.[10] Rather than speaking directly to the American people, Gray suggested de Valera send an emissary to the United States to explain the Irish government's problems.

The Irish need for arms was possibly more psychological than real. In November 1940 the Germans had offered to supply Ireland with British arms captured at the time of the Dunkirk evacuation, but de Valera rejected the offer because it was imperative that Dublin avoid any suggestion of any kind of collaboration with the Germans, lest this provide the British with a pretext for seizing Irish bases and thus dragging Ireland into the war.

Although the British had appeared to pose the greater danger for most of the second half of 1940, German behaviour gave rise to a serious crisis around Christmas. At 5.00 p.m. on 19 December, Hempel called on Walshe urgently to say that a German civilian passenger plane would land additional German diplomats from the United States at Rineanna (now Shannon) airport at daybreak two days later. Walshe insisted the landing could not be permitted for political reasons. He said that William Warnock, the Irish *chargé d'affaires*, would explain the situation to the Foreign Ministry in Berlin. 'Herr Hempel asked with great insistence that we should not wire Mr. Warnock, that we should deal with the matter through him, and that, pending consideration of the general questions, the airport should be cleared 'in order to save time' and we should let him have at once the call sign and wave-length of the airport wireless station.'[11]

After discussing the matter with de Valera, Walshe telegraphed Warnock to explain to the German foreign ministry the obvious reasons why Hempel's request 'concerning the staff of the German Legation here is politically impossible from our point of view. It would add enormously to our difficulties.'[12] For months the British press had been spreading rumours of the

German Legation being an overstaffed espionage centre, so increasing the staff at this time might provide the British with a pretext to act against Ireland. Warnock was instructed to tell the Germans the 'proposal might be reviewed at another time', but it was 'quite impractical at the moment'.[13]

Next day Hempel called on Walshe again. 'He argued with considerable emphasis that the German Government had the technical right to increase the staff,' according to Walshe. 'He referred at one point to the possibility of a break of diplomatic relations.'[14]

'We did not deny the technical right,' but contended the time was not appropriate. 'Its exercise in present circumstances would occasion us serious political embarrassment,' Walshe argued. Nothing further was heard from the Germans until the day after Christmas, when Hempel said he had received instructions from Berlin, insisting 'there was no room for discussion'. Walshe again pointed out that the whole thing 'would furnish propaganda against Irish neutrality'.[15]

Terry de Valera, the Taoiseach's nineteen-year-old son, believed his father feared that the arrival of the Germans would provide the British with an excuse to seize Irish bases. 'He feared a British invasion was imminent,' Terry wrote.[16]

Following a conversation with Maffey, John Hall Kelly warned Ottawa that the British might occupy Irish ports. 'I consider such action would be ill-advised and suggest that Canada be consulted before any action is taken,' Kelly telegraphed Mackenzie King.[17] Next day de Valera asked Hempel to have Berlin withdraw the request for landing facilities for additional legation staff, or it would be rejected.

As Hempel waited for further instructions from Berlin, he was seriously embarrassed by a number of incidents during the first three days of the new year when German aircraft bombed a number of Irish areas. Three bombs were dropped at Colpe, near Julianstown, County Meath, and five bombs at Duleek, County Louth, on the night of 1 January, but nobody was injured. In the early hours of the following morning two bombs were dropped at Rathdown Park, Terenure, Dublin, where two houses were demolished and seven people injured. Two other bombs were dropped on waste ground in the same district. The same morning three bombs were dropped on the Curragh Racecourse, and that afternoon two large magnetic mines were dropped by parachute at Glencormac, near Enniskerry, County Wicklow; neither mine detonated. Both were positively identified as being of German origin before being destroyed by the Irish Army. Three further bombs were dropped that evening at Ballymurris, about seven miles south of Enniscorthy, County Wexford. In little over twenty-four hours some twenty bombs had been dropped on Irish territory.

About fifty houses were seriously damaged early the following morning at Donore Terrace, South Circular Road, Dublin, and twenty people were injured. The bombs struck on the pavement in front of a terrace of houses just across the street from one of the country's few Jewish synagogues, which suffered some broken windows and other damage. Two houses, in which twelve people were sleeping, were demolished, but there were no fatalities in the densely populated area. The only fatalities in the series of bombings were in an isolated farmhouse at Knockroe, near Borris, County Carlow. Three people, two sisters and a daughter of the owner, were killed when a bomb hit the home of the Shannon family while they slept in the early hours of 3 January 1941.

The Government announced that the 'Chargé d'Affaires in Berlin has been instructed to make an energetic protest to the German Government against the violation of Irish territory by German aircraft, and the loss of life and destruction of property which took place as the result of bomb explosions and fire'.[18] This was initially refuted in Germany. 'These bombs are English or they are imaginary,' Associated Press reported from Berlin. 'Our flyers have not been over Ireland, and have not been sent there, so someone else will have to explain these bombs.'[19]

Many people suspected the British had dropped German bombs. Gray learned that the IRA was 'certain' the British were responsible, and he noted 'a general majority' of the Irish people 'appear to think it probable'. The Canadian High Commissioner reported that there were persistent rumours that some drunken Canadian members of the Royal Air Force had dropped the bombs.[20]

'I have not the slightest doubt they were dropped by the Germans,' Frank Aiken told Richard Mulcahy.[21]

If the Irish authorities suspected British involvement in the bombing, they would hardly have secretly agreed, on 21 January 1941, to allow British sea planes based on Lough Erne to fly due westward through what was known as the Donegal Corridor over the land from Beleek in County Fermanagh to Ballyshannon on the coast of County Donegal. This was nominally to facilitate air–sea rescue operations, but there was no way of checking the purpose of those flights, so the agreement afforded the British at least 100 miles' extra range in the mid-Atlantic area in providing air cover.

In the midst of his embarrassment over the German bombings, Hempel withdrew the request for landing facilities for extra staff. The Germans asked if de Valera would accept the German diplomats being transferred from the United States, 'if they came by ordinary means of travel'.[22] The Taoiseach promptly agreed. The only commercial route from the United States at the time was via Portugal, to Britain and then on to Ireland. This, of course, killed the project. It was just another of the many subtle, and not so subtle, ways that de Valera slanted his policy in favour of Britain. But some of the British press was still giving Ireland little credit.

Although Churchill had decided to exert economic pressure on the Dublin government, he rejected a plan to cut off virtually all shipping to Ireland. Instead, licensing laws were introduced to prohibit the export of specified items to Ireland, like feeding stuffs, fertilisers, spare parts, various metals, paper, chemicals and electrical products. The British also terminated the informal understanding to provide Ireland with shipping space equivalent to forty whole-time ships in return for an Irish agreement to refrain from chartering neutral ships. That arrangement had been requested by the British in 1939 to keep chartering rates down by eliminating Anglo-Irish competition for neutral shipping. By the beginning of 1941, however, Britain had gained control of Greek and Norwegian ships. As a result the Chancellor of the Exchequer estimated the Irish would be lucky if they could charter enough ships to fulfil a quarter of their needs. Churchill told his Cabinet that supplies would be scaled back gradually, and they would say the action 'was taken in no vindictive spirit and only dire necessity forced us into such a step'. Ministry of Information was to 'inform the press that the government viewed this measure with profound regret, and that it had been taken only because the pressure on our own shipping space was severe'.[23] Lord Cranborne was put in charge of implementing the economic pressure, and Churchill asked to be informed every few days 'as to how the screw is being applied to Ireland'.[24]

Irish Military Intelligence intercepted a letter in which Senator Frank MacDermot wrote to his wife in the United States that Gray had told him 'that he had no doubt that the USA would ultimately come into the war and that this country, he was sure, would be invaded'.[25] The international press was adding to the anxiety. 'If the Irish-ports question becomes a matter of life and death,' the Economist declared, 'the only thing to do, as the Economist remarked before, is to seize them. There will be plenty of moral justification for the act.'[26]

There were news reports from the Continent that Britain or Germany was about to invade Ireland. On 8 January the Press Association reported a British plan to invade 'from Ulster in a few weeks', according to the Swedish newspaper Dagens Nyheter. 'In such an event,' it added, 'Berlin is determined to act in the same manner as in the case of Norway and Belgium.'[27] The Zeesen wireless station broadcast a story from the Swedish newspaper Social-democraten: 'The Reich Government have just come into possession of information according to which the British government have the intention of carrying out the military occupation of Ireland during the coming weeks, or at least occupying the western ports.' The Times of London concluded that such reports had probably been planted by the Nazis 'simply to frighten Ireland'.[28]

With the British refusing to sell arms or provide an assurance to respect Irish sovereignty, de Valera told Maffey the Germans might not meet with as spirited a resistance as they would have met with six months earlier. Maffey again urged London to provide weapons.

'Hateful as their neutrality is,' Maffey added, 'it has been a neutrality friendly to our cause. I need not give in detail what we have got and are getting in the way of intelligence reports, coded weather reports, prompt reports of submarine movements, free use of Lough Foyle and of the air over the Donegal shore and territorial waters etc., etc.'[29] Even in Britain's darkest hour, Irish 'plans and details were revealed to us with the greatest frankness', Maffey noted. 'The catastrophic fall of France stiffened the country's resolve to maintain neutrality, but the Éire Government continued to help in every way which did not expose them to German action.'[30]

Walshe was still confident that Irish-American opinion would keep the British in check. 'The resentment of the Irish people in the United States would be such that Britain would lose more than she would gain by such an action,' he told Canadian High Commissioner Kelly.[31] The latter suggested to Ottawa that Churchill should provide an assurance.[32]

The Canadians had a realistic grasp of the Irish situation. Oscar Skelton, the head of the Department of External Affairs in Ottawa, wrote to the Canadian censor that Irish neutrality did not stem from an anti-British bias or sympathy for the Nazis, but from a war-weariness. The Irish had been through three wars in the past quarter-of-a-century—World War I, the war of independence and civil war. 'The country is anxious, if at all possible, to avoid getting into another war,' he wrote.[33]

Churchill was unwilling to make concessions to de Valera. 'I do not at all wonder that Mr de Valera regrets the disappearance from power of Mr Chamberlain who gave him the Irish bases and a good many other things for nothing.'[34] Unless Dublin was prepared to enter the war, Churchill was not about to placate Irish fears. 'We do not wish them to have further arms, and certainly will not give them ourselves,' he explained to Lord Cranborne.[35] 'I could under no circumstances give the guarantee asked for.'[36] Churchill continued:

No attempt should be made to conceal from Mr de Valera the depth and intensity of feeling against the policy of Irish neutrality. We have tolerated and acquiesced in it, but judicially we have never recognised that Southern Ireland is an independent Sovereign State, and she herself has repudiated Dominion Status.

Maffey reported:

> There is no reason whatever that we should sell anything we cannot spare.
> That is quite well understood here. Our best hope of achieving anything
> here lies and always will lie in the actions and thoughts of America and of
> Irishmen overseas. For that reason we must be careful not to work the
> economic pressure in such a way as to revive that fatal sympathy for
> Ireland by lending colour to the cry that we are blockading her out of
> resentment.[37]

Although it is not possible to determine what proportion of the American
people would have supported British seizure of Irish facilities, a Gallup poll
conducted in the first week of January 1941 indicated 63 per cent of the
American people believed Dublin should allow Britain to use the ports, and
only 16 per cent opposed the idea, with the remainder undecided. Of first-
generation Americans whose fathers were born in Ireland, a majority of only
52 per cent opposed the suggestion, with 40 per cent in favour of it. These
figures, which Gray gleefully passed on, could hardly have been reassuring to
those who were relying on American opinion as the trump card against a
British attack.[38]

On 20 January 1941 Maffey found de Valera 'in an exceedingly nagging
mood', which he presumed had been brought on by the trend of American
public opinion. Knowing that Churchill suspected him of being too anxious
to mollify de Valera, Maffey had to pander to Churchill's prejudices in order
to get a proper hearing in London. Maffey wrote:

> Mr de Valera is more uneasy today than he has ever been in any stage of
> his non-stop political career. Ireland being Ireland, in the mass ignorant
> and responsive to old hatreds, he is still the chosen tribal leader for their
> feuds. But Mr de Valera hitherto has used this Irish fanaticism on a bigger
> stage than his platform today. Through it he has achieved prestige in
> America, in England, and Geneva. He could stir worldwide interest in the
> soul of Ireland. But it is the soul of England which stirs the world today,
> and Éire is a bog with a petty leader raking over old muck heaps. He has
> in the past enjoyed world prestige, he is vain and ambitious, but the task
> he has followed without looking either to right or to left is now leading
> into insignificance.

It was Roosevelt's courageous speeches that were stirring the Irish in America.
'These Irish-Americans are the pillars of Mr de Valera's temple. They created
him, preserved him, and endowed him,' according to Maffey, who felt the

Taoiseach was therefore worried about the loss of this constituency. But Maffey's invective was as a further attempt to impress Churchill in order to have him consider the next part of the message. 'Mr de Valera is telling the truth when he says that if we arm Éire we shall create a most powerful weapon against a German invasion and establish a good friend on our flank,' Maffey continued.[39]

'Certainly it would give me personally considerable pleasure to be able to say to Mr de Valera that he and Éire could "stew in their own juice".' Maffey wrote, but he realised that the Irish Army was not strong enough to deter a German invasion, so the Irish people had little choice. 'In the present unarmed state the vast majority cannot but support de Valera's neutrality,' he explained.[40]

As an astute judge of what was happening in Ireland, Maffey realised British economic pressure would lead de Valera to conclude Ireland was being blockaded, and he would appeal for American help. 'The belligerents in blockading each other are blockading us,' de Valera explained in a radio address the following week. 'How far directly and how far indirectly, how far designedly and how far undesignedly, we need not wait to estimate. The results are the same, and they are serious. We have not a moment to lose in preparing for the worst in regard to all those supplies that come to us from abroad, and we shall be foolish in the extreme if we prepare for anything less than the worst.'[41]

There were 'indications that there is a crisis on', Aiken told Mulcahy at a Defence Conference meeting that day. Mulcahy did not think the British were deliberately turning the economic screw, but de Valera told him next day that Head Line, a British-owned company, had been instructed in the United States not 'to take stuff for Ireland'. The Irish knew Maffey had failed to persuade Churchill to promise to respect Irish neutrality. The Taoiseach said he was looking for such a promise in order to publicise it so the people could concentrate on the German danger.[42] He was concerned about Germany's recent interest in Ireland. On 22 January he told Gray he was convinced the Germans were going to invade, and he said Ireland was in desperate need of American arms to ensure the Irish Army could hold out until British help could arrive.

When Gray asked for an assurance that Ireland would ally with Britain and hand over naval and air facilities for the duration of the war if Germany attacked, de Valera said he would be unable to commit himself until the occasion arose. Unless the Irish government was willing to give such a commitment, Gray said he would not recommend allowing Dublin to purchase American equipment. De Valera could have told Gray that military arrangements had already been made with the British, but he apparently did not trust him because the American Minister had been appallingly indiscreet. An Associated Press correspondent had recently reported that Gray had told him that de Valera threatened Hempel with expulsion following the recent German bombing incidents. This was further distorted by American press reports that Hempel had actually been expelled.

Gray was dismissive when de Valera mentioned Ireland's rights. He told the Taoiseach his only right was to believe in his religion and be burned for it, if necessary. 'Every other right depended on the force to maintain it.'[43]

'He called my views the greatest exponent of force he had ever met,' Gray noted. 'I made it clear that it was a case of facing realities.'[44]

The American Minister had developed a particularly low opinion of the calibre of Irish politicians. With only one or two exceptions in the Cabinet, he compared them to the local politicians he used to cover in Monroe and Duchess Counties in New York during his days as a newspaper reporter. If he was going out on a limb, he suggested the President warn him to be careful. 'I feel that I only can be helpful to you and to Ireland by trying to interpret your policy AND ITS IMPLICATIONS to this government,' he explained. 'It is better that they get their feet on the ground even if they blame me for the shock than that they should go on in the world of unreality in which they are existing.' [45]

'You need not "be careful"', the President replied. 'I think', he added rather pointedly, 'you are unfair to the Board of Duchess County or of Monroe County. Almost all of them were highly practical people.'[46]

Although scathing about de Valera in some of his reports, Gray wrote to First Lady Eleanor Roosevelt that de Valera was very good in the area of social legislation. 'The great thing the de Valera government has done and is doing, is to govern in the interest of the under-privileged as far as possible,' he wrote. 'They have a real new deal here.' In foreign policy, however, he complained that de Valera 'lives in a dream-wish world'. He and his colleagues did not realise a small country like Ireland, without mineral resources, could not 'be free and independent in a sense that a continent wide state or federation of states can be independent and free'. Yet in spite of what he saw as shortcomings, Gray still professed a personal affection for de Valera. 'I like him very much,' he wrote, 'though I despair of coping with him.'[47]

| DISTINGUISHED VISITORS

In early 1941 the debate was raging in the United States over the lend-lease proposal to further amend the American neutrality laws. As the Bill was going through Congress, Irish-Americans were on both sides of the issue. The United Irish Societies—the umbrella organisation for all local ethnic Irish-American groups and clubs—passed resolutions condemning the lend-lease proposal in New York, Philadelphia, Chicago and San Francisco. Senator David I. Walsh led the fight against the Bill in the US Senate, where Senator James Murray of Montana was one of his strong supporters.

Former Ambassador Joseph P. Kennedy adopted a somewhat contradictory public attitude. He had committed one of his legendary indiscretions only days after Roosevelt's re-election, in which he had played such a significant part. He told reporters of the *Boston Globe* and *St Louis Post-Dispatch* that 'democracy is all finished in England' and 'it may be here as well'.[1] On a commercial air flight to Washington in early 1941 he was talking rather loudly to President Roosevelt's son, Franklin Jr., when somebody with an English accent asked him to keep his voice down. 'I hate all those goddamned Englishmen from Churchill on down,' Kennedy snapped.[2] Nevertheless, the President sought his help. 'He would like to have a long talk with me about the Irish situation which, according to Welles, I was the only one who could help in straightening it out.'[3] After all, Kennedy had played a significant role in bringing about the agreement in which the British had handed over the ports. Roosevelt met Kennedy on 16 January, but nothing came of the meeting. Kennedy broadcast another speech a couple of days later. 'I favour that we give the utmost aid to England. By helping Britain we will be securing for ourselves the most precious commodity we need—time to—time to rearm,' Kennedy said. 'Therefore we ought to arm to the teeth and give as much help as we can. But let us do it on the basis of preserving American ideals and interests.'[4] A few weeks later he testified in the US Senate against the Lend-Lease Bill.

There were 3,600,000 Americans with at least one parent born in Ireland.

About 20 per cent, or 700,000 of them, were bitter and irreconcileable Anglophobes who were 'intense and even militant in their hatred of Great Britain', according to Sir Gerald Campbell of the British embassy in Washington. The remainder were generally anti-British, he added, but their sympathy was 'neither extreme nor easily to be turned into actions'.[5]

There was some vocal Irish-American support for the President's policies. Professor Maurice S. Sheehy, a distinguished priest who was head of the Department of Religious Education at the Catholic University of America, delivered an emotive radio address over CBS, announcing that he was joining 'the fighting force of our nation' as a Navy chaplain. Speaking as one whose 'Irish blood clamours for vengeance against England', he paid tribute to the British for their gallant stand against Nazi tyranny. 'Today I am convinced as a matter of calm reason, with all my in-born prejudices pulling to an opposite conclusion, that England's cause is the cause of freedom, of the United States and of Christianity.'[6]

John McCormack of Boston, the Majority Leader of the House of Representatives, and Senator James F. Byrnes of South Carolina were principal sponsors of the Lend-Lease Bill. It was actually McCormack who first introduced the legislation.

'I never knew I would live to see the day when a good Irishman like John McCormack from Massachusetts would openly admit that Great Britain is our first line of defence,' Congressman Newey Short of Missouri exclaimed. McCormack thanked him for the compliment of characterising him as an Irishman. 'There is', he added, 'one greater compliment that he could give me—by characterising me as "the American of Irish descent from Boston"!' Most Irish-Americans considered themselves Americans and their Irish prefix was indicative only of their ancestry, not their allegiance.[7]

Lend-lease had a relatively easy passage in the House of Representatives, where it passed by 260 votes to 165. Congressmen with Irish names like Buckley, Byrne, Delaney, Fitzgerald, Flanagan, Kelley, Kennedy, McCormack, McGranery, O'Brien, O'Toole and Sullivan—to mention only some of the more than seventy Congressmen with Irish surnames—voted in favour of the Bill by a three-to-one majority. The Senate then passed by bill by 60 votes to 31, with the majority of Irish-American Senators supporting the legislation.

A group of 129 prominent Irish-Americans sent an open letter to de Valera. It was, they noted, a critical time for Ireland, the United States, and the world:

Therefore, we, a group of Irish Americans appeal to you and through you to the Irish people to allow Great Britain to use the Western ports of Ireland. The lifeline between Britain and America has become the lifeline of civilization. This lifeline is threatened. It is the declared policy of the

United States to keep it intact and Ireland has it in her power to take the greatest step toward making this policy effective. We ask you to do this for the sake of that Irish freedom, which our ancestors fought to win. We ask it also as Americans because the freedom of America is threatened, and what we ask of you America is preparing to do herself by opening her ports to the British fleet ...

It may seem strange for Irishmen to say it, but only if England survives can Ireland be free. It took Ireland centuries of bitter struggles to win her liberty, but Ireland will lose all she has won and more, by a Nazi victory ...

For her own security America is sending all the arms she can produce to England, but it depends partly on Ireland whether these arms ever arrive, otherwise all America's effort may be in vain ... We ask Ireland to grant the use of her ports not only for the sake of England, but for Ireland, for America and for the world.[8]

Among those who signed the letter were former chancellor of the University of New York James Byrne, Professor Francis E. McMahon of Notre Dame, Charles C. O'Donnell of DePaul University, William Agar of Columbia University, and the former Police Commissioner of New York City Major General John F. O'Ryan, along with Christopher T. Emmet, a great-grandnephew of the Irish patriot Robert Emmet. All would later figure prominently in an organisation established to offset the influence of AFIN. The British essentially orchestrated the whole thing as part of the activity of the Special Operations Executive (SOE), which was Britain's wartime sabotage and subversion organisation, formed in July 1940. It was established with the amalgamation of departments from Special Intelligence Service, Military Intelligence Research and the propaganda section of the Foreign Office. The Executive's operations in the United States were under the British Security Coordination (BSC) Office in New York, headed by the Canadian William S. Stephenson, who better known by his codename, Intrepid. The BSC's responsibilities were far-ranging, including intelligence, propaganda, recruitment, counter-espionage and security.[9]

Paul O'Dwyer, chairman of AFIN, promptly denounced the appeal. 'The sentiment expressed in the letter does not represent the Irish-American sentiment in this country,' he warned. 'The Irish societies from coast to coast are on record as unalterably opposed to any interference with Ireland's neutral position.'[10] The whole thing was just a stunt, and the *Irish Advocate* exposed a further stunt a couple of months later when it published a letter that William Agar wrote urging certain Irish-Americans to write to their local newspapers calling for Irish bases to be made available in the fight against

Hitler. He wrote to one particular woman with the following explanation:

I am enclosing a copy of a letter which I am sending around quite widely
to Irish Americans or to Catholics who might know other Catholics of
Irish descent asking them if they will see to write to their local newspapers.
I would like you to do even more than that, if you will, and write directly
to one of the following newspapers in Ireland: The *Irish Independent* of
Dublin, the *Cork Examiner*, the *Irish Times*, Dublin, and the *Irish Press* of
Dublin.

I have been informed on good authority that Joseph Walshe, head of
the Department of External Affairs, who acted as de Valera's deputy during
his recent eye troubles, and apparently passed on to de Valera just what he
wanted him to know, must be disabused in the idea that the United States
will back Ireland against England ... I realise that none of these things will
be published but I think that it may do some good in breaking the
outrageous point of view over there.'[11]

While the British orchestrated these activities, the people involved
undoubtedly believed in what they were doing. James Dillon spoke out on
similar lines within Fine Gael in Ireland. He came out forcefully at a party
gathering in January: 'I pray Germany and its rulers may be smashed by the
Anglo-American alliance. I also pray that they day will dawn when a united
Irish people will play their part.'[12] At a front-bench meeting on 4 March 1941,
Dillon sparked a debate by suggesting that Ireland should join the fight for
democracy before the United States got involved, as it was likely to do shortly.
'We have got to be belligerent,' Dillon argued.[13]

Dan Morrissey contended the government would reject the idea, but
Dillon thought some members of the government, especially Seán T. O'Kelly,
Gerald Boland, Seán MacEntee and Erskine Childers, might favour it, though
they might not be prepared to split the Cabinet. John Marcus O'Sullivan
argued that they would first have to persuade de Valera to go along with the
idea, as it would otherwise damage the country. Fine Gael would not get 10
per cent support for going to war, according to T.F. O'Higgins, who said it
might make a difference, however, if they could point out that otherwise
specific industries would have to shut down. As ever, Fine Gael was keeping
an eye on the views of Catholic Church leaders. Paddy McGilligan noted that
nearly all the Catholic bishops supported neutrality. Two of the bishops
appeared to lean towards Germany, while Bishop Patrick Morrisroe of
Achonry was highly critical of the Nazis, but the censors ensured his
comments did not appear in the press. He put religion on the battlefield:

We know what the Poles are suffering and we know how the Dictator has treated the Church in Germany. Can we look with indifference on God dethroned from His rightful place in the universe? Can Catholics view with easy minds the possibility of a victory which would give brute force the power to control Europe and decide the fate of small nations? Thoughtless persons give no heed to these prospects, yet they may become very real. Such an attitude of indifference to the religious outlook of the future is treason to our faith. This mentality is caused by the persuasion that anything that injures a hereditary enemy is good for us. Even if true, political expediency should not weigh in the balance against Christianity.[14]

Wendell Willkie, the man Roosevelt defeated in the 1940 presidential election, visited Dublin on 4 February to talk to de Valera. At the time it was generally assumed he was on a mission for Roosevelt, but he had in fact made the trip on his own initiative, almost as an afterthought, because he was being criticised by Irish-Americans for being too pro-British. On the second-last day of an eighteen-day visit to Britain, he flew to Dublin for a brief meeting with the Taoiseach in order to ask him to allow the Royal Navy to use Irish ports. This would be a waste of time, Churchill warned, but Willkie went anyway and had a 'brutally frank' discussion with de Valera.[15] He told the Taoiseach the Irish were making fools of themselves by thinking they could remain neutral. Hitler would attack wherever it suited him.

'You want Britain to win?' Willkie asked.

De Valera agreed.

'And yet you are making it more difficult for her,' Willkie said. Ireland should join with the British at once and give them the ports. If he gave ports to Britain, de Valera replied, Dublin would be bombed.

Willkie reportedly could not conceal his contempt at this timidity. 'American opinion', he said, 'will not be with you.'[16] American sentiment was responsible for Irish freedom, Willkie argued. Ireland would stand condemned in the United States, if Britain were defeated.

After the short meeting with the Taoiseach, Frank Aiken accompanied Willkie to the airport. Gray had only the briefest of opportunities to talk to Willkie when they were momentarily alone in a toilet. How did the meeting with de Valera go? Gray asked.

'I handed him a couple of jolts,' Willkie whispered.[17]

That night, back in England, Willkie told the British that they had not placed a toe, much less a foot wrong in their propaganda campaign against Ireland.[18] When Maffey returned to London for consultations the following week, he found the Dominions Secretary particularly happy with the way

Britain's Irish policy was developing.

'Against the world background de Valera's creed looks mean and parochial,' Cranborne wrote to Churchill on 17 February. 'To re-assert himself he turned to his one and only technique—the working up of feeling against England. He is not pro-German, but you cannot teach an old dog new tricks.' Thus Cranborne was happy with the policy of turning the economic screw. 'The trade restrictions we have imposed have served and are serving a very useful purpose,' he continued. 'The Fools' Paradise has come to an abrupt end. There is every reason why the policy should not be relaxed.'[19]

Australian Prime Minister Robert Menzies was in London at the time, where he had some candid conversations with prominent British politicians about Ireland. 'All present are plainly anti-R[oman] C[atholic],' he noted in his diary. Ernest Bevin suggested some federal scheme was the only way out of the partition impasse. Menzies agreed: 'Now is the time for a commission from the dominions, chaired by USA, to offer to settle the matter!'[20] He noted, however, that Churchill 'enjoys hatred, and got a good deal of simple pleasure out of saying what he thought of de Valera, who is (inter alia) a murderer and perjurer'. Menzies thought there was trouble ahead. 'We may as well get ready for squalls,' he wrote. 'I endeavoured vainly to get his mind on the question of the ultimate solution of Ireland. War? Federal Union? Should the Dominions offer to intervene?'[21]

With the British exerting economic pressure and both the Roosevelt administration and the putative leader of the Republican opposition clearly in agreement with the British pressure, de Valera sought to bolster the protection that American opinion was providing against British aggression. He informed Gray on 24 February that he was sending Frank Aiken to the United States to explain the Irish situation and to try to purchase arms and ships. It was Gray who first suggested sending an emissary to explain Dublin's predicament, rather than delivering broadcasts to the American people. The Taoiseach asked Tánaiste Seán T. O'Kelly to go, but he declined. Frank Aiken was then chosen. Although de Valera's authorised biographers wrote that Gray was unhappy with the choice of Aiken, this was not so.

The American Minister welcomed Aiken's selection as a way of educating the Irish Cabinet about the reality of American policy by impressing on Aiken that the Irish should not expect American help if they were not prepared to be more helpful to Britain. Aiken had the reputation of being anti-British, so it would be all the easier for Washington to reject his overtures. 'It has seemed impossible', Gray wrote to Roosevelt on 4 February 1941, 'to make any of these people realise what was going on in the USA or that the American people had very little understanding or sympathy with Mr de Valera's academic contentions.'[22] Aiken was a particularly apt choice from the American standpoint because Gray had been bitterly critical of him in his correspondence. As the Minister in charge of censorship, Aiken had not only been playing down the assistance the British had been giving Ireland but was also, as far as the American Minister was concerned, preventing things being published that were critical of the Nazis. Gray had already informed Roosevelt that James Dillon had described Aiken as 'having a mind, halfway between that of a child and an ape'. He added that Aiken had 'the imaginations and vanities of a physically huge man with the mentality of a boy gang leader playing at war with real soldiers'.[23]

Aiken planned to travel through Britain to Portugal for a flight to the United States. 'Aiken is anti-British, but certainly not pro-German,' Maffey telegraphed the Dominions Office. 'He is not impressive and is rather stupid. I hope that every assistance will be given. It will help to dispel idea that our economic measures are punitive.' Maffey added that the idea for the mission 'originated in a suggestion by u.s. Minister here who hinted that useful purpose would be served by dispatch of envoy from here. He tells that in his view the main purpose served would be educational. He does not think any of the Minister's objectives will be achieved.'[24] Maffey added in a further telegraph that preliminary steps should be taken by the British Embassy in Washington to ensure Aiken 'should return in chastened mood'.[25] The British Embassy staff should be prepared, he warned, to counter likely Irish arguments.

While the State Department would try to facilitate Aiken, Secretary of State Hull instructed Gray to tell de Valera that it was going to be very difficult to get any orders filled because American arms production 'is already pre-empted by prior orders for periods varying from a few months to more than a year'. As a result Aiken would be 'unable to get quick delivery without British support'; therefore the Americans suggested he should work through the British Purchasing Commission in the United States.[26]

'Last summer I endeavoured to enlist your good offices to procure arms for the Irish Government direct from America,' Gray telegraphed the State Department. 'I wish formally to recede from this position in view of changed conditions and fuller knowledge. This is not to be taken as an alarmist warning but as common prudence in view of unfortunate possibilities. If, as I suspect, you believe the decision to arm Ireland to be primarily a British responsibility, I agree entirely.' The same day Gray also wrote a covering letter to Under Secretary Welles, explaining that being able to exploit anti-British sentiment was so important to de Valera's 'political existence that he is unwilling to abandon it. He would like Britain to survive, but rather than contribute to her survival with any sacrifice of his political position which he considers synonymous with Ireland's best interests, he would have Ireland go down in general ruins.'[27]

While Britain was unwilling to arm the Irish for fear the weapons might eventually be used against British troops in the event Britain decided to seize Irish bases, the Germans were offering to supply weapons. Hempel was engaged in secret talks with a member of the Irish Army, but de Valera was still unwilling to avail of the Germans' offer for fear of giving the British a pretext of charging that there was some kind of collusion between Dublin and Berlin, especially when they were already tightening the economic screw.[28]

If all imports were cut off, much of the country's industry would grind to a halt and there was a danger of serious food shortages, especially as a foot-and-mouth epidemic was already causing many cattle to be slaughtered. The obvious way out of this predicament was to bolster Ireland's shipping capacity so the country could undertake transportation of her own supplies. Nine Irish ships had been lost since the start of the war, de Valera informed the Dáil. Eight ships had been attacked from the air, and seven of the attacking planes had German markings. Four of the ships had been sunk, with the loss of twenty lives. Three other ships had gone down after striking mines, while two had disappeared due to causes unknown. Preparations were therefore made to establish Irish Shipping Limited, a nationally owned shipping company.[29]

Four more Germans were interned in November after their aircraft came down off the Kerry coast, bringing the German complement at K Lines to ten. But the next dozen airmen to come down were all Allied, with the result that there were more British than German internees. Hempel suggested, on 26 January, that the Irish repatriate an equal number of British and German airmen. Maffey liked the idea, so he went to London for consultations, but the authorities there would not hear of it. They were afraid the Germans would be able to provide valuable information about Ireland. Hence the whole idea was scrapped, though the German Minister would bring it up again several times during the war.

On his return to Dublin, Maffey told Walshe that they were very annoyed in London over the internment of British pilots in Éire, even though the terms of internment were improving. The internees were allowed out on parole each day, provided they remained within the triangular area formed by the three nearby towns and promised not to try to escape while on parole. The Germans tended to settle in better, as they would have little chance of getting back to Germany even if they did escape. The Allied internees, on the other hand, were always restless as they were only 70 miles from Northern Ireland.

Maffey gave rise to the first of three crises in Dublin during the first half of 1941 when, on 19 February, following four or five days in London, he candidly told Joe Walshe that the British could not declare without mental reservations that they would not invade Ireland. If Germany 'had them by the throat', they would take whatever measures were necessary in the circumstances, as they saw Irish neutrality as an advantage to the Germans and a danger to Britain.[30] 'No matter how friendly we might feel towards the British,' Walshe was insisting, 'we had a fundamental duty to maintain the people's defences against all possible aggressors.'[31]

Colonel William J. Donovan, who was one of the growing number of Irish-Americans who strongly supported Roosevelt's policy, visited Ireland on 8 March as part of a fact-finding mission for Navy Secretary Knox on behalf of the President. He came to find out if there was any possibility of de Valera allowing Lough Swilly, County Donegal, to be used for an American base. This was in connection with secret Anglo-American talks being conducted in Washington, where it had been decided that the United States would build a base in Northern Ireland for Americans to use once the United States entered the war. When it came to selecting a site for the base, however, Lough Swilly appeared more suitable than any port in Northern Ireland.

Donovan had been led to expect a long-winded historical lecture on what England had done to Ireland over the centuries, but the Taoiseach made no reference to past grievances. Instead he came to the point at once. 'De Valera seemed worried and disturbed and yet anxious that I understand that in this cause he and his government were friendly to England,' Donovan reported. The Taoiseach said he was opposed to ending partition by force, 'as he felt that only by evolution could they have unity'. If Ireland were properly armed, he said the country could successfully resist a German invasion and 'save England a diversion of troops'. To give Donovan a perspective on his difficulties, de Valera requested Cardinal MacRory to discuss matters with Donovan. As an Irish-American Catholic, de Valera obviously hoped Donovan would realise that the Dublin government had to be careful in open dealings with the British, because of the power and influence of Church figures like the Cardinal. 'There are dangerous elements which may have consequences of a very serious nature to British defence if not dealt with,' Donovan continued. 'It is my opinion that they can be dealt with if we and the British act rapidly.'[32]

Realising that de Valera would not agree to hand over Lough Swilly, Donovan never actually asked for the port. A few weeks later Secretary of State Hull played down its significance. 'Lough Swilly would be scarcely any improvement over Lough Foyle, twenty miles away over the border in Northern Ireland and already being used by the British,' Hull said.[33]

After leaving Dublin, Donovan met Churchill and the Australian Prime Minister at Chequers. Donovan reported:

I expressed my belief to them that the center of trouble lay in the North and that this trouble was emphasised by de Valera's failure to permit the Irish people to be enlightened of what was taking place in the outside world, but I felt throughout that he would wish to be in on Britain's side if he were free. I was asked to express my views as to the remedy. I told them this was not a job of fighting but rather one of statesmanship: that the fear of the Irish that the proper arming would not be permitted by the British as they intended to seize the ports; that if force were used, it would be necessary in order to hold the bases for the occupation of Ireland; that this would be worse than non-use of the bases as it would play into the German hands, and it would mean diversion of British troops needed badly at home. In addition the situation in the United States would be endangered. Menzies agreed with all of this …[34]

The Australian Prime Minister added that controversy would have implications for Australia, where 23 per cent of the population were of Irish origin. Donovan outlined, 'with emphasis', six ways in which relations with Dublin could be improved. First, some kind of liaison should be established between de Valera and Churchill as 'there appeared to be a curtain of asbestos hanging between England and Ireland'. He said that 'de Valera constantly referred to the absence of this liaison'. Secondly, that Churchill 'should look into the veracity of the complaints against the Northern Irish and that irritation whenever possible should be removed'. Thirdly, the opinions and speeches of James Dillon should be publicised as he was urging that Irish people had 'an obligation to civilization and Christianity to join England and declare war'. Fourthly, he thought members of Roosevelt's Cabinet should meet with Frank Aiken in Washington and impress on him 'that the United States was only furnishing with arms those countries of whose intention to help the democracies there was no doubt'. Fifthly, 'it is necessary for us to get rid of the veil of unreality under which Ireland is living if we really intend to influence her,' Donovan argued. He suggested the United States should try to bring Ireland into its sphere of military influence by carrying 'our naval, military and governmental representatives to Foynes from Boston by air'. Sixthly, 'if anything is to be accomplished we must bring Ireland into our sphere and it might be a good plan, not an inconceivable one, to issue an invitation to de Valera to come to America.'[35]

Churchill promised to do what he could to improve relations with Dublin. 'Although he was for a united Ireland,' he said, 'he would not compel it.' As things stood, he would have to back up Northern Ireland, but the situation would change if de Valera aligned with Britain. In that event, he would use all his influence to end partition. If de Valera agreed to come in, he would grant sufficient defence protection before a base was set up, and he would 'establish an all-Ireland defence commission' as a preliminary step towards a final settlement.[36] Donovan concluded his report with the observation that Churchill and Menzies agreed that the latter should go to Ireland the following week to discuss the matter personally with de Valera.

Menzies believed fighter aircraft would provide better protection for the convoys from the skies, but the fighters were confined to a relatively short range. Hence he thought the British needed Irish airbases rather than ports. 'If pressure continues to grow I will not be surprised to find very drastic measures being seriously considered by Cabinet here,' Menzies reported. He hoped to avoid this by going to Ireland to persuade de Valera to facilitate the British. 'My hand would be greatly strengthened if Cabinet in Australia could arm me privately with most emphatic expression of opinion that this problem concerns the security of the whole British Empire and that Australia cannot and will not remain indifferent to the continuance of a policy which materially helps Germany and may vitally injure us.'[37]

Maffey clearly did not think anybody would be able to influence de Valera to change his attitude, and trying to replace him was not a realistic option because there was no one of stature to carry on. 'Col Donovan made no impression whatever on Mr de Valera,' Maffey reported. 'It is difficult to conceive of this country carrying on at all if the reins fall from Mr de Valera's hands.'[38]

Brutal candor was hardly what Donovan was suggesting, but this was the immediate approach adopted by the British. On 14 March Maffey sparked a further crisis by telling de Valera and Joe Walshe that the British could not rule out the possibility of using force against Ireland in an emergency, with the result that they would not supply arms, as they could not be sure that those would not be used against British forces. 'We must realise the time might come—indeed he believed it certainly would come—when Britain or America, or perhaps both, would have to bring pressure to bear upon us.' Maffey explained, according to Walshe. 'It would be better for us to prepare for such an eventuality.'[39]

Chapter 14 ∾

AIKEN MISSION IN
CONTEXT

Ostensibly Frank Aiken went to the United States to purchase arms and ships, but Colonel Dan Bryan, head of Irish Military Intelligence, noted there was another main objective, i.e. 'to mobilise u.s. or Irish-American support' against the threat being posed by the British. The Americans had already told Dublin that Aiken would need British support to obtain arms or ships in the near future, and the British had made it clear they were opposed to providing arms. Thus the main purpose in sending Aiken to the United States was to appeal for American support over the head of the Roosevelt administration.[1]

Aiken arrived in Washington on 18 March 1941 and met with Under Secretary of State Sumner Welles the following day. 'Aiken has the narrowest Irish point of view,' Welles noted. 'No cooperation with England while Ulster question remains unsettled.'[2]

De Valera's St Patrick's Day broadcast about the blockading of Ireland again fit neatly into the so-called Starving Europe Campaign being waged by former president Herbert Hoover. Although this was merely coincidental, it took on added significance in the following days when leaders of the Roman Catholic Church in the United States came out vocally in support of Hoover's efforts. 'I can't understand why any power should prohibit the sending of food to old women and little children,' Cardinal O'Connell of Boston said on 29 March.[3] The cardinal, along with two other archbishops and seventeen bishops, signed a letter in support of Hoover's campaign, which became inextricably linked to anti-war moves on behalf of Church members. One of the archbishops was John T. McNicholas, a native of Kiltimagh, County Mayo, whose whole family had immigrated to the United States when he was just three years old. The other bishops included men with Irish names like Duffy, Gibbons, Gorman, Griffin, Kelley and O'Hara.[4]

John Cudahy, who still fancied himself as a statesman, had harboured further diplomatic ambitions, but he got no further call from the President after the election. In February he had an article published in the *New York Times* arguing that the transfer of Irish bases to Britain was strictly an Irish consideration. 'There is as much relevancy for everything-short-of-war shouters to dictate to the Irish their course of action as for the Irish to determine what we should do if the British sought refuge for their battleships on our shores,' he contended.[5]

Life Magazine commissioned Cudahy to return to Europe as a special correspondent. 'Those of us who early last summer predicted famine conditions were called "sensationalists",' he wrote. 'The situation is really more tragic than the sensationalists predicted.' He decried the food conditions in Spain, Belgium, Poland, and France.[6]

Cudahy reported that Spanish Foreign Minister Ramón Serrano Suner, a brother-in-law of the Spanish Dictator Francisco Franco, said the United States was making an irretrievable error by taking sides in the war. This seemed to bolster the remarks of Cardinal O'Connell, who had not confined himself to the famine situation. 'Some sort of secret manoeuvres are bringing us nearer and nearer war all the time,' the Cardinal warned.[7] Archbishop McNicholas had earlier complained that a 10 per cent minority 'is forcing America subtly and cleverly into the world conflict and the majority of 90 percent favouring peace is standing by silent and helpless'.[8]

'Stop the War Makers,' the *Gaelic American* thundered in a banner headline quoting Fr Edward Lodge Curran, who warned there were only two powers that could keep the United States out of the war: the pulpit and public opinion.[9]

Aiken got a boost on 4 April when the State Legislature in New York passed a resolution calling on the White House to facilitate his mission. Although all the leading officials of the Roosevelt administration—Vice President Henry Wallace, Secretary of State Hull, Under Secretary Welles and Assistant Secretary Dean Acheson—accorded him the courtesy of a hearing, he made little headway. At first Aiken reportedly associated mainly with supporters of Roosevelt and shied away from the White House's many Irish-American critics. The *New York Daily Mirror* noted that he was loud in his praise of both British courage and Roosevelt's policy of making the United States the 'arsenal of democracy'. He initially avoided Irish-American Congressmen, who had opposed lend-lease, and 'hobnobbed' instead with supporters of the Bill, such as John McCormack of Boston and James Patrick McGranery from Philadelphia.[10]

There was, however, a limit to Aiken's willingness to show sympathy for Britain. He was not prepared to give details of the secret Anglo-Irish military talks to State Department officials. On 2 April 1941, when Assistant Secretary of State Dean Acheson asked him if any arrangement had been made with the

British to repel a possible German invasion of Ireland, Aiken said such preparations might provoke an attack. The best way of helping the British, he argued, was to have a strong Ireland, fully prepared to resist a German invasion. If he could get adequate arms from the United States, Ireland could increase five-fold the 50,000 men already under arms. As those men would be defending their homeland, they would be worth a further three to four times their number of foreign troops.

Aiken was dismissive about the importance of the Irish bases. 'The British had greatly exaggerated the utility of Irish ports, since the convoy routes were around the north of Ireland instead of the south of the island as had been the case in the last war,' he explained.[11] The American Joint Chiefs of Staff would make the same point a couple of years later, but the diplomats did not appreciate the validity of that argument in 1941.

The British Foreign Office notified the Roosevelt administration that 'information has been received from most secret sources indicating that Aiken is not only anti-British but also hopes and believes in German victory'.[12] Aiken had reportedly said in Lisbon that 'there is no reason why I should not wish for a German victory'. Churchill told Ambassador Winant in London that the purpose of Aiken's mission was not to obtain arms but to rouse American sentiment in support of Irish neutrality.[13]

Aiken was kept waiting in Washington for almost three weeks before he finally got to meet Roosevelt in the White House on 7 April 1941. Just before the meeting, the British Ambassador personally informed Roosevelt of what London believed was the true purpose of Aiken's mission and what he had reportedly said in Lisbon. The President therefore began his meeting with Aiken by accusing him of saying that Ireland had nothing to fear from a German victory.

Robert Brennan, who was also present, reported that Aiken denied the charge, but then Roosevelt launched into a long oration on Britain's need for Irish help. Aiken had hardly had a chance to speak by the time a presidential aide entered the office, which was the prearranged signal to terminate the meeting. But Aiken had not come 3,000 miles to be brushed aside that easily. Instead of leaving, he tried to persuade the President to accede to the Irish requests, and he was not even put off when a servant entered and arranged a tablecloth and cutlery on the President's desk for lunch.

Roosevelt suggested at one point that some aircraft might be furnished for submarine spotting, but Aiken replied that he was not concerned about submarines; he was worried about the danger of an invasion and he assumed Ireland could anticipate the President's sympathy.

'Yes,' replied Roosevelt. Ireland could expect his sympathy against German aggression.

'Or British aggression?' Aiken asked.

There was no danger of a British attack, Roosevelt snapped.

'If that is so, why cannot they say so?' Aiken replied. 'We have asked them.'

'What you have to fear is German aggression,' Roosevelt insisted.

'Or British aggression,' Aiken added defiantly.

'I have never heard anything so preposterous in all my life,' Roosevelt snarled, jerking the tablecloth from his desk in temper, sending the cutlery flying and effectively ending the argument.[14]

Before leaving, Brennan suggested that much of the Anglo-Irish tension could be eased if the President could get a commitment from the British not to invade Ireland. Roosevelt replied that he would get one in the morning, but he never did.

Finding Aiken 'strongly anti-British' when he met him four days later, Secretary of State Hull sought to impress on him that the United States was fervently opposed to the Nazis. 'All countries alike', Hull said, 'are now in danger from Hitler, whether they are peaceful or otherwise. Hitler has no friends and is not a friend of anybody, and he would sacrifice any of his most loyal followers or sympathisers just as quickly as he would an enemy if it would serve any small purpose for him to do so.'[15]

American officials were upset by Aiken's attitude, which they considered fanatically anti-British. This was compounded, following his departure from Washington, when he began touring the United States and associating with some of Roosevelt's bitterest critics, and addressing Irish-American groups, many of which were actively opposing the President's aid to Britain. During those speeches, from Boston to San Francisco, he stressed that Ireland was 'the most blockaded country in world'.[16]

'When the Axis powers included Ireland in the blockade zone, it became increasingly difficult to obtain supplies,' Aiken told a gathering in Boston on 18 April. 'We protested against being included in the zone, but it was of no avail. They sank some of—our ships and ships which we had chartered.' Nevertheless Ireland was determined to remain neutral. 'Neither economic pressure nor threat of military aggression nor promise of an Irish Utopia after the war are going to shift us.'[17] Even though the British had made no demand for the Irish to hand over bases, Aiken complained there had 'been persistent propaganda by the British newspapers, magazines and platform agents, both at home and over here to compel Ireland to do so. To do that, would in my opinion, plunge peaceful Ireland into this terrible European war.'[18]

'Irish bases for England are out of the question,' the *Philadelphia Public Ledger* quoted him as saying. He said he had found no sentiment among Irish-Americans for giving Britain the use of Irish bases. 'On the contrary,' he said, 'I have been deluged with letters which said in effect, "for God's sake, don't give up our bases or we will lose our independence".[19]

During a press conference at AFIN headquarters in New York on 23 April, Aiken complained that Britain was violating an agreement made at the start of the war to provide Ireland with a certain amount of shipping space. 'England has not been giving us a fair share of the goods from overseas,' he said. 'There is no acute shortage of petrol in England.'[20]

Although Gray admitted there was no proof, he told de Valera he strongly suspected that AFIN 'was composed largely of German sympathisers and very probably financed by German funds'.[21] In fact, it was run by people like Paul O'Dwyer from Mayo, Mike McGlynn from Kerry and Seán Keating from Cork. They had been born and reared in Ireland and were motivated by a desire to help their native land. But in the circumstances it was probably not the best time or place for Aiken to accuse the British of violating their trade agreement with Ireland because the charge fitted neatly into the anti-British picture, as it was made only hours before a large anti-war rally in the city.

That evening, Charles A. Lindbergh addressed his first rally in New York since joining the America First Committee. He quickly became the main attraction of America First, and there was an overflow crowd of some 25,000 people to greet him. 'Most of the people were middle-class, middle-aged Americans of Irish descent,' according to *PM Daily*, the quality New York tabloid, which described the gathering as 'one of the most fascinating fascist meetings ever held in the USA'.[22] In view of the make-up of the crowd and the fact that other speakers at the rally included prominent Irish-Americans like Senator David I. Walsh and John T. Flynn, Aiken's remarks earlier in the day were most untimely as far as the Roosevelt administration was concerned.

Aiken privately encouraged opposition to American aid for Britain. Immediately after the New York rally, he was a guest of honour at a dinner given by Flynn, the head of the New York chapter of the America First Committee and author of *Country Squire in the White House*, the unflattering biography distributed by the German Embassy during the 1940 Presidential election campaign in an effort to defeat Roosevelt. Lindbergh was also present at the dinner and Aiken expressed complete agreement with the famous flyer's views. He added that Britain's plight was really much worse than was commonly believed in the United States, because British shipping losses were greater than was generally reported. Aiken's assessment of Britain's position was correct, but this explains all the more the Roosevelt administration's reaction to him. Britain was on the verge of defeat during the spring of 1941. The Germans were sinking British ships twice as fast as the combined building output of the United States and Britain. At that rate it was obvious the British could not survive for long without further assistance, such as the introduction of American convoys.

In the circumstances, it was important for Irish officials in the United States to tread delicately on issues likely to exacerbate the Anglophobia of Irish-Americans. De Valera was clearly aware of the need to choose his words carefully because in his American addresses he avoided referring to the British by name when mentioning the danger of invasion or blockade. He simply said that Ireland would resist any attacker, or that in the process of blockading each other, the unnamed belligerents were blockading Ireland.

Aiken, on the other hand, made imprudent references to the British with over-simplified and exaggerated charges. He not only accused them of occupying Northern Ireland and blockading the rest of the island, but also touched a nerve by referring to the Black and Tans, and even worded some remarks so vaguely that they could be interpreted as questioning Britain's motives in fighting the Germans. The *Irish World* reported on 12 April, for example, that in justifying Irish neutrality, Aiken had said a quarter of a million Irishmen had fought for democracy in World War 1 and had been rewarded by having Britain foist the Black and Tans on them.

Secretary of State Hull informed the British Ambassador there was an 'Irish uprising in Congress, starting with the average Irish extremist who knows nothing about the fundamentals of the British or the American, or even the Irish situation'.[23] Due to the Congressional hostility, Roosevelt decided on 10 April to shelve for the time being his plans to convoy materials to Britain.[24]

Not wishing to antagonise the Irish-Americans by leaving himself open to the emotive charge of deliberately permitting the British to create another famine in Ireland—as many Irish-Americans believed they had done during the mid-nineteenth century—Roosevelt decided to sell two ships to Ireland. On 25 April the State Department instructed Gray to tell de Valera the United States would negotiate the transfer of the ships with him personally, but not with Aiken. Since Aiken's attitude was one of blind hostility toward the British, on whom Ireland's freedom depended, the Roosevelt administration said it would not do business with him 'unless and until the Irish government is prepared to adopt a more cooperative attitude'. Although the United States did not wish to question Ireland's right to remain neutral, Hull insisted that 'there is a clear distinction between such a policy and a policy which at least potentially provides real encouragement to the German Government'.[25]

Gray delivered the message during a somewhat stormy meeting with the Taoiseach on 28 April 1941. Gray came prepared for a showdown; he read from notes drafted for the occasion. The United States was determined to aid Britain until the Fascists were defeated, with the result that de Valera's Christmas and St Patrick's Day messages to the American people depicting Britain as equally guilty as Germany for Ireland's shortage of supplies was antagonistic to the policy of the United States government. What was more, the Irish charge was untrue because the British had been supplying Ireland. Using statistics quoted by Dillon in the Dáil, Gray said the value of Ireland's exports during the first full year of the war had been greater than before the outbreak of hostilities. Furthermore, he noted that the latest British imports were running at three-quarters of the previous year, despite British shipping losses.

> In framing your statement as you did you intended to put a responsibility on Great Britain for Irish privation equal to that imposed on Germany and to withhold credit for Great Britain for her services in suppling you in the measure that she has. The effect of creating such an impression on your American audience as you must see, whether or not it was so intended, could only be to excite antagonism against that nation which it is our national policy to aid, and thus to weaken popular support in America for that policy. It is obvious that in the present emergency policies antagonistic to the British war effort are antagonistic to American interests.[26]

The Taoiseach flushed angrily and snapped that it was impertinent to question his statement, but Gray replied that he would not expect to go unchallenged because the St Patrick's Day address broadcast to the United States appealed mainly to anti-British elements, who had opposed Roosevelt, his lend-lease programme, and who were 'now engaged in sabotaging American aid for Britain'.

What seemed to annoy de Valera most was that Gray had not objected for more than a month, and then so much of his case appeared 'to be a rehash of the attacks which were made in the Dáil and the Senate'. The Taoiseach explained his real intention had been to let the British know he believed they were considering a blockade of Ireland by making it impossible for the Irish to get ships. And he also hinted that Gray was acting more British than the British and would do well to mind America's interests.

'I, of course, denied that I had any intention of trying to influence the American public against the American Executive,' de Valera noted.[27]

For the remainder of the war, Gray said he 'considered British interests the same as American interests'. While he hoped his blunt approach would have a 'sobering' effect, Gray warned the State Department that henceforth relations with de Valera would likely be much less amicable. 'I no longer hope to get anything from him by generosity and conciliation,' Gray wrote, but he was convinced it had been necessary to impress on the Taoiseach the gravity of the situation. 'If it be essential to survival,' Gray warned, 'his ports will be seized with the approval of the liberal sentiment of the world.'[28] In that event, he said, Dublin would only have the choice of fighting on the side of Britain or Germany.

Disturbed by what amounted to an insensitive lecture from the American Minister, de Valera instructed Robert Brennan to reject the offer of the two ships. Thus even though the ships were needed, de Valera said he could not accept them under the circumstances.

While Gray was annoyed at Aiken playing politics in the United States, he seemed conveniently oblivious to his own behaviour in Ireland. He had been behaving even worse, not only in associating with de Valera's opponents but also in trying to influence members of his Cabinet in a most naïve way. Just the week before his meeting with de Valera, for instance, Gray invited P.J. Ruttledge, James Ryan, Gerald Boland, Seán MacEntee and Joe Walshe to a dinner at his residence to meet Thomas Campbell, an American wheat expert and friend of Roosevelt. Campbell brought up the issue of American convoys. 'In all this Ireland could give great help and he felt sure she would do so in this great fight for freedom and democracy,' Campbell said. 'When he sat down, there was a general look of puzzlement on all the Ministers' faces,' Walshe wrote, 'arising, no doubt mainly from the realization that David Gray had brought them there to put them on the defensive and to influence them through this powerful friend of Roosevelt. I had personally never seen such an example of incorrectness and undiplomatic behaviour, and I think it should never be forgotten for Gray, who once more showed himself as the worst enemy of the policy of neutrality which he knows to be that of the Irish people.'[29]

Aiken, meanwhile, continued to irritate the Roosevelt administration official by speaking out tactlessly in what turned into a coast-to-coast tour of the United States. In Chicago on 27 April he referred to the Twenty-Six Counties as 'the free portion of Ireland', thereby implying that the people of Northern Ireland were being kept in subjugation—despite the fact that the clear majority of the people there consistently favoured the British presence.[30] The following week in San Francisco he not only criticised Britain over partition but also talked about a possible British invasion of the rest of the island. If the British invaded Ireland, he warned, the Irish people would fight. In the same speech he reportedly reiterated the charge that Ireland was the most blockaded country in Europe, but he went a step further and accused the British of introducing the blockade first. The Germans had only followed, he said.

Fine Gael leaders seemed to be echoing Gray when they complained that Aiken was antagonising Washington by his actions. Richard Mulcahy, who did not believe the British were deliberately exerting economic pressure, denounced de Valera's Christmas and St Patrick's Day broadcasts to the United States. He also denounced Aiken for getting leading American isolationists to patronise Ireland. In fact, Mulcahy asked for Aiken to be recalled, but the Taoiseach refused. He actually blamed Gray and said he would demand Gray's recall if it were not for his relationship with Roosevelt.[31]

De Valera seemed to be starting a campaign to get rid of Gray, according to Maffey, who told the Dominions Office that Gray had arrived in Dublin 'with somewhat alarming prejudices, but he very soon and very rapidly lost sympathy with its present leadership and trend. Mr de Valera has always looked to certain sections of American opinion for support in every conflict with Great Britain and he has not been disappointed.' Gray was speaking his mind in Dublin with 'sincerity and complete frankness', Maffey continued. He was not saying what Americans usually said and 'Mr. De Valera does not like it'. The previous week the Taoiseach 'went out of his way' to impress on a couple of people that Gray 'was little less than a disaster' as American Minister. 'I should hate to feel his reputation was damaged by intrigue originating in the de Valera-Aiken group,' Maffey wrote.[32]

Maffey's report was shown to Foreign Secretary Anthony Eden. Although the Americans were annoyed with the de Valera government, this did not mean that the British could do what they liked with Ireland. On 9 May Winant warned Eden that the United States expected to be informed if any actions were contemplated against Ireland.[33] The Dominions Office reassured Eden: 'As you know, we are not contemplating any such violent action at the present time. If we do, we will certainly let Washington know, but I do not anticipate our forcibly taking over the ports.'[34]

Initially the Foreign Office planned to have Ambassador Halifax speak to the State Department in support of Gray, but the Foreign Office feared that in 'taking up the cudgels too vigorously on the latter's behalf, we should give rise to a suspicion that there is some foundation for the Irish complaints against him'. Instead, it was decided that Eden would speak to Ambassador Winant in London.[35]

Mulcahy publicly denounced Aiken's behaviour in a speech given at University College Dublin:

It is appalling that an Irish minister should go to America—on the most important diplomatic mission yet—and use 'soap-box diplomacy' on American platforms. It was lamentable that an Irish Minister should conduct his business in such a way that he would hand himself over to be espoused by the isolationists—people who were fighting against American policy. That is not the way to get supplies for Irish industry.[36]

White House officials bitterly resented Aiken's references to Anglo-Irish disputes, when those references could harden the attitude of Irish-Americans towards the administration's foreign policy. The *New York Daily News* reported, 'An anti-British wave of sentiment is sweeping the country'.[37] Ignoring de Valera's rejection of his offer of the two ships, Roosevelt announced the offer at a White House press conference on 20 May 1941. He also said he had instructed Norman Davis, president of the American Red Cross, to inform Brennan that Washington was also willing to give Ireland $500,000 worth of medical supplies. When asked about arms, however, the President stated that American weapons could only be spared for 'those nations which are actively waging war on behalf of the maintenance of democracy, and there isn't anything left over'.[38]

There was no overt criticism of Aiken or of Irish policy in Roosevelt's remarks at the press conference, so the Irish government accepted the offer. The *West Hematite* and the *West Neris* were chartered to an American shipping company, which in turn chartered them to Irish Shipping, and the vessels were renamed *Irish Pine* and *Irish Oak*, respectively.

Aiken was neither placated nor impressed, however. 'I'd hate like hell to think our nuisance value was only half a million dollars,' he remarked to Lindbergh over dinner on 24 May.[39] He obviously did not care that he was making a nuisance of himself by appealing directly to Irish-Americans, or openly associating with critics of the administration like Lindbergh, who was becoming more radical in his pronouncements. The following week, in Philadelphia, the local Irish-American boss John Kelly organised an America First rally at the Arena auditorium, where Lindbergh trenchantly denounced Roosevelt before a crowd of 16,000 people.

'Is it not time for us to turn to new policies and to a new leadership?' Lindbergh asked.

There was thunderous applause when somebody shouted, 'What are we waiting for?' Others roared, 'Impeach Roosevelt!' Many were giving the Nazi salute amid cries of 'Are we going to let the Jews run this country?'

'Most amazing of all', the Philadelphia *Daily News* reported, 'was the smile that spread over the face of United States Senator David I. Walsh of Massachusetts when the Arena rang and re-echoed with the booing of President Roosevelt. Instead of protesting, instead of resenting the disgraceful exhibition, Senator Walsh sat in his chair beaming on the half-frenzied crowd.'[40]

Even though Gray had protested to de Valera about Aiken's behaviour, the emissary remained in the United States for the best part of another month, during which he continued to associate with people like Lindbergh, Flynn, Walsh and even John Cudahy, with whom he shared a reviewing platform during an Irish-American parade in mid-June.[41]

In his efforts to stop Roosevelt's drift towards war, Cudahy went all the way to Berlin, where he tried to enlist the help of the top Nazis. Cudahy advised German Foreign Minister Joachim von Ribbentrop to warn Roosevelt that Germany would sink any American vessels escorting North Atlantic convoys.[42] Since Roosevelt had been able to increase his aid to Britain by exciting American fears that Hitler's next objective, after the conquest of Europe, would be South America, Nazi Propaganda Minister Josef Goebbels arranged a meeting so that Hitler could personally assure Cudahy that Germany would respect the Monroe Doctrine and keep out of the American hemisphere. According to Walther Hewel, the Foreign Minister's liaison officer with the Führer, Hitler dismissed as 'ludicrous' the suggestion that Germany would wish to become involved in the Americas. 'That is on a level with claiming that America plans to conquer the Moon!' he said. Hewel noted that Cudahy was 'deeply impressed'.[43]

At their meeting on 23 May 1941 Cudahy urged the Führer to warn the United States that Germany would sink any ships attempting to convoy material to Britain. In his publicised account of the interview, Cudahy reported that Hitler harboured no hostility towards either North or South America and that Germany would respect the Monroe Doctrine, but would nevertheless sink any American ships convoying with supplies bound for Britain. His unquestioning report provoked widespread criticism because he seemed to be suggesting that Hitler's veracity could be taken for granted. His behaviour was an example of the pains to which he was prepared to go to prevent further American aid to Britain, for fear such aid would lead to American involvement in the war. By openly associating with Cudahy and others whom the Germans had already found useful, Aiken was behaving in a manner that was certainly not calculated to win friends in the Roosevelt administration.

Despite Cudahy's efforts, some Americans were making assiduous preparations for American convoys to carry material to Britain. In line with the Destroyer-for-Base deal, the Americans set up the first of their bases in January 1941 in Newfoundland, which had not yet joined the Confederation of Canada. On 9 April 1941 the Americans agreed to establish a base on Greenland, guaranteeing its security. This was followed by plans to garrison American troops in Iceland and in Northern Ireland. It was decided that the Americans would build a naval base in Derry and a flying-boat base on Lough Erne, the most westerly lake in the United Kingdom. Contracts were signed on 12 June, and on 20 June 362 American technicians set sail from Halifax, Newfoundland. The first of them arrived in Derry ten days later. Initially, only Sir John Andrews, the Prime Minister of Northern Ireland, was informed about the true nature of the technicians' work.

Chapter 15 ❧

BOMBING AND
CONSCRIPTION CRISES

In the four weeks from 8 April to 6 May 1941, Belfast was blitzed four times by the Luftwaffe. On the night of 16 April more people were killed in Belfast than in any single air raid on any British city outside of London.

The first raid began shortly after midnight on the morning of Tuesday, 8 April 1941. Six German Heinkel 111 bombers, which had detached themselves from a raid on Glasgow, attacked Belfast, killing thirteen people. This was possibly just an exploratory raid to test the city's defences, which consisted of just two balloon barrages, sixteen heavy and six light anti-craft guns; the city had no searchlight. An RAF squadron of Hurricane fighters was stationed at Aldergrove, but they were not equipped for night flying. To make matters worse, there was no underground system in which people could shelter. Indeed, there were no air-raid shelters for three-quarters of the population.

The anti-aircraft fire was ineffective because the German bombers were flying at 7,000 feet (2,133 m), which was above the two balloon barrages but well below the 12,000 feet (3,657 m) at which the anti-aircraft shells were exploding. One of the bombers taunted the gunners by turning on its lights.

Two days later a British Lerwick flying boat put down in Bundoran Bay while running low on fuel. Instead of interning Pilot Officer Denis Briggs, Irish Army officers entertained him while fuel was brought for the aircraft from Northern Ireland. After the plane was refuelled, Briggs returned to his base on Lough Erne.

The following Monday was Easter Monday, and Dublin celebrated the twenty-fifth anniversary of the 1916 Rising. People had reason to be thankful for Irish independence—just how thankful would become apparent within a matter of hours, when some 180 German bombers attacked Belfast the following night. The first wave of aircraft dropped flares. The area was lit up 'brighter than at noon in summertime', one witness recalled.[1] Residential areas of the city were hardest hit. At least 745 people were killed, compared with the highest estimate of 554 people killed in the infamous bombing of Coventry the previous November.

With fires blazing out of control across Belfast, John MacDermott, the Minister for Public Security at Stormont, telephoned Sir Basil Brooke for permission to ask authorities in Dublin to send fire brigades to help fight the conflagrations. 'I gave him the authority as it was obviously a question of expediency,' Brooke noted in his diary.[2] MacDermott asked the operator in Dublin to have 'someone in authority' send fire brigades to Belfast. The message was passed to the Taoiseach, who promptly directed that all but one of Dublin's fire brigades proceed to Belfast without delay. They were joined by fire brigades from Dun Laoghaire, Dundalk and Drogheda, bringing the total to thirteen fire engines in all. De Valera also sent ambulances and instructed Defence Minister Oscar Traynor to ensure roads were cleared for the emergency vehicles heading North.

'Is that not liable to have serious consequences?' Traynor asked.

'I have thought over the matter carefully and have decided that whatever the risk we must send aid,' de Valera replied.[3]

There was an even bigger raid on Belfast on the night of 4 May. Around 200 German bombers dropped over 95,000 tons of bombs, mostly incendiaries, on central, north and east Belfast. Fire brigades from the South helped out again. The loss of life was not as great this time, however, because many people had moved from the city and thousands of others had taken the precaution of sleeping in the open countryside at night rather than risk death in their beds. As a result, the death toll in the largest raid was down significantly—150 people were killed. A fourth raid the following night was much smaller; it was assumed that the planes involved were off-course and hit Belfast by mistake.

A total of 1,100 people died in the four German raids. About 3,200 houses were destroyed and 56,000 others damaged. About 220,000 people abandoned the city to live elsewhere, at least temporarily. They scattered throughout Northern Ireland and beyond. About 10,000 fled south of the border.

De Valera's decision to send fire brigades to Belfast on the two occasions was a courageous gesture because a German invasion of Britain was expected imminently. The Taoiseach made no apologies for his actions. 'They are all our people,' he told a gathering in Castlebar. 'Any help we can give them in the present time we will give to them wholeheartedly, believing that were the circumstances reversed they would also give us their help wholeheartedly.'[4]

Hempel adopted an understanding attitude. He was 'clearly distressed by the news of the severe raid on Belfast and especially of the number of civilian casualties', according to Joe Walshe, who did not protest against the bombing, but did voice regret to Hempel. 'I said to him it was a pity that the German

Government had departed from its policy of leaving the Six Counties alone,' Walshe reported. 'I was afraid that the casualties were very heavy and that the bombing had been indiscriminate.'

Berlin must have felt compelled to act because of Belfast's importance to the British war effort, Hempel explained, but he said he would ask Berlin 'to confine the operations to military objectives as far as it was humanly possible'. He made no objection to sending the fire brigades to Belfast.[5]

'I think we could have protested, but it would have been cruel,' Hempel told an Irish journalist afterwards. 'I know that the Irish Government felt a bit uneasy that the German Government might protest, but it was a deed of sympathy for your people, and we fully understood what you felt.'[6]

'Nobody from Germany protested and I had no intention of doing so,' Hempel said. 'Your own people were in danger.'[7]

Cardinal MacRory asked Hempel to get Berlin to exclude Armagh as a bombing target; the German Minister endorsed the request, as the town had no military significance. Moreover, he added, the Cardinal was a good friend, a strong supporter of Irish neutrality and had good relations with the Italians.

On 12 May Ernest Bevin, the British Minister for Labour and National Service, suggested at a Cabinet meeting that conscription should be implemented in Northern Ireland in conjunction with a Bill being prepared to conscript Allied nationals in Britain. Churchill liked the idea, but Home Secretary Herbert Morrison had reservations.

'When I was leaving, Churchill walked with me and put his arm through mine,' Morrison noted.

'Now you'll do this for me, won't you?' the Prime Minister said.

'I can't give you any promise,' Morrison replied. 'I don't know. It's a big thing and I must think more about it.'[8]

When the British introduced a conscription Bill for Ireland in 1918, the legislation dealt a lethal blow to the Irish Parliamentary Party. De Valera enlisted the help of the Catholic hierarchy to denounce the conscription, which roused such opposition that it was never implemented. In 1941 de Valera again opposed the introduction of conscription in Northern Ireland in order to prevent radical elements exploiting the issue, as Sinn Féin had done in 1918.

Guy Liddell, the head of MI5's counter-intelligence, went to Dublin on 21 May with his brother, Cecil, head of MI5's Irish operation. They met with Colonel Liam Archer of G2 to discuss the recent capture of Gunter Schultz, a German spy who had been dropped in Ireland, in County Wexford, on the night of 12 March. He was to make his way to the Dublin home of a former *Abwehr* agent, Werner Unland, who had fled from England with his British wife just before the outbreak of the war. Since then he had been extracting money from Berlin to fund a fictitious spy network that he had supposedly set up. Schultz was carrying a radio-transmitter and was supposed to report on weather conditions, but he was arrested before he reached Dublin. He was carrying a message for Unland, along with a photograph of him, so Unland was also arrested and interned.

The German spy operations had been 'singularly ill-conceived' and poorly implemented, according to Archer, who warned that there was great anxiety over possible conscription in the North. 'If it were enforced there would undoubtedly be bloodshed,' he warned. He reminded Liddell of the way the Irish had been turning a blind eye to the British aircraft flying over the Donegal Corridor. They were flying so low it was 'impossible for the Éire authorities to say that they could not recognise their markings'. Guy Liddell went on to note:

> Troops from the North constantly wander across the border and instead of being interned are shepherded back. There are moreover a number of other things which the Éire Government are doing to render assistance. If conscription is enforced in the North a large number of Catholics will refuse to register and if any attempt is made to prosecute them they would go on the run and join the IRA. Feeling in the South will be extremely bad and it seems quite likely that the Éire Government will try to enforce stricter neutrality. We told Archer that we would certainly represent his views to higher authority as soon as we got back.[9]

Ernest Bevin produced a Cabinet memorandum arguing that 40,000 men would be conscripted in the next nine months, 'and the number might well be 60,000 or even higher'.[10] But there were reservations. 'The Government must be prepared to deal with large scale resistance,' Home Secretary Morrison warned. 'The prison accommodation in Northern Ireland is limited and nearly full already and as a last resort the Government must be prepared to set up concentration camps for thousands of resisters.'[11] The Cabinet therefore decided to consult authorities in Belfast, but there was mixed opinion there, too.

'The Government of Northern Ireland is emphatically of opinion that conscription should be applied to Northern Ireland,' Sir John Andrews telegraphed.[12] James Beattie, leader of the Northern Ireland Labour Party, warned that 'If Mr Churchill forces conscription on Northern Ireland his action will prove one of the biggest blunders in the history of Ireland or England. It can only lead to strife and tragedy, and I warn Mr Churchill not to be led into this trap by an unrepresentative junta like the Ulster Unionist Council.'[13]

Dulanty feared the whole thing would be implemented in a sectarian way, compelling Catholics to serve while a great many Protestants would be exempt because they were members of the police reserve or employed in war work. Churchill was unmoved. 'The decision on Monday will be in favour of conscription,' Machtig warned Maffey.[14]

Gray advised the State Department that conscription would probably have harmful repercussions for American interests because de Valera would exploit the situation for his own political advantage at the expense of Fine Gael. Gray still wanted the Irish opposition strong enough to be able to split the country, if the British ever delivered an ultimatum for the ports. He therefore sought Washington's help in opposing compulsory military service in Northern Ireland. 'It will seriously hamper the opposition on which we must rely,' he predicted. Consequently, he could 'discover no reason why Ulster conscription should not wait for several months.' James Dillon predicted de Valera would rouse anti-British feelings and would use the crisis to escape from economic and political realities by enlisting the support of the Roman Catholic cardinal for 'a Holy War'.[15]

'All classes of opinion here unite in condemning the move as calamitous,' Gray added. 'It appears to be a repetition of the same fatal blunder made during the last war. The weak and failing Ulster government is probably seeking to sustain itself by provoking a crisis. Unless Great Britain is prepared from a military point of view to seize the whole country it appears to be madness. So little can be gained and so much lost.' There would be few nationalist conscripts, and thousands of Irish volunteers in the British forces would become disaffected. The Irish government, a majority of the Irish people and the Irish Army, all of which had hitherto 'been inclined to be friendly' towards Britain, would become definitely hostile and possibly give active support to Germany. But what was 'most important of all', he continued, was that in the process Fine Gael would be undermined 'and the opportunity for dividing the country on the question of the ports will be lost for the duration' of the war.[16]

Ireland, which had been 'made one by God, was partitioned by a foreign power', Cardinal MacRory complained. 'Conscription would now seek to compel those who will writhe under this grievous wrong to fight on the side of its perpetrators.'[17] There were public demonstrations in Derry, Armagh, Newry, Omagh, Dungannon, Enniskillen and Belfast.

There was considerable disquiet in the British press. 'Our experiences in the last war proved the folly of seeking to conscript unwilling Irishmen,' warned the *News Chronicle*. 'The number of men conscripted would have to be offset by a considerable number of troops required to keep order.'[18] Moderate nationalists in Northern Ireland would join the IRA, the *Daily*

Express predicted. *The Times* questioned whether enough men would be conscripted. Only 200,000 men would be eligible for conscription in Northern Ireland, but this included those who had already volunteered for military service, as well as many of those who were already engaged in vital defence work, which was almost exclusively reserved for Protestant unionists. As a result conscription would fall heavily on Catholic nationalists, which possibly explains why the unionist authorities were so in favour of the idea. The *Daily Telegraph* estimated that only 60,000 men would be eligible.

The controversy received extensive publicity in the United States, especially in the *New York Times*. Paul O'Dwyer of AFIN deplored the whole affair: 'It is a political move by the Churchill government to intimidate the Irish people into giving up their ports and bases, thus inviting destruction by German planes. Following the Axis pattern, provocative incidents undoubtedly will be created to provide an excuse for aggressive action against the Irish.'[19]

'The British Government has no right to occupy six counties of Ireland and then go on to commit the monstrous outrage of conscripting men in an army they allege is fighting for freedom and democracy,' Frank Aiken told the New York State Convention of the American Association for Recognition of the Irish Republic on 25 May.[20]

'Opposition to conscription', the Belfast correspondent of the *New York Times* observed, 'has brought about almost complete unanimity between the various factions in Southern Ireland, as well as nationalists and those with nationalist tendencies in Northern Ireland.'[21] For one of the few times since the Anglo-Irish Treaty was signed in 1921 various segments of the Irish nationalist community were in agreement. Even the *Irish Times* was opposed to the move: 'Writing as Irishmen who always have stood for the British connection, we would appeal to the British government not to persist in its plan. The effect of conscription in the North to our domestic relations would be deplorable; in the long run its effect on British interests would be equally bad.'[22]

The British Cabinet met at Chequers on Saturday, 24 May. Sir John Anderson, who had been Under Secretary for Ireland in Dublin Castle during the Black and Tan days, wished to press ahead. 'Trouble in last war had arisen not so much out of the proposal to apply conscription to Ireland but through our having failed to carry it through,' he argued.[23] It was none of Dublin's business, so he argued that Irish objections should not be considered. Anderson and Churchill seemed to have learned nothing from their Irish mistakes of earlier years.

John J. Hearne, the Irish High Commissioner in Ottawa, called on the Canadian Prime Minister on the same day with a message from de Valera warning that conscription in Northern Ireland could have disastrous consequences. 'I did not wish to make any commitment with respect to what he had said,' Mackenzie King noted in his diary. 'I could read between the lines of his communication and he, doubtless, would read between the lines of mine.' Hearne's warning struck a chord with the Canadian leader. 'Though I did not say so,' he wrote, 'I agree with him and further feel that it would have repercussions in Canada which would be unfortunate.'[24] Conscription already provoked such intense feelings among the French-speaking population that talk of civil war in Canada was not uncommon. As a result the Canadian government dared not draft men for service abroad until very late in the war. Mackenzie King was therefore anxious that trouble over the issue should be avoided in Northern Ireland.

After discussing the issue in Cabinet, Mackenzie King said his colleagues 'were unanimous' that the imposition of conscription in Northern Ireland would have a bad effect in Canada.[25] He warned Malcolm MacDonald, the new British High Commissioner, that it would provoke intense resentment among Irish-American elements in the United States, as well as among the Irish in Canada.[26]

'I am sure', Mackenzie King telegraphed Churchill, 'you will not misunderstand my motive if I suggest that, in case the step has not already been taken, it would be well to seek from the Ambassador at Washington an expression of his views as to the possible effect, especially at this very critical moment, upon Irish-American opinion and the attitude in the United States of a decision by the British government to enforce conscription in any part of Ireland.' He added that he would be grateful if the possible repercussions on Canadian public opinion were also considered. 'We are at the moment engaged in a recruiting campaign for further voluntary enlistments in Canada's armed forces for overseas service,' he explained. 'The more it is possible to avoid the conscription issue becoming a matter of acute controversy, the less difficult, I feel sure, will be the task of maintaining Canadian unity.'[27]

Prime Minister Robert Menzies, who had just returned to Australia, was even more critical of what was happening. Already facing an internal party crisis that would lead to his ouster as Prime Minister within days, he feared that a conscription crisis in Northern Ireland had the potential to cause disaffection among Australians of Irish extraction. Archbishop Daniel Mannix of Melbourne, a native of Charleville, County Cork, had become one of the most influential public figures in Australia by opposing conscription during World War I. While the archbishop was not nearly as critical of Australian involvement in World War II, Menzies still had to be wary about Mannix's attitude if there was trouble over conscription in Northern Ireland.

'The greatest difficulty is the prevailing lunacy,' the Prime Minister complained. 'They are mad in Dublin, madder still in Belfast, and on this question perhaps maddest of all at Downing Street. Blind prejudice, based on historical events, is the most intractable and almost the most dangerous thing in the world.'[28]

Roosevelt asked Ambassador Winant to discuss the problem with Churchill, while Gray tried to persuade de Valera to accept a compromise. The Taoiseach initially accepted Gray's suggestion that the Roman Catholic minority be exempted from conscription in Northern Ireland, but he telephoned Gray a few hours later to say that, on thinking it over, he could not agree to any form of conscription in the Six Counties.

'In the interest of saving a tragic situation,' Gray warned de Valera, 'if he were not willing to accept a compromise without prejudice to his position he was taking a dangerous course and skating on thin ice.'[29]

An escape clause would not be acceptable to the Taoiseach, Cosgrave said, because he was looking for a political issue. Gray was talking with him when de Valera telephoned again, saying that since their previous conversation had been so unsatisfactory, he was sending over a letter explaining his position. 'This', Gray wrote, 'was a very temperate, reasonable document.'[30]

'Why at this critical time this new apple of discord should be thrown in, I cannot understand,' the Taoiseach wrote. 'If Mr Churchill is determined, as he seems to be, to go ahead with the proposal, the prospect is indeed as dark as it can be ... Almost inevitably this will lead to a new conflict between Ireland and Britain in which we shall all be involved. We are truly in a world gone mad.'[31]

'A feeling of better understanding and mutual sympathy, which held in it the promise of an ultimate close relationship, had grown up between our peoples in recent years,' de Valera wrote to Churchill on 25 May. 'The imposition of conscription will inevitably undo all the good that has been done and throw the two peoples back into the old unhappy relations. The conscription of a people of one nation by another revolts human conscience. No fair-minded men anywhere can fail to recognise it as an act of oppression upon a weaker people, and it cannot but do damage to Britain herself.'[32]

Dulanty, who delivered de Valera's message to Churchill, described his meeting with the Prime Minister as 'exceedingly unsatisfactory'. Churchill fulminated as he asked if de Valera desired a public answer. 'If he does,' Churchill said, 'I will give it and it will resound about the world.'[33]

Fine Gael leaders were complaining that conscription would 'present de Valera with a scoop and weaken their position', Maffey warned London in an urgent telegram:

All classes of opinion here united in condemning that move as calamitous. It appears to be a repetition of the same fatal blunder made during the last war. Unless Britain is prepared from a military point of view to seize the whole country it appears to be madness. So little can be gained and so much lost. Eighty thousand Irish volunteers in British Army will be disaffected. A Government, a popular majority and an army inclined to be friendly to Britain rather than the Axis will become definitely hostile possibly giving active aid to Germany and, most important of all, the pro-British Opposition will be helpless and the opportunity of dividing the country on the question of the ports will be lost for the duration.

My view is that we shall not get any move forward here till we have a clash with de Valera. When that comes we shall need the Opposition and we should avoid taking any step that weakens them and strengthens de Valera. Facilities on the West Coast are presumably vastly more important than Ulster's present needs. If we do not put a foot wrong we may have less difficulty than is expected in making a forceful approach to the solution of the ports question.[34]

Andrews telegraphed that the opposition to conscription in Northern Ireland would be stronger than he had previously suggested, while Sir Charles Wickham, the Inspector General of the Royal Ulster Constabulary, emphasised that it would pose a difficult and dangerous task for the police. 'Conscription will give new life to the IRA and will attract into its ranks many who to-day are keeping well clear of it,' he warned the Home Secretary.[35] 'The whole thing was a political ramp, by politicians in N. Ireland,' Wickham told Guy Liddell. 'They wanted to appear as great loyalists, but in actual fact hoped that their suggestion would not be acceptable to the home government. Had it been accepted they intended to conscript the Catholics and leave the Orangemen in the factories,' he said.[36]

'A very gloomy and unpleasant cabinet' met in London.[37] Churchill read the letter from de Valera to the meeting, and the message from Mackenzie King was also read. Cranborne mentioned that a telephone call from Maffey had just been received. Even though de Valera's speech to the Dáil had been moderate, Machtig informed Cranborne that things in Dublin were 'pretty well ablaze'.[38]

By this stage the Cabinet had gone distinctly cold on the idea, but the Prime Minister wished to push ahead. Alexander Cadogan, Permanent Under Secretary at the Foreign Office, noted that Churchill had a habit of jumping to ill-considered decisions and then arguing that backing down would demonstrate weakness, whereas, Cadogan wrote, 'it shows stupidity to jump to them'.[39] In the face of strong opposition from within the Cabinet, Churchill postponed a final decision until the following day. Afterwards, over dinner, he told Winant, 'The Cabinet is inclined to the view it would be more trouble than it was worth to go through with conscription.'[40]

At the time the focus in the Atlantic was on the naval conflict. The British had suffered a dreadful blow when the German battleship *Bismarck* sank the *Hood*, the pride of the Royal Navy, in an engagement that lasted only minutes. Despite a frantic search, the British and Americans lost track of the *Bismarck* in the following days. It was eventually located by an American Catalina flying boat loaned to the RAF and flying out of Lough Erne. The pilot was PO Denis Briggs, who had been released after he landed in Bundoran Bay while running low on fuel on 10 April. The steering mechanism of the *Bismarck* was damaged in an ensuing air attack.

On the morning of 27 May the Cabinet decided to forget about conscription in Northern Ireland. Churchill told his colleagues that *Bismarck* had received four hits from torpedoes and was virtually stationary. He was expecting to receive word soon that the battleship had been destroyed.

In the House of Commons he gave full play to his sense of the dramatic as he announced that the Royal Navy had damaged the *Bismarck* and was moving in for the kill. He then announced that plans for conscription in Northern Ireland were being dropped because 'it would be more trouble than it was worth'.[41] His tactics in switching from the *Bismarck* drama to conscription 'left the House with a sense of *coitus interruptus*', Harold Nicolson noted.[42]

'I saw one of the secretaries in the official gallery make a violent sign with a small folded sheet to Brendan Bracken,' Nicolson continued. Bracken took the paper and passed it to Churchill.

'I crave your indulgence, Mr Speaker,' Churchill said. 'I have just received news that the *Bismarck* has been sunk.'[43] The chamber erupted into wild cheering. This was the most positive war news Britain had received since the conflict began. Amid the ensuing euphoria, the conscription crisis passed into history.

'That such a project was ever seriously considered under present conditions makes one wonder whether the British cabinet has any competent adviser on Irish affairs,' *The Round Table*, the influential journal on British Commonwealth Affairs, concluded.[44]

Two German aircraft bombed Dublin shortly after midnight on 31 May. They had apparently become disorientated while on a bombing mission over either the Mersey or the Bristol area, both of which were bombed that night. The first plane arrived after midnight. A flare was sent up to denote neutral territory, but the plane dropped a bomb off the North Circular Road. It fell on soft waste ground and did little more than excavate a huge crater. About 30 minutes later another plane dropped four bombs in the North Strand area, doing enormous damage and leaving a 1,000-yard swathe of destruction. Twenty houses were demolished, and some fifty-five other houses were rendered virtually uninhabitable. In the process thirty-four people were killed, hundreds of others wounded and over 400 made homeless. The bombs were identified as German and a diplomatic protest was lodged in Berlin. If their aircraft were involved, the Germans said, it was an accident as 'there can be no question of any intentional attack on Éire territory'.[45]

The Taoiseach made no effort to exploit the bombing to rouse any passions. 'I don't think de Valera is going to change his line unless forced to do so,' Gray wrote to Roosevelt on 9 June 1941. 'He has deliberately passed up the chance to excite anti-German feeling over the recent bombing. He has in fact clamped down on expression of anti-German feeling. He either has an understanding with the Germans on which he relies or what is more likely he is blindly taking the thousand to one chance that he can escape involvement.'[46]

Unbeknownst to Gray, the Dublin government made another quiet concession to the British in June, allowing them to station the *Robert Hastie*, a lightly armed tugboat with a crew of eleven, in Killybegs, County Donegal, for air-sea rescue purposes. The crew wore Royal Navy uniforms at sea, but wore civilian clothes in port, where the boat's Lewis gun was covered.

Colonel Thomas McNally, the officer in command of the Curragh, had tried to improve morale within the K Lines internment camp by promoting friendly exchanges between the internees and the Irish Army. He arranged with the Curragh Race Committee to provide free passes for the German and British officers to attend the Irish Derby, which was being run for the first time since any of them had been interned.

Flight Lieutenant Hugh Verity, the senior Allied officer, went out of his way to act contented. Sergeant Sydney Hobbs brought over his English girlfriend and they got married at the Curragh, which was the occasion of a great celebration. Verity ostensibly made arrangements for his wife to come over to live in the Curragh area, but he was secretly planning to escape, with the help of the British escape organisation, MI9, which had established an Escape Club in Éire to help the Allied internees.

The escape was planned for the night of the Irish Derby as there would be many visitors in the area, which would enhance the chances of getting away safely afterwards. The internees managed to overpower two guards at the gate and nine got out. One was arrested within minutes and two others within a matter of hours, but six managed to make it to Northern Ireland with the help of the Escape Club. Hugh Verity, Paul Mayhew and Sidney Hobbs were among those who escaped successfully. All three rejoined their units. Mayhew and

Hobbs were subsequently killed in the war, while Verity survived to rise to the rank of Wing Commander.[47]

| SPIES AND GHOSTS

Looking back after the war, Joe Walshe concluded there were eleven crises in relation to Irish neutrality during wartime: nine of those were in the first twenty-one months of the war, with only two occurring during the remaining four years of the conflict.[1] The real threat to Ireland had passed after the Germans launched their invasion of the Soviet Union. Thereafter the Germans were unlikely to invade Britain or Ireland until they defeated the Russians, and that never happened.

Following Gray's help during the conscription crisis, Joe Walshe approached him again about supporting further Irish efforts to secure American arms, but Gray said he would only help if de Valera would guarantee Ireland would get into the war 'without reservation' and would make Irish facilities available to both Britain and the United States, if Germany invaded. As things stood, Gray wrote to Roosevelt on 9 June, de Valera would probably only put up token opposition because neither Britain nor the United States had been willing to arm Ireland properly.[2]

A group of prominent Irish-American politicians, which included Senators James Mead of New York and Joseph O'Mahoney of Wyoming, along with House Majority Leader John McCormack of Massachusetts and Congressman Eugene Keogh of New York, called on Roosevelt to provide arms for Ireland. At a press conference on 27 June the President said some rifles might be available, but no ammunition, because the Irish had failed to give 'some fairly definite assurance that they will defend themselves against any German attack'.[3]

'Have you received any such assurance, Mr President?' a reporter asked.

'No. No,' Roosevelt replied.[4]

The Irish were indignant. De Valera had given Gray assurances on a number of occasions. Gray said he had personally passed this information to the State Department, but he had given a very different account in his letter to Roosevelt on 9 June.

Robert Brennan protested to the State Department that Aiken had personally emphasised that Ireland would fight during his conversations with Roosevelt, Wallace, Hull, Welles, Acheson and others. As a result the Irish government was at a loss to understand Roosevelt's remarks. Sumner Welles later explained that Roosevelt had not meant to question the Irish willingness to defend themselves but, rather, their ability to do so successfully. Since Dublin had not made proper preparations to receive British help in the event of attack, the President was opposed to arming Ireland because those arms would be likely to fall into enemy hands.

In the letter that apparently prompted Roosevelt's remarks, Gray had again reiterated the importance of being able to use Fine Gael to divide the Irish people, in case the United States should decide to seize Irish facilities. He suggested, for instance, that Roosevelt should publicly offer Ireland some anti-aircraft guns in order 'to combat "German barbarism".' He believed de Valera would refuse such an offer, but it would nonetheless make a favourable impression on the Irish people. 'Keep the people behind us and the Opposition,' Gray advised. 'Then if you have to do anything, you can split the country.'[5]

If the British cut off all supplies and allowed famine conditions to develop in Ireland, Gray suggested in his next letter to Roosevelt on 26 June 1941, the Americans could sail in with food aid. It was certain de Valera would refuse naval and air facilities to protect those ships, but he argued the United States could seize bases as part of saving the Irish people from the obstinate stupidity of their government.

Gray believed James Dillon would command enough influence to ensure Fine Gael would accept the Allied seizure of Irish ports, and that a majority of the Irish people would then agree—even though they would oppose giving up the ports if consulted in advance. Before the war Dillon had told the Dáil he favoured giving 'the United States of America or Great Britain any facilities they wanted'.[6] It became apparent, however, that Gray had greatly exaggerated Dillon's influence.

Dillon acknowledged in the Dáil on 17 July 1941 that the government's neutrality policy had the support of a majority of the Irish people, the majority of the Dáil and even a majority of Fine Gael, but he nevertheless contended the policy was wrong. He said Ireland should provide whatever facilities the United States and Britain desired:

Air and naval bases are required in this country by the United States of America and Great Britain at the present time, to prevent the Nazi attempt to cut the lifeline between the United States and Britain now. At present we act the part of Pontius Pilate in asking, as between the Axis and the Allies, 'What is truth?' and washing our hands and calling the world to witness that this is no affair of ours. I say we know, as between those parties, what the truth is—that, on the side of the Anglo-American alliance is right and justice and on the side of the Axis is evil and injustice.[7]

'I do not think we have got any responsibility for the present war,' de Valera told the Dáil.[8] 'If a neighbour's house was on fire, surely you would allow the firemen to get up on your roof to put out the fire next door?' people were essentially arguing. 'Of course we would,' de Valera said, 'but that is not an analogy to what we are being asked to do. What we have been asked to do is to set our own house on fire in company with the other house. We have been asked to throw ourselves into the flames—that is what it amounts to.'[9]

Members of Fine Gael were surprised that Dillon spoke out. Richard Mulcahy immediately disassociated himself from the views expressed. 'We are united in the view that neutrality is the best policy for the country at the moment,' Cosgrave told the Dáil. 'We are united in the view that, if aggression comes, a united country will meet it.'[10] In contrast with Dillon's speech, Cosgrave's remarks were well received. As a result, Gray found it necessary to reconsider his advice about the best way of securing the ports. When he outlined a plan for Roosevelt the following month, he did not mention using either Dillon or Fine Gael.

Gray's next suggestion to the President was for the British to supply Ireland with 'mediocre elderly rifles, a balloon barrage and such other out of date conspicuous equipment as could be spared by the Home Guard as they get equipped with modern stuff'. The gift would be publicised by having someone object to it in Parliament, and the government would respond by suggesting that it had handed over the equipment in accordance with a secret agreement reached with de Valera. By broadcasting this on radio a few times, either the IRA or the Germans might be provoked into taking action, which would bring Ireland into the war. 'You have to fight fire with fire,' Gray explained to Roosevelt, 'and glory be to God you understand this situation.'[11]

Gray discussed the latest two schemes with Senator Ross McGillycuddy, who was better known as The McGillycuddy of the Reeks. He had retired from the British Army as a lieutenant colonel in 1923, and went on to become an independent member of the Irish Senate. In order to ensure his views were not misunderstood, McGillycuddy sent Gray a memorandum outlining the main points of their conversation. 'The occupation of the ports and the development of airfields would turn a lamentable weakness into a source of strength, from which an offensive could be developed,' he wrote. But he dismissed the famine idea or the use of calculated broadcasts: 'A *fait accompli* was the one and only way of dealing with the Éire people and the Éire Government. This must be staged by the hereditary friend and not the hereditary foe.' In order words, the Americans should seize the bases. The political situation was such in the United States, however, that President Roosevelt could not yet risk direct involvement in the war.

'I am fully aware of the difficulties which confront the President,' the senator continued, 'but I offered the suggestion that the press in America should begin to draw attention to the unfortunate attitude of Éire.' He suggested launching a propaganda campaign in the American press to justify an American invasion of Ireland, while the Germans were engaged on the Russian front. 'An occupation of the ports could be effected with a minimum of difficulty during the time that the enemy is engaged elsewhere,' he wrote. It would be difficult to estimate the extent of Irish resistance, but 'in any eventuality the want of equipment and ammunition in Éire would make it a matter of little difficulty for an American force to hold such areas as they required for the prosecution of the war.'[12]

The day after Dillon stunned the Dáil with his call for bases for the Americans, the Germans dropped another spy, Joseph Lenihan, whose family would play a major role in Irish politics in succeeding years.[13] He was dropped by parachute near Summerhill, County Meath, on Friday, 18 July 1941. His mission was to radio weather information to Germany. He arrived with money, the necessary radio equipment, a cipher, secret ink and an address in Spain for communication purposes. He was to establish himself in Sligo and if everything went satisfactorily, some trained meteorologists would follow. He made his way to Dublin, where he telephoned his younger brother, Gerard, a civil servant in the Department of Industry and Commerce. Joe had been something of the black sheep of the family. Educated at St Flannan's College, Ennis, he won a county council scholarship to university, studied medicine for a short time, but quit to enter the Customs Service, from which he was dismissed in 1931. After a brief stint in the United States he returned to Ireland. In 1933 he was sentenced to fourteen days in jail for causing a public disturbance. He lived for some months with his brother Patrick, but they fell out over money. 'I was fed up with his general conduct,' Patrick recalled. Joe was subsequently convicted of forgery and sentenced to nine months in jail.[14]

On emerging from prison, he emigrated to England and moved on to Jersey in May 1940, shortly before the Germans seized the island. He offered his services to the Germans as a spy. He first left for Ireland on the night of 29 January 1941, but the heating apparatus broke down on the aircraft and he and four of the crew got frostbite. He lost three toes and spent three months in hospital.

The day after he was dropped successfully, he visited his brother Patrick in Athlone and then went by bicycle to visit a sister in Geashill, County Offaly. On the Monday he returned to Dublin and deposited a large sum of sterling in Ulster Bank, which promptly notified the authorities. Next day he proceeded to Dundalk, with the Special Branch just one step behind him. He crossed the border into Northern Ireland at Goraghwood on 23 July, and promptly offered his services to the British as a double agent. He demonstrated a phenomenal memory by giving 'more fresh and accurate information about the Abwehr in the Netherlands and Paris than any other single agent', according to Cecil Liddell.[15]

Later, when the British asked if Lenihan could return home on a holiday, Freddy Boland said there would be no objection, but he would be watched because of his 'habits and character'.[16] De Valera balked, however, at allowing Lenihan to set up a transmitter to send messages to Germany from Sligo.

Meanwhile, every chance Gray got he stressed resentment at Aiken's interference in American politics. Conveniently oblivious to his own interference in Irish politics, he complained that by associating with Irish-American groups opposed to Roosevelt's foreign policy, Aiken had given what was tantamount to the Irish government's approval to White House critics; therefore the Roosevelt administration would not be willing to make any sacrifices for Ireland. 'It is a great shock to them', Gray wrote, 'that we have a grievance and that we do not take kindly to their playing their politics in our yard.' It was not that Washington was questioning Ireland's right to remain neutral, he explained, but that 'majority opinion in American would not sanction our making sacrifices for people who will do nothing for us.'[17]

A clash between de Valera and Gray was probably inevitable. The American Minister thought Irish independence was little more than sublime nonsense, because Ireland was too small to be really independent. The country relied on Britain for both economic stability and political freedom, seeing that without the British to stave off the Nazis, Hitler would overrun Ireland. As a result Gray thought the Irish should recognise their dependence on the British and support them.

'If Britain completely shuts off coal and gasoline, this place would be a disorganised and howling wilderness in three months,' Gray wrote to Roosevelt on 11 August. 'There would be no transport except by water and horse and Dublin is a city of 600,000 people with distribution problems which you can picture for yourself. It probably would be a wise thing to do to explode this nationalistic dream of 'self-sufficiency' and this glorification of non-cooperation and opposition to federation with their neighbours. It's all pathetic.'[18] Whether pathetic or not, the Irish government's opposition to a federation with Britain was certainly understandable in 1941. It was barely twenty years since de Valera and his colleagues had been engaged in a life-and-death struggle to withdraw from a union with Britain.

Gray realised he was making himself very unpopular in Dublin, but he was not worried because he was confident Roosevelt approved of his actions. 'Praise the Lord,' Roosevelt wrote to him on 2 August 1941, 'you have got the number of certain persons in the emerald Isle!'[19] This was in response to a letter in which Gray had been particularly critical of de Valera and Aiken. Three weeks later the President echoed Gray's sentiments about the economic situation in Ireland. 'It is a rather dreadful thing to say,' Roosevelt wrote, 'but I must admit that if factories close in Ireland and there is a great deal more suffering there, there will be less general sympathy in the United States than if it happened six months ago. People are, frankly, getting pretty fed up with my old friend Dev.'[20]

Gray deluded himself into thinking American pressure was helping to promote better Anglo-Irish relations, which were much better than he realised. In September 1941 he noted British policy was 'to conciliate the Irish army and to obtain its goodwill by procuring from time to time equipment, which it greatly needs, but of a nature which in the event of an Anglo-Irish crisis would not seriously threaten Britain.'[21]

'I have been slow to realise that a conviction of German victory is very general in government circles and among the professional classes,' Gray wrote to Roosevelt on 21 October 1941. But he had actually been so indiscreet that the Irish preferred to confide in the British.

De Valera told Maffey on 11 October that 'he had never held any strong views about any particular form of Government, but he realised, from what he had himself seen, that dictatorship, even when it starts with all the chances in its favour as in Italy and in Germany, leads inevitably to disaster. With all its faults, democracy seemed to him to be the best form of Government. It might go through dark or disappointing chapters, as in America, where the rapid growth of wealth enabled the forms of democracy to be abused, but it had in it inherent qualities which kept the ship of state on or near its course.' In the short term, however, he thought deadlock was the most likely outcome of the war because it would be difficult to drive Hitler from occupied territory on the Continent. His hold would be uneasy, however, so he believed the British should stay heavily armed and wait for German control to disintegrate. 'He had no doubt whatever that a Hitler domination of Europe would have no permanence as it was essentially evil,' Maffey reported.[22]

A few days later Cardinal MacRory called for a negotiated peace during an address in Maynooth. 'I asked him how a negotiated peace with Hitler was to be guaranteed,' Gray reported.[23]

'Whatever Hitler may be,' the cardinal replied, 'you ought to try to make peace with him now, because you may have to later on.'[24]

'Besides believing that Hitler cannot be beaten, they are only just beginning to believe that we mean business,' Gray continued in his letter to

Roosevelt. 'They had absolute assurances from Boston that we would never do any shooting.'[25]

By the autumn of 1941 American naval vessels and planes were reporting any sighting of German u-boats to the British. On 11 September the American destroyer *Greer* was tracking a u-boat, which eventually fired on the *Greer*. Five days later the US Navy formally began convoying British and American ships as far as Iceland, from where the British took over the convoying duties. By early October Churchill was talking in terms of 'when' rather than 'if' the United States entered the war. 'When they come in', he said to W.P. Crozier, editor of the *Manchester Guardian*. It was 'as though he regarded it as certain', Crozier noted.[26]

Two weeks later, on 17 October, the US destroyer *Kearney* was torpedoed while on convoying duty off Iceland. Eleven sailors were killed. Before the end of the month another American destroyer, *Reuben James*, was sunk in similar circumstances, with the loss of 115 lives. The United States was effectively involved in an undeclared war with Germany. In between those sinkings, Gray again suggested Japan would be the catalyst for bringing America into the war openly. 'Before you get this,' he wrote to Roosevelt on 21 October, 'Japan may touch things off. You have handled that situation miraculously as every other as far as I can see.'[27] He seemed to be congratulating Roosevelt for bringing the United States to the point where the Japanese were going to attack. This was still more than six weeks before the assault on Pearl Harbour.

John D. Kearney, who took over as Canadian High Commissioner in August 1941 following the death of John Hall Kelly, provided a fresh perspective on Irish neutrality. He adopted a more understanding approach than either Gray or Maffey. Kearney, whose parents were both Irish, had visited Ireland a number of times. It looked briefly like Canadian Prime Minister Mackenzie King might visit Ireland that August. He was in Britain, and Kearney told de Valera at their first meeting that Mackenzie King was considering a quick visit. 'After my chat with Mr de Valera I feel that his desire to see you is so genuine that he would be, to say the least, disappointed if you did not come,' Kearney wrote to Mackenzie King.[28]

'I have all along cherished the hope that it might be possible for me to visit Éire and, in particular, to have a friendly talk with the Prime Minister,' Mackenzie King replied.[29] But he changed his mind, apparently as a result of Churchill's hostility to Ireland. When Mackenzie King informed Churchill that he hoped to meet de Valera at Foynes on his way home, Churchill fumed that 'the Irish had put themselves into an incredible position which would not be forgiven for generations'.[30] As a result the Canadian leader seized on an excuse to fly back directly to Canada.

Ironically, Kearney found that the Irish authorities distrusted the

Americans more than the British. The State Department did not understand Ireland's problems, de Valera complained, but the real Irish ire was reserved for Gray.[31] He had been telling journalists that there was 'every reason' to believe the Germans were getting valuable espionage from Ireland, but he admitted to Walshe he had 'no means of knowing whether the Axis spy system is effective'.

'What a pretty story!' Walshe exclaimed in exasperation, 'all founded on acknowledged ignorance.'[32]

Walshe became so disillusioned with the American Minister that he actually wrote to him suggesting he reconsider his position in Ireland: 'The whole character of your notes forces the conviction upon me that your prejudices make it impossible for you to be the instrument through which a proper balance of goodwill can be established between our two Governments.'

Generally, Walshe tried to be agreeable with diplomats. He was at the heart of the secret cooperation with the British, but they were suspicious of him. They informed William J. Donovan on a visit to London that they had learned from 'an entirely reliable source, which must on no account be compromised' that Joe Walshe had advised the Italian Minister in April 1941 'that a decisive attack by the Axis on the British islands should not be too long delayed and not later than the beginning of next Spring, because the main concern in governing circles in Éire lay in the possibility, which was considered to be more and more certain, that America would intervene in the war, which would render the position of Éire even more critical than at present. This conversation indicates, even under the most favourable interpretation, a tendency on the part of Mr. Walshe towards re-insurance with the Axis.' The 'entirely reliable' source in this instance was probably an intercepted diplomatic report. Donovan was told, 'The Italian Minister is extremely unreliable, but as it confirms the impression gained from previous reports you may care to show this message to the President for his strictly personal information as showing the unsatisfactory attitude of some at any rate of the Irish authorities in regard to this country.'[33]

If Gray were recalled, Walshe told Kearney that another representative would probably be able to secure Irish bases for the Americans, provided the United States entered the war and could guarantee an end to partition. Maffey and Gray warned that Walshe was probably not reflecting de Valera's attitude on the ports. They were convinced the Taoiseach would not give up the ports. Kearney therefore asked the Taoiseach on 20 November.[34] 'I ascertained that even a promise of unity of Ireland would not alter his attitude,' Kearney reported.[35]

Some of Gray's advice to Roosevelt around this time came from bizarre sources, such as supposed ghosts. His dabbling in spiritualism reveals more about his personality and his relationship with Roosevelt than anything else, but this is important because understanding Gray, with all his eccentricities, fears and prejudices, is vital to understanding the deterioration of relations between the United States and Ireland, as well as the whole series of distortions that eventually developed around Irish policy during World War II.

Gray had become involved in spiritualism as a student at Harvard University before the turn of the century. In the 1930s he met Geraldine Cummins while visiting the west Cork home of writer Edith Somerville. Cummins wrote *The Scripts of Cleophas,* on the early Christian period, under supposed spiritual guidance. She would go into a hypnotic-like state and begin writing automatically, up to 1,500 words an hour. Her writings on the period totalled over a million words. Scholars were intrigued by the extraordinary knowledge of first-century terminology found in the writings, and a number of experts were convinced her work was inspired by an unnatural phenomenon.

Cummins became a particularly famous writing medium. On meeting her again in June 1941, Gray persuaded her to hold a séance. She obliged and began writing out messages, one of which supposedly came from Gray's late father. Gray was greatly impressed.[36] 'It was instantly evident to me', Gray later wrote, 'that there could be no question either as to the genuineness of the phenomena or of your complete good faith.' Her automatic writing at 'a speed beyond normal powers of composition, seemed to me to constitute a supernormal phenomenon of first importance'.[37] He was satisfied with her *bona fides.*

Born in 1890, Cummins was a daughter of W. Ashley Cummins, a professor of medicine at University College, Cork. Her brother and sister were both respected doctors. Geraldine accepted an invitation to hold further séances at the American Minister's official residence in Phoenix Park, Dublin, on 7 November 1941 and again the following day. Only she and Gray were present at each session, during which she transmitted messages purportedly coming from President Roosevelt's late mother, who had died earlier that year, from former President Theodore Roosevelt and from former British Prime Minister Arthur J. Balfour, as well as members of Gray's own family. As the different ghosts were supposedly sending their messages, the handwriting would change. Gray explained to Roosevelt that the communication from Theodore Roosevelt 'is quite suggestive of his writing and so is my father's'.[38]

'My boy will have to make an important decision in the next two months,' Roosevelt's late mother supposedly warned. 'I want him to throw down the gauntlet.'[39] This was a month to the day before the Japanese attacked Pearl Harbour.

It was probably no surprise to Gray that Balfour's ghost should turn up at a séance, as the building had been his official residence while serving as Chief Secretary of Ireland from 1886 to 1892. Shortly after his arrival in Dublin, Gray had mentioned to Roosevelt that he found the house endearing because of 'the memories and the ghosts that are here'. He added, 'Arthur Balfour was here eight years nearly.'[40] Balfour had been a believer in spiritualism and had actually taken part in sittings with Cummins.

The Balfour message, which concentrated on Irish politics, began with an apparent reference to James Dillon, who had lunched with Gray earlier in the day:

He's a clever fellow. You can trust him but there are others you must not trust. I saw a man here, dark with a strong face in the last six months. Some name like Walsh. Is there a Joe Walsh? He, from what I can see is hand and glove with the German Minister. He and his colleague Dr Murphy. If you meet those two again lay false tracks for them. Never let them know the slightest inkling of your real intentions. The organisation of the Fifth Columnists in this country is now complete. Walsh is a leading quisling. There are two divisions in this column—the IRA who are not in the inner council but who stand aside waiting to be used by Hitler when the time comes to strike. Second division, the intellectuals co-ordinated with the people of German nationality scattered through the country, some holding key positions. Of this group the authorities know practically nothing. But from among them come the men who will make a Hitler's quisling cabinet if there is ever one.[41]

Gray believed the message referred to Joe Walshe of the Department of External Affairs and Seán Murphy, the Irish Minister in Vichy, France.[42] 'I am no prophet,' Balfour purportedly warned. 'I merely can see into the minds of certain leaders.' He did not know whether the Germans would invade. They had supposedly planned to do so the previous September, but this was postponed because German forces had failed to conquer the Soviet Union in time. Now, the message added, a plan 'hatched at Berchtesgaden' envisaged invading Ireland the following spring. Balfour supposedly continued:

I presume you cannot change the attitude of the USA government. If only your people would occupy the island before the blow falls—ruin, death and disaster of a very horrible kind would be averted. I don't say it will fall, for circumstances may yet save this poor ignorant people. But H.Q. have planned the coup for next spring. I believe de Valera will go down on his knees and thank God if the USA takes forcible possession of this country.

There will be no resistance only welcome, and it will be a sound strategic stroke in the war. Are the Allies always going to be late in moving? That is what you have got to ask Washington.[43]

At a further séance with Cummins on 2 December 1941, the late President Theodore Roosevelt supposedly advised that Hitler was considering an offensive in the west, so Gray should 'build up confidence with the Éire authorities'. If any approach were to be made to the Dublin government, the message suggested Gray should be careful about reporting it to Washington because there was a leak in the government and the Germans might easily discover what was happening.

'De Valera is likely to keep his own counsel,' the message continued. 'He is in his heart anxious to keep in with the Allies so be friendly to his cabinet but keep the essential moves concentrated on de Valera.'[44] This communication contained one prediction, however, that was very wide of the mark. The former President supposedly belittled the danger of a Japanese attack. 'I want to tell you,' he purportedly said, 'that I think Franklin will hold the Japs for a while; at any rate from our country's point of view. I see no immediate Armageddon for young America, possibly not at all.'[45]

This was the Tuesday before the Japanese attacked Pearl Harbour. But Gray's reaction was to conclude that the ghosts were not very well informed. 'Four days after this communication,' Gray wrote to Roosevelt, 'the Japs attacked Pearl Harbour. They had T.R. fooled. I suspect that if these communications come through pretty much as given, our friends on the other side don't know very much more than they did on this side.'[46]

Chapter 17 ∾

IRISH-AMERICANS
AGAINST THE WAR

A s Roosevelt was moving towards war in the autumn of 1941, his isolationist opponents were becoming shriller in their opposition. 'The three most important groups who have been pressing this country toward war are the British, the Jewish and the Roosevelt administration,' Charles Lindbergh complained in Des Moines, Iowa, on 11 September.

America First had tried to keep Father Coughlin and the Christian Front at arm's length because many were embarrassed by the anti-Semitic approach of those elements decrying aid to communist Russia. Coughlin and the Christian Front essentially depicted communists and Jewish people as much the same—enemies of Christianity. Francis P. Moran launched an anti-Semitic campaign in Boston during the summer with the showing of a Nazi propaganda film, *Sieg im Westen* (Victory in the West). His Christian Front activities at the Hibernian Hall in the Roxbury district attracted gatherings of up to 500 people. Moran used the '*Heil, Hitler*' salute and highlighted threats supposedly posed by Communism and Zionism. He lauded the activities of America First, which attracted, but did not always welcome, support from other anti-Semitic Irish-Americans, such as Henry Ford, the car man-ufacturer.

Organisations such as the Committee to Defend America by Aiding the Allies and Fight for Freedom, Incorporated, which were inspired, funded and controlled, to a degree, by British Security Coordination (BSC), sought to exploit the religious implications of the war. The prime aim of William A. White's Committee to Defend America by Aiding the Allies was to facilitate aid to Britain, while Fight for Freedom, Inc., carried the idea a step further in calling for an American declaration of war on Germany. Those organisations ensured that publicity was accorded to the views of people who were taking issue with isolationists. Just as Irish-American isolationists enlisted the support of the Catholic clergy at the outset, interventionists were now using people like Bishop James P. Hurley of St Augustine, Florida, Monsignor John

A. Ryan of the Catholic University of America and other prominent Catholics.

Bishop Hurley admitted to thinking at one time that communists were the main enemy of Christianity. 'Until a few years ago that was true,' he said, 'but today the first enemy of our humanity, killer of our priests, despoiler of our temples, the foe of all we love both as Americans and as Catholics—is the Nazi.'[1] Fight for Freedom, Inc., arranged for the bishop to deliver a radio address on 6 July. 'With the example of all the countries of Europe before us, let us pray for peace but prepare for war,' the bishop said. 'We shall sooner or later be forced into the war by the Nazi lust for world domination.' He wound up denouncing the 'small but noisy group of Catholics' which obviously included Coughlin and his supporters. 'Years ago they established the crank school of economics, latterly they have founded the tirade school of journalism; and now they are engaged in popularizing the ostrich school of strategy.'[2]

'Hitlerism is the number one menace to religion, culture and American liberty today,' Professor Francis E. McMahon of the University of Notre Dame declared over WBYN of Brooklyn, New York. 'Aiding Russia to fight and weaken this menace is not only ethically permissible, but a matter of great practical urgency. Americans should not be misled by the apostles of obstruction who would paralyze the national will to stop Hitler by a perverted application of ethical principles to justify their own prejudices and emotions.'[3]

His broadcasts were obviously designed to counter the influence of Coughlin and AFIN. BSC was behind the appeal of the 129 Irish-Americans who asked de Valera, in March 1941, to allow Britain to use Irish bases. This eventually led to the establishment of an interventionist American Irish organisation. Most of those involved may not have known the BSC essentially controlled the organisation. 'Contact with it was maintained by a good cut out, a man who followed directives from the BSC office and kept the BSC posted on every move,' according to the BSC's official history.[4]

McMahon, chairman of the Notre Dame chapter of Fight for Freedom, became chairman of the Midwest branch of a new national organisation, which established other branches in New York, Washington and Boston during September and October 1941. James Byrne of New York University, who led the list of 129 Irish-Americans in March, was appointed honorary chairman, while the writer Christopher T. Emmet (a great-grandnephew of the early-nineteenth-century Irish patriot Robert Emmet) was national treasurer, and James Tumulty of Jersey City was national secretary. The new organisation was so hastily established that it called itself by different names—Committee for American Irish Defense (CAID), American Irish Defense Committee and American Irish Defense Association (AIDA).

Regardless of which name was used, each listed the same national officers. Rossa F. Downing—who had approached Cardinal Dougherty and various Irish-American bishops the previous year on behalf of the Committee to Defend America by Aiding the Allies in the hope of getting them to use their influence to persuade de Valera to give bases to the British—became chairman of the CAID branch in Washington, D.C., and was soon appointed national chairman in place of Byrne, who became honorary chairman. Downing's previous involvement in ethnic politics afforded him a stronger platform from which to appeal to Irish-Americans. His involvement went back to the Friends of Irish Freedom (FOIF) during the Irish war of independence. After de Valera broke with FOIF in 1920, Downing played a leading role in de Valera's new American Association for Recognition of the Irish Republic.

Others prominently linked with the new organisation included William Y. Elliott of Harvard University and Henry Grattan Doyle of George Washington University; industrialists Bernard J. and Paul J. Rothwell of Boston; and the former Police Commissioner in New York City, Major General John F. O'Ryan, who was also a veteran of World War I. The services of Edward J. Flynn, National Chairman of the Democratic Party, were also enlisted.

The *Washington Post* reported the formation of AIDA on 15 September. Helen Peck, the local secretary, said the organisation had been set up 'to offset the discredit that has fallen on some Irish societies in the United States that have swallowed Hitler propaganda'.[5] The new organisation proclaimed twin aims of refuting the isolationist stance taken by ethnic Irish newspapers and seeking to galvanise American influence to persuade the Dublin government to allow Britain to use Irish bases, or at least obtain such bases for American forces to protect shipping once the United States began convoying material all the way to Britain. 'Our Association was formed chiefly because the great majority of Irish-American opinion was not finding its expression, the small minority with the loud voice was trying to pass itself off as a majority,' a Washington spokesman for the organisation explained.[6]

CAID published a pamphlet, *No Blarney from Hitler*. 'One of Hitler's most audacious lies and the most fantastic is that he is fighting for Western Christian civilization,' the pamphlet proclaimed. It went on to note that Pope Pius XII depicted Nazi Germany as the real menace to the Catholic Church. Bishop Hurley of St Augustine asked Irish-Americans to 'urge our President and our country to take every step necessary to defeat Nazi schemes for world conquest'.[7]

AFIN wished to compete with this propaganda, but could not match the resources of the new group, whether calling itself CAID or AIDA. They suspected it was financed by the British, in collusion with the Roosevelt administration. 'I have reserved effective control of the organization,' Sandy

Griffith of the BSC reported. 'The proposed activities have been discussed informally with people in the Administration, with Secretaries Knox and Welles, and with Colonel Donovan.' He noted that the BSC was subsidising AIDA 'at the rate of $1,500.00 per month'.[8]

It was ironic that while Gray was annoyed at the Irish government for involving itself with the likes of AFIN, members of AFIN were bitterly critical of the fact that they were getting no help from the Irish government or the Irish Legation in the United States. 'One of our difficulties is lack of funds,' Mike McGlynn told an executive council meeting of AFIN in New York on 18 September 1941. 'We haven't the money to go through and combat this propaganda.' Seán Keating, a Cork-born member of the executive, was bitterly critical of Brennan and his staff.[9] 'They have failed to cooperate with us in any way,' Keating complained. 'I refuse to be a fall guy for either the Minister at Washington or the Consular Service here. We have been entirely too silent. The government needs strong men. We are trying to do a job for Ireland but can't get an ounce of cooperation.'[10]

Usually people in Ireland looked to America for funds, but AFIN was looking to Ireland. The Irish Legation had been keeping its diplomatic distance. In June the secretary of the Legation, Denis Devlin, complained to McGlynn regarding the announcement that 'Mr Brennan had informed the National Headquarters of the American Friends of Irish Neutrality' about negotiations to purchase the two American ships. 'Should the impression spread that we were delegating our functions to organisations whose members are American citizens, operating under American municipal law, it would place us in an ambiguous position and would certainly be viewed with disfavour by the authorities,' Devlin warned. 'Further there is the danger that we might be ourselves obliged to repudiate certain statements which you may issue.' If the Legation used AFIN for propaganda purposes, AFIN would be required by law to register with 'the State Department as foreign agents, which you could not do unless the Irish Government authorised it'.[11]

At a meeting of the AFIN executive on 18 September, McGlynn complained that the Legation did not have contact with organisations 'who have the pulse of the people'. Keating and McGlynn were particularly critical of Senator Frank MacDermot, who was visiting the United States. McGlynn questioned MacDermot's Irish *bona fides* because of his Oxford education and his service in the British Army during World War I, but the Irish Consulate in New York refused to intervene against MacDermot. 'They wouldn't approve of any approach to MacDermot, until he had done us harm,' McGlynn said.

MacDermot had arrived in August 1941 to visit his American wife and young son, who had moved to the United States for safety after the outbreak of war. He had recently tabled a resolution in the Senate calling on the government to 'take immediate steps to obtain the full and effective cooperation of the government of the United States', but he withdrew it due to lack of support. The new American Irish committee took MacDermot under its wing, and William Agar accompanied him to Boston.

'A certain number of people in the United States who love Ireland are under the impression that it is good Irish patriotism to obstruct aid to Britain,' MacDermot told a Boston gathering on 16 September. 'They are misguided for if England is overwhelmed by Hitler little Ireland will suffer the same fate.' He was not critical of Irish neutrality. 'No government could follow any other policy,' he explained.[12] During a radio address over WJSV of Washington, D.C., an affiliate of the CBS network, the following night, he welcomed the 200,000 British troops garrisoned in Northern Ireland because they provided protection for the whole island against a German invasion. 'There are few citizens of Éire who do not feel happier and more secure because these forces are near at hand,' he said.[13]

This was not the kind of Anglophobic fare Americans might have expected to hear. 'Neutral though we are,' MacDermot said, 'substantial numbers of our youth have crossed to England and Northern Ireland to take part in the British war effort.' He actually called for America to provide arms for the Irish Army to defend neutrality. 'It is in your own interest that we should be helped effectively to secure ourselves against attack, and perhaps you might reasonably do more for us than send arms,' he said.[14]

AFIN published a mimeographed newsletter on 22 September, calling for support for a petition aimed at concentrating 'the attention of Congress and the American people on the plight of the Irish people' in order to help the Dublin government 'to purchase food, arms and ships'. Irish people were going to go cold, according to an editorial in the *Irish World*, 'because England refused to deprive herself of coal, and peat cannot be transported by railroad without coal, nor by truck without gasoline'.[15] The following week nine Irish-American organisations met in Chicago under the umbrella of the Irish-American Alliance Organisation to discuss ways of helping Ireland. 'Several references were made to the last famine in Ireland and all the gruesome details were dwelled upon for a considerable length of time,' according to a report of the meeting. 'This, without a question, was to stir up the sympathetic nature of the Irish, who could at this point picture every family in Ireland as not having eaten for months and practically dying from starvation.' There were various suggestions about ways of helping.

'Should we not have to see Mr Churchill, who can confer with Mr Roosevelt as to whether or not we can do this?' one woman asked, much to the amusement of the gathering, which was described as definitely anti-British.[16]

MacDermot told a luncheon in Boston on 26 September that it was a mistake to rake up old prejudices against England. He personally did not like neutrality, but the Irish government had decided on that course and it was endorsed 'by a large majority of the Irish people, so I accepted the decision'. Americans should not be misled, however. 'Because Ireland has declared her neutrality does not mean that Ireland wants Hitler to win,' he said. 'On the contrary, only a handful of Irish people want to see him victorious. They realise that if he should defeat England, he would want to subjugate Ireland as a military necessity and Ireland under Hitler, would be a sorry spectacle and not a desirable place to live.' People were not allowed to enlist in British forces within Éire because 'that would be un-neutral', but, MacDermot said, 'more young Irishmen in Éire have joined the English colours than in the North with all their boasted devotion to the Union Jack.'[17]

'On the way to America,' he continued, 'I stopped a few days in London and came in contact with Irish Catholic officials in the War Office, the Foreign Office, the Committee of Information and other important government agencies. In Lisbon and Bermuda, I came across Irish Catholic officials in high government positions. The latest recruit to the British Cabinet, Brendan Bracken, hailed from Tipperary.'[18] He was personally very close to Churchill, and had become Minister for Information. Although born and reared in Ireland, he was ashamed of his Irish background and frequently tried to pass himself off as an Australian.

MacDermot did not attack Irish neutrality: 'I am against giving England military bases in Ireland. That would mean the breaking of the neutrality law and invite German aggression.'[19] But he was critical of Irish-American opposition of aid for Britain. 'Americans of Irish descent should remember, if they play Hitler's game by obstructing either America's defence or American aid to Britain they are, however unconsciously, hurting the interests of the people living in Ireland,' MacDermot said in a radio address over the New York City station, WEVD, which was owned by the Jewish *Daily Forward* newspaper.[20] He was not trying to pave the way for the British to get Irish bases, but he was trying to weaken the isolationist influence of Irish-Americans, much to their annoyance.

MacDermot raised eyebrows with his reference to Irish people he had met 'in the British foreign office, the war office, the ministry of information, and even in the intelligence service'.[21] Niall Oran Meagher of the *Irish Echo* was incensed. 'I have never, in all my life, listened to such treachery,' he wrote. 'I never knew that an Irishman could be such a modern Judas and Benedict Arnold at one and the same time. MacDermot is a traitor to Éire and should be removed forthwith from office by President de Valera, the man who appointed him.'[22]

McGlynn wrote to Robert Brennan on behalf of AFIN, demanding the senator's immediate recall to Ireland: 'We consider it a treasonable act on the part of Senator MacDermot to advocate that his country's sovereignty should be sacrificed in order to further the aims of a foreign government; and we consider it equally treasonable for him to be conspiring with known propagandists of an alien power.'[23]

'If Mr MacDermot knew Irish Americans as well as he pretends to do, he would know that they are American citizens and that their first allegiance is to the United States,' the *Gaelic American* complained. 'It is because of their love of America that they are so strongly opposed to its involvement in a foreign war which has no concern for the people of this country. They shudder at the thought of hurling three or four million young Americans into an imperialistic war which has no concern for any citizen, young or old. This war is not America's war and our men and treasure should not be expended in the age-long bickerings and conflicts of imperialistic and totalitarian nations.'[24]

Although MacDermot disassociated himself from efforts to get de Valera to give bases to the United States, the new organisation in Chicago asked Catholic priests in the area to make parish halls available for meetings to 'crystallise the influence of Catholics of Irish descent'. The plan was to organise Irish-Americans to lobby Congress to occupy Irish bases, 'assuming this would be the wish of Mr de Valera's government'. Terence O'Donnell, secretary of the Midwest branch, sent an appeal to 380 local Catholic priests to enlist their help, and he planned to contact other clerics the following week. Letters were signed by the branch chairman, Professor Francis E. McMahon, another of the 129 Irish-Americans who had signed the open appeal to de Valera in March. He thought that appeal had backfired because people were not ready for it. 'We were—and in certain areas of the United States still are—prophets without honour even among our own family, our parishes, our brethren in the Faith, our fellow-Americans,' he wrote. 'But fortunately this is no longer the case.' There was, he suggested, 'good reason to believe' de Valera would welcome an American initiative for bases.[25]

The form letter—each of which was individually addressed to the different priests—continued:

Our object in addressing you—regardless of any personal opinions you may entertain in this matter—is to secure as a loyal Irish American your active support for a movement to ensure *for the United States* the use of the western ports of Éire 'for the duration'. We have not much inclination to relight or engage in an age-old controversy, because none of us have any time to lose: For yourself, ourselves and the United States it is later than we think.

We therefore invite cooperation from you as a priest with parochial, teaching or similar influence. What form should such cooperation take? We might suggest:

1. Use of the parish hall for an immediate get-together meeting, where as in a forum led by yourself, we can crystallise the influence of Catholics of Irish descent in your parish, and who are favourable to the United States' occupation of the Éire ports 'for the duration', and naturally assuming this would be the wish of Mr de Valera's government.
2. Supply to such parishioners as are adept in public-speaking literature and speech-material that they may act as minute-men addressors of similar forums in adjoining parishes. We will supply such literature free on request, if you can advise the quantity you can use to advantage.
3. Utilise a supply of declarations like the enclosed and which we will send free of charge, for all those parishioners willing to write their congressmen at Washington to support United States' acquisition of the ports of Éire as the better solution of a present very critical and vexing problem.[26]

Although AFIN was critical of the Irish Legation's failure to confront MacDermot or his Irish-American backers, Brennan published a well-reasoned article in *America* magazine on 25 October. He skilfully defended de Valera's policy. For years before the war, the Irish government had stated it would take no part in the forthcoming conflict. 'I have heard Americans dwelling on the foolishness of Ireland's attitude, but it is hardly conceivable that, on a question so vitally affecting the interests of Ireland, all the Irish people should be wrong and a handful of people three thousand miles away should be right.' Any Irish government that tried to abandon neutrality would be ousted overnight. He went on to dismiss the significance of Irish ports. 'The value of these ports is grossly exaggerated,' Brennan argued. 'The occupation of the French coast by the Germans make the southern route for ships impossible, and all the traffic now goes by the northerly route past the Northern Ireland and Scottish coasts. The British have in these waters all the bases they need.'

By this stage AIDA was already changing tack somewhat, playing down the issue of the ports and looking instead for Irish-American support for the President's foreign policy. Christian Front elements were more critical than ever, especially after the sinking of the destroyer *Kearney* with the loss of eleven lives. 'Roosevelt murdered the seamen on the *Kearney* and should hang for it,' Francis Moran told a Boston meeting, according to a police report. He later denied using those words, but he did admit saying that 'Roosevelt was responsible for the deaths of the seamen on the Kearney and should be placed on trial for it, and if convicted should be made to pay for it'.[27] Another Irish-American, Oklahoma Governor William 'Alfalfa Bill' Murray, accused Roosevelt of being a dictator and predicted a revolution 'to return the country to the people'.[28]

AIDA was launching a campaign to collect 100,000 signatures to demonstrate Irish-American support for Roosevelt's foreign policy. The initiative was referred to as a roll call of Irish-Americans and the campaign slogan was 'You can count on the Irish, Mr President.'[29] They were being asked to subscribe to the following declaration:

> As an American of Irish decent, I hereby affirm that I support the declared foreign policy of the President and Congress of the United States. I am unalterably opposed to the Axis Powers, and will work to the utmost for an Allied victory. Therefore: I wish to join with like-minded people of Irish heritage in promoting national unity in America and in urging the utmost cooperation between Éire and the United States.[30]

'We don't intend to try to influence Ireland to give up her bases,' Rossa Downing said. 'She doesn't want to give them up for the simple reason that she could be annihilated. Hitler could make another Coventry out of Ireland. Anyway, let Ireland handle her own affairs.'[31] William Y. Elliott, head of the Political Department at Harvard University and a member of Roosevelt's famous 'Brain Trust' of advisers, stressed the same theme in regard to the bases: 'It is not in any way our place to urge de Valera to go to war until we do.'[32]

AIDA was essentially contending that 'the small minority with the loud voice' had drowned the voice of the quiet majority of Irish-Americans. Hence the 100,000 signatures were designed to demonstrate that Irish-Americans were in the mainstream of American sentiment behind the President. 'We feel that the isolationism expressed by the so-called Irish press is the child of America First and Nazi propaganda,' a spokesman contended. 'The very reason for the Defense Association's existence is to end once and for all the notion that the American Irish stand apart from the mainstream of American opinion, which is definitely anti-Hitler.'[33]

The roll call was launched in New York City at a rally held in front of the statue of Fr Francis P. Duffy in Times Square. He had served as a chaplain in World War I, in the mainly Irish-American Fighting 69th Brigade. Speakers at the rally included General John F. O'Ryan, William Agar and Francis

McMahon. About 1,000 people turned out, which some opponents ridiculed.

'Any time a man cannot stop in Times Square and gather that much of a crowd about him by just looking up in the air, New York will have changed considerably,' the *Irish Echo* observed. 'The high-pressure campaign to get 100,000 signatures and force Ireland into the war will probably fail as dismally. It is now up to the honest-to-goodness Irish to show the President of the United States where the Irish really stand.'[34]

Irish-American isolationists and interventionists were soon vying with each other in a propaganda contest. Isolationists controlled the ethnic press, which defended Irish neutrality with enthusiasm, while AIDA switched the emphasis of its campaign from the earlier call for Irish bases to a call on Irish-Americans to support the President's foreign policy. On 10 November Senator Burton K. Wheeler of Montana, one of the leading isolationists in Congress, released minutes of a meeting of government officials held at the Office of the Coordinator of Information on 8 October, at which plans for the AIDA roll call initiative were discussed. Those attending included William Yandell Elliott, representatives from the Navy Department, Civilian Defense and Intelligence. W.J. Donovan was supposed to be there, but was unable to attend for some reason. Two of his aides were present, however. The meeting was told that Rossa Downing would lead the AIDA roll call, which was to begin on 27 October.[35]

American Federation of Labour, the Congress of Industrial Organizations, the Committee to Defend America by Aiding the Allies, and Fight for Freedom, Inc., announced their support for the campaign. The American Council for Public Affairs was to publish a pamphlet on 27 October with 'The Case for American Irish Unity', by Mayo-born Terence O'Donnell, secretary of the Midwest branch of AIDA. Isolationist Irish-Americans were endangering not only 'America's and Ireland's cause, but also the cause of political and religious freedom everywhere', O'Donnell contended.[36] Supreme Court Justice Frank Murphy provided an introduction, ridiculing the idea that Germany was fighting the godless Soviet Union on behalf of Christianity. Having served as Mayor of Detroit and Governor of Michigan, Murphy was obviously used to counteract the views of the Detroit-based Coughlin, and he did so from a religious perspective. The Christian Churches, in their 'present form, must disappear from the life of our people', the Nazi ideologue Alfred Rosenberg told a Nuremberg rally in 1936. 'It should be abundantly clear to anyone that under Nazi rule no religion would remain free,' Murphy contended. 'Any concessions thus far made to religious bodies have been made solely for reason of convenience and opportunism.'[37]

On 23 November AFIN held a rally at the Manhattan Centre to counter the AIDA campaign. The *Irish Echo* noted in advance:

Ireland's position is daily growing more perilous and unless her friends in America raise their voice in protest against any effort to involve her in the present European war, the outlook will be indeed dark. Certain groups in this country are circulating literature with the deliberate intent of misleading people of Irish sympathies as to the issues at stake and there is no doubt that their ultimate object is to jeopardise the safety of the Irish people by attempting to induce them to make concessions which would immediately terminate Ireland's neutrality.[38]

'If Ireland wants to go to war, that is her business, and the business of nobody else,' Mayo-born Congressman William B. Barry told the crowd. 'And if she wanted to remain neutral, and of course she does, that also is her business.' Some 5,000 people turned out for this meeting, which was five times the turnout for the AIDA gathering in Times Square, with the result that the isolationists seemed to be winning the propaganda contest. While AIDA was aiming to collect 100,000 Irish-American signatures, the isolationist *Gaelic American* thundered in a bold front-page headline: 'Thirty Million Irish Americans support Ireland's Neutrality'.[39] This was hyperbole, of course. A total of 129 Irish-American organisations were supposedly represented at the Manhattan meeting, which contrasted starkly with the 129 individuals who had signed the open letter to de Valera in March. The implied threat to Irish independence had clearly galvanised the Irish in America, and this undoubtedly explains why Downing and Elliott emphasised that the roll call had nothing to do with bases.[40] The roll call was officially wound up on 3 December, but Francis McMahon told an AIDA luncheon in Chicago three days later that the occupation of Irish bases was the prime aim of the organisation. He branded those who preached appeasement towards Hitler as the perpetrators of 'the most traitorous act in the history of western civilisation'.[41]

AIDA tactics had fallen flat. 'The bitter truth was that the President could not count on the Irish,' according to Thomas E. Mahl's study of the largely British efforts to influence American public opinion. 'The masters of deception were left complaining that the Irish had "distorted" AIDA pronouncements.' AIDA was reduced to whining about 'vicious attacks by the Coughlinite Irish organisations and press'.[42]

AFIN and the other anti-war Irish elements had won the battle, but were on the brink of losing their war. This was only days before the Japanese attack on Pearl Harbour. Within days, all would be changed utterly.

Following the Pearl Harbour attack, America First immediately decided to disband, and the executive of AFIN decided likewise the following Friday 'because of the necessity of concentrating every effort on the successful prosecution of the war in which our country is engaged'.[43] Father Coughlin vanished from the national stage. Bishop Edward Mooney of Detroit ordered him to make no further political pronouncements, and the Roosevelt administration withdrew mailing privileges from *Social Justice*. The stark implication of this was that Irish-Americans were now behind the war, and Ireland was on her own.

Chapter 18 ～

| IN A WORLD AT WAR

On hearing of the Japanese attack on Pearl Harbour, Churchill was elated. Henceforth the United States would be fighting alongside Britain against the Axis powers. In his exuberance he fired off telegrams around the globe. One was to de Valera:

> Now is your chance. Now or never. 'A Nation Once Again.' Am ready to meet you at any time.[1]

Maffey telephoned Joe Walshe after midnight to arrange an urgent meeting with de Valera. 'I demurred at the idea of ringing up Mr de Valera at such an unseemly hour, unless the message was to the very first order of importance,' Walshe later recalled. 'Maffey replied that he had been instructed to deliver it immediately.'[2]

De Valera suspected it was some kind of ultimatum, and he asked that the Army be alerted. 'I telephoned the Chief of Staff to take all necessary precautions against an advance across the border,' Walshe noted. 'It was a night of great alarm in the country.'[3]

Maffey did not get to de Valera's home until around 2.00 a.m. Hearing a noise in the corridor, de Valera's nineteen-year-old son, Terry, opened his door to find his father in a dressing-gown in the hallway in a rather agitated mood. 'He looked in my direction and said in a strong, stern voice: "Go back to your room and do not come out unless I call you".'[4]

The Taoiseach had no intention of accepting what amounted to an invitation from Churchill to go to war with Germany and Japan. He had no mandate for war, even in return for a deal to end partition—not that the message was intended to imply such an offer. In referring to 'A Nation Once Again', the anthem of the old Irish Parliamentary Party, Churchill was simply implying that Dublin could make progress towards unity by cooperating in the struggle against Fascism.

'I concluded it was Churchill's way of intimating "now is the chance for taking action which would ultimately lead to the unification of the country"—rather than offering a deal to end partition,' he later explained. 'I indicated to Sir John Maffey that I did not see the thing in that light. I saw no opportunity at the moment of securing unity, that our people were determined on their attitude of neutrality, etc.'[5]

The Taoiseach and Walshe concluded that Churchill had probably been drinking too much following the news of Pearl Harbour, 'and that his effusion flowed in the message'.[6] The version of the telegram later published by Churchill ended, 'Am ready to meet you anywhere,' whereas the message delivered by Maffey concluded, 'Am ready to meet you any time.' De Valera understood 'it was an invitation to go over to see him'. The Taoiseach decided against this.

'I was not in favour of it,' de Valera noted, 'because I considered it unwise, that I didn't see any basis of agreement and that disagreement might leave conditions worse than before.' De Valera suggested instead that a visit by Cranborne to Dublin would be 'the best way towards a fuller understanding of our position here'.[7]

After reading Maffey's report of the meeting, Churchill said 'he certainly contemplated no deal over partition.' What he meant by the phrase—'a nation once again'—was that Ireland could 'regain her soul' by entering the war. In Churchill's own words, partition could only be ended 'by consent arising out of war comradeship between North and South'.[8]

Roosevelt warmly welcomed Churchill's initiative. 'Delighted to know of message to de Valera,' he cabled Churchill.[9]

During a speech in Cork on 14 December the Taoiseach publicly sympathised with the United States on being dragged into the conflict while reaffirming his determination to stay out the war. 'We can only be a friendly neutral,' he said, before going on to warn of the dangers ahead. 'In a world at war,' he said, 'each set of belligerents are ever ready to regard those who are not with them as against them.'[10]

As there was little hope of persuading de Valera to abandon neutrality, Cranborne toyed with the idea of cancelling the proposed trip to Dublin, but Maffey encouraged him to come anyway. Shortly after arriving in Dublin on 16 December 1941 the Dominions Secretary met with Gray, who was clearly delighted the United States was in the war at last. Having anticipated a Japanese attack, he actually welcomed word of the assault on Pearl Harbour because he realised Roosevelt would no longer have to contend with the opposition of the isolationist lobby. 'My dear Franklin,' Gray wrote. 'Our first reaction to the news that Japan had attacked us was "Thank God! the country is now behind the President".'[11]

The vast majority of Americans of all ethnic persuasions, including even

Anglophobic Irish-Americans, would rally to the flag. Previously, Dublin could legitimately contend it had to be careful in its public dealings with the British for fear of fuelling speculation about secret Anglo-Irish deals that might inflame Anglophobic elements. Now Gray advocated the United States should 'carry the ball for a bit'.[12]

Without even waiting for instructions from Washington, he began openly advocating the sale of American arms to Ireland. 'In particular,' Cranborne noted, 'he referred to the desirability of the supply to Éire of a small number of fighter aircraft.'[13] The proposal had nothing to do with helping Ireland. He believed the delivery of a dozen aircraft could promote cooperation with the Irish military, whose pilots would need Allied training. He also hoped it could be used to suborn the head of the Irish Air Corps, Colonel Patrick Mulcahy, a brother of Richard Mulcahy, one of the Fine Gael representatives on the inter-party Defence Conference.

Cranborne reported that Gray told him, 'The present head of the Éire Air Force was extremely sympathetic to the Allied cause and would no doubt be very willing to carry out such plans as he could behind the facade of neutrality by way of preparing for future cooperation with the Allies.'[14] The machinations of the American Minister did not end there. Writing to Roosevelt next day he explained he was only thinking of allowing the Irish to purchase 'token arms', and this would be highly publicised. 'If the Germans protest,' Gray wrote, 'it will push the Irish our way.' He thought Roosevelt could further excite the situation by referring to the thousands of Irishmen serving in Allied forces. 'If you ever have a reason to speak publicly on the subject,' he wrote, 'you may say that there are 150,000 Irish volunteers from Éire fighting the Axis.'[15]

When they met the next day, de Valera told Cranborne that he could have brought Ireland 'into a defensive alliance with Great Britain' before the war, if partition were ended. But now that opportunity was gone. Cranborne argued that de Valera's political position was so strong, he could lead the people to do anything he wished, but the Taoiseach said it was only strong because he was representing the will of the people. 'If he tried to lead them in a direction in which they did not want to go, his influence would be gone and the country would be split from top to bottom,' Cranborne reported. 'Until the question of partition was settled, there was no chance of Éire abandoning neutrality.'[16] De Valera realised the British needed the Northern ports at that stage, so he accepted that a solution to partition would therefore have wait.[17]

An RAF Wellington bomber landed at the Irish Army camp at Gormanston on 21 December, but it was quietly allowed to leave. But there was no question of releasing any of the four-man crew of a German bomber that crash-landed near Waterville, County Kerry, the same week. They were promptly interned.

There was an unfounded rumour that Field Marshall Walther von Brauchitsc, the recently deposed Commander-in-Chief of the German Army, was on board, but there was in fact no one with a military rank above sergeant.[18]

On 2 December the Toronto *Globe and Mail* reported that an aircraft of the Royal Canadian Air Force, with three men on board, got lost for a time over Éire. 'Although short of gasoline they decided to make for Northern Ireland rather than be imprisoned in a neutral country until the end of the war,' according to the report. 'As a result there was a crash and all were killed.' In fact, the aircraft, which was being delivered from Canada to Northern Ireland, had landed at the Irish military airfield at Baldonnel on 27 September 1941. The Department of External Affairs instructed that the plane should be refuelled. The crew were fed and allowed to rest for some hours. After taking off again, they crashed near Jenkinstown.[19]

Hearne was instructed to secretly inform the Canadian authorities what had happened and to ask them to inform the newspapers that the press reports were misinformed. Dublin asked that Ottawa ensure that Canadian censorship prevented the publication of 'such foul calumnies' about Irish neutrality. It was, of course, 'quite out of the question to give publicity to a true story'.[20] Kearney confirmed this account and the Canadian Department of External Affairs asked the editor of the *Globe and Mail* to retract the story.[21]

On 22 December 1941 Roosevelt thanked de Valera for the expressions of sympathy in Cork, but he went on to intimate this was not enough. While the desire to avoid involvement in the war was understandable, it merely played into the hands of the aggressors by allowing them to choose the time and manner of their attack, according to the President. 'If freedom and liberty are to be preserved, they must now be defended by the human and material resources of all free nations,' he added. 'Your freedom too is at stake. No longer can it be doubted that the policy of Hitler and his Axis associates is the conquest of the entire world and the enslavement of all mankind.'[22]

Nex day Maffey raised the possibility with de Valera of Ireland providing bases for the Americans to protect Atlantic shipping. The Taoiseach had invited the United States to proclaim the defence of Irish waters vital to American interests in May 1940. He would probably have welcomed American warships in Irish waters then, but Roosevelt had decided against this. Now it was too late. De Valera showed 'considerable nervous excitement' when Maffey suggested the possibility of an American request for bases. De Valera replied:

Let it be clearly understood the answer to any such approach would be a plain 'No'. Éire has the right to choose her own way. She did not start the war, nor does she wish to get into it. The war was caused by the blunders of the great powers. I have seen opportunities missed, but the little powers could do nothing. Why should Éire suffer? If there is a conflagration why should she be thrown into the fire?[23]

De Valera delivered a radio broadcast to the United States on Christmas Eve. 'I would like you to know that, in the difficulties that lie ahead for you,' he said, 'you will have the understanding and sympathy of our people.' But he reaffirmed his own determination to stay out of the conflict. 'Today,' he said, 'we are a people united as perhaps never before in our history. Unless we are attacked, any change from neutrality would destroy this unity. It is our duty to Ireland to try to keep out of this war.'[24]

Gray described it as a 'fatuous broadcast'.[25] He called on the Taoiseach on New Year's Day. While waiting in an outer office he had a pointed exchange with de Valera's private secretary, Kathleen O'Connell.

'Who would have thought a year ago that America would be in the war!' she exclaimed.

'That is what Mr de Valera, Mr Walshe, and all the Government people have thought,' Gray replied. 'Where did they get the information that made them take that view?'

She said nothing.

'For a year and a half I've been telling you that we couldn't keep out and you all laughed at me. On whom have you been relying?'[26]

'It is significant of the whole twisted and blinded viewpoint here that the Irish mind wishfully refused to accept the fact that American interests were bound up with British survival,' Gray wrote to Roosevelt next day, arguing on the same lines as he had with Cranborne a couple of weeks earlier. 'Perhaps economic pressure will make them realise at long last that their survival is bound up with that of Britain.'[27]

'There is no reason why American and British interest should be sacrificed for a government which refused all help,' he explained. The Allies could exert economic pressure by cutting off their supplies to Ireland, and they could conceal their motives with a much-publicised offer of arms. 'The severer these pressures the better,' he added, 'as it is the only way in which the Irish people can be made to realise the fatuity of their Government's program. But the severer they are the more need for expressions of good-will and token offerings similar in spirit to the sterile friendliness of de Valera.'[28]

Britain supplied about 90 per cent of Ireland's imports; therefore British cooperation was necessary for the economic pressure to work. But London showed no inclination of following Gray's lead, because most of the British officials did not have the same jaundiced view of Irish policy. In the midst of his incessant scheming, Gray was in the dark about the extent of secret Irish cooperation. On the same day that he was complaining about the 'sterile friendliness of de Valera', Maffey was ironically writing that the Taoiseach 'will make his neutrality as friendly as possible, but he has to tread warily where overt actions are concerned'. He added that de Valera was promising to bring 90 per cent of the Irish people on the side of Britain, if Germany attacked, provided the British had not poisoned things by 'ill advised' action.[29]

'We have a system of intelligence which works for our purposes,' Maffey reported to the Dominions Office on 27 January 1942. 'When the principle of neutrality is not publicly and violently outraged,' he explained, 'the Éire authorities endeavour to solve the problems which the war brings in a manner favourable to us (stranded aircraft, deserters, etc.)' Moreover there was a close liaison with the Irish military and many Irish people had joined the British services. 'It had been the policy of his Government to put no difficulty in the way of this recruitment,' but there was a limit to how far he would go. 'Mr de Valera said that if he were Hitler and Éire joined the ranks of his enemies the first thing he would do would be to bomb Dublin, Cork and Limerick,' Maffey continued. The Irish people strongly supported the policy of keeping Ireland out of the conflict. 'In the country at large neutrality is no longer merely a policy. It has become a principle, almost a faith.'[30]

'Let there be no doubt that if America and England laid violent hands upon Éire they would meet with 100 per cent opposition and any hold we effected would be subjected to unceasing attacks.' Maffey warned. He therefore wished to be in a position to be able to secure further help by economic pressure. 'An acute shortage in the field of supplies is now developing and nothing should be done to mitigate it, except in return for definite services,' he continued.[31]

'It has been demonstrated that the Irish government will do almost anything to help us short of involving themselves in the war,' Canadian High Commissioner Kearney assured his government. With Dáil approval necessary for a declaration of war, the Dublin government had no choice but to remain neutral because the Irish people were clearly opposed to involvement in the conflict. 'The only thing that could unite them for war purposes is invasion,' he wrote, 'just as it required a declaration of war by Japan to unite the Americans.'[32]

The Americans were not as confident of de Valera's goodwill because they were not aware of the secret cooperation. The Coordination of Information Bureau under William J. Donovan decided to send Robert Rowley Patterson on a thinly disguised spy mission. He had spent ten years as a Vice-Consul in Cobh during the 1930s and had helped with arrangements for Americans sailing from Galway after the outbreak of the war in 1939, as well as the American passengers who were picked up by the *ss Washington* in June 1940 before he returned to the United States. He set out for Ireland on 23 December 1941 with a considerable supply of silk stockings, lipsticks, sugar, coffee and tea—all of which were in short supply in Ireland. His ship to Liverpool took much longer than expected and he did not arrive in Dublin until 14 January 1942.

Patterson hired a car, and Gray supplied him with petrol coupons to travel about the island for three weeks under the cover of trying to interest provincial newspaper editors in publishing excerpts from a daily bulletin from the US Embassy in London. During his travels he distributed his supplies liberally in an effort to prompt contacts to speak more freely. Nearly everybody he talked with about Irish neutrality brought up the thorny issue of de Valera's refusal to allow the British to use the ports.

There was a great deal of talk about fighting anyone who dared to invade the country. 'We'll repel any invader, no matter who,' Patterson was told, but he dismissed such talk as 'bunk'. Yet he thought it pointless for Washington to try to persuade the Irish to enter the war because they were 'scared as hell'. The Americans should just seize anything they needed in Ireland. 'If the United States wants to go in,' he wrote, 'just go.'[33]

Patterson was told several German parachutists had been picked up going to Dublin and Killarney. One can only wonder why anyone would have thought the Germans were interested in Killarney, which had no strategic significance whatever. Yet later the same year Washington asked Dublin for an official explanation about the rumoured presence of hundreds of Japanese tourists.

As a result of a conversation with Garda Chief Superintendent Harry O'Meara in Tralee, Patterson described Kerry as 'the hot spot' of German activity. O'Meara said someone from the German Legation made a trip to the vicinity practically every week and visited 'homes all round Tralee'. A German radio-transmitter had been picked up about a year earlier, he added, and another was believed to exist but had not yet been located.

'I don't know what the hell you're doing here,' O'Meara said to Patterson, 'but you're welcome.'[34]

'He may be quite all right but, as his visit here seems strange, I thought I'd let you know,' O'Meara informed the Garda Commissioner. 'He can make himself very popular and would be useful for intelligence work if there is any such thing going on.'[35] Gardaí, who kept an eye on Patterson, noted his passport was marked 'on a special mission to U.S. Legation, Dublin Éire'.[36]

In the nearby seaside resort of Ballybunion, Patterson called on another friend, Jack Walsh, who had been active in the old IRA. They had been close friends and Patterson was actually godfather to Walsh's eldest son, Seán, who would later become well known as the Secretary Manager of Ballybunion Golf

Club from the early 1970s to late 1990s. After some duck-shooting together, Jack Walsh 'agreed to report on German activities' in the Kerry area to the American Military Attaché in Dublin. He was assured, in return, his 'travelling expenses would be paid'.[37]

Patterson went on to Foynes, where he called on Army Captain Stapelton, whom he had met in 1939. While at the air base he talked freely to Captain Stapelton and a lieutenant, who noted that Patterson's 'manner would suggest he had quite a few drinks'. They concluded, 'his mission is to report on the reaction of Ireland to America's entry into the war', but especially to evaluate the possibility of America taking over the ports. He stated confidently that America would win the war, although it might take up to eight years. 'We may have to call on you for some assistance,' he said before asking Captain Stapelton what would happen if American planes flew over Ireland.

'Any plane that was not here on its lawful business would be fired on, no matter its nationality,' Captain Stapelton replied.[38]

From Galway, the local G2 commander reported that Patterson talked quite freely about being interested in the attitude of Irish people toward the United States following her entry into the war. 'He said he wanted to meet the editors of most of our papers to arrange to have them supplied with American war news,' G2 reported. 'He also said that some Irish papers were pro-German and he had instructions to pay particular attention to these editors—*The Kerryman* was an example of the type he meant.' He asked to meet J.A. Power, editor of the *Connaught Tribune*, but Power refused to meet him. He said he was already plagued with British and Axis propaganda and did not want 'American stuff' as well. The G2 officer persuaded Power to agree to meet Patterson, but the meeting never took place because Patterson had been drinking so heavily that he had to dry out over the weekend in St Bride's Nursing Home.[39]

Patterson returned to the United States by air and wrote an alarmist report that fit neatly into the critical picture of Irish neutrality that was already being formed in Washington. Ireland was beginning to take on a much more important role in the thinking of the Americans. Churchill and Roosevelt had decided to station three divisions of American troops in Northern Ireland, where they could complete their training, while the trained British troops stationed in the area could be used elsewhere. It was also hoped the replacement of British troops by Americans might help to further improve Anglo-Irish relations.

On 6 January 1942 President Roosevelt announced American forces would be stationed in the United Kingdom. Sir John Andrews was summoned to London, where Sir Alan Brook, the Chief of Imperial General Staff, explained Operation Magnet, in accordance with which the US Navy would take over the base already built by the Americans on Lough Foyle. There were also unfounded rumours of some kind of deal for bases in the Twenty-Six Counties.

'There are rumours being spread about bargains,' the Taoiseach told a gathering in Navan on 12 January. 'Now there are no bargains. When this war started I said there was no inch of our national territory for sale, and I hope that that will be sufficient for our people.' He denounced the role of the foreign media:

> This country at different times since the war began has been the subject of violent articles in different newspapers in foreign countries. All sorts of suggestions are being made. Everything that could be said to inflame other people against us is being used. You do not see these things, because we have adopted a policy not to let into the newspapers anything that would go to stir up bitterness and ill-feeling.[40]

The first American servicemen arrived, unheralded, in Northern Ireland on 21 January 1942. They were the crews of four US Navy destroyers—*Wilkes*, *Roper*, *Madison* and *Sturtevant*. They put into the new base in Derry after completing escort duty with convoy HX169. The base, which was officially commissioned as an American naval base on 5 February, became the first such American facility in European waters. It was used to repair damaged ships, refuel escorts and service British vessels.

Two American troop carriers, *Chateau Thierry* and *Stratford,* arrived in Belfast Lough on 26 January 1942 as part of Operation Magnet. The plans were to announce their arrival with great fanfare, as if they were the first American servicemen to arrive. The Governor, the Duke of Abercorn, was at the Belfast Docks, along with Prime Minister Andrews and Sir Archibald Sinclair, the Secretary of State for Air, to welcome the American soldiers under the commands of Major General Russell P. Hartle. The whole operation was to be carefully orchestrated. When the tender docked, an American colonel came on board to select somebody who would supposedly be the first American soldier to step ashore. Private Milburn H. Henke of Hutchinson, Minnesota, was selected to be photographed as the 'first' American soldier setting foot in Northern Ireland. To ensure this, arrangements were made to delay the arrival of other tenders with troops. As the first American 'was about to come down the gangway', they could hear the strains of a band at the head of a column of American troops from the second tender passing down the Dock Road from another quay. Private Henke walked down the gangplank wearing a new helmet, blouse, necktie, full field pack, M1 rifle, gas mask, and canvas leggings. He posed on the dock for pictures that later appeared in

American newspapers as supposedly the first American soldier to land in Northern Ireland, but he was more likely the 501st. The military press were not about to allow the truth to get in the way of a good story.[41]

Maffey informed de Valera of the arrival of the Americans and pleaded with him not to object to the landing. De Valera previously tried to insist that his government should be consulted, if the Americans decided to assume control of any facilities in Northern Ireland. His demand was sparked by reports of Americans building bases in Northern Ireland. Roosevelt had said those American technicians constructing the bases were working as ordinary citizens, and the British were paying them. De Valera told Gray that while he recognised the 'de facto occupation' of the Six Counties by the British, he was not waiving Dublin's claim to sovereignty over the area. Gray indignantly suggested that Dublin should raise the matter with the State Department through Brennan. Realising the Americans were building a base for themselves, Gray began telling people the United States was putting its 'defences into Northern Ireland and that Ireland could in effect get its own supplies and arms'.[42]

When the *Daily Mail* suggested in October 1941 that the Americans occupy the Lough Foyle base, de Valera instructed Brennan to enquire about Washington's intentions. The President duly authorised the State Department to tell him the 'inquiry related to territory recognised by this government as part of the United Kingdom, and to suggest that the Irish Government address its inquiry to the United Kingdom government'.[43]

Although effectively told that this was none of his business, de Valera seized on the arrival of the Americans for another of his ritualistic denunciations of partition. While the Irish people harboured no hostility towards the United States, he emphasised, he had a 'duty to make it clearly understood that no matter what troops occupy the Six Counties, the Irish claim for the union of the whole national territory and for supreme jurisdiction over it will remain unabated'.[44]

Robert R. Patterson, who was still in Ireland on his spy mission, thought 'de Valera had no choice but to make his statement about the invasion of the North of Ireland by American troops' because of Dublin's claim to sovereignty over the whole island.[45] But Gray deeply resented the allusion to the troops as occupiers. De Valera was playing petty politics in the midst of the war. Gray again wrote to Roosevelt, advocating an embargo on all petroleum supplies to Ireland. He also added that Britain should embargo coal deliveries. The Dublin government had forbidden the export of all the food Ireland needed, so he thought it natural to treat the Irish in the same way. 'The British are boobs not to adopt the same policy,' he wrote. 'Why should coal be rationed in Britain yet exported to Éire, or why should gasoline that we need be sent to Éire? It is not coercion; it is simple justice.'[46]

Within hours, however, there was an example of why the British were unwilling to pursue such a stringent policy. An American, Sergeant Salvatore Walcott of Rhode Island, who had been serving in the Eagle Squadron of the RAF for the past three months, made an emergency landing in his Hurricane fighter at Dublin airport. He had got lost and was almost out of fuel. Initially it was intended he should be interned along with the thirty-three other Allied and thirty-five German airmen being held at the Curragh. He was held overnight, but de Valera ordered his release. His plane was re-fuelled next morning and he was allowed to leave.

Gray viewed the release as de Valera's way of indicating that Dublin was not really bitter over the arrival of the American troops. As a result there was some confusion over whether or not the Taoiseach actually intended his statement should be considered an actual protest against the arrival of the American troops. Although most Irish newspapers and the international press generally featured the word 'protest', de Valera's own newspaper, the *Irish Press*, simply carried the caption 'Statement by Mr de Valera'.[47] The three Allied representatives in Dublin decided among themselves that the Canadian Kearney should seek a clarification from the Taoiseach, who told him, on 31 January, that it was just a statement. Kearney reported:

Mr de Valera made it clear that he felt obliged to make some statement in case silence might be interpreted as acquiescence in the status of partition. He also told me that he feared a worsening of relationships between Ireland and the United States by reason of the presence of the American troops in the North, because the American soldier would not understand the Irish the way the British soldier did, and if the nationalist minority … showed resentment at the arrival of the American troops, they might take offence—whereas the British soldier, under similar circumstances, would not.[48]

Chapter 19 ∾

BEYOND REASONABLE
BELIEF

S ome in the United States resented the Taoiseach's remarks about the
arrival of American troops in Northern Ireland, and this again focused
a spotlight on Irish neutrality. *The Nation* had twenty-three pages of
articles, adorned with a number of cartoons ridiculing Irish neutrality. One
article, by William L. Shirer, contended that British fighter planes operating
out of southern Éire could play havoc with the German bombers flying from
Brest. The Germans used to fly one day from France to Norway around the
coast of Ireland to attack Allied shipping as it funnelled together off the
north-west coast of Ireland. Next day they would fly the reverse route back to
France. Shirer concluded that Hitler had not attacked Ireland in 1940 for three
reasons: (1) the Luftwaffe had failed to gain air supremacy, (2) an attack on
Ireland would bring America into the war and (3) a neutral Éire gave the
Germans a great advantage in the Battle of the Atlantic. But Shirer did not
think Éire could stay out of the war: 'Mr de Valera's refusal to grant bases to
the Allies will not save his country from attack by Hitler in the end, any more
than Norway's or Holland's or Belgium's strict neutrality saved them from
attack when Hitler found it expedient to smash them.'[1]

German seaplanes were sheltering in many small Irish inlets before
attacking Allied shipping, according to the London *Daily Herald*. The report
indicated that Heinkel seaplanes 'have been observed several times. One
skipper reports that they land on the water, wait for shipping to enter the
vicinity, then take off again to attack.'[2] The idea of seaplanes sheltering in
Irish inlets and then ambushing Allied ships as they passed by the Irish coast
was ridiculous. Whatever chance planes might have of sighting shipping from
the air, they had practically no chance from the water. Nonetheless the
readiness of reputable newspapers to believe such nonsense gave rise to
tensions.

Pilot Officer Roland L. 'Bud' Wolfe of Ceresco, Nebraska, was interned in κ Lines on 30 November 1941 while serving in the RAF's Eagle Squadron, which consisted of American volunteers. He bailed out of his plane as it was about to run out of fuel in heavy fog over County Donegal. Within two days of being interned he applied for a general parole that would allow him to return home to the United States, where he would take no further part in the war. The attack on Pearl Harbour was then only five days away. Before the Irish government could respond, America was at war, so his application was turned down.

Wolfe signed out of the camp on parole on 13 December. When he did not return by the following morning, camp authorities complained to the senior Allied officer, who telephoned Maffey's office to report what he believed was a serious parole violation. Those at the camp assumed the twenty-three-year-old American had absconded in an apparent effort to get back home, but that afternoon he reported back to his unit at Eglington Air Force Base, County Derry, where he denied violating parole.

Maffey asked for Wolfe to return immediately to the Curragh to straighten matters out. 'I entirely concurred with his decision,' Gray wrote.[3] Wolfe was probably the only American of the whole war ordered to return to a concentration camp because his superiors had doubts about the manner of his escape. Wolfe said he had signed out on parole at 9.10 p.m. on 13 December, but after going out had immediately returned because he had forgotten his gloves. By re-entering the camp he fulfilled his parole obligations. 'I was then automatically off parole,' he argued.[4] Consequently, he was free to escape minutes later, when he was allowed to leave again without signing another parole form.

None of the other internees had seen Wolfe return for his gloves, but a colleague, who was visiting him from his outfit at Eglington, had witnessed proceedings. He provided an affidavit supporting Wolfe's story, but camp guards contended Wolfe had not returned. The Taoiseach and the Army authorities accepted the word of the guards. Henceforth the parole procedure was changed to have internees sign in before their parole would be terminated.

The competence of the guards in relation to the Wolfe affair was called into question on 21 January 1942 when one of the German internees, *Leutnant* Konrad Neymeyr, simply vanished from the German camp. He escaped by tricking the guards at the gate. An Irish Army officer with IRA sympathies helped him to stow away on board the s.s. *Lanarone*, bound for Portugal, but Neymeyr was discovered and handed over to the British when the ship put into Welsh port for a navicert. He was the only German to escape from Ireland, but he spent the remainder of the war in a British prisoner-of-war camp.

Wolfe spent the next two years at κ Lines, seething with frustration. On weekly visits to Dublin he would meet American servicemen visiting from Northern Ireland to enjoy steak dinners. They were free to stay overnight and take the train back to Belfast, but Wolfe had to return to the Curragh by the last bus each night. He became a kind of celebrity in the Curragh area, riding with the Kildare Hunt in a cowboy hat and Western attire. He raised many eyebrows in those staid circles as he charged ahead of the hunt with a distinctive one-handed style of riding.

Wolfe had travelled over 4,000 miles to fight, not to sit out the war being treated like some kind of wayward schoolboy. Life became all the more frustrating for the Allied internees with the gradual realisation that they were being held just to placate the German internees and to preserve the illusion of strict Irish neutrality. Although the internment of Allied airmen had been allowed to remain in the background as far as international relations were concerned, it suddenly threatened to explode in February 1942. On 7 February the Department of External Affairs in Ottawa asked Kearney to enquire about conditions at the camp, which was holding nine Canadians at the time. The two most senior Allied officers—Flight Lieutenants John Leslie Ward of Vancouver and J. Grant Fleming from Calgary, Alberta—were both Canadians. Fleming took over from Ward as the senior officer in December 1941 after his aircraft came down in Galway Bay on 3 December 1941. He and one member of the crew, both strong swimmers, managed to make it ashore; seven others perished. From the outset Fleming was determined his stay in Ireland would be as short as possible. In January 1942 he began working on an escape plan that involved all thirty-three Allied internees. In addition to the Canadians and the American Wolfe, there was a New Zealander, a Frenchman, two Poles and nineteen men from various parts of the United Kingdom. Since the camp opened in September 1940, surrounded by just a 10-ft-high barbed-wire fence, three further barbed-wire barriers had been added.

The German part of the camp 'did not seem to be as heavily wired', Kearney reported on first visiting κ Lines. 'Of course the inducement for them to escape is not as great as for our boys because it is much more difficult for them to return to their units,' he wrote. The Germans organised education classes and had their own self-imposed daily routine. 'On the whole, the Germans seem to have settled down for the duration of the war,' Kearney added. 'Our boys, rightly or wrongly, feel that if they organise classes it might be interpreted as acquiescence of their lot, whereas they want it known that they are doing all they can to rejoin their units.'[5]

On Christmas Day 1940 Pilot Officer Aubrey Covington climbed over the compound gate. The sentry outside the gate called on him to halt and threatened to shoot him. But Covington gambled that the guards were ordered not to shoot any internee. No such order had been issued, but the sentry could not bring himself to shoot in such circumstances, especially on Christmas Day. Covington ran off, but other soldiers stopped him before he got very far. Thereafter the guards were supplied with batons and given 'definite authority to use these batons vigorously in the case of an attempted escape'.[6]

The Allied internees came up with a plan to use wire-cutters to get through the first fence of stranded barbed-wire and then use a couple of special ladders to cross the next two, 14ft-high fences of thickly coiled barbed-wire, which stood 8ft apart. The two specially made ladders would be 16ft-high ladders, with a second, 9ft-long ladder hinged at the top of each. The first part would be put against the second fence, while the other part would be swung over to form a bridge between the two coiled barriers. The men were confident they could then roll over the smaller outer fence using mattresses.

They smuggled wire-cutters into the compound and a friend on the outside secured enough steel strips for them in 2.5ft sections for the ladders. They smuggled these into the camp in their golf bags. The steel strips were hidden under Captain Kasimierz Baranowski's mattress, while the Polish captain was given the task of pretending to be sick. They plied him with drink and had him stay in bed for a week.

The break was planned for the night of 9 February 1942. That day Kearney happened to talk to Fleming on the telephone about conditions at the camp. Fleming indicated everything was satisfactory: rules were lenient and the health of all the men was excellent. They were housed in well-heated quarters, had plenty of good food and were well treated. 'The boys have no complaints and appreciate the treatment but find life boring,' Kearney noted. [7]

During the afternoon the steel strips were bolted together to form the required ladders, and the men organised themselves into various groups, each with specific tasks. There was a diversion party to secure the inner gate in order to prevent guards entering the compound. They armed themselves with flash bombs and smoke-screen material to distract the attention of the guards away from the east fence, where the escape bid was to take place. A hole was quickly cut in the inside fence and the three sentries subdued on the east side. Initially things went well, until another guard rushed to the scene and began shaking the wire, forcing one of the crosswalks to collapse and leaving Fleming entangled on top of the third fence. By the time he had extricated himself and jumped to the ground, the place was swarming with guards, some with a baton in each hand. They flailed anyone who got in their way.

One of the gun-posts was blazing away. 'Only blank cartridges were used,' Kearney reported. The firing continued even when the guards came on the scene, so it was obvious to all that the shooting was only for effect.[8]

Five men reached the other fence, where the heaviest fighting took place. The five resisted, hoping thereby some of their colleagues might escape. Afterwards guards and internees accused each other of using excessive force. The internees were a sorry sight—a mass of cuts and bruises from the barbed-wire and the batons, with their clothes in tatters. Six needed hospital treatment, as did one of the guards, but none of the injuries was serious.

Kearney, Maffey and Wing Commander Malcolm Begg, the British Air Attaché, visited the camp in the following days. De Valera indicated he was anxious every facility and comfort, not incompatible with international duties, should be accorded to the aviators. He later told representatives from the Departments of Defence and External Affairs that there should be a strong guard at the camp at all times, but they should take 'the utmost precaution to ensure that none of the internees is shot'.[9]

On the day after the mass breakout attempt, James Dillon publicly denounced the government's neutrality policy at the national convention of Fine Gael. His father and grandfather had both sought refuge in the United States and his brother was now working there. 'Whoever attacks America is my enemy,' he declared. 'The survival of the Irish nation depends upon the maintenance of the Irish-American alliance,' he added. 'Without that alliance, at the present moment this nation cannot survive.'[10]

The speech caused considerable embarrassment within Fine Gael. There was virtually no political support for Dillon's calls for the country to go to war. Afterwards W.T. Cosgrave and Dick Mulcahy encouraged Dillon to resign from the party rather than wait to be expelled. He dutifully quit and became an independent deputy. Ironically, on the day of his controversial speech a brother of one of his Fine Gael colleagues was awarded the Distinguished Service Order in Britain for his role in leading the air attack in which the battleship *Bismarck* had been crippled.

Lieutenant Commander Eugene Esmonde—elder brother of John Esmonde, the Fine Gael deputy from Wexford—was reared near Borrisokane, County Tipperary, and educated at Clongowes Wood College, County Kildare. He served in the Fleet Air Arm of the Royal Navy before becoming a commercial pilot. He later rejoined the Royal Navy as lieutenant commander at the outbreak of hostilities. On the day after receiving the DSO, Esmonde was killed leading the attack on the three German battleships—*Scharnhorst*, *Gneisnau* and *Prinz Eugen*—in their dramatic dash through the English Channel in broad daylight on 12 February 1942. He was posthumously awarded the Victoria Cross for his part in that engagement.

There was considerable uneasiness in Dublin over press reports that the German Legation had sent weather information that helped the three battleships in the Channel Dash. Three radio messages were monitored from the German Legation in Dublin on 10, 11 and 12 February. Some British newspapers suggested the Germans were assisted with meteorological information from the Legation in Dublin, but Cecil Liddell of MI5 thought it more likely the weather information came from German aircraft in the Atlantic.

For over twenty years de Valera had consistently maintained that Irish territory should not be used for any attack on Britain. He therefore instructed Walshe to lodge a strong protest with Hempel. 'Up to now, I have used evasive terms, but this time I thought it better to be quite blunt and to call a spade a spade,' Walshe reported to de Valera afterwards. 'In any case, your instruction obliged me to take this course.'[11]

'The greatest danger which threatened our neutrality was the use of a transmitter by the German Legation,' Walshe warned Hempel. 'Nothing was so calculated to give the British, and the Americans (especially since their troops arrived in the Six Counties) a better excuse to demand that we should break off diplomatic relations with the German Government.' Walshe insisted the Germans 'must cease absolutely using the transmitter'. If they used it again, de Valera would insist on its transfer to Irish custody.[12]

Hempel 'looked very troubled while I was speaking', according to Walshe. He had previously insisted the German Legation was legally entitled to use the equipment, but he agreed not to use the transmitter again. He still had the use of a telegraph line to Berne, although his telegrams were taking four days to get to Berlin. The line passed through London, so the British could, if necessary, always cut the cable to the German Legation in Dublin, but they left the cable line open as a *quid pro quo* for the Germans in occupied France not blocking messages for Britain from Berne.

The renewed international press attention increased tension in Ireland by lending credibility to German propaganda that the Americans were making industrious preparations to invade the Twenty-six Counties from Northern Ireland. Berlin had already used such propaganda to justify pre-emptive invasions of neutrals like Norway, Belgium and Holland, with the result that there was renewed speculation about Hitler's intentions towards Ireland.

Gray thought the Germans might make a desperate effort to gain control of Ireland in order to knock Britain out of the war before the United States could mobilise properly. He feared, for instance, that Germany might be able to seize Irish airfields with an airborne invasion. Then, with the aid of air cover, the Germans would 'undoubtedly' be able to land an invasion convoy on the south coast of Ireland and, if they gained control of the island, would have little difficulty defeating Britain.[13]

Gray, who had still not learned about the secret cooperation that de Valera and Walshe had agreed with the British, was alarmed by another communication from the supposed ghost of Arthur Balfour. On 15 February Gray sent Roosevelt the transcripts of further séances, during which Balfour supposedly warned again about a group of prominent Irish people having made preparations to establish a quisling-style government. 'Balfour said that there was, beside the IRA, an organisation of Irish quisling intellectuals opposed to the Government and ready to take over,' Gray noted.[14]

W.T. Cosgrave later told Gray that the story about the 'would-be quisling intellectuals' fit in with what he had heard. 'This is hard to account for except as a supernormal phenomenon,' Gray wrote.[15] MI6 considered Joe Walshe a potential quisling, along with two former members of Cosgrave's government from the 1920s: Ernest Blythe and J.J. Walsh.[16]

Faced with the Nazi menace and the possible treachery of would-be Irish quislings, the American Minister again suggested his government improve its popularity in Ireland by making 'a token gift to sweeten the Irish people' with some equipment. 'A few airplanes would do this best,' he again noted. If the Irish became difficult, the Allies could always ground the planes by cutting off their fuel. For the time being, however, he believed the American priority should be to deal with the Nazi menace in relation to Ireland. 'You can attend to Dev later on,' Gray wrote. 'German propaganda is spreading the story of our intending to invade Éire industriously. We should do something to counter it without much delay.'[17]

What he was advocating ran into strong opposition, but not from the White House, where Roosevelt described Gray as having done 'exceedingly well' in Dublin.[18] The British were the main stumbling block. They were satisfied with their policy of using economic pressure to secure Irish concessions.

'No arms for de Valera 'till he comes in (except a few trifles by the RAF in return for conveniences),' Churchill insisted after Ambassador John Winant inquired about the British attitude towards Gray's suggestions. 'We request most incessantly that no arms be supplied by the United States. This would spoil the whole market.' The position was explained to Maffey, but he was told not to inform Gray.[19]

As a result the 'something' that Gray asked for to counter German propaganda came in the form of a personal assurance from Roosevelt to de Valera on 26 February that the United States never had 'the slightest thought or intention of invading Irish territory or threatening Irish security'. Instead of posing a danger to the Irish people, he contended, American troops in Northern Ireland 'can only contribute to the security of Ireland and of the whole British Isles, as well as furthering our total war effort'.[20]

The Irish gradually began to feel the British economic squeeze in 1942 as factories were forced to close because they could not get sufficient fuel or raw materials. The transportation system was seriously disrupted as the shortage of coal supplies hit the railroads, and the decline in petrol forced the government to ban the use of private motorcars. Authorities had to ration bread and clothing, in addition to the earlier rationing introduced on sugar, tea and fuel. By the end of 1942 the country's normal requirements of tea were cut by 75 per cent, textiles by 78 per cent, petrol by 80 per cent, coal gas by 84 per cent and paraffin by over 85 per cent. An intensive turf-cutting campaign partly eased the energy shortage. While native peat was sufficient to keep homes warm, it was a poor industrial substitute. Meat, eggs and dairy produce were in plentiful supply and the government pursued a programme of compulsory tillage. In October 1941 it ordered that 25 per cent of arable land-holdings of 10 or more statue acres should be cultivated. Later, as yields fell due to fertiliser shortages, the minimum area of cultivation was increased to 37.5 per cent. The country thereby produced ample vegetables and about three-quarters of its normal wheat requirements. The food situation was good enough in March 1943 that the government sent a much-publicised cargo of potatoes, sugar and other supplies to refugees in Spain. This, of course, had the political impact of suggesting to Irish people that they were fortunate in comparison with others.

A couple of basic factors prevented the overall economic situation from deteriorating to the extent Gray believed possible. The unemployment situation was never as grave as it might have been because an army recruiting campaign absorbed many of those who lost jobs due to factory closures. Others found employment in turf-cutting or tillage, and many migrated to Britain. Between 1940 and 1945 some 124,500 men and 58,000 women migrated to Britain and Northern Ireland.

The severity of the economic dislocation was also mitigated by Britain's reluctance to introduce a complete embargo on supplies to Ireland, because they were anxious to continue their Irish trade. The parliamentary secretary to the British Minister of Transport explained, for instance, that 'drastically reduced' exports of petroleum were being sent to Ireland in order 'to ensure the continued export to the United Kingdom of valuable agricultural products received from Éire'. [21]

In March 1942 Gray learned, to his dismay, that the British had concluded a deal for Irish beer in return for 30,000 tons of wheat. Since this wheat fulfilled some of Ireland's most pressing needs, he told Maffey the deal undermined the chance of using 'economic pressure and postpones the only position which is favourable to our obtaining our greatest *desideratum*, "the ports"'. The American people, he added, would not understand why Britain had used shipping for the benefit of Ireland when the Irish government was unwilling to help the Allies. If beer had been essential, he said, 'the wheat should have been given as a highly publicised humane gesture.'[22]

Gray found the ingratitude of some people around de Valera particularly exasperating. Martin Corry, a Fianna Fáil deputy from Cork, was gloating that the British were so badly off that they were importing crows from Cork for food. 'They have eaten all the rabbits,' Corry told the Dáil, 'and now they are on the crows.'

'What about rats?' Captain P. Giles of Fine Gael asked.

'That may happen before this war is over, and I for one will not cry,' Corry replied.[23]

In the circumstances Gray could not understand London's reluctance to adopt more stringent economic measures against Ireland, but his condemnation of the beer-wheat deal finally prompted the British to confide in him about the secret cooperation. He was genuinely surprised. On 23 March 1942 he informed the State Department 'that a mutual good feeling and confidence have been established between the Irish and British Military chiefs beyond what might reasonably have been believed possible'. [24]

With the aid of Colonel John Reynolds, the American Military Attaché, Gray prepared an extensive report on the Irish military situation. He allowed Irish authorities to study the document, which put a great deal of emphasis on the danger of a German attack, as well as the importance of helping the Dublin government to maintain the morale of the Irish Army. 'The concession of such armament to the Irish Army as may be available,' he wrote, 'is the most practical way of attaining this end.' The report was written partly 'for Irish consumption', Gray explained in covering letters to Roosevelt and Hull. He was only asking for 'token' concessions. The proposal was 'purely a political gesture for political ends'.[25]

When there was no word from Washington by 20 April 1942, de Valera wrote to Roosevelt. His letter was ostensibly to thank the President for the assurance that American troops would not invade Ireland, but it was obviously intended to highlight the armament situation. Stressing the need for weapons, the Taoiseach wrote there were 250,000 Irishmen prepared to defend their country, if they could only get the necessary arms.

Roosevelt was unmoved. He decided to ignore the letter. In a memorandum to Under Secretary of State Sumner Welles, the President complained about de Valera:

> If he would only come out of the clouds and quit talking about the quarter of a million Irishmen ready to fight if they had the weapons, we would all have a higher regard for him. Personally I do not believe there are more than one thousand trained soldiers in the whole of the Free State. Even they are probably efficient only in the use of rifles and shotguns.[26]

Allied internees visiting Dublin were meeting servicemen on leave from the North, who told them stories of airmen being spirited across the border. In the first nine months of 1942 twenty-six belligerent aircraft crashed or landed on Irish territory. Only four of those were German and all eight of their survivors were interned, while the forty-five airmen who survived twenty RAF crashes and landings were promptly freed. Any doubts the internees may have had about such stories were dispelled in the early hours of 25 April 1942 when Pilot Office Donald N. Kennedy of the RAF was taken to K Lines after he came down near Arklow. Within hours, however, he was picked up at the camp by British Air Attaché Malcolm Begg, and driven to the border. Begg advised that RAF air crews flying near Ireland should be told to say, if they came down in Éire, that they were 'engaged in air-sea rescue operations in response to an SOS from an unidentified aircraft believed to be German'.[27] The Allied internees therefore concluded they were really little more than window-dressing to placate the Germans next door.

After the Germans invaded Crete, Gray again became concerned about the danger of a German invasion of Ireland, and his uneasiness was intensified by reports of the activities of Hempel and Henning Thomsen, the secretary of the German Legation in Dublin. They had been meeting with prominent Republicans like Dan Breen and Tom Barry, two of the more famous names from the War of Independence. On 8 May 1942 Gray wrote to Roosevelt:

> Certain information has come to me which suggests or might suggest that the Germans mean to move in here next month. The German Minister has been in Cork where he entertained twice a former gunman and IRA leader, Tom Barry, and another well-known pro-German, Seamus Fitzgerald, a port commissioner who has just been fired by the Government.
>
> In Dublin, Thomsen, the Secretary of the Legation, has been entertaining at the Gresham Hotel Dan Breen, a former IRA gunman and present deputy from Galway, known to be pro-German and suspected of being on the German payroll. He also gave a party in a private room for some members of the Italian Legation and several pro-Axis Irishmen. They had a lot to drink, and late in the evening began to say: 'Let us drink tonight. Next month it will not be so happy.'[28]

The actions of the German diplomats may have been designed as a veiled threat to keep the Irish government from making too many concessions to the Allies. When Hempel asked how he would react to a British or German invasion of Ireland, Tom Barry said the Irish would resist any invasion by either country. Hempel impressed him as a 'real friend of Ireland', Barry wrote. 'It was clear to me then that the greatest danger of invasion came from the USA, urged on by the scoundrel, Gray.'[29]

The American Minister did indeed pose a threat to Irish neutrality at the time. Even though he looked on de Valera as a 'malign genius' who was 'blind to handwriting on walls and deaf to the rumbling of approaching catastrophe', Gray still thought the Taoiseach could be pressurised into co-operating with the Allies. He had 'bowed to events in the past and probably will again', Gray wrote to Churchill on 11 May 1942.[30] Believing that the overwhelming majority of Irish people wished to stay out of the war due to an 'undue fear of an air attack', Gray suggested an impressive American air display might be sufficient to frighten the Irish into giving up the ports to the Allies.[31]

'I have never seen any people so desperately afraid of being bombed,' wrote Colonel Jack Reynolds, the American Military Attaché. 'I am quite sure if an election were being held tomorrow on the issue of neutrality, 90% of the Irish people would support de Valera's policy.'[32]

Following James Dillon's resignation from Fine Gael in February, Gray abandoned any hope of dividing the Dáil. He wrote to Roosevelt on 20 May 1942:

He has lost the advantage of an organised party following and Cosgrave has been jockeyed by de Valera into a position of impotent assent to de Valera's foreign policy.

I think, therefore, that the *fait accompli* procedure would be best, accompanied by simultaneous publication of our demands and of their justification to the Irish people. Probably a great flight of planes dropping leaflets would be the best way of doing this at about the time that the demands were presented to de Valera.

At the same time, ships, small ones, would move into the ports and land troops, or not, according to conditions. If Mr de Valera refused to accept the situation and ordered his troops to fire, I think a few well-placed bombs on the Irish barracks at the Curragh and in the Dublin area would be the most merciful way of shutting off opposition.

I feel pretty sure that you would decide that de Valera ought to be kept in power and everything possible done to support his government. If he refused to go on and went to the hills, as Aiken would probably advise him to do, then the Cosgrave people should be invited to form a government.

If they refused I would ask General [Michael J.] Costello, commanding the southern area, to take over as a temporary measure to preserve public order with the civil service. If he also refused, I would put an American general into Dublin in charge till an Irish government could be formed.[33]

Chapter 20 ◡

| FDR'S COLD SHOULDER

The Irish censor was blocking Allied propaganda, and G2 reported that James Dillon had discussed the recent issue of *The Nation* with Gray on the telephone. 'It is the most strikingly effective thing I have read,' Dillon told him.[1] If the Allies invaded, they would hardly have time to conduct propaganda, so Gray suggested steps be taken as soon as possible. He was therefore anxious that articles like those that appeared in *The Nation* should be re-issued in Ireland. 'If we get a big propaganda shop going here,' he wrote to the President, 'it might very likely prepare things.'[2]

There was little chance of propagating the American viewpoint through ordinary Irish channels, because Frank Aiken would 'make any propaganda job here a difficult one as he is about as friendly as a disappointed rattlesnake', Gray wrote.[3] He thought Aiken was undermining the influence of the two or possibly three members of the Irish cabinet who 'would like to come in on our side, and I believe would strongly oppose firing on us if we sailed into the ports'. Aiken 'keeps crowding Dev to the left whenever he wavers'. Of course, he added, the decision on whether or not the Irish would resist an American invasion 'would be one man's—that is Dev's'.[4]

The Taoiseach was already worried about American propaganda. He complained about excessive publicity being given to the completion of the American base in Derry, fearing it was designed to provoke a German attack on Northern Ireland without regard to 'the lives of Irish non-combatants'. On 6 July 1942 Gray found him 'in a sour, discouraged mood, evidently labouring under some acute apprehension of hostile conspiracy'.[5]

After assuring him that the United States was not trying to provoke a German attack, Gray raised the issue of talks arranged between Major General Hartle, the Commander of US forces in Northern Ireland, and Lieutenant General Daniel McKenna, Chief of Staff of the Irish Army, even though he knew de Valera did not wish to discuss the matter or even acknowledge officially that he was aware of the talks. 'I did not wish,' Gray wrote, 'ever to give Mr de Valera the opportunity to disavow all knowledge of the liaison and

De Valera with members of Irish diplomatic service. (*Front*) John W. Dulanty (High Commissioner in Britain), Joseph P. Walshe (Secretary of the Department of Foreign Affairs), Eamon de Valera, Robert Brennan (Minister to the USA), and T.J. Kiernan (Minister to the Vatican). (*Back*) John J. Hearne (High Commissioner to Canada), Frank Gallagher (Editor of the *Irish Press*), F.H. Boland (Assistant Secretary of the Department of Foreign Affairs), Michael MacWhite (Minister to Italy), Sean Murphy (Minister to France), Leo Kearney (Minister to Spain), and Michael Rynne (Legal Advisor, Department of External Affairs).

Survivors from the *Athenia* landing in Galway after their passenger liner was sunk on the day Britain declared war. (*Getty*)

One of the look-out posts which were built around the Irish coast. Each was numbered and the 'Éire' sign was to warn military aircraft that they were flying over neutral territory. (*Irish Military Archives*)

Éire prepares: Ford Mk vi armoured cars in Ireland preparing for possible attack. (*Getty*)

Rifle practice: infantryman on manoeuvres. (*Getty*)

Machine-gun practice. (*Getty*)

18 November 1940. The Garda, the Irish police force, on parade with their gas masks and helmets. (*Getty*)

One of the country's few searchlights. (*Irish Military Archives*)

German war aircraft crash-landed in County Waterford on 1 April 1941, after it was attacked by British forces over the Welsh coast. (*Irish Military Archives*)

Anti-aircraft defences in Dublin. (*Irish Military Archives*)

President Franklin D. Roosevelt proudly announces America joining the war. (*Topfoto*)

Eamon de Valera and David Gray, US Minister to Ireland, 1940–47. (*Getty*)

Sir John Maffey, British representative to Ireland, 1940–47. (*Getty*)

De Valera inspecting the guard of honour outside the GPO in O'Connell Street, Dublin, 1 June 1940. (*Getty*)

Col. Dan Bryan who became head of G2, Irish Military Intelligence, during the Emergency. (*Irish Military Archives: Mark Hull, J. Carolle Carter and Michael Kennedy*)

The Dublin bombing. Workers clearing up bomb damage on 3 June 1941, following the German bombing of Dublin. (*Getty*)

30 October 1941, Manhattan, New York. Speakers at the America First rally in Madison Square Garden, pictured on the rostrum. (*Left to right*) Senator Gerald Nye, Senator Burton K. Wheeler, Charles A. Lindbergh, and John Cudahy, former United States Minister to Éire. (*Corbis / Bettmann*)

General William J. Donovan decorating Colonel David K. Bruce, head of the oss in the European Theatre of Operations.

Some Allied internees in their bar at κ Lines internment camp. (*Left to right*) Flying Officer (fo) Charles Brady of Toronto, Canada; Sgt Roswell Tees of Niagara Falls, Ontario, Canada; Sgt Victor Jefferson of Belfast; fo Aubrey R. Covington of Kingston-on-Thames, Surrey; Sub. Lt Bruce N. Girdlestone of Wellington, New Zealand; Sgt Stanislaus Karniewski of Poland; Fl. Lt Leslie Ward of Vancouver, Canada; and Pilot Officer (po) Roland 'Bud' Wolfe of Ceresco, Nebraska. (*Photograph courtesy of Bruce Girdlestone*)

Allied internees from κ Lines at the marriage of Sgt Ros Tees to Eileen Lewis of Newbridge, 14 September 1943. (*Back row, left to right*) Sgt Stanislaus Karniewski, Sgt James Holloway, Sgt Robert Harkell, Sgt David Sutherland, Sgt Victor Jefferson, Sgt Eric Ross, Sgt Duncan Fowler, Sgt Norman Todd, ғо John Shaw, Sgt William Ricketts, Sgt David Reid, Sgt Frank Thomas, Sgt William Barnett, Sgt George Slator, Sgt James Wakelin, Sgt Leslie Diaper. (*Front row, left to right*) Sgt James Masterson, ᴘᴏ Roland Wolfe, Sub. Lt Bruce N. Girdlestone, Sgt Frederick W. Tisdall, Sgt Ros Tees, Eileen Lewis Tees, Fl. Lt Leslie Ward, ғо Charles Brady, ғо Denys Welply; ᴘᴏ David Midgeley, ᴘᴏ Aubrey R. Covington. (*Photograph courtesy of Roswell Tees*)

Ervin R. Marlin was sent to Ireland as an oss spy in September 1942. (*Photograph courtesy of John Tepper Marlin*)

Martin S. Quigley arrived in Ireland as an OSS spy in May 1943.

Carter Nicholas, head of the Éire Desk at OSS headquarters, visited Ireland on a secret mission in September 1943.

Allen W. Dulles was given German documents which gave the mistaken impression of a serious security leak in Dublin. Aspects of those documents were misinformation planted and forwarded by the British. (*Getty*)

charge me, and possibly also Sir John Maffey, with tampering with his General Staff without his knowledge.'[6] Gray's distrust was such that he had no confidence of goodwill even in cooperation.

The possibility of trouble in Northern Ireland surfaced in a serious way in August 1942, when six IRA gunmen were sentenced to death for the murder of a policeman. 'Hanging six for one would shock public opinion,' Gray warned the State Department.[7] As the danger of sectarian violence was of direct concern to the United States with its troops stationed in the area, Winant expressed concern to the British, while Maffey made strong representations at de Valera's behest. He noted the Taoiseach was 'not moved so much by sentiment as by practical considerations'.[8]

The sentences of five of the six men were commuted. (One of those reprieved was Joe Cahill, who became a leader of the Provisional IRA during the late 1960s and early 1970s.) The execution of the other man, Thomas J. Williams, on 2 September 1942 gave rise to a wave of anti-British demonstrations throughout the island and sporadic violence, including the stoning of cars carrying American troops in Belfast. The British flag was burned during a demonstration in O'Connell Street, Dublin. The British took the burning in their stride. 'Of course, if they did this to the American flag,' Gray wrote to Roosevelt, 'I should have a formal apology before night or leave the country. But the English have lost all sense of touch about Ireland. They are strong at the wrong time.'[9]

In the midst of the unrest over the execution of Williams, Joseph Cardinal MacRory denounced Britain and the United States for occupying the Six Counties: 'When I read, day after day, in the press that this war is being fought for the rights and liberties of small nations, and then think of my own corner of my country overrun by British and United States soldiers against the will of the nation, I confess I sometimes find it exceedingly hard to be patient.'[10]

Gray protested to MacRory that his remarks played 'directly into the hands of the IRA and might reasonably be expected to incite the murder of American troops in Northern Ireland.' The Irish reaction to the arrival of the American troops had shocked and pained the American people, he explained. 'And now your utterance, which indicates that you regard us in effect as invaders, I feel will intensify the unhappy impression made by Mr de Valera's protest.' Gray continued:

Some Americans understand that Mr de Valera in protesting the arrival of American troops may have wished to emphasise his claim to sovereignty over the Six Counties, but they ask why he protested American troops coming as friends for the protection of Ireland, and did not protest German bombers coming to bomb Belfast and kill Irish nationals. They feel that his attitude has been more friendly to Germany, from whom he obtains nothing but bombs, than to Americans and their Allies from whom he receives what is needful to maintain Irish economy.

The Allies had been generous to Ireland, but this was not appreciated, Gray complained. Faced with such ingratitude, he predicted American resentment 'will last for generations and be inscribed in history, unless we can find some means of arresting this tide of tragic misunderstanding'. There was a danger some misguided members of the IRA might take the cardinal's words as encouragement 'to drive the invader' from Irish soil. 'If murder follows,' Gray wrote, 'the consequences to Irish-American friendship will not be pleasant.' He therefore asked for a meeting with the Cardinal to discuss the situation.[11]

Although the German Minister had privately described Cardinal MacRory as a bitter enemy of the British Commonwealth, Gray had an amicable meeting with MacRory at the Gresham Hotel, Dublin, on 16 October 1942. He 'was most grateful for the friendly tone of my protest for apparently he is used to having bricks and dead cats thrown at him', Gray wrote. 'He is really a dear old man with an understandable obsession about the wrong of partition. The war means little to him as long as "the Nation which God made is divided by man". I told him he must not be naughty and rock the boat while the war was on. He said my letter was a fine letter and presented the arguments on my side very strongly, but that it had not changed his mind one bit.'[12]

Irish people knew he never encouraged violence, the Cardinal argued, so it was his 'firm conviction that not a hair of the head of any American soldier will be injured on account of anything I have said.' Partition was 'about the greatest possible violation of a nation's rights', the cardinal contended. 'The United States has virtually condoned partition by sending armed forces into the Six Counties without the nation's consent.' The presence of Allied forces was 'bound to make that part of Ireland a cockpit; and may well lead to [a] German invasion of Southern Ireland, thus making a cockpit of an entire country that ardently desires to remain out of the war', he added. 'Has Great Britain or the United States for selfish reasons any right before God to involve a helpless nation in such a calamity?'[13]

'I didn't ask him for any promises,' Gray reported, 'but he made me feel that he was really friendly and perhaps a bit apprehensive and would not make trouble in future.'[14] Gray knew the Dublin government had no control over the Cardinal. Seán T. O'Kelly had actually asked him a year earlier to speak to MacRory about the necessity of playing down partition during the war. However, Gray felt the government effectively sanctioned the Cardinal's remarks by not censoring them.

The censor had earlier blocked the *Irish Press* and *Irish Times* from reporting that *Osservatore Romano*, the Vatican newspaper, had denied rumours of Papal support for the Axis powers. The censor had prevented the publication of those rumours in the first place, so it was logical to suppress the denial. The censor also stopped the *Irish Independent* from reporting the Lenten pastoral of Bishop Morrisroe of Achonry, who criticised Germany's 'godless plans' and asked whether Catholics could 'view with easy minds the possibility of a victory which would give brute force the power to control Europe and decide the fate of small nations'.[15] Since those remarks had been censored, Gray protested to de Valera: 'Observing one policy towards publication of sentiments inimical to the Axis Powers and another toward publication of sentiments inimical to the United States, is scarcely observing the benevolent neutrality which Your Excellency proclaimed upon our entry into the war.'[16]

'The nucleus of anti-American and anti-British influence in Éire is the censorship group controlled by Frank Aiken,' Gray reported.[17] He actually complained to the Minister for Local Government, Seán MacEntee, who was a Northern Catholic. Gray wrote to Roosevelt:

> I told him frankly that I thought the Aiken group running the censorship and playing up anti-American sentiment were getting the country into danger if it were dangerous to loose American friendship. I gave him a copy of my letter to Cardinal MacRory ... To my surprise he asked me why I did not circularise the Government with the letter. I told him I had got it before de Valera in a note of complaint about censorship for anti-American discrimination but did not care to go farther though I would give him copies to distribute. He then named the cabinet members for whom he wanted copies. He left out Aiken and Little (Posts and Telegraphs). This confirmed my suspicion that a majority of the cabinet are against Aiken but are unable to move Dev away from him and are glad when we do anything to indicate to Dev that he is on a dangerous course. The key to Dev's attitude was disclosed when he told me that he could not stop the publication of reports of agitation for the reprieve of IRA boys who killed an Ulster policeman, reports which were helping to build up anti-American feeling, and that HE WOULD NOT IF HE COULD.[18]

Gray also complained to British authorities about their failure to censor some scurrilous accusations in *The Ulster Protestant*, which contended that Roman Catholic convents were brothels and that one nun, who had been molested by a priest as a thirteen-year-old, had supposedly escaped from such a brothel in Canada. Gray had previously complained about other articles in the same journal, including one that proclaimed, 'Papists are Traitors'.[19] John Winant, the American ambassador in London, thought the *Ulster Protestant* was so offensive that German agents were behind it. The publication was never banned in the Twenty-Six Counties, because its total circulation in the area was only seventeen copies. In truth, its publishers would probably have welcomed the publicity of being banned.[20]

Aspects of Irish censorship plumbed absurd depths. Books of the country's most eminent writers were banned, including George Bernard Shaw, Seán O'Casey, Frank O'Connor, Seán O'Faoláin and James Joyce. Among American books banned were Ernest Hemingway's *For Whom the Bell Tolls* and *A Farewell to Arms*, William Faulkner's *Sanctuary*, John Steinbeck's *The Grapes of Wrath* and Sinclair Lewis' *Elmer Gantry*. The censoring mentality reached a ridiculous extreme when the records of Bing Crosby were banned from the air because the controller of Radio Éireann thought 'crooning' might harm Irish youth.[21] 'Ireland is a puritanical country with a clergy many of whom have never been away from the island and whose reading and general culture is limited,' Gray explained. 'It is honestly believed by these elements of the clergy that the Irish people must be protected from what in America seems innocent and amusing fun.'[22]

The censorship was often absurd, but de Valera thought it was necessary. 'We think that a great deal of the trouble in the world is caused by newspapers stirring up antipathies between people,' he said.[23]

'Anti-British feeling was the dynamic of Irish opinion, always there though often latent,' Maffey reported after one conversation with the Taoiseach. 'Propaganda produces counter propaganda and the mind of the younger generation, brought up in an age and atmosphere of bitter hostility to England, would respond more rapidly to propaganda directed against us.'[24]

To circumvent Irish censorship, Gray suggested an American publicity bureau be set up in Ireland. He recommended Helen Kirkpatrick should head it, but she was overlooked in favour of the American press attaché Richard Watts, a former drama critic with the *New York Herald Tribune*. Watts was working for the Office of War Information (OWI), but he was instructed to confer with Gray in publishing *Letter from America* from the United States Legation in Dublin. The first issue was published on 30 October 1942. Each week thereafter the press attaché sent out copies, free of charge, to people on a mailing list that included clergy, teachers, lawyers, government officials and anyone who requested it. The list grew from around 18,000 at first to about 30,000 by the time the last issue was published, in April 1945.

Letter from America devoted considerable space to pro-war speeches by prominent Irish-Americans and accounts of heroism of both Irishmen and Irish-Americans serving in the Allied forces, such as Captain Colin P. Kelly, who was considered the first American hero of the war. He stayed at the controls of his stricken bomber until his crew had time to escape. The aircraft then blew up with him on board. He was actually mistakenly credited with crashing his plane into the Japanese battleship *Haruna*, thereby supposedly becoming the first suicide pilot of the war. The newsletter also celebrated Lieutenant Edward 'Butch' O'Hare, who became the first American ace and the first pilot to be awarded the Congressional Medal of Honour during World War II. In a fighter he shot down five Japanese bombers in an engagement on 20 February 1942. He was later killed in the war, and O'Hare Airport in Chicago was named after him. Charles E. Kelly won the first Congressional Medal of Honour in the Italian campaign at Salerno. There was also the tragic story of the Fighting Sullivans—the five sons of Thomas F. Sullivan of Waterloo, Iowa. They all perished when their ship, uss *Juneau*, was sunk off the Solomon Islands. *Letter from America* also reported the story of a British war hero, Lance Corporal John Patrick Kenneally of the Irish Guards. He was awarded the Victoria Cross for gallantry in North Africa, of which there will be more shortly. In an amazing piece of undiplomatic candour, Gray wrote to Richard Hayes, who was a cryptologist for Irish military intelligence as well as Director of the National Library of Ireland, that *Letter from America* was designed to 'tell the Irish people what their censorship did not want them to know'.[25] It included frequent articles about Nazi tyranny, including gruesome pictures of the opening of the concentration camp at Lublin, Poland.

Although Aiken was the minister responsible for wartime censorship, Belfast-born Joe Connolly oversaw the civil servants who implemented it. Connolly's duties should not have been of any concern to Gray, but this did not stop Gray interfering. 'Our neutrality outraged all his sentiments and I think nothing would have pleased him more than to see us dragged into the conflict,' Connolly wrote in his memoirs.[26]

One clandestine British operation came unstuck following a mass escape attempt from K Lines on 17 August 1942. Nine men escaped from the camp. Three made it to Northern Ireland—Canadians Flight Lieutenant J. Grant Fleming of Calgary and Pilot Officer Ralph Keefer of Montreal, along with Sergeant Vic Newport of Bristol. Sub Lieutenant Bruce Girdlestone from Wellington, New Zealand, managed to stay at large for five days before he was caught. He was being aided by Irish members of an Escape Club, set up in conjunction with MI9, the British escape organisation; G2 had been aware of its existence after its members helped six men to escape in June 1941. Members of the Escape Club were put under surveillance following the latest escape. As petrol was heavily rationed at the time, doctors and priests were essentially the only private citizens with motorcars. Hugh Wilson, an Irish doctor, set out to drive Girdlestone to the border along with a friend, Dicky Ruttledge, but they quickly realised they were being followed. Girdlestone managed to escape on foot during a car chase through some Dublin slums, but he was caught the following day in the centre of Dublin.

Wilson and Ruttledge were arrested and charged with helping Girdlestone. Maffey was instructed to intercede with de Valera on their behalf. Although he had no connection with the Escape Club, Maffey told the Taoiseach it would be difficult for him 'to maintain an attitude of "complete disinterestedness" regarding these individuals, as they had been led into the mess as tools of a British organisation'.

Maffey was afraid of the implications if the details of the group became public. 'I gather that the ramifications of the plot are wide and deep,' he reported. He therefore tried to play down the arrests. De Valera was under pressure from the Irish security forces, which resented the attitude of some members of the Escape Club. They talked recklessly about having 'nothing to fear' because Maffey 'would have supplies cut off from Éire if a finger were laid upon them'.

Maffey tried to persuade de Valera to quash the case against Wilson and Ruttledge because they had merely become involved 'in a sporting spirit' at the behest of the British. 'In the assistance rendered to the internees there was nothing sinister, nothing un-Irish, not even necessarily anything pro-British,' Maffey argued. 'The matter wanted looking at from a human angle rather than from the political angle. Enough had surely been done to produce the deterrent effect which was required.'

Late that afternoon an RAF Spitfire landed near Oulart, County Waterford, and de Valera ordered the internment of the pilot, a Pole, Jan Zimek, who had been on a mission to intercept some German aircraft over the Irish Sea. 'Walshe asked me not to oppose a decision which was Mr de Valera's personal decision in the light of difficulties confronting him as a result of the Wilson case and also increased IRA activities,' Maffey reported.

Wilson was fined £300 and sentenced to two years in jail, but the sentence was suspended pending his future good behaviour, while Ruttledge jumped bail and fled the jurisdiction. Maffey's office paid Wilson's fine, and the whole thing was quietly forgotten.

Gray frequently acted on his own initiative without getting State Department approval, but he did report fully on his actions in personal letters to Roosevelt. He did not even confine his hardline views to Irish affairs. He was, for instance, bitterly critical of Roosevelt's 'isolationist' opponents, especially those in Irish-American circles. 'These isolationist bastards are still trying to crucify you,' Gray wrote to the President on 16 September 1942. 'Take a leaf out of Dev's book and start a good big concentration camp at Chi[cago] with an annex in S[outh] Boston.' Gray felt those Irish-Americans were acting unpatriotically because they were bolstering the Taoiseach's determination to withstand Allied pressure to adopt more cooperative policies:

> I am more and more convinced that Mr de Valera is stiffened in his policies by the reports that he gets from Boston. Why isn't it about time to open on the Irish racketeer and smoke him out of business. You have proved that nobody can deliver the Irish vote so why let these blackmailers continue to do business. ... Over here the IRA racketeers go to jail. Why should they be allowed to hamper our war effort in America?[27]

Gray was confident in acting on his own initiative because there had never been a word of reproach from the White House. In fact, the same day that he was writing his latest letter to the White House, the President was writing that many people had commented on 'what a perfectly magnificent job' Gray was doing in Ireland. 'I did not have to be told that because I knew it,' Roosevelt wrote, 'for the very simple fact that you have not given me the remote shadow of a headache all these years.'[28]

Roosevelt's policy was essentially to ignore Ireland and to advise prominent Americans to avoid the country. 'I am inclined to think that my policy of giving Dev the absent treatment is about as effective as anything else,' Roosevelt explained. 'The other day one of his friends over here—a typical professional Irish-American—came in to tell me about the terrible starvation among the people of Ireland. I looked at him in a much interested way and remarked quietly, "Where is Ireland?"'[29]

'I do wish', Roosevelt continued, 'the people as a whole over there could realise that Dev is unnecessarily storing up trouble because most people over here feel that Dublin, by maintaining German spies and making all the little things difficult for the United Nations, is stirring up a thoroughly unsympathetic attitude towards Ireland as a whole when we win the war. That is a truly sad state of affairs.'

'While you remain aloof in the recesses of the W[hite] H[ouse],' Gray advised Roosevelt, 'it might be a good thing to have the American press come out with the plain facts about Ireland.' Otherwise, he felt, de Valera might escape the deserved consequences of his policy after the war. 'At that, Dev may get away with it,' Gray wrote.[30] During the following weeks and months the American Minister became virtually obsessed with the need to dramatise what he believed was de Valera's unhelpful attitude.

By contrast with the 'absent treatment' method of the Americans, John Betjeman, the British press attaché, was bringing over famous British people to Ireland to promote better relations. The Ministry of Information concluded this tactic had 'clearly been justified by the results'.[31]

With the approach of winter in 1942, there was a marked increase in the number of American planes getting lost over Ireland. Gray feared some American airmen would inevitably be interned. 'This luck cannot last,' he warned the State Department. He therefore suggested the Irish be asked to agree to some kind of formula to release American pilots. 'While the right to intern cannot well be questioned,' he wrote, 'it would be unfortunate to accept internment without protest.' He advocated retaliating in the form of an embargo on coal, petrol, steel, wheat, and chemical supplies to Ireland. 'I know inside me that this is simple justice,' he wrote to Roosevelt, 'but I haven't the ability to frame the formula that you can, which will cover the case.'

Gray was instructed to discuss matters with American officials in London. Ambassador John Winant thought it might be best to leave well enough alone. 'Why not let sleeping dogs lie?' Winant asked. But Major General Hartle 'could see no objection' to exploring the question with Irish authorities. 'A somewhat stronger line taken by us', he argued, 'would tend to induce more favourable action toward the British.'

While in London, Gray had lunch at 10 Downing Street with Churchill and the Free French leader General Charles de Gaulle, who joked about Gray being 'Ambassador to Mr de Valera'.[32] Churchill, for his part, seemed content to forget about Ireland. 'At great disadvantage we have conducted the war at sea without Irish bases which would have been so valuable to us and I believe now we can win the war without the help of Mr de Valera's Éire,' Churchill said.

This was the first time any senior Allied figure told Gray that Irish bases were not needed and it opened the avenue for a whole new approach towards Dublin. In the past he had believed it was necessary to keep as many friends as possible in Ireland, in case Irish bases had to be seized. 'As you know, I have always had to contemplate the possibility of a necessary intervention,' Gray wrote to Roosevelt. 'Now we can study a policy with that factor left out.' The Allies no longer needed Irish help, so the Irish could be told to go and fend for themselves.

'I said in my view,' Gray reported, 'both the British and American Governments should accept the Irish claim to separatist independence, but should then say, in effect, "Supply and protect yourself," as any independent state is supposed to do. I said that this was the only antidote that I could see to the decade of de Valera's preaching to Irish youth that Éire was essentially self-sufficient and self-reliant.' In short, Gray told Churchill and de Gaulle that self-government, with all its difficulties and responsibilities, should be imposed on the Irish. 'It may appear reckless, but it is not,' Gray wrote to Roosevelt. 'You must crowd Dev mercilessly when you have a grievance and prevent him choosing his own line and issue.'[33]

'I like your thought that Ireland must have self-government imposed upon it—with all the responsibilities that that implies,' the President replied. 'With all the responsibilities they will realise they cannot exist alone in the world—and, at the same time, they must be told that because of their geographical situation they will never be permitted to allow any other nation to use them in a military way or otherwise against the United States or Britain.'[34]

'It seems to me that during all these years it has been a pity that Ireland has lived in a dream under the rule of a dreamer,' Roosevelt continued. 'They do not know the facts of life and it will take a rude awakening to teach them.' He left little doubt about his intention to ensure the Irish were awakened out of their dream. 'If and when we clean up Germany,' he wrote, 'I think that Churchill and I can do much for Ireland and its future—and I think that he and I can agree on the method with due consideration of firmness and justice.'[35]

The State Department instructed Gray to approach the Irish informally about possible American landings. 'American planes which may come down in Ireland', the State Department contended, 'will ordinarily be on training or transit flights and not at the time engaged in any hostile activity nor any hostile mission.' The same could not be said of German flights. 'In view of distances from Germany and German occupied areas,' Secretary of State Hull continued, 'it cannot even remotely be supposed that such German planes have lost their way on peaceful flights.'

On 30 November 1942 Gray asked Joe Walshe if the Dublin government would 'recognise, in principle, the distinction between such non-combatant transport or training flights and flights which were manifestly combatant'. Walshe replied that the government was ready 'to recognise this distinction and suggested the terms operation and non-operational as better expressing the nature of the two classes of flights'.

'Walshe's attitude was extremely friendly and cooperative,' according to Gray. He agreed to Gray's suggestion to formalise an understanding, with an exchange of diplomatic notes, that would be kept secret. All German planes that came down in Ireland would be considered to have been on operational flights, but Walshe said he would have to consult with de Valera about Gray's request that any American planes that landed while on operational missions should be treated like stricken surface vessels and given 24 hours to make repairs and fly away.

After consulting de Valera, Walshe informed Gray it might be best to leave well enough alone on the understanding the Irish government would adopt the friendliest attitude possible towards the Allies. 'In practice,' he wrote, 'our attitude of friendly neutrality towards the United Nations results normally—in so far as aircraft and their crews are concerned—in the internment of only such crews as are on operational flight. After full consideration of the matter, I am inclined to think that the existing relatively satisfactory situation should be left as it is. New and formal regulations or agreements are more likely to create difficulties than lessen them.'

'I am as much concerned as you are over the necessity of keeping the friendly cooperation of the Irish government as little discussed as possible at present, and that is one of the reasons for my concern over the possibility of Americans being interned on the Curragh,' Gray wrote to Walshe on 22 December. He accepted that Dublin intended to implement as favourable a policy as possible. 'I appreciate deeply not only your cooperative goodwill towards both our Allies and ourselves in this matter but also the difficulties which confront you,' Gray wrote. He was confidently assured by the State Department that American pilots who landed in the Twenty-six Counties would not be interned if they declared they were on non-operational flights.[36]

The Irish agreed to apply the same formula to British and Canadian airmen. According to Winston Churchill's son, Randolph, the 'non-operational' argument was merely a 'convenient fiction' to help the Allies while still preserving the appearance of neutrality.[37]

Gray thanked de Valera personally on 23 December for accepting the non-operational principle.

'It was very difficult to work out a rule which would give neither side an advantage,' de Valera replied.

'But', exclaimed Gray, 'we want an advantage, a great advantage which we think we deserve.'

'Naturally you do,' de Valera laughed.

Whatever gratitude Gray felt vanished almost immediately. The Taoiseach's talk about giving neither side an advantage irritated Gray so much that he felt he should seek another meeting to demand an explanation. Gray wrote to Roosevelt:

> I would enumerate all that he gets from us and from our ally, the things that keep his country going and ask whether he feels no obligation to accord us a different treatment from that which he gives Germany from whom he gets nothing but bombs. I would suggest that it makes no difference to us for we are winning the war without his help but that if he believes in the moral law as I do, failure to meet his moral obligations, he must recognise as a dangerous course, for the moral law never forgets or forgives. In this case the Truth ultimately will be disseminated and will lose him the support of American opinion if he has not already lost it.[38]

Chapter 21 ∿

OSS AGENTS IN IRELAND

WHEN President Roosevelt referred to the Irish 'maintaining German spies' in his letter to Gray of 16 September 1942, he was apparently referring to the staff of the German Legation. In time it would become apparent that this view of what was happening in Ireland was grossly distorted.

The newly formed Office of Strategic Services (OSS), the wartime forerunner of the Central Intelligence Agency (CIA), was divided into five branches. Secret Intelligence (SI) was charged with procuring information by clandestine means and was the largest and most important branch, as well as the first to establish an 'Éire Desk'. Research and Analysis (R&A) consisted mainly of academic experts, who interpreted and analysed reports from SI agents, and it, too, set up an 'Éire Desk'. Counterintelligence (CE), which was later called X-2, was the branch that, in effect, spied on spies; it did not establish an 'Éire Desk' until comparatively late in the war, when it stationed its first agent in Dublin. The other two branches—Secret Operations (SO), which dealt with dropping agents behind enemy lines, and Morale Operations (MO), which engaged in black propaganda—had no involvement with Ireland.

The SI branch quickly recruited three agents. General William J. Donovan, the Director of the OSS, initially recommended sending the Hollywood actor Errol Flynn to Ireland to drum up support for the war effort. Flynn had volunteered for the mission. Although he was Australian, his father, Professor T. Thomson Flynn, had been Dean of the Faculty of Science at Queen's University, Belfast, before emigrating to Australia. Donovan suggested to Roosevelt that Flynn should be sent to Ireland in uniform.[1] Nothing came of the idea, however, because Flynn's loyalty was suspect due to earlier Fascist contacts.

Roland Blenner-Hassett was possibly chosen to investigate Patterson's alarmist report about happenings in the Tralee area. A native of Tralee, Blenner-Hassett had emigrated to the United States during the Troubles of the 1920s when one of his sisters, Julie Hassett, was active in the Republican movement. He still had relatives in Ireland, among them his sister and the popular comedian Jack Cruise, who was a first cousin on his mother's side. While in the United States, Blenner-Hassett obtained a doctorate in philology.

The other agent selected was Ervin Ross Marlin, who was better known by his nickname, 'Spike'. Code-named Hurst, he was selected as agent-in-charge. Born Irving Hirsch into a poor Jewish family in New York City in 1909, he became a Protestant and formally changed his name to Ervin Ross Marlin in 1928. He had been attending Hamilton College in Clinton, New York, but became disillusioned with the discrimination and snobbery within the college. He heard about Trinity College Dublin, and worked his passage to Ireland and enrolled there in 1929. He took a degree in history and political science over the next three years. While living at the college his roommate was a Dutch student, Willem von Stokum. Marlin married Willem's sister, Hilda, who was a student at Dublin School of Art. Their father was a naval officer and their mother was the daughter of a prominent Dutch newspaper editor and publisher, Charles Boissevain, and his Irish wife, the former Emily MacDonnell. Emily was the daughter of a Dundalk lawyer and the granddaughter of Richard MacDonald, who was Provost of Trinity College Dublin. The von Stokum children spent time in Ireland growing up.

After graduating from Trinity College, Marlin returned to the United States with his wife in 1934 and helped to establish the Social Security System. Later both he and Hilda were active in the Washington chapter of CAID. As a result he was headhunted to serve as an OSS agent in Ireland under the cover of a Special Assistant on economic matters to Gray. Before going to Dublin, Marlin trawled through available government documents on Ireland. Ray Atherton, head of the Western European Division of the State Department, suggested Marlin was wasting his time examining the State Department files. 'After two weeks in Dublin you will now just as much or more than you would from a study of our files,' Atherton told him.[2] There was some interesting material on Ireland prepared by MI6 in the OSS files, but this did not include any recent reports, despite requests for updates.[3] There were eleven organisations collecting information, either trying to influence Irish-American opinion or planning to do so, but Marlin found there was no proper co-ordination between them, and the Office of War Information had as yet done nothing in relation to the attitude of Irish-Americans.

Initially it was planned that the other two agents would serve under Marlin, but this idea was scrapped before they went overseas because Marlin and Blenner-Hassett could not get along with each other due 'to certain incompatibilities of temperaments'.[4]

'My instructions', Marlin later wrote, 'were to study the problems of economic self-sufficiency and other specific aspects of the Irish scene, to collect information on matters as directed by the Minister and in general to make myself useful to the Legation.'[5] He considered his task fairly innocuous, because he did not know Gray had been advocating economic sanctions to force Dublin to hand over bases. Hence Marlin, who liked Ireland, did not recognise the sinister undertones of his mission when he arrived in Dublin on 12 September 1942.

Blenner-Hassett arrived two weeks later, on 25 September, using the code-name 'Train'. His cover was as a fellow of the American Council for Learned Society to study Irish folklore, supposedly under James H. Delargy, Professor of Folklore at University College Dublin. Blenner-Hassett first spent five days in his native Tralee, where he stood out like the proverbial sore thumb. With his acquired British accent, he no longer really fit into the society he had left two decades earlier. While Marlin actually thought Blenner-Hassett was 'an English academic', his former colleagues in Tralee considered him a social climber who was ashamed of his humble origins, especially with the 'Blenner' prefix to his surname. It seemed he was trying to pass himself off as part of the old, wealthy Protestant gentry in the Tralee area; the Blennerhassett family owned Ballyseedy Castle, near Tralee. The fact that he also tended to be out-spokenly critical of the Catholic Church, of which he had once been a member, did little to endear him to the largely Catholic community.

One former classmate, Micheál Ó Ruirc, who was very active in the local Gaelic Athletic Association, was shocked; he categorised Blenner-Hassett as 'a frightful snob'. The spy's cover was so thin that even his sister ridiculed the idea that he would be sent to Ireland to collect folklore. 'Yeah,' she would exclaim, 'and a war on!' She all but openly described her brother as an American spy.[6]

Blenner-Hassett met two old friends who were members of the IRA. 'I made no attempt to discuss political matters with those two persons, although they, on their part, made it abundantly clear that they regarded my presence in Ireland at the present time as somewhat strange.'[7] He then moved to Dublin and got a flat in Upper Pembroke Street. He hoped to get information from three categories of people: former friends in government positions, or in the IRA, and academics he would meet under his cover. However, he was clearly looked upon with suspicion by just about everybody. Two of the people he knew growing up in Tralee had become highly influential civil servants: Maurice Moynihan, who was both Cabinet Secretary and Secretary of the Taoiseach's Office, and J.J. McElligott, the Secretary of the Department of Finance. Both men kept their distance from him.

'My telephone was tapped, all mail reaching me from points within Éire was opened and, on at least three occasions, I was absolutely sure that I was being followed,' he reported. 'Apparently this surveillance was put into operation immediately on my arrival and I think a similar procedure is adopted as a purely routine measure towards any foreigner landing in Ireland.' Even Delargy distrusted him. The professor 'was quite unable to conceal either his suspicion, or the embarrassment which my presence in Ireland caused him', Blenner-Hassett noted.[8]

While Blenner-Hassett was suspected from the outset, Marlin was exposed by the first letter he received from the United States. He had requested some literature on the Social Security System be forwarded to him, but when it was mailed from Washington it included a covering letter stating that material was being sent 'in compliance with the instruction of Mr. John Megaw of Strategic Services in this city'.[9] The Irish censor opened the letter and recognised its significance.

Even though all German spies were rounded up and jailed for the duration of the war, no effort was made to impede Marlin or arrest Blenner-Hassett. Freddy Boland of the Department of External Affairs—who had studied at Harvard and at the University of California—had a particularly friendly meeting with Blenner-Hassett. 'He is keenly aware of the necessity for preserving cordial Irish-American relations and, while I think he was under no illusion that the purpose of my presence in Ireland was wholly academic, he was, however, sufficiently intelligent politically to take the situation at its face value.'[10]

This was essentially what had happened earlier when G2 and the Garda Special Branch detected people working for MI6 in 1940 and 1941, or the Escape Club functioning in conjunction with MI9. A few of the MI6 agents were arrested in the provinces, but for the most part the Irish were content to keep British agents under surveillance. Members of the Escape Club were detected after the first successful escape from K Lines in June 1941, but no action was taken until Hugh Wilson and Dicky Ruttledge were caught trying to help Girdlestone following his escape in August 1942.

Boland arranged for Blenner-Hassett to meet Joe Walshe, but this turned into something of an ordeal. 'I was shown into Mr Walshe's office at Iveagh House one day in November, and found him seated at his desk, turning over the pages of a document which, during the course of the interview he consulted, and which was a police dossier of my movements,' Blenner-Hassett reported. Walshe accused him of being a propaganda agent for *Letter from America*, the first issue having recently been published. Blenner-Hassett had never even heard of it, but Walshe did not accept his denial. Blenner-Hassett described the ensuing scene:

At this point he became violently excited and, pounding the table with his fist, harangued me for 15 minutes, at times screaming that I was, and must be a propaganda agent. The only interpretation I can put on this somewhat curious performance is that he hoped by this violent outburst of temper, which I suppose may be regarded as a kind of 'emotional Third Degree,' to force from me some kind of explanation of my presence, other than the ostensible one.[11]

Walshe was apparently irritated by wild rumours circulating in the United States about German espionage in Ireland. On 29 October 1942, for instance, Robert Brennan protested to Sumner Welles at the State Department about a statement in the *Pocket Guide to Northern Ireland*, a booklet published by the War Department and issued to every American soldier going to Northern Ireland. It declared:

Éire's neutrality is a real danger to the Allied cause. There, just across the Irish Channel from embattled England, and not too far from your own billets in Ulster, the Axis nations maintain large legations and staffs. These Axis agents send out weather reports, find out by espionage what is going on in Ulster ... [12]

The Axis missions were under constant surveillance, and Irish authorities were sure no further radio messages had been sent since February. Welles asked if it were not true that the Axis legations were greatly oversized. Brennan denied this, as he had on numerous other occasions, and pointed out that even the London *Times* had refuted that rumour. Welles took up the issue with the War Department, but it stood over the booklet and refused to retract the offending statements.

The most absurd rumour was the supposed presence of hundreds of Japanese tourists in Ireland. Although the oss knew the story was without foundation, it was anxious to learn the exact number of Japanese people in the country, so it asked the State Department to enquire through diplomatic channels. John D. Hickerson, the head of the European Affairs Division of the State Department, later said he considered the rumour a joke when he asked Brennan for an explanation. But the Irish Minister took him seriously, or at least pretended to do so.[13]

There were only four Japanese people in the whole country: the Consul General, his wife, a vice-consul and one stranded seaman. According to Sumner Welles, the Irish Minister said his government 'was deeply irritated by the inquiry', which showed that Washington was determined to believe the Irish were 'permitting every kind of Axis subversive activity to be going on in Ireland notwithstanding the frequent and official denials on the part of the Irish government'. Although Gray had nothing to do with the rumour, Irish officials felt the State Department would never have made such a ridiculous inquiry if he had been reporting properly. Brennan therefore asked for Gray to be replaced by someone who would be 'an independent and unprejudiced witness to seek and make known the truth'.[14] Those strong sentiments provoked an equally strong response from the State Department, which rejected Brennan's request as 'offensive in the extreme'.[15] Consequently, if the Irish wished to get rid of Gray, they would have to demand his recall formally, which was out of the question at the time.

The Irish were not the only ones having problems with Gray. Marlin found it virtually impossible to work with him. As part of his cover as a Special Assistant, Marlin was supposed to help Gray and even carry out tasks assigned to him. On 21 November 1942 Marlin went to London to report on his conclusion after his first ten weeks in Ireland:

1. Éire will continue to be neutral, and any policy we undertake with regard to Éire must begin with the acceptance of this knowledge.
2. The occupation by Allied military forces of any part, or the whole, of Éire would probably result in trouble for ourselves immediately, and in the future when the war is over.
3. There is undoubtedly Axis activity in Éire. How much there is I do not know because I have only been in Dublin, and the Axis works almost exclusively outside of Dublin. I have personally observed propaganda at work among the lower classes. Swastikas being sold at pro-German jewellers and Swastikas and anti-Ally slogans being chalked up on the walls, and rumour spreaders and word-of-mouth propagandists. I am told there is much more of this down in the country, and it is my hope that I shall be able to report more substantially in the near future on this matter.
4. The Irish Government spends large sums of money in espionage and counter-espionage of German activity and other subversive elements. The British are kept informed of official operations, whereas we seem not to be, an omission that should be corrected.
5. Train's experience emphasises the difficulty of placing oss men from outside in Éire at this time and suggests the advisability of employing Irish men on the spot as agents.
6. IRA activity is at present mostly conducted in the north of Ireland, and it seems evident that a liaison with the authorities in the north would be of considerable assistance in carrying on our work in the south.'[16]

Blenner-Hassett had been ordered not to divulge his mission to anybody, so he told Gray his visit 'was of an exclusively academic nature'. Gray was therefore furious when the State Department requested him to afford Blenner-Hassett the privilege of using the diplomatic pouch. This was tantamount to admitting Blenner-Hassett was an intelligence agent. 'The anti-American group in the government is in an ugly mood and will make trouble and compromise American interests,' Gray warned. He called for 'the immediate severance of any secret service operating with the Ministry'.

'Blenner-Hassett was recognised as a spy shortly after his arrival,' the OSS was informed. 'The local Irish have excellent secret service facilities and shadow all strangers. They have developed a complete file on Marlin and Blenner-Hassett. The trail leads to the embassy and will certainly compromise us.' Gray contended the Legation 'has better sources of information than Marlin or Blenner-Hassett'. Of course, he believed his sources were better because they were telling him what he wished to hear, but he obviously had more influence with the White House. The State Department therefore requested the OSS to defer to Gray's wishes, unless it could refute them.[17]

'In retrospect,' Carter Nicholas, head of the Éire Desk of the SI Branch of the OSS, concluded that 'securing the privilege appears an error as it made Train stand out too much.'[18] Gray agreed, somewhat reluctantly, that Marlin could retain his diplomatic cover on 'the understanding that he was not to develop any underground contacts'.[19]

Marlin was authorised to buy a car and he was given coupons for 15 gallons of petrol per month. This would allow him to evaluate supposed Nazi activity outside Dublin.

He avoided overt propaganda when he gave a public lecture to the Irish Transport and General Workers' Union on the Social Security system in the United States. 'If there were any in the audience who expected war propaganda they were disappointed,' Marlin wrote. Somebody in the audience did make a snide reference to the Statue of Liberty as a 'memorial to the dead', but this provoked the ire of some of the audience. 'The opposition roused by this pointless critic did more to win us friends than anything I could have said.'[20]

While Marlin clearly appreciated the importance of playing down propaganda, Gray did not. 'I think it would be good propaganda to get American entertainers over here,' Gray had the temerity to tell Erskine H. Childers, then a junior minister in the Fianna Fáil government.[21] But that indiscretion must have seemed mild to Childers in comparison with other remarks.

Marlin was able to use his contacts within the labour movement to draw up a thorough evaluation of the Labour Party. This was the first of a series of reports. As he was working from the Legation, he had to work out an arrangement with Gray to transmit his reports, which Gray was allowed to read. But this proved problematical when Marlin submitted a report on the attitudes of members of the Irish government. He reported that Minister for Posts and Telegraphs P.J. Little was pro-German, as were, he claimed, two of the men credited with starting the war of independence, Dan Breen and Tom MacEllistrim, both serving Fianna Fáil members of the Dáil.[22]

Gray demanded the identity of Marlin's source in regard to Little. At first Marlin refused to say, but Gray insisted on being trusted if the two of them were to continue working together at the Legation. Marlin reluctantly divulged that Erskine Childers had told him, only to be confronted by Childers in a very agitated state a couple of days later. It seemed that Gray had not only complained to an Irish official that Little was pro-German but went on to commit the appalling indiscretion of citing Childers as the source of the information.[23]

In the circumstances, Marlin developed deep reservations about Gray's discretion. 'How can you conduct security matters when your nominal boss— Gray—insisted on knowing everything, including sources of information, and then informs the Minister concerned of them!' Marlin exclaimed.[24] There was a further confrontation between them when Marlin reported that an American told him us troops in the North got on better with local people— both nationalists and unionists—than with the British servicemen. 'What I said to Gray', Marlin recalled, 'was that the only trouble experienced by our troops in the North arose from fights between British and American sailors in Derry.' When Gray demanded to know who had told him this, Marlin flatly refused to disclose that it had been Colonel Reynolds, the Military Attaché. [25]

Before long Marlin realised his initial report about supposed pro-German activities outside Dublin was without foundation. Most stories about German spies in Ireland were ludicrous, he concluded.

'The whole thing was a kind of joke,' he later recalled. 'I spoke to J.P. Walshe, who told me that there were between fifty and a hundred thousand British sympathisers in Éire who were straining at the leash to report anything they heard about German spies.' Marlin never uncovered any, nor did he find any indication of the existence of any spy centres. 'I assume that Irish intelligence had the place buttoned up,' he explained. 'Once they realised it was in their interest to keep us informed, they were very good to us.'[26]

'In the ordinary course of friendly talks, in no sense official,' Walshe noted, 'Mr Marlin and I came to the conclusion that a lot of doubts and difficulties between our two countries could be effectively removed by the establishment between our security services of a free and friendly intercourse.'[27]

On 4 January 1943 Walshe approached Gray and Marlin with an offer to put security relations on a 'more official and comprehensive basis'. It was an offer to cooperate formally with the oss, as they had been doing with mi5.

Marlin wished to avail of the offer, but Gray—knowing that Roosevelt and Churchill were no longer concerned about Ireland—was unenthusiastic because he wished to be able to say the Irish had been uncooperative.

When asked, for instance, the Irish supplied 'police dossiers on IRA, for transmission to the FBI in America, where such information would be correlated with that on the activities of the IRA in America'. Blenner-Hassett believed he was wasting his time in Ireland because the Irish were ready to provide extraordinary cooperation: 'It became clear to me that my continued presence in Ireland was not only useless for the purposes for which I was sent there, but might easily prove embarrassing to members of the American Legation and Consular Staff. So long as the American Government secures all the information it desires about the activities of the IRA in Ireland, it is a matter of indifference how, or by whom, this object is achieved.'[28]

An open telegram was sent to Blenner-Hassett to report to London in person. He told people in Dublin that he had been called up for military service, and he was amused by the Irish reaction. 'For the fortnight while I was waiting for a British visa to London,' he wrote, 'I was inundated with invitations from people who were aware that I had been in Dublin for over three months.' Those people now came up with 'all kinds of various excuses as to why they had been unable to see me before then, and asking me to have lunch and dinner with them before I left. I accepted a number of those invitations, and it was quite clear that most people now accepted as true the reasons for my presence in Ireland which I had given on my arrival, and all seemed to be painfully embarrassed by the social ostracism to which they had subjected me.'[29]

Maurice Moynihan even invited him to meet de Valera on 18 January 1943. As a result of this meeting, which lasted for 90 minutes, Blenner-Hassett concluded that de Valera was labouring under a 'major misapprehension' that he could manipulate a considerable body of Irish-Americans for his own political ends. Although the spy did not try to disabuse de Valera of the notion that the Irish-Americans could be easily manipulated, he advocated that Washington should undermine the Irish leader's ability to exploit the situation.

Three days later Blenner-Hassett went to London and wrote a full report of his findings in Ireland. He concluded the IRA had been driven 'completely underground' by the policy of internment, and the executions in Ireland, Northern Ireland and Britain:

From a four-months residence in Dublin, and conversations with people in all walks of life, and of various political opinions, it is my firm conviction that the IRA is completely discredited socially, possessed of very little financial strength, and certainly in Éire completely lacks anything resembling cohesion, organisation or discipline. I do not believe that it is over-optimistic to state that the problems which the IRA offers for America, Britain, Éire and Northern Ireland is, or should be within a very short space of time, an almost negligible one in the conduct of the Allied war effort.[30]

'His information and conclusions about the IRA proved subsequently to have been very accurate,' according to Carter Nicholas.[31] Fears prompted by Patterson's report were therefore placated. 'All the parties are genuinely committed to the policy of Éire's neutrality, and in doing so reflect quite accurately the sentiments of the vast majority of the population of Éire,' Blenner-Hassett noted. 'Despite the existence of a very rigorous news, movie and radio censorship, which prevents the population of Éire from having any understanding of the true nature of Nazi-ism and Fascism, it can be said quite truthfully that the sympathies of the vast majority of the people are on the side of the Allies. This is especially true since America's entry into the war, and the turning of the tide of battle in favour of the Allies.'[32]

There was, however, a certain amount of disillusionment with economic conditions. He predicted Fianna Fáil and Fine Gael would lose seats in the next general election. Those would be picked up by the Labour Party and independents, but there was 'no real alternative' government. 'A second general election may well become necessary within a year,' he wrote.[33] All of this proved remarkably accurate.

In his report Blenner-Hassett was particularly critical of the influence of the Catholic Church, which enjoyed enormous power in Ireland. He was especially disparaging about the influence of Maynooth College on the training of the secular clergy:

Since the curriculum is largely theological and dogmatic rather than intellectual and empirical, the lack of self-enlightenment is little short of appalling… The attitude of the Church arises directly and logically from its immemorial and still very strongly active detestation of all forms of liberalism, all manifestations of the rights of the individual conscience… Nothing is more detestable to the Catholic Church in general, and especially the Irish Catholic Church, than liberty of the individual conscience.

He was disgusted, for instance, by the controversy surrounding the appointment of Robert Corbett, the Master of the Coombe, as professor of gynaecology at University College Galway. Bishop Michael Browne of Galway, whom Blenner-Hassett characterised as 'an outspoken clerical fascist', objected to the appointment 'because Dr Corbett had been educated at Trinity College Dublin, the only non-Roman Catholic institution of higher learning in Ireland'. Corbett was actually a Catholic, but he turned down the post because of the bishop's opposition and emigrated instead.[34]

'In the eyes of the Irish Catholic Church, the Allied Nations, especially America and Britain, are, if anything, only slightly less desirable than Germany,' Blenner-Hassett noted. He obviously meant 'slightly less undesirable' as he thought members of the hierarchy were virtually Fascist in outlook. 'I am convinced that what the Irish Church hopes to see as the outcome of this war is the military defeat of Axis, followed by peace between the Allies and semi-authoritarian regimes in Italy and Germany.'

He warned that de Valera would later seek to end partition by the twin approach of attempting 'to exploit to the full the nuisance value which the IRA will possess after the war' and by contending that partition should be ended in line with the principles of the Atlantic Charter. Blenner-Hassett concluded:

I am sure that Mr de Valera intends to appear at the post war Peace Conference and basing his claim on the Atlantic Charter will seek the repeal of partition. We may therefore expect an intensified campaign immediately at the end of the war to mobilise British liberal sentiment and Irish and Irish-American sentiment in the US. To counteract this I should advise that great emphasis be given in the American press to Irish and Irish-American names in American casualty lists and that an intensive campaign be carried on in the American Press to point out the difficulties which Éire's neutrality creates for the Allies, especially in the maintenance of the Atlantic Patrol. The object of this should be the complete disillusionment of certain Irish and Irish-American elements with Ireland's domestic troubles, so that the American delegation to the Peace Conference could quite truthfully reply to Mr de Valera that Ireland's problems, because of Éire's neutrality, had ceased to interest anyone in America.[35]

The report was well received in Washington. 'It was extremely well written, and of considerable value with the exception of the part concerned with the Church, which was tendentious and prejudiced,' according to Nicholas.[36] Maffey later essentially echoed the views that Nicholas had dismissed as tendentious.[37] It may well have had a profound influence later, when Gray argued that de Valera should be discredited in order to ensure that he would not be able to cause trouble over partition either between Britain and the United States or for the American government among Irish and Irish-American elements in the United States.

Chapter 22 ❧

GETTING MAXIMUM
COOPERATION

Although Gray had sought to frustrate the Irish offer of cooperation with the oss in January 1943, Washington decided that David K. Bruce, head of the oss operations for Europe, should visit Dublin. Accompanied by Stacy Lloyd, he met with Walshe, Garda Commissioner Paddy O'Carroll and Colonel Dan Bryan, the head of G2, on 15 March 1943. The weekend-long talks convinced Bruce the Irish were serious about helping.

'Bruce recognised our frankness and real desire to be helpful,' Walshe noted.[1] Consequently it was decided Marlin should come 'out from under what was left of his "cover" at the Legation' to act as a liaison with the Irish on intelligence matters. He was ordered 'to work round the clock' collecting whatever information Dublin was prepared to hand over.[2]

Gray wrote to Walshe that Bruce and Lloyd were 'very well satisfied with your kindness and cooperation and hopeful that some mutually useful arrangement may come out of it'. He added rather pointedly, however, 'I am not responsible for Mr. Marlin.'[3]

The Irish supplied Marlin with voluminous reports on such matters as IRA strength, radio interceptions, daily, weekly and monthly reports on aeroplane and submarine sightings, the names and addresses of people in America to whom German nationals living in Ireland or pro-German Irish people were writing, and files on German spies already captured. The material was so detailed that the 'Éire Desk' at oss headquarters in Washington found it necessary to prepare an index card on each individual mentioned in the reports. These quickly totalled over 4,000 names.[4]

The information included the cipher of the spy Goertz and details of how his code was broken. There were also ongoing reports on the activities of a Dubliner named Joseph Andrews, who had been in contact with Germany using Goertz's code. He had sent a number of messages through the German

Legation in Dublin, offering to set up a sabotage organisation in Northern Ireland, where he claimed to have established a friendship with a supervisor at Shortt Brothers and Harland, the aircraft manufacturer in Belfast. He also mentioned Major General Hugo MacNeill as sympathetic to the Germans. Andrews asked to be picked up by Germans either by plane or by submarine so that he could explain his plans further.

The Germans had difficulty in deciphering the messages initially, and when they did were deeply suspicious of Andrews as a possible *agent provocateur*. Hempel was particularly wary because Andrews had been arrested shortly before Goertz and then released soon after the spy was captured. The German Minister correctly suspected that Andrews might have betrayed Goertz.[5]

When Berlin failed to reply after four months, Andrews tried another route. He asked an Irish seaman to deliver a coded message to the German Legation in Portugal, but the seaman handed it over to an intermediary, who gave it to British intelligence before handing it to the Germans. Bletchley Park had not been able to break Goertz's code, but Richard Hayes did, and G2 co-operated with MI5 in stringing along Andrews and the Germans. 'The two organisations were not simply exchanging information: they were running a joint counter-intelligence operation,' according to historian Paul McMahon.[6]

In this message Andrews tried to interest the Germans in his scheme by mentioning that the Weymouth area of England had been evacuated and taken over by Allied troops. The Germans acknowledged receiving this message, but they made no effort to pick up Andrews, who sent a further message in March 1943. This time he explained that General Eoin O'Duffy, who had organised the Irish Brigade to fight on Franco's side during the Spanish Civil War, was now supposedly ready to organise a 'Green Division' to fight for the Germans against Russians. He also mentioned that he had been approached with a scheme to spring Goertz from jail, but that he needed funds to put the various plans into operation. 'With money,' he explained, he would have 'men ready for sabotage, etc., in occupied Ireland'.[7]

Convinced O'Duffy had nothing to do with Andrews, G2 concluded the whole thing was merely a confidence trick to extract money from the Germans.[8] Marlin was briefed about the activities of Andrews and was kept abreast of further developments by G2, which was so cooperative that Marlin no longer saw any point in remaining in Dublin. He was sure there was no need to keep an eye on the Irish, as he was convinced of their good faith. Anxious to make a greater contribution to the war effort, he was frustrated at not having enough work to keep him busy in Dublin. For one thing, he found 'working with Gray was impossible' because he considered him 'a hypersensitive paranoid type of person'.[9]

Gray was trying to block secret Irish offers of cooperation for political reasons. As a result Marlin found his position had become 'difficult if not impossible. On the one hand we were getting maximum cooperation from the Irish, while on the other Gray fulminated against de Valera and his policies. It was all I could do to get his approval of our cooperation and to maintain it.'[10]

Marlin thought it was a waste of time trying to help Gray because there was little mutual trust between them. 'I couldn't get out of Dublin fast enough,' he explained.[11] He moved to London on 30 April 1943. 'I was relieved of my assignment under Gray,' he noted. 'He wanted me out also so we were at last in perfect agreement on one point.'[12]

The oss wished to send a new man to Ireland under cover, but was having difficulty in getting a passport for the specially selected agent, who had already been trained. In order to keep the new agent's identity secret from Gray and the State Department, the oss did not want to use any influence with the State Department to get a passport for him, so it was another few months before that agent could take up his duties in Ireland.

In the interim R. Carter Nicholas, the head of Secret Intelligence's Éire Desk at oss headquarters in Washington, considered a couple of different approaches. One idea was the possibility of sending an Agricultural Mission to Ireland as a cover. Lloyd Steere, the United States Agricultural Attaché to Britain, visited Ireland and warmly approved of the oss proposal. But the plan had to be abandoned 'because of British objections to stimulating vegetable production in Ireland'. The British contended the money needed for experts, seed and fertiliser could be better spent in England.[13] The oss next considered the possibility of recruiting James Dillon's brother, Myles, who was in the United States on business at the time. Nicholas personally asked Myles about 'doing a reporting job for us in Ireland'. After considering the approach Dillon declined the job, because it would have required him to divide his loyalties.[14]

The Anglo-Irish intelligence cooperation established before the war continued to develop. Guy Liddell was so content with the help that he considered it unnecessary to avail of an Irish offer to station intelligence officers in Dublin to keep an eye on the Axis representatives. In April 1943 Maffey wrote to the Dominions Office that he felt comfortable asking Walshe 'if he saw anything through his European window which would interest me and which he could tell me I should be grateful'.[15] In short, he felt he could ask the Irish to pass on anything of value they might learn from their diplomats in Germany, Italy or France.

Marlin made arrangements to return to Dublin periodically. Between visits the Irish agreed to forward future material to him through John Belton, the Secretary of the Irish High Commission in London. 'It is indicative of the degree of Irish cooperation', Nicholas wrote, 'that these reports and other reports were sent to Hurst [i.e. Marlin] in London through the Irish pouch from Dublin.'[16] In fact, it was also indicative of the deep distrust the Irish had of the American Minister in Dublin. They preferred dealing with Marlin, on whose discretion they could rely.

Within a month the new agent took up his post in Ireland. He was Martin S. Quigley, who had been personally recruited by William J. Donovan, the director of the oss, to serve in both Ireland and the Vatican. Quigley was an Irish-American whose parents had some business involvements in the Carlow area. His father was publisher of the *Motion Picture Almanac* and several motion picture periodicals. The new agent had visited Ireland with his father a couple of times before the war. When he returned on 25 May 1943, he came under the cover of a representative of Motion Picture Producers and Distributors of America Incorporated. This allowed him to travel extensively about the country visiting cinemas.

Quigley was to keep his eyes open and report what he saw rather than to go digging for secret information. 'You will go to Dublin as the representative of the Motion Picture Producers of America, Inc, to carry on continuing negotiations with respect to the Irish censorship of American films, to make study of films which in the past have been found objectionable to the censorship authorities and to the people of Ireland and to advise the association on how trouble may be avoided in the future. This work will continue for a considerable period, perhaps as long as a year'.[17] His reports were to be sent by regular mail, with the result that they would pass through the regular mail censorship. They were to be written in such a way as not to rouse any suspicion about him. No strings were to be pulled to facilitate Martin Quigley travelling to Ireland. He had to make his own travel arrangements and obtain a visa through normal channels. He was also ordered to keep his oss connection secret from everyone, including Gray and Marlin, though the latter was notified that someone was being sent. Quigley was given a secret means of identifying himself to Marlin in case he needed emergency help.

'Do you happen to know where the Gallow Glasses originated?' Quigley was to ask Marlin, who would reply, 'The Hebrides.' But it never became necessary to divulge his identity to Marlin while in Ireland.[18]

Given the code-name Harte, Quigley was to report what any intelligent American might be expected to observe in Ireland. As part of his cover he was also supposedly researching a book. 'My final orders were phrased in a lengthy series of questions to which I should seek answers,' he recalled. The first group of questions dealt with attitudes: 'What is the true attitude of the Irish Government towards the us? Towards us troops in Northern Ireland? Towards Germany and the other Axis powers? What is the power of the

Roman Catholic hierarchy in Ireland? What is the attitude of the Catholic hierarchy in Ireland with regard to Germany and the us?" Other questions concerned the effectiveness of propaganda directed at the Irish people and the attitude of the IRA, labour unions and labour leaders.[19]

On his third day in Ireland Quigley telephoned Gray to apprise him of his presence. He was surprised that Gray answered the telephone himself, but nothing else about the Minister's behaviour prompted Quigley to change his attitude. Some in Washington had expressed the view that Gray 'was too close to the Anglo-Irish commercial interests and Protestant community in general', Quigley noted. 'His social contacts did not include "the common people" or their opinion-makers and leaders.'[20] Gray, who was about to return to the United States for consultations, was rather melodramatic when he met with Quigley. 'Should the Germans invade Ireland,' Gray said, 'I plan to take up a position here at the embassy gate with a rifle in hand and resist the Nazis as long as I am alive.'[21]

While in Dublin, Quigley stayed at the Shelbourne Hotel, where he paid £1 a day. He travelled about extensively and met a wide range of people, including de Valera, Frank Aiken, W.T. Cosgrave, Richard Mulcahy, Seán T. O'Kelly and Gerald Boland, as well as many newspaper editors and a selection of bishops, including the Roman Catholic Archbishop of Dublin, John Charles McQuaid, and Michael Browne, the bishop of Galway.

In light of Blenner-Hassett's experiences, Quigley was warned to expect questions like 'Why wasn't he in some branch of the us military?' and 'What was a single young American doing in a civilian film job in Ireland in the midst of the war?' The only person who ever asked him those questions was Archbishop McQuaid.[22] He had been rejected for military service because he was very short-sighted, which was obvious from the thickness of his spectacles.

From the outset Quigley realised his mission did not have the cloak-and-dagger implications frequently associated with espionage. 'Should I be so unlucky as to be revealed as an American intelligence agent, I felt it would be an embarrassing situation that was likely to become something of an international incident,' Quigley admitted. 'Very likely de Valera would have made a strong objection to the us State Department and had me expelled. In the circumstances I had no fear that a failure would result in a long jail sentence or worse.'[23]

At the start of his second week in Dublin he met with de Valera, whom he had met at the Dublin Horse Show in 1939. At that time Quigley, then in his early twenties, was travelling with his father. The latest meeting with the Taoiseach, on 1 June, was to discuss the film industry. 'De Valera said that he believed that the motion picture was the most potent force for instruction in the world,' Quigley reported. 'He said he thought it was much more powerful than the press or books because it demanded so much less of its audience.' He was hopeful that films could be used to promote the Irish language by the use of token phrases. 'He had instructed people running the Irish Radio Station to produce programmes that would elevate the tastes of the audience. This is done even though, as he remarked, people who do not wish to listen to such a program twist the dial and tune into another station.'[24]

Although Gray tended to see slights against the Allies in the Irish censorship, Quigley realised things were not so straightforward. 'I asked de Valera about the censoring of the film *The Eternal Gift*, which is merely the Catholic High Mass produced by the Servite Fathers in Chicago and bearing the endorsement of the Archbishop of Chicago and a commentary by Monsignor Fulton J. Sheen of the Catholic University,' Quigley noted.

'This country is so Catholic that representations of a Catholic religious service, no matter how treated, would be objectionable,' de Valera explained. During the civil war he had defied the bishops and he might have feared that Quigley would therefore suspect his Catholic credentials, so in his own subtle way he let Quigley know that his half-brother, Thomas Wheelwright, was a priest. 'At the door of his office Mr. de Valera asked whether I had met his brother, a priest in the United States,' Quigley noted.[25]

The first picture that was rejected in its entirety while Quigley was in Ireland was a Bob Hope comedy, *They Have Got Me Covered*, which was about espionage in Washington. However, two war movies, *Fight for Freedom* and *Aerial Gunner*, were each passed 'with relatively minor cuts'. He could have anticipated about three-quarters of the cuts, but the other quarter surprised him. Those included cutting dance scenes from movies, with the result that their entertainment value was often impaired. Quigley had many meetings with the film censor, Richard Hayes, who was, ironically, working very closely with Irish military intelligence in his role as a brilliant code-breaker. Hayes told him, for instance, that he was 'very much against South American and South Seas type dancing', on moral grounds. When Hayes went on holiday during the summer his replacement, Michael J. Dolan, who was better known as an actor with the Abbey Theatre, cut the word 'war' from every film, no matter in what context it was used.[26] Hence it quickly became apparent to Quigley that there were all kinds of influences on censorship, ranging from the taste of the film censor to the attitude of influential politicians and Church leaders.

'Hardly a film goes by in which there is not at least one or more cuts under the Emergency War Powers Orders,' he reported.[27] Frank Aiken told Quigley on 15 July that the Irish people were united behind neutrality and the government was anxious that nothing should be shown on a cinema screen that 'might disturb that unity in any way'. The motivation was purely an internal consideration, having nothing to do with 'avoiding anything that might seriously annoy a belligerent nation'. During one movie a woman in the audience cheered when the British Air Raid Protection service arrived on the scene in the film. Other patrons then began to boo and hiss. The censorship aimed at avoiding such demonstrations. 'It seems that films come in for the strictest censorship of all,' Quigley noted. 'Aiken told me that the censorship of the press need not be so strict because if a person does not like a newspaper story he need not read it but in a cinema he may create a disturbance.'[28]

'Although Ireland is neutral, the people here feel the war quite personally and I was told by the county exhibitors almost every family has either a relation or a good friend either in the service or in war work in England,' Quigley had already reported. 'This is further extended by the well-known fact that practically everyone here has relations or intimate friends in the United States. That also makes people feel the effects of the war.'[29]

Quigley quickly realised the Irish authorities were favourably disposed towards the Allies. 'The Irish Government's position in World War II was a peculiar form of neutrality,' he explained years later. 'Openly the position was that of pretending neutrality in the classic sense. Actually it was a neutrality against the Axis and for the Allies.'[30] In his book *A U.S. Spy in Ireland*, he made it clear that 'the use of the term "neutral" as applied to the twenty-six counties of Éire was a misnomer'[31] because the Dublin government provided a great deal of secret help to the Allies, whereas it never gave any help to Germany. He was therefore baffled by Gray's attitude. 'He never knew what was really going on, or if he did, he refused to accept the truth,' Quigley wrote.[32]

The Irish were so helpful that Quigley—like many other Americans who visited Ireland during the war—thought it would be possible to arrange a deal for Irish bases in return for the ending of partition, the causes of which he analysed in some depth. He enlisted the help of Emmet Dalton, who was nominally the supervisor of the Paramount Film distributing branches in Britain and Ireland. Dalton had served in the British Army in World War I and returned home to take an active part in the war of independence and later in the civil war. He was an advisor to Michael Collins during the 1921 Treaty negotiations and had taken part in the negotiations on defensive matters between Collins and Churchill. Hence he now had access to Downing Street.

'He did not know I was with the oss,' Quigley noted. 'He did know, however, that I had contacts in the film world who had excellent access to President Roosevelt, through his father's friend William J. Donovan.'[33]

Quigley went to London for three weeks during late August and the first half of September 1943 to report fully on his findings in Ireland. While there he met with his superior, Carter Nicholas, who came over to finalise a secret approach to the Irish in line with some talks that Marlin had been having.

'I arrived in London in early September,' Nicholas recalled. 'I conferred with Col. Bruce and Hurst [i.e. Marlin] about the future course of SI work with respect to Éire.' After meeting with Bruce and Marlin, Nicholas met Quigley. 'I conferred with him fully over a period of two or three days about his work, the difficulties that had developed in it, and certain communication problems,' Nicholas noted. 'He had prepared there and delivered to me part of a very full report entitled "NOTES ON ÉIRE".'[34]

Quigley's information fit neatly with what the others had reported. 'My work was helpful in establishing—along with other material Nicholas had—that the Irish situation was not hurtful to the Allied cause,' Quigley noted.

'Dalton's report was that the British Imperial General Staff was quite content with the existing situation with regard to the treaty ports and wanted nothing to change the situation,' according to Quigley. 'The word was, "Leave things as they are".'[35]

Ironically, Gray was in the United States at this time meeting with Roosevelt and Churchill and railing against de Valera's policy, while the OSS was on the brink of establishing some extraordinary cooperation with the Irish. 'David Gray never really understood the Irish,' Quigley contended.[36]

During one of his periodic visits to Dublin in July 1943, Marlin approached Walshe about securing Irish help 'in communicating with Switzerland or any other part of Europe' where the Irish had diplomatic missions. 'Walshe replied', according to an official OSS report, 'that if the material consisted of a single sheet of paper without identification as to its origin or destination, in short, a document that might be going to an Irish representative in case it should be picked up by the enemy, he would aid us by having one of his men take it personally, or by sending it through the Irish pouch.'[37]

Since this opened the possibility of using Irish diplomats as American spies, it was decided Nicholas should visit Dublin for exploratory talks. On Saturday, 25 September 1943, he and Marlin arrived in Dublin. The following is Nicholas' account of what happened after they checked into the Hibernian Hotel:

They immediately telephoned Mr Joe Walshe, Secretary of External Affairs, and conferred with him at our hotel that evening. Mr Nicholas told Mr Walshe that the information which had been received as a result of the liaison had been very useful and that the source had been scrupulously protected. Quite naturally Walshe had been somewhat concerned over the possibility that the source might be revealed in one way or another. I then said that the rapid progress of the war was fixing attention more and more on information from the Continent and I wished to sound out the possibility of Irish help, including particularly, the possibility of our receiving information from Irish diplomatic sources. It was intimated that other neutrals had gone as far. He said he thought he would be able to give an answer on Monday morning and we made an appointment at his office.[38]

Next day Nicholas and Marlin met with Colonel Dan Bryan. They asked him about 'the possibility of using an IRA man or any other Irishman who had or might possibly establish contact with the Germans'. Nicholas later reported, 'No one but Andrews was suggested.'[39] Both Bryan and Marlin thought he was too unreliable. He was, in fact, a serial double-crosser and, anyway, they also believed he was distrusted by the Germans. Moreover Irish authorities had moved to put an end to his intrigues by arresting him. Nevertheless Bryan promised 'to be on the look-out' for a suitable candidate, although he was not optimistic. On the following day, Monday, 27 September, Nicholas and Marlin again met Walshe, who read them reports in which they might be interested from Irish diplomats on the Continent. This extraordinary meeting was summarised by Nicholas:

1. Mr Walshe permitted us to take notes on reports received from Irish diplomats.
2. He agreed to transmit to Hurst the substance of future reports.
3. He agreed to transmit to the Irish *Chargé d'Affaires* in Berlin a request for information on the political situation in Germany at the top, and to transmit the substance of the answer to Hurst, and to ask Irish diplomats suitable questions which we might in the future originate.
4 He agreed to have Miss Walshe, Secretary to the Irish *Chargé d'Affaires* at Berlin, interviewed and to transmit a report of the interview to Hurst.
5. Mr Walshe's opinion of the reporting abilities of his men was subsequently checked against a similar report obtained by Hurst from Mr Belton in London and served as a good basis for evaluation.[40]

Upon his return to London, Nicholas forwarded his expanded notes on the Irish diplomatic correspondence to William J. Donovan in Washington. These notes included extracts from messages describing conditions in Germany, Italy and France. The British were already surreptitiously reading the Irish diplomatic messages as they had broken the Irish code, but having the diplomats' answers posed by the oss was something else. In the following weeks Marlin supplied questions to Walshe for the respective Irish representatives in Berlin, Rome and Vichy. Walshe then forwarded the replies to Marlin. In effect, the Irish diplomats were being used as American spies.

Meanwhile Quigley returned to Ireland on 15 September with a two-month visa, but he found the climate in relation to film censorship had changed. 'The fundamental reason for this is not very clear,' he reported. 'In the latter part of September the Irish censorship authorities decided to tighten up on the film censorship. Why, I do not know.'[41]

The problems began with the movie *A Yank in the RAF*, which was a love story. It had passed the censor and began showing in the Savoy cinema in Dublin two days after Quigley's return. Aiken decided to see it on 20 September, and the censor announced a couple of days later that it was being withdrawn. Some 41,000 people had seen it during its seven-day run. Quigley protested to de Valera, who told him to talk to Aiken. 'While there was nothing in the film to which exception can be taken while in the cinema, when people went home and thought about the picture they did not like it and protested to him,' Aiken explained.[42]

There were also problems with *Army Chaplain*, a 20-minute feature on the training of army chaplains of various denominations at Harvard University. It highlighted a Catholic chaplain going into battle in the Pacific. It had been showing for six weeks when it was withdrawn, after some 70,000 people had already seen it. A cut in the movie *Bombardier* involved the line 'There are three things a bombardier must remember—hit the target—hit the target—hit the target.' Quigley found the film censor's decision to cut the second and third 'hit the target' inexplicable. 'Don't ask me why!' he exclaimed.[43] Mystified moviegoers were left to figure out for themselves the two censored things that should be remembered!

After failing to make any headway with Aiken, Quigley encouraged the cinema-owners and Fine Gael and Labour representatives to put pressure on the Minister. He should not have been surprised, then, to learn that Aiken was annoyed with him. 'Aiken saw red' when a labour delegation mentioned Quigley's name. Members of the delegation had called on him to complain that film censorship was a threat to their jobs, and they suggested Hempel had some influence on the matter of censorship.

'I do not care any more for the German Minister than I do for Martin,' Aiken exclaimed forcefully.[44]

Thereafter Quigley found that a distinct strain had developed in his relationship with Hayes, the film censor, who no longer welcomed Quigley's visits. 'My presence embarrassed him,' Quigley noted, 'because he probably blamed some of the increased pressure from some of his superiors on me.' There was nothing that Quigley could do about that situation. 'The film censor's office has previously served as a fair source of good information and a routine business cover and I had previously spent three or four mornings a week there.'[45]

One of Quigley's main tasks had been to evaluate the influence of the Irish bishops. He was able to demonstrate the power and influence of the hierarchy by simply reporting on censorship. Archbishop John Charles McQuaid of Dublin had a French film on the Passion of Christ banned. The Papal Nuncio, Archbishop Pascal Robinson, told Quigley that although he would not care to see such a film himself, he would not object to others seeing it. But McQuaid was almost a law unto himself, even in the early days of his reign. 'Other bishops resented the fact that his influence with the Film Censor achieves control of films in their dioceses,' according to Quigley. The Bishop of Limerick may not have had much influence with the film censor, but he managed to have all movies banned in Limerick on Sundays. 'One is frequently told the story in Ireland about there not being "26 bishops there but 26 popes",' Quigley noted.[46]

With his visa about to expire, Quigley planned to return to the United States. 'I would not have been very surprised had I been asked to leave Éire, and I feel pretty sure that any request for an extension of my stay beyond November 15 would not have been well received,' he reported when he got to London.[47]

During his final days in Dublin, Quigley was invited to visit the Kildare Street Club by H.E. Guinness of Guinness & Mahon Bank. 'The Anglo-Irishman in Dublin, even after generations, evidently does not understand the native Irish at all,' Quigley reported. They essentially considered themselves as foreigners in Ireland. 'That is perhaps somewhat natural, as the boys are regularly educated in England or partly in England and partly at Trinity College which looks to England,' he added. 'It will be many years before the Kildare Street Club type has the same viewpoint as the native Irish.'[48]

Those were the people with whom Gray was associating, but Quigley thought Gray was right in arguing 'that there should be no secret intelligence use of the legation'. Quigley suggested the telephones at the American Legation were being tapped.[49] This was before automated telephone exchanges, so there was always the possibility nosy operators might be listening in. In fact, it would have been surprising if G2 and the Garda Special Branch were not getting information from operators.

Following his return to the United States, Quigley published a booklet, *Great Gaels: Ireland at Peace in a World at War*, the research for which had been part of his cover in Ireland. It was published in 1944. Some Americans might have been surprised at his conclusion that 'the great majority of [Irish] citizens had lost all sympathy with the IRA'. He clearly had difficulty hiding his frustration with the censorship in Ireland.[50]

Chapter 23 ∿

WITHOUT SO MUCH AS 'THANK YOU'

A lthough the Irish agreed not to intern Allied airmen on non-operational flights, they did not even bother to check the claims in most instances. 'Under the circumstances,' Canadian High Commissioner Kearney wrote, 'the meaning of the words "non-operational flight" has, sometimes, been stretched almost beyond recognition. Since the above attitude has been adopted by the Irish government, many American air crews have made forced landing but none of them has been interned.'[1] The crew of five of the first six American warplanes that came down in Ireland failed to claim 'non-operational' status, but all thirty-four men on board were released anyway.

Lieutenant Vernon Yahne of Mitchell, South Dakota, was on a training mission when he got lost and landed on Phoenix Park Race Course, Dublin. He was preparing to destroy his plane until some locals informed him of his location. The plane was dismantled and moved to Baldonnel, and a British pilot flew it back to Northern Ireland.

On 23 December 1942 Lieutenant Arthur L. Brodhead from Strousburg, Pennsylvania, landed his fighter on the beach at Ballyvaughan, County Clare, after getting hopelessly lost on a flight from Eglington to Liverpool. He was put up at the nearby home of P.J. O'Loghlen, a Fianna Fáil member of the Dáil, and was guest of the O'Loghlen family for Christmas dinner.

There was a sensational forced landing of a Flying Fortress on the grounds of an agricultural college in Athenry, County Galway, on the morning of 15 January 1943. The sixteen men on board included Lieutenant General Jacob Devers, then senior American commander of the European Theatre of Operations, along with three other generals, Major General Edward H. Brooks and Brigadier Generals J.M. Barnes and C.D. Palmer. They were en route from North Africa to a military conference in London. After a meal at a local hotel, the American party was transported to the border at Beleek in two trucks and a convoy of cars.[2]

The sixth of those aircraft, a Flying Fortress piloted by Lieutenant Cecil Waters, was actually fired on by an Irish anti-aircraft battery on 17 April 1943 before he landed at Dublin airport. 'The crew had not been briefed to claim non-operational status,' Gray complained.[3]

The war in the Atlantic took a dramatic turn in early 1943 when the Germans intensified their U-boat campaign. News of recent Allied successes in North Africa and on the Russian front had been received in Ireland with 'a satisfaction approaching enthusiasm' and the Irish government had 'given additional tangible evidence of a willingness to help the Allies', according to the Canadian High Commissioner. Many Irish people had begun to worry about the country's post-war position, so Kearney thought de Valera might now be willing to provide bases, if President Roosevelt asked for them:

> At least some support either from the electorate at large or the opposition parties would be forthcoming should a request for facilities be made in the near future. Mr de Valera had repeatedly stressed the importance of unity in regard to Ireland's attitude towards the war, and I believe he would stretch a point to maintain such unity, and in case he is doubtful as to what course to pursue he might be influenced in favour of acceding to the request if such a course found favour in other quarters.[4]

Maffey liked the idea, so he and Kearney approached Gray, who was positively enthusiastic. It would afford the opportunity he desired to publicise Irish policy in the United States. If the request were rejected, all three Allied representatives felt it should be publicised. Gray thought the Allies could then take whatever action 'as seems needful, presumably occupation of the areas of land and water required but with a minimum of interference with [the] Irish Government'.[5]

'Maffey, Kearney and I agreed', Gray wrote to Roosevelt, 'that after the publicised request had been made, in view of the tide the war has taken and the corresponding orientation of Irish opinion toward the bandwagon it would [be] almost impossible for de Valera to order his troops to fire on naval forces occupying the areas in question. It would be a very lucky solution for him of a situation which he cannot like, but does not know how to get out of. He would of course prefer a German attack.'[6] Maffey went to London to discuss the idea.

Clement Attlee, who was Dominions Secretary and Acting Prime Minister in Churchill's absence, noted that neither military nor naval authorities had mentioned Irish bases for some time. He therefore informed Foreign Secretary Anthony Eden that he would be opposed to taking any chance of de Valera complying with such a request, lest Britain become obliged to defend

Ireland, which would 'probably' be more trouble than the facilities were worth.[7]

'The Dominions Office considers that the situation, from the Allied point of view, might easily be a great deal worse than it is, and that it is best to leave well enough alone,' Kearney reported.[8] 'Sir John said that the Dominions Office was of the opinion that, since the Military Services were no longer clamouring for Irish bases, it was thought better not to raise the question at present,' Gray wrote to Sumner Welles. While Kearney was ready to forget about the idea, Gray was only postponing it. 'The proposal is therefore *in suspenso*,' he wrote.[9]

Paradoxically, the British belittled the value of Irish bases while the Allies were in the midst of their gravest crisis in the Atlantic. The Admiralty later recorded that 'the Germans never came so near to disrupting communication between the New World and the Old as in the first twenty days of March, 1943'.[10]

Although some members of the British government were quietly satisfied with Irish policy, others still played up their annoyance with the Irish. Foreign Secretary Anthony Eden was distinctly cool towards John J. Hearne, the Irish High Commissioner in Canada, when they were guests of British High Commissioner Malcolm MacDonald in Ottawa on 2 April. 'Eden was aloof and hardly courteous,' Hearne noted.

'When are you people going to come into the war?' Eden asked. 'If you do not come in soon you will be too late. Do you not think that your country should be in the war?'

'No,' Hearne replied.

Eden said there were 300,000 Irish people in British forces; he seemed to be suggesting the Dublin government was missing out by not getting actively involved. 'They sent Walshe over to see me to talk if you please about postwar cooperation,' Eden continued. 'I liked Walshe very much; I even like de Valera. But I can tell you I made it clear to Walshe that there was absolutely nothing doing. This is a club and if you are in it you either keep the rules and play the game or you do not, that is all.'

'I did not expect this barrage and feel at a disadvantage,' Hearne replied.

'It is hardly fair,' MacDonald interjected. As the host, he seemed 'somewhat embarrassed', but he agreed with Eden that if the Irish did not get into the war soon, it would be too late.

'You should advise your Government to get into the war,' Eden said.

'I am afraid you overestimate my influence and you certainly mistake my views which, as you should be aware, do not differ from those of my Minister.'[11]

When Kearney travelled to London the following week, however, Attlee encouraged him to keep up his friendly attitude towards the de Valera government. He said he realised it would be impossible for Kearney 'to lure the Irish into the war'. In fact, Attlee said the British 'were wrong in assuming that anyone could convince the Irish to denounce their neutrality'.[12]

Tommy Church asked in the Canadian parliament the following week if the Ottawa government had made any effort to 'secure the use of the Éire bases which belong to the Empire, for immediate use so as to help in the Battle of the Atlantic?'

'This question should not have been permitted,' Prime Minister Mackenzie King replied. 'It is certainly a question to which a reply could not be given at this time.'[13]

While members of the British government had different attitudes towards Ireland, there was no doubt Churchill was spoiling for a confrontation with the Irish, and did not seem to care on what issue he started it. On 11 April 1943 he suggested to Eden that Ireland and other neutrals should be excluded from a forthcoming international conference on food. 'Southern Ireland is neutral, and this is the moment to make her feel her isolation and the shameful position she will occupy at the peace,' Churchill wrote. 'I will appeal personally to the President not to send an invitation to Southern Ireland while they remain in the present position. It is only by making them feel the ignominy of their conduct that we may being them along.'[14]

Churchill wrote to President Roosevelt that day:

1. About 2 years ago the Government of Northern Ireland wished to have conscription in its own area and I favoured the policy. However at the time American opinion was adverse and I received both from you and from Winant strong advice to the contrary. The situation is now changed. United States forces are in Ireland in considerable numbers and we have the spectre of young Americans taken by compulsion from their homes to defend an area where young fellows of the locality loaf about with their hands in their pockets. This affects not only recruiting but the work of important Belfast shipyards which are less active than the British yards.

2. I am thinking therefore of re-opening the question and asking the Northern Ireland government whether they would like me to have another try. A loud caterwaul may be expected from Valera, and I should like to know first of all how you feel about it and whether you could do anything to help.[15]

After considering the issue carefully, Roosevelt replied:

The situation has, I feel, changed as regards public opinion in the United States since this matter was under consideration by the Government of Northern Ireland two years ago. I frankly doubt whether it would create much of an issue in this country. I do not feel that I am in a position to express any opinion concerning the effect in Éire and Northern Ireland of the reopening of the question. Your information is, of course, much better than ours and you are doubtless in a position to weigh the advantages and disadvantages of such a move.[16]

Of course, it was not just the American, Canadian, Australian and Irish leaders who had objected to the introduction of conscription in Northern Ireland in May 1941. Most of Churchill's own Cabinet were also opposed, so nothing came of the idea. Within weeks Churchill was taking another tack with Attlee in a supposed effort to save the Irish from themselves.

'Their conduct in the war will never be forgiven by the British nation unless it is amended before the end,' the Prime Minister wrote. 'This in itself would be a great disaster. It is our duty to try to save these people from their selves. Any proposals you make to terminate the enemy representation in Dublin will be immediately considered by me. We ought not to shirk the difficulties unduly for the sake of a quiet life.'[17]

Gray was thinking on parallel lines with Churchill. Even if Irish bases were not needed, he wished to ask for them as a means of initiating a propaganda campaign to dramatise what he believed were the obnoxious aspects of Irish neutrality. During his visit to London in November 1942, Gray had talked about the need to educate the American people concerning Ireland's neutrality. American ignorance in the matter had since been highlighted with the publication of some Gallup polls conducted in October and December 1942. Half of the people in the United States did not even know Ireland had not 'gone to war against Germany'.[18] For Gray, who was anxious to undermine the influence of those Roosevelt considered professional Irish-Americans, the poll figures had positive aspects that showed a real potential for exploitation. Of the half that knew Ireland had not gone to war against Germany, 90 per cent said they would like to see the Irish hand over bases and 71 per cent said Ireland 'should' join the Allies. Among Irish-Americans who realised Ireland had not gone to war, 72 per cent said they 'would like to see Éire let the Allies war bases along the Irish coast' and 56 per cent felt that Ireland should 'join the Allies in declaring war against Germany'. Only 32 per cent of Irish-Americans expressed the opinion that Éire should stay out of the war.[19]

Unless the Irish situation were dramatised, Gray feared de Valera would escape the consequences of his policy by contending Irish neutrality had been favourable to the Americans and had never refused any assistance to them. To avoid this happening he suggested Roosevelt ask de Valera for help as the latter's refusal 'would at least put him on record for the purposes of post-war adjustments and would prevent him from saying that he had been with us all along which is probably what he will say if he is not put on record'.[20]

During the following weeks the genesis of what seemed like an anti-partition campaign surfaced as Robert Brennan, Cardinal MacRory and de Valera made pronouncements about the Ulster question. Brennan put forward a strong defence of Irish neutrality in an article in the *New York Times*. The British had handed back the ports long after de Valera had made clear that Ireland would remain neutral in the coming war. 'If their occupation had been so vital as is now pretended,' he argued, 'the British would not have surrendered them, especially with war on the horizon.' He cited the partition problem as a justification for staying out of the war. There was, he complained, a great deal of discrimination against Catholics in Northern Ireland, which was highlighted by the Prime Minister of Northern Ireland publicly apologising for the presence of even one Catholic on the staff of thirty-one messengers employed in public offices.[21]

The same day Cardinal MacRory stated publicly that the Atlantic Charter's guarantee to restore the rights 'to those who have been forcibly deprived of them' amounted to a promise to end partition.[22] Gray blamed the Taoiseach for the Cardinal's statement. 'I think Dev is in this,' he wrote to the President next day. 'He is using the Cardinal.'[23]

De Valera got into the act himself on 8 May by contending partition was the one problem that had prevented Irish cooperation with Britain. The British reacted by publishing a letter in which Churchill assured the retiring Prime Minister of Northern Ireland, Sir John Andrews, that Belfast's gesture in providing Britain with the use of much-needed facilities during the war had cemented ties between Britain and Northern Ireland into an unbreakable bond.

Gray was becoming obsessed with a fear that the Ulster question would be used to disrupt Anglo-American relations after the war, in much the same way de Valera had helped to wreck Woodrow Wilson's peace plans after the Paris Peace Conference of 1919 had not recognised Ireland's claim to independence. On 14 May 1943 Gray sent the State Department a long memorandum evaluating the significance of Irish political affairs and outlining the various alternatives open to Washington to place the de Valera government on record. There were at least three areas in which American interests were 'gravely prejudiced by the policy of the Irish government', he explained. One, the Allies had been denied Irish facilities to protect Atlantic shipping. Two, Axis diplomatic and consular missions in Ireland posed an espionage threat to the

Allies. And three, de Valera was apparently planning to use the partition issue to create a post-war rift between Britain and the United States for his own selfish political ends. 'Whatever the rights and wrongs of partition,' Gray wrote, 'it should be clearly understood that a solution on any basis of reason and compromise is not the primary object of the de Valera leadership at this time.' Instead, the Taoiseach was simply exploiting the issue to stay in power, with the result that the partition grievance was politically more important than finding a solution.[24]

De Valera was unlikely to accept any solution short of Irish unity, which Northern Unionists were unwilling to consider. There was therefore little chance of a settlement in the near future. Gray believed Americans were morally obliged to support the Unionists for providing much-needed bases during the war, but he feared de Valera would appeal to Irish-Americans to force Washington to put pressure on the British to abandon Northern Ireland. As things stood, de Valera could distort matters by arguing that the Twenty-six Counties had also been helpful to the Allies, and he would thus be in a position to open a rift in Anglo-American relations by feeding Roosevelt's opponents with anti-British and anti-partition propaganda. 'It has become increasingly apparent', Gray wrote, 'that he intends to use the alleged wrong of partition to open this rift and to enlist the sympathies and support of the Irish-American groups to this end.'[25]

The disruptive potential of Irish-Americans should not be underestimated. Those who had been prominent in isolationist circles right up to the attack on Pearl Harbour were now facing the political oblivion to which Hitler's appeasers were condemned, and there was a danger they might try to use the partition issue to stir up popular support in a desperate effort to salvage their waning political influence.

To ensure that Irish affairs could not be exploited, Gray suggested dramatising negative aspects of Irish policy. Possible alternatives were to ask the Taoiseach for bases, to request the expulsion of Axis representatives from Ireland, or to demand that the Irish clarify whether or not the country was a member of the British Commonwealth. A fourth alternative simply consisted of generating a crisis by enacting conscription in Northern Ireland.

All of the suggestions were designed to create a climate conducive for a propaganda campaign in which de Valera could be discredited in the eyes of the American public. 'The important thing from the viewpoint of Anglo-American cooperation', Gray wrote, 'is to bring to the notice of the American people the unfair and destructive policy of the de Valera politicians at the time when British and American interests are essentially the same and to obtain a verdict of American disapproval which will remove the pressure of the Irish question from Anglo-American relations.'[26]

Gray returned to the United States for consultations on 5 June 1943. Two days before leaving he received what he believed was further confirmation of de Valera's intention to raise the Ulster question after the war, when the Taoiseach said a solution to partition was not beyond the bounds of good statesmanship since 'exchanges of populations were not impossible in these days'.[27] Gray took the remark as an indication the Taoiseach was looking for an ethnic-cleansing solution, whereby Protestants in Northern Ireland would be moved to Britain and replaced by Roman Catholics of Irish extraction from Britain. It was hardly surprising the American Minister never seriously considered this a workable solution, because the Protestants in Northern Ireland could trace their ancestry in the area back to the early seventeenth century, which was much earlier than the vast majority of Americans could trace their ancestral roots in the United States.

In the following weeks Gray had meetings with various American officials and spent time with Roosevelt at both the White House and his family home in Hyde Park, New York. At these meetings he emphasised the need to undermine de Valera's political appeal in the United States, and suggested the best way would be to get the Taoiseach on record as refusing to allow the United States to use Irish bases.

'I think we might consider asking for a lease of ports in a manner similar to the lease of eight bases from Great Britain in 1940,' Roosevelt wrote to Hull. 'I think Mr Gray is right in his desire to put de Valera on record. We shall undoubtedly be turned down.' He was obviously influenced by Gray. 'We are losing many American and British lives and many ships in carrying various supplies to Ireland without receiving anything in return, and without so much as "Thank you".'[28]

The Secretary of State advised Roosevelt to be cautious for fear of becoming embroiled in a purely Anglo-Irish dispute:

The Irish and British have fought one another for seven hundred years. They suspect and distrust one another. Each tries on suitable occasions to obtain the support of the American people and Government against the other. We must be careful, therefore, to be sure that any action which we take in this regard has a sound military basis in the opinion of our own Chiefs of Staff. It seems to me that this is of fundamental importance to make it impossible for anyone to maintain that we took sides with the British against the Irish and 'pulled British chestnuts out of the fire.'[29]

While Gray was in the United States, de Valera called a general election in Ireland. Ironically, neutrality was not an election issue. Even James Dillon came out strongly in support of neutrality during the campaign. 'No one is so foolish as to bring upon himself all the horrors of war,' he told a gathering in Monaghan. 'Nobody in the last election supported abandoning neutrality.'[30]

The outcome of the general election was as Blenner-Hassett had earlier predicted. Fianna Fáil and Fine Gael lost seats, while the Labour Party and a plethora of smaller parties made gains. De Valera was re-elected at the head of a minority government when the new Dáil convened on 1 July 1943. There were some ominous rumblings and a frightening degree of intolerance exhibited among the small parties. J.J. Walsh, a Postmaster General in the first government of W.T. Cosgrave, wrote to the *Sunday Independent* calling for the formation of a new nationalist party, promising 'the elimination of half-breeds and crossbreeds. There is no room for these types in the new Ireland'. Oliver J. Flanagan, a newly elected Monetary Reform deputy, denounced the Emergency Powers being invoked against the IRA:

> We do not see any of these acts directed against the Jews, who crucified Our Saviour nineteen hundred years ago, and who are crucifying us every day of the week. There is one thing that Germany did, and that was to rout the Jews out of their country. Until we rout the Jews out of this country it does not matter a hair's breath what orders you make. Where the bees are there is honey, and where the Jews are there is money.[31]

He accepted there was a war on, so the government had to take precautions. 'But I cannot see why they are letting the banks go scot free and the Jews and the Masons,' he complained. 'Surely, the Republicans are not worse than they are?'[32]

While in Washington, Gray received a disquieting letter from his predecessor in Dublin, John Cudahy, who contended there was 'growing bewilderment among our people concerning the real issues of this war'. Many Americans were puzzled about being asked to fight for the principles of the Atlantic Charter when it was obvious the Soviet Union had no intention of upholding those principles in regard to Poland, where Cudahy had served as Ambassador during the early 1930s before going to Dublin. Cudahy was now so critical of Roosevelt's leadership that he asked Gray to try to persuade the President not to seek a fourth term in 1944, because there was a danger of 'something almost approaching a civil war'.[33]

Gray visited a number of Irish-American strongholds to evaluate the likely reaction in the United States if the Irish launched an anti-partition campaign. He was particularly anxious to learn the kind of support people like Fr Charles E. Coughlin and Fr Edward Lodge Curran might have within the United States. 'The day is coming when this country will need a Coughlin and need him badly,' Fr Edward Brophy had said in June 1942. 'We must get and keep organised for that day.'[34]

Gray talked with Archbishop Samuel Stretch in Chicago, before going on to Detroit, where he met with Archbishop Edward Mooney. In New York City he met with Bishop Joseph Hurley of Florida and Bishop John Francis O'Hara, who was a former President of the University of Notre Dame. He then went on to Boston to meet Joseph P. Kennedy.

After those talks Gray was more perturbed than ever. He wrote to Cudahy that he did not believe there could 'be more bitterness against F.D.R. than there now is'.[35] In another letter to an American intelligence officer, he explained 'that Pearl Harbour had not scotched the venomous minority groups, whether Irish, German, Italian, or purely lunatic Americans'.[36] This only served to strengthen his conviction about the need to weaken the potential American support for an anti-partition campaign.

Gray discussed the problem with Roosevelt and Churchill over dinner in Hyde Park on 14 August 1943. The only record of the meeting is an inconclusive memorandum written by W. Averell Harriman, who noted Gray argued his case, but Churchill 'seemed unimpressed'. Harriman later explained he attended the dinner just to discuss his own forthcoming assignment as Ambassador to the Soviet Union, so he paid little attention to the conversation regarding Ireland.[37] From a letter Gray wrote to Roosevelt a couple of days later, however, it is apparent the point of disagreement with Churchill concerned the tone of the note. Gray thought it was 'very important to keep a friendly ending', but Churchill objected to telling de Valera that if he went his separate way, the Allies would wish him well.[38] In the end it was decided Gray would draft the kind of letter he wished Roosevelt to send to de Valera, and the President and Churchill would then consider it.

Gray submitted the draft letter two days later. It was in the form of an invitation to Ireland to join the Allies in the fight against Fascism. He outlined a magnanimous American policy towards Ireland, thanks to which the 'normal standards of living have been less impaired in Éire as the result of war than in any other country in Europe'.[39] But the Dublin government made 'no contribution to the safety and maintenance of a supply line by which in so important measure your national economy is maintained'. In fact, it had adopted policies that were less than generous towards the United States by protesting against the American use of Northern Ireland bases and permitting the Irish newspapers to publish protests against the American presence in the Six Counties, while censoring items critical of Germany for bombing Ireland. Moreover, he went on, the Irish government allowed Axis diplomats to remain in Ireland, where they could spy on Allied war efforts.

In the past Americans would not have been justified in asking the Dublin government to abandon neutrality because they could not adequately assist in defending Ireland against German attacks. 'Now, however,' he continued, 'the outcome of the war is no longer in doubt. Our victory is assured though it is not yet won, and it appears to the American government to be a friendly act to offer the Irish people a share in that victory as we have given them a share of our supply.' This part of the letter was clearly designed to provoke a refusal from de Valera. The draft document pointed out that America's 'offer cannot be construed as a plea for aid or an effort to purchase cooperation'. It was simply supposed to be a generous offer to share the glory of victory. The outcome of the war was not going to be affected by Ireland's participation, but the country could 'play a notable and honourable part in contributing to the shortening of its duration by leasing us bases for the protection of the Atlantic supply lines and by the elimination of Axis spy centres on Éire territory'.[40]

Along with the draft letter, Gray sent the President a covering memorandum outlining his reasons for advocating the proposed approach. If the Irish accepted the offer, the United States would obtain bases and the removal of Axis diplomats, and would be able to control Irish representatives at the post-war peace conference. But this was all pretty much academic because, Gray noted, it was 'probable' that de Valera would reject the approach as he had told Maffey some months earlier that Ireland could not jump on the Allied bandwagon.

'They would mock me,' the Taoiseach declared, 'if I changed after it appeared certain that you were going to win.'

'It is', Gray wrote, 'this egotistical vanity which apparently in the past inspired his refusal to accept the [1921] Treaty ... and thus precipitated a wholly needless civil war.'[41]

'De Valera could easily abandon neutrality without incurring much risk for Ireland,' his authorised biographer noted. 'But that was not his way.'[42]

'The note is composed primarily for the American public and designed to reveal to them how generously Éire has been treated and how little the government of Éire had done in return for the people of America,' Gray wrote.[43] In short, it was a propaganda exercise.

Roosevelt told Halifax, the British Ambassador, that he had a good mind to ask for Irish bases. He did not think de Valera would accede, but it would set the record straight and evidence of his refusal could be useful.[44]

But the Cabinet in London was distinctly cool about the idea. It telegraphed Churchill not to do anything about Gray's proposed note until he had discussed the matter in Cabinet upon his return home.[45]

Chapter 24

ǀ LIVING THE LIFE OF RILEY

Despite his absent treatment policy towards Ireland, Roosevelt encouraged Archbishop Francis Spellman of New York to visit Dublin and stay at the American Legation in April 1943. The archbishop had been visiting American troops in Britain and North Africa as part of his duties as head chaplain to the armed forces. He turned down an invitation to stay with Archbishop John Charles McQuaid of Dublin. Spellman had meetings with de Valera, Cardinal MacRory, the Papal Nuncio and Archbishop McQuaid during a four-day stay in Dublin.[1]

'They can hardly shoot old uncle Gray when His Grace stopped with him,' Gray noted gleefully. 'From what he told me of his talk with de Valera,' Gray reported, 'he took the line of saying that what de Valera did was his own responsibility entirely but that thus and so was the policy of America and that he, Spellman, was a hundred percent behind it.' Gray took a vicarious delight in feeling he had outsmarted the Taoiseach:

> I have never seen him so sour and depressed as he was during the four meals that I took in his company last week. The only comment he ever made on Spellman was that his ancestors were Irish. I think he is undergoing great inward suffering and if our Archbishop could have said to him what he recently, as a priest, said to de Gaulle, to purge his soul of vanity it might help. In his addresses at mass our Archbishop slipped in the American viewpoint continuously but of course the Government through its press has soft pedalled all this and claims the visit as a compliment paid by America to Ireland.[2]

'Of course Dev knows that we put this over on him,' Gray added, 'and that is one thing that makes him so sour. He considers the support of American Catholics for his Nationalistic policies his RIGHT.'

Gray drove North with Spellman to meet Cardinal MacRory and the Governor of Northern Ireland. The Cardinal appeared to resent the presence of Gray, who had given the press copies of his letter to the Cardinal of the previous autumn without consulting him. MacRory felt that the American Minister should have balanced it by also giving his letter to Gray. He was so annoyed that he ignored three letters from Gray. He obviously overreacted to Gray's presence, however, because he later expressed regret for being rude to Spellman.[3] Although happy with the Spellman visit, Gray still thought it best that the United States pursue the absent treatment. 'Keep everybody of importance away from Éire from now on much as it makes life dull for this legation,' he advised.[4]

Although a news blackout had been ordered on the Athenry crash involving the four American generals, Hans Becker, a German national who was living in Ireland since before the war, happened to pass the crash scene on the day and he informed Hempel, who asked for an explanation from the Department of External Affairs about the release of those on board. He mistakenly believed General Dwight D. Eisenhower was one of them.

Frederick Boland replied the aircraft was effectively a passenger plane carrying military personnel. 'Very occasionally, these passenger planes made forced landings here and we had spoken to the British about them but, of course, in view of their passenger character, there was no question of our being able to intern them,' Boland reportedly explained. He advised the German Minister not to listen to rumours. 'The way rumours travelled around here', Boland said, 'was simply extraordinary and there was always the possibility that some of them were put around for the expressed purpose of causing difficulties to our neutrality.'[5]

Within a fortnight, however, a British Wellington bomber made a forced landing in the Killbarry area of County Waterford with five men on board. They were returning from a bombing raid on Lorient. Coming so soon after the Athenry incident, members of the crew were interned. They were, in fact, the last Allied airmen to be interned. Less than a fortnight later six others were freed when they came down in County Roscommon while returning from a bombing raid on St Nazaire.

In the first six months of 1943 sixteen belligerent aircraft landed in Ireland. All were Allied—eight British and eight American. All sixty-two American survivors were released, along with eighteen of the twenty-three other survivors. The Germans protested indignantly with a formal note.

'We were unable to answer that note because it took as its headline those legal rules which we have been gradually forced by British pressure (tacit as well as overt) to leave far behind,' noted Michael Rynne, the legal advisor of the Department of External Affairs.[6]

The British initially accepted internment without protest. 'There were many good reasons for requiring the maximum restraint on our side,' Maffey wrote to Walshe in May 1943. 'We had preoccupations so immense that we could not afford to enlarge the field of controversy.'[7] That was in 1940, but by mid-1943 things had changed. The Allied internees were deeply frustrated because they realised they were little more than window-dressing to placate the German internees in the adjoining compound. One of the Canadian internees, Pilot Officer John P. Calder from Owen Sound, Ontario, had been making a name for himself as part of an elaborate escape attempt. His plan was to feign madness in order to be transferred to hospital without signing parole. He felt he would then have a much better chance of escaping from the hospital.

The twenty-seven-year-old Calder, who had been a journalist with the Canadian Press wire service before the war, withdrew socially and began writing a book. Before his internment he had written about a tour of Windsor Castle with fifty-four other airmen from various parts of the British Empire. The group had been invited to afternoon tea with the Royal Family. This article made front-page news across Canada, as did his account some weeks later of a daylight bombing raid on the naval yard in Brest. He also wrote an account of the events leading up to his internment for the influential *Maclean's* magazine.

Part of Calder's plan was to refuse parole and to spend most of each day writing. At meals he would often get into heated arguments with his New Zealand colleague, Bruce Girdlestone, who was the only one in on Calder's scheme. Although staged, their arguments were convincing, and it was not long before Calder's anti-social behaviour was attracting the attention of both colleagues and guards. By June 1943 he was ready to implement the final stages of his plan. It seemed a particularly appropriate time to play on the humanitarian feelings of the Irish authorities, as they had been particularly amenable to approaches on compassionate grounds in recent weeks.

On 12 June Sergeant James Wakelin of Newcastle was given an extended two-week parole to visit his mother in England following the death of his father. Ten days later the senior Allied officer Flight Lieutenant John Leslie Ward of Vancouver, Canada, was given a similar parole to visit his wife, who was ill in England.

Calder had prepared for the final stage of his scheme by bolstering his profile with five more articles to the Canadian Press. These articles, which began appearing in newspapers throughout Canada during June, infuriated some of his colleagues, who resented his depiction of K Lines as a virtual holiday camp. They were 'almost living the life of Riley', he wrote. The *Toronto Star* actually headlined its article, 'Interned Canadian Fliers Live Life of Riley in Éire.'[8]

Parole conditions were such that they could sign out at 8.00 a.m. and did not have to be back until 8.00 a.m. next morning. They were free to go anywhere within a 10-mile radius of the camp and could go to Dublin once a week. Seven of the Allied airmen actually got married while interned. Five of those marriages were to local Irish women, while two of the British internees married their English girlfriends, who came over to Ireland. Married men could avail of all-night parole three nights a week; they only had to sign in at the camp by noon the following day. By Irish standards they had some of the best recreational facilities in the country, with access to the Irish Army swimming pool, squash courts, handball alleys, gymnasium and golf course. The Curragh racecourse, on which the country's horse-racing classics were held, was literally across the road, and some of the men became so friendly with local trainers 'that race goers frequently approach us for tips', Calder wrote.

The ten remaining commissioned officers—who included an American, two Canadians, a New Zealander and a Pole, with the other five coming from various parts of Britain—had a room each, and they shared three Irish Army orderlies to look after their needs. Within the compound, the internees had their own bar, selling beer and spirits at duty-free prices.

'Because of parole conditions, a reasonable plenitude of good food and excellent recreation facilities, our internment is in striking contrast to usual prisoner-of-war treatment,' Calder wrote. 'So friendly are some Dublin merchants that we are able to maintain a first-class bar in the camp. We may bring in as much food as we can buy. It would be a luxurious way of living through the war, for we remain on full pay. Those who want to may study for post-war activities.'

His colleagues, all grounded airmen, were deeply frustrated at missing out on all the actions of the war. They could not understand him depicting the place in this 'luxurious' light, especially as it would likely weaken pressure on the Dublin government to release them. Calder's articles bolstered his notoriety among his colleague and drew attention to himself and his own peculiar behaviour. On the night of 25 June 1943, as a guard was making his rounds, Calder flew into a rage and destroyed his typewriter and tore up his book manuscript before dissolving into tears. 'Even I was awed at the display,' wrote Girdlestone, who knew it was an act.[9]

Guards were concerned as Calder began to drink heavily, or at least pretended to do so. In the next three days he emptied three bottles of brandy at a rate that he might have drunk them. He washed out his mouth and brushed his teeth with brandy. His breath was foul and his drunken display convincing. Then, on the night of 28 June, he pretended to try to commit suicide by taking some iodine. He was rushed to hospital without signing parole, and he was transferred to Sir Patrick Dun's Hospital in Dublin.

Although Kearney suspected it might be part of an escape attempt, he asked the Department of External Affairs to release Calder on humanitarian grounds. A couple of consultants with strong Allied sympathies examined him and played along with him. 'His condition is serious,' H.J. Eustace, the consultant psychiatrist at the Adelaide Hospital, Dublin, concluded. 'He requires constant supervision as he certainly will repeat his suicidal attempt.'[10]

The Irish did not want the bad publicity that would inevitably follow if their most famous internee should commit suicide. They therefore readily agreed to his release. Calder was moved to hospital in Britain on 1 July 1943. He told his family he had more trouble convincing the British doctors he was sane than he had in persuading the Irish that he had gone mad.

Jan Zimek, a Polish Sergeant, was also released five days later. He had been causing some trouble between the two sets of internees. At a dance in Newbridge on 16 May 1943, he publicly upbraided his colleague, Sergeant Karniewski, for talking to two of the German internees. Four of the Germans roughed up Zimek outside afterwards. There was a further incident on 1 June over a girl that Zimek fancied, when she and a friend left the hall with two of the Germans. Zimek began hassling them and they retaliated by knocking him off his bicycle and giving him a few punches. He suffered a fractured skull in the fracas.

Wing Commander Begg, the British Air Attaché, visited Zimek in hospital and advised him to act crazy. Dr Eustace was called to examine Zimek, who acted distressed. Eustace asked him if he wanted to be transferred to England.

'No' Zimek said. He wished to go back to the Curragh.

Why? Eustace asked.

He replied that he intended to kill all the German internees.

'If he is not released,' Eustace warned, 'he will do himself a serious injury.'[11]

'There is obviously a good case on all counts for getting him out of the country without delay,' Maffey wrote to the Department of External Affairs. 'I hope this course will be followed.'[12]

'The Department of Defence would be glad to be rid of this Pole,' de Valera was informed, so he duly authorised Zimek's transferral to Northern Ireland next day.[13]

When Kearney mentioned to de Valera the following month that internment had been evoking most criticism of Irish neutrality, 'Mr de Valera said that anybody who knew the facts would say that Ireland had adopted an attitude of benevolent neutrality.'[14] The Taoiseach even agreed to apply the non-operational argument retrospectively to those already interned, but it was first necessary to move the Allied internees away from the Germans and to a new camp in Gormanston, County Meath. Both the British and the Germans had asked for the camp to be split up, and the incidents involving Zimek provided a further justification for separating the two sets of internees.

Maffey tried to persuade de Valera to release not just the twenty men he had agreed to free but also the other eleven who were due to move to Gormanston. 'We were not going to worry about eleven airmen as being in any way a practical manpower question,' Maffey explained. 'I was looking at things from his point of view. Not only was he keeping a bad card in his hand. He was running the risk of an embarrassing "show down" when American airmen on operational flight tested his principles.'[15]

The Irish had indicated they 'were going to give a liberal interpretation to the phrase "non-operational flight". One of those being released was Pilot Officer Roger Emile Motte (alias Maurice Remy), a Free French pilot who had actually shot down a German bomber near Kilmacthomas, County Waterford, on the day he was interned.[16]

Holding on to British internees merely to placate the Germans was courting trouble, Maffey warned.[17] 'He said he knew perfectly well that if we interned any American airmen, we might get a very "bloody" Note,' Walshe noted. 'I felt I could not let that remark pass, and I said that, if we got a "bloody" Note, we'd send back a Note more "bloody" still.'[18]

'It was no argument in our eyes for their retaining our eleven airmen to keep the Germans quiet,' Maffey explained. 'If other methods were difficult, why not allow the eleven men to escape?' Walshe did not commit himself on this point, but he did give 'the impression that we shall be able to work matters out this way if no better way presents itself'.[19]

When de Valera and Maffey met again two days later, the Taoiseach explained he could release all of the Allied airmen only if the British agreed to the release of their German counterparts at the same time. He 'seemed obsessed by the "fifty-fifty" neutrality idea,' Maffey noted as he went on to accuse the Irish leader of possessing 'Himalayan obstinacy'.[20] 'I left him in no doubt for the fiftieth time as to the complete unacceptability of any such plan, and I took the opportunity of ramming in for the fiftieth time our grave apprehensions regarding any German in Éire,' Maffey continued.

The Allied airmen left the Curragh camp for the last time on 18 October 1943. They travelled to Dublin in a military convoy, which split up in Phoenix Park, Dublin. The men being released headed for Northern Ireland, while the others went on to Gormanston. Their families were notified that they had been freed, with no details other than a suggestion that they had actually escaped. 'I have to ask that you will treat this information as confidential and do your utmost to ensure that no mention of his escape appears in the press,' the New Zealand naval secretary informed Girdlestone's parents.[21]

While the idea of a note inviting de Valera to join the Allies was being discussed in Washington, Gray returned to Ireland in early September and informed Maffey and Kearney about his initiative. 'I explained that the object of my recommendation was to prevent the Irish partition issue being injected into post-war American politics by de Valera and exploited by the subversive elements in America which tried to block preparedness and lend-lease in order to oppose your plans for cooperation with the British Commonwealth and other nations,' Gray reported. 'We know these forces are still active and organised.'[22]

'If it is in any way doubtful whether we can at this stage of the war make full use of any facilities Éire may concede,' Maffey argued, 'I am in favour of not accepting concessions or cooperation from Éire but of leaving her to stew in her present isolation so that her moral weight in the peace settlement may be negligible.'[23]

'You have looked at this business through English eyes—God bless you,' Maffey wrote to Gray. 'I must now look at it though American eyes.' If de Valera did not make the predictable reply, the note could prove embarrassing for Roosevelt, because it could provoke an international incident in which 'Mr de Valera, having the last word in the debate, will get the best of the argument.'[24]

Gray said Roosevelt wanted a 'No' answer from de Valera, but Maffey warned the proposed approach 'has the smell of an attempt at being clever and when it comes to that Mr de Valera is no novice'.[25] He could respond by making lavish demands for defence equipment as a precondition to accepting the Allied offer. Then if the Allies refused such armaments, he would say he could not accept the offer for fear of putting Irish women and children at risk when the country was virtually defenceless. If the Taoiseach adopted this approach, Roosevelt would be in a weaker position than ever in the quest to discredit de Valera and his Irish-American supporters.

'It would be a historic confrontation,' Maffey warned. 'This is the spotlight for which Mr de Valera is craving. On a world platform he will stand level with the President of the United States and enjoy a right of reply.'

Having stoked Gray's indignation for years, Maffey now found himself in the embarrassing position of trying to dampen the American Minister's ire. 'Throughout,' Maffey wrote to the Dominions Office, 'it has been my aim to assist in getting America into a state of irritation against Éire and now that this irritation seeks to find expression in specific action it is disconcerting to find myself suggesting difficulties and dangers in the method proposed.'[26]

Gray seemed to be almost paranoid. For instance, he complained to Maffey about an article in the *Ulster Protestant*, which asked, 'Will the Pope be on the list of war criminals?' Such sentiments were standard in that bigoted publication, but Gray somehow suspected 'German agents' were behind it.[27]

When Maffey predicted Ireland was going to have a shortfall of about half her needed supplies, Gray foresaw another problem. 'I don't have to tell you what will start in Irish-Americans circles when Éire really begins to feel the pinch,' he wrote Roosevelt on 17 September. 'If you don't nail Dev's hide on the fence NOW, you will be in a bad way, unless you want to give in to him and supply him without ever getting a thank you.'[28]

Gray's proposal had already run into strong opposition from the military in Washington. Army Chief of Staff General George C. Marshall noted that bases in the Twenty-six Counties would not be of much use as long as the French coast was under German control—a point the Irish had been arguing for almost three years. 'Naval bases will not significantly reduce the existent submarine threat because present bases in southwest England are closer to the Bay of Biscay,' Marshall wrote. 'However, naval bases will be useful when it is considered safe enough to route convoys south of Ireland and when invasion operations start in western Europe.'[29]

If de Valera acceded to a request and handed over ports, American forces would possibly be handicapped because they would be morally obliged to divert personnel and equipment to protect defenceless Irish cities. Instead of asking for the ports, therefore, the Joint Chiefs of Staff advised the President to ask the Irish government to guarantee that bases would be made available, if needed. The State Department drafted a new note, which Hull forwarded to Roosevelt. Instead of an offer, this was drawn up as a request stating that in planning strategy it would be helpful to know if America could count on being able to use Irish facilities should the occasion arise in which their use would 'help to save American lives and the lives of nationals of those countries associated with us in the war'. Ireland would be asked 'to grant to the United States, for the duration of the war and six months thereafter, permission to use existing air and naval facilities in Ireland at any time these facilities should be required and also as may be needed by American forces'. It was 'entirely possible' the United States would not need any facilities, the document emphasised, but 'it would be of real assistance to us *now* in planning our war strategy to be able to count upon the use of such bases if they should be needed.' Roosevelt approved the new approach, and the proposed note was forwarded to London for British consideration.[30]

Gray thought the note's 'extremely mild phrasing' tended to play down Washington's resentment over de Valera's remarks about American troops being stationed in Northern Ireland at a time when the Irish were permitting Axis representatives to remain in Dublin. Moreover, he warned that the Taoiseach would simply reply that Washington should ask for bases if they were needed, at which time Dublin would consider the request. If he did this, the Americans would have neither the promise of facilities nor the record of a refusal.[31]

Maffey, who considered the new draft an improvement, still felt that 'the political advantages on this exchange would probably rest with Mr de Valera and on the practical front nothing would happen'.[32] He disagreed with Gray's view of de Valera being motivated by 'a dynamic militancy aimed at provoking bloodshed in the North on the question of Partition and embittering Anglo-American relations by injecting into them the factor of renewed trouble in Ireland'. The British Representative thought it would be better if de Valera ignored the partition issue, 'but he is not in an easy position politically, and having interned several hundred men pledged to violence, I am convinced that he would regard an outbreak as disastrous to his Government and his hopes'.[33]

Gray asked two of the Taoiseach's colleagues—Seán MacEntee and Conor Maguire—if there was any way de Valera could be persuaded to enter the war. 'They each looked at each other and then at me and laughed, indicating I must be crazy,' Gray reported.[34]

Hull argued the amicable tone of the revised note actually made the document more potent for future publication, in the event the Irish rejected it, because it would mean they would have refused a limited request made in the 'friendliest terms'. If de Valera accepted, on the other hand, the United States 'would then be in a much stronger position to ask as a next step the removal of Axis representatives as a necessary security measure'.[35]

On realising that the new draft would only be one step in a series of moves that could be used in preparing a political position to counter Irish attempts to undermine the Anglo-American relations, Gray 'heartily' approved of it. 'But believe me,' he wrote to Roosevelt, 'you will have to face this situation and handle it without gloves later on. Dev's political survival depends on his injecting the vitality of hate into this issue of partition.'[36]

The Taoiseach had recently provided confirmation of his intention to make an international issue of partition. At the annual Fianna Fáil árd fheis in late September, he declared: 'We will try to do everything we can in order that the wrongs of this partition of our country would be brought to the notice of all those who would have any power to remedy it.'[37]

Gray wrote to Undersecretary of State Edward Stettinius on 22 October:

The evidence is now conclusive that Mr de Valera is planning to tie his political fortunes to the issue of partition and intends to appeal to all anti-British elements in the United States for support. It must be remember in this connection that Mr de Valera and the responsible party leaders associated with him know as well as we do that Britain cannot and will not coerce Ulster and that, consequently, all agitation to this end will only create ill feeling and postpone to an indefinite future the beginning of conciliation between North and South and of recognition of their common economic interest within the framework of the Commonwealth.'[38]

On being told the Americans would consider an evasive Irish reply a refusal, Maffey approved of the new American note. 'If we can rely on this line being firmly held,' he telegraphed the Dominions Office, 'my previous objections would not apply and I should be in favour of the *demarche* suggested.'[39]

The Canadian High Commissioner was stunned by these arguments. He had had different reasons for suggesting an American approach in the first place, back in January. 'I had in the forefront of my mind the winning of the war,' he told Maffey, 'and not post-war relations between Great Britain and the United States of America, and not at all the part certain Irish elements in the United States of America might play in post-war relationships.' Kearney was convinced the Taoiseach would reject the proposed note. 'Although it contained some honeyed phrases,' he argued, 'it was almost tantamount to an indictment.' In spite of Gray's assurance to the contrary, the Canadian High Commissioner concluded the document 'seemed to be drafted in such a way as to provoke a refusal'. He therefore objected to it.

'If a refusal were received, which was the only answer one could anticipate,' Kearney wrote, 'I foresaw that resentment would replace any benevolence which Ireland had heretofore exhibited, and the elimination, or curtailment of acts of goodwill could not be of any advantage in so far as the Allied war-effort was concerned.'[40]

On 12 October 1943 Churchill announced that Antonio Salazar, the dictator of neutral Portugal, had given Britain bases in the Azores. Hempel reported that Walshe complained about British insinuations that Ireland might follow Portugal's example in allowing the Allies to use the Azores. Walshe ruled out Irish 'participation on the side of the Allies' and he thanked Hempel for 'Germany's sympathetic appreciation' of Ireland's difficulties.[41] This report was intercepted by the British and passed to Churchill as an apparent example of Irish treachery, but it was typical of Walshe's diplomatic approach. In recent weeks he had been involved in the secret arrangements for releasing the bulk of the Allied internees, had allowed the oss to read Irish diplomatic reports and had agreed to question Irish diplomats on the Continent on behalf of the oss, while he merely offered empty platitudes to the German Minister.

Gray thought Salazar's action afforded an ideal backdrop for the proposed request to de Valera, but the British procrastinated. Churchill was sorely disappointed that it had been toned down considerably from Gray's original draft, given that he had even opposed the friendly ending of that draft. 'I have now read for the first time the new proposed letter from the President to Mr de Valera, and it is certainly very different from that which he showed me at Hyde Park,' Churchill wrote to Cranborne on 2 November. 'I agree that we cannot accept this policy.'[42]

Some members of Churchill's government thought de Valera's existing policy was discrediting him sufficiently in the United States already, and they were afraid the Taoiseach would comply with the request in order to be in a stronger position to demand an end to partition. 'They do not seem to appreciate that a generous offer refused by de Valera would go far toward eliminating him as a trouble-making influence after the war nor will they believe that he definitely nailed his flag to the mast of neutrality and will under no circumstances whatsoever join with the United States,' Gray telegraphed Hull. 'This irrational obstinacy is his fundamental weakness and should be exploited by the United States.'[43]

Hull thought the British possibly feared the American proposal might be intended as a step to help de Valera to end partition. He therefore sought to assure the British that the United States had no intention of being dragged into the partition controversy and the proposed note was intended to 'serve an extremely useful purpose not only with regard to our domestic situation and our relations with Ireland but particularly with reference to certain vicious influences which may otherwise be brought to bear on Anglo-American relations after the war'.[44]

The note was a purely political initiative and had nothing to do with the military or naval people. Guy Liddell of MI5 noted: 'The naval authorities do not regard the Irish bases as of any great importance.' [45]

Chapter 25 ∿

AS AN ABSOLUTE
MINIMUM

I t was not until 7 December 1943 that Churchill finally told Roosevelt, at the Cairo Conference, that London wished to forget about the Irish ports. The British were afraid de Valera would avoid a direct refusal and would cloud the issue by raising the partition question in a manner that would embarrass them. While Roosevelt still thought it would be 'a good thing to have an American protest to Ireland on record', he understood the British attitude.[1]

Gray was already thinking of other ways to discredit de Valera and undermine his Irish-American supporters. 'It would', he wrote to Roosevelt on 4 November 1943, 'be a logical development for the record when and if Dev turns down the request for the ports to follow up with a request that he at least get the Axis spy missions out of the country.' The Axis representatives in Dublin were in a position to learn about American troop movements in Northern Ireland. The American forces 'might just as well be in Vichy France', Gray noted. When he discussed the problem with the Canadian High Commissioner the following week, however, Kearney expressed complete satisfaction with Irish security, because the Irish had been cooperating with the Allies on intelligence matters and had been using radio-detection equipment supplied by the British to make sure the German Legation was not using its radio-transmitter. Kearney added that Walshe offered that the Irish would also work with Canadian intelligence.[2]

In the second half of 1943 a total of twenty belligerent aircraft came down in Ireland. Two were German and all eight survivors were interned, while all sixty-six survivors from eighteen Allied planes were released. Those included forty-four Americans, twelve Poles, seven from the United Kingdom, two Australians and one Canadian. In addition, two BOAC civilian aircraft crashed—one on landing at Rineanna and the other en route from Lisbon to Foynes. There were no casualties on the first aircraft, but ten of the twenty-five people on board the second plane perished when it crashed into Mount Brandon. Sixteen of the Americans released were on two American military planes that got lost flying from Morocco to Britain. The planes landed at Rineanna within a couple of hours of each other, and the crews remained there overnight before flying out next day. Much to the surprise of the Irish, the American crews refused to associate with each other. One crew complained that the others were 'Damned Yankees'.[3]

Hempel quickly learned of the release of the bulk of the Allied internees in October. Only one German was released during the war. *Feldwebel* Max Hohaus had been the lone survivor when the plane in which he was flying crashed into a hill in Cork, in February 1941. He spent over two years in hospital being treated for horrific burns. He was handed over to the British for repatriation home through the Red Cross in October 1943. In addition to Calder and Zimek, Sergeant Frank Thomas from Lancashire, England, was released on compassionate grounds. Calder quickly returned to action. In August 1943, while returning from a bombing mission, his plane crashed into a mountain in Scotland. He was the only survivor. He wrote an article about the hospital where he was treated, and he was interviewed on the BBC's World Service.

Hempel learned about Calder and protested about the discriminatory release of Allied airmen. Earlier protest notes of 23 May 1942 and 27 July 1943 questioning the release of Allied aircraft had been ignored, along with his request for the release of a similar number of German airmen. 'I told him that we could not complain about that attitude,' Walshe reported. 'He was, of course, perfectly free to report to his Government on his failure to obtain a reply but he should remind his Government about the much more serious matters relating to which no reply had been received by the Irish Government from them.'[4]

The Irish attitude was further evidence of the Dublin government's bias towards the Allies. While returning to Ottawa for consultations in November 1943, Kearney was surprised to learn in London that Vincent Massey, the Canadian High Commissioner to Britain, was highly critical of the Irish. He also found Malcolm MacDonald, the British High Commissioner in Canada, equally critical. Ireland was being seen as a 'diplomatic pariah', but Kearney could not understand how adopting such an attitude was in Canada's interest. He was therefore pleasantly surprised at the attitude of Prime Minister Mackenzie King, who desired strong ties with Ireland. This bolstered Kearney's determination to ignore MacDonald's advice to 'leave Ireland alone'.[5]

Gray suggested the State Department formally ask de Valera to expel Axis diplomats. He forwarded a draft for a formal note contending Irish neutrality favoured the Axis powers because Ireland's geographic location gave their representatives an opportunity for espionage. It was common knowledge at the time that Allied troops in Northern Ireland and Britain were preparing for the invasion of Europe, so Gray argued the success of the operation and the lives of thousands of men would be endangered by the possibility that the invasion plans could be betrayed from Ireland. He therefore suggested the Irish government should be asked to make its policy 'truly neutral' by expelling the German and Japanese representatives.[6]

In a covering telegram, Gray explained that Maffey shared his belief de Valera would reject the request. This would afford the United States 'an important political advantage' by placing him 'on record in such a manner as would strengthen our defence against pressure group attempts to involve [the] United States in the partition question'. Although the whole thing was primarily motivated by political considerations, Gray warned the State Department that the German Minister might indeed get hold of vital information, which could then be forwarded to Berlin in an emergency by using the Legation's radio-transmitter. The transmitter had not been used for over a year, but he warned, 'it remains ready for use for the immediate transmission of any message deemed important enough to risk complications with the Irish government.'[7]

Walshe said to Hempel 'quite frankly and in the most friendly way that the presence of a wireless transmitter in the German Legation was giving us more worry in our relations with the British and American Governments than any other factor'. The time had therefore come to request the Germans to hand over their transmitter, Walshe told Hempel on 15 December 1943. 'As the crisis of the war drew nearer, my minister and I felt that at any moment we might receive from these two Governments an ultimatum calling upon our Government to give his papers to the German Minister.'

'Dr Hempel said that, if he gave up his wireless transmitter, he would feel that he had given up everything,' according to Walshe. 'To this I replied that he, in fact, had no right to have a wireless transmitter, that it was not allowed in any country in time of war. For that reason it was a luxury.'[8]

German espionage in Ireland became a live issue a few days later when the Germans dropped two Irishmen as spies in County Clare. The two men, John Francis O'Reilly and John Kenny, had been among seventy-two Irish people working in the Channel Islands when the Germans invaded in 1940. After working in Germany for some time, they volunteered to go to Ireland to transmit weather information.

Born in Kilrush, O'Reilly was reared in Kilkee. He spent some time in the Customs Service, but he was obviously restless. He entered Buckfast Abbey as a novice in March 1939, but quit after just three weeks. He then went to work for an amusement park and a number of different hotels. On 7 May 1940 he went to Jersey and worked as a farmhand. The following month, when the island's authorities arranged for the evacuation of the island, O'Reilly decided to stay rather than risk being called up for military service in England. He was still on Jersey when the Germans invaded the following month.

Islanders were instructed not to fight, so there was no resistance. The Germans knew O'Reilly was Irish, and he found them friendly. He got a job working for them in a civilian capacity. He perfected his German and in March 1941 was employed as an interpreter between the soldiers and the workmen. 'I went to the Commander of the Island and I requested permission to go to Germany,' O'Reilly later explained. 'I told him I was prepared to work there. He consented to facilitate me.' O'Reilly helped to persuade some seventy of the Irish contingent to go with him to Brunswick in Germany, where they worked in a steel plant, while he was employed as an interpreter and bookkeeper.[9]

'Life in Germany is quite normal,' O'Reilly wrote to his parents in July 1941. 'The food situation is good and the shops are well-stocked with every commodity. The people are as well mannered as their soldiers in Jersey led me to believe; all expressed curiosity as to how I arrived here from Ireland (as they believed). The weather is wonderful and all my spare time is spent sun-bathing.'[10] His letters had to pass through censorship, so G2 took a particular interest in him and photocopied all of his correspondence.

He was invited to Berlin for an interview with the Ministry of Propaganda. 'I went there on September 24, 1941, and made a voice test on radio,' he wrote. 'I was offered employment by the Ministry as they said they wished to start news features for Ireland.'[11] He broadcast to Ireland on the short wave radio station three times each evening under the name of Pat O'Brien, which he shared with a couple of other commentators. In October 1941 when he applied for a passport at the Irish Legation in Berlin, he told William Warnock, the Irish *Chargé d'Affaires*, he would not say anything to endanger Irish neutrality in his broadcasts.

His job allowed him to hear radio broadcasts from home. 'I hear the news from Athlone every night; it is rather amusing to hear them talking about the price of pigs in the Dublin market, just as if there was nothing of greater importance, as far as Éire is concerned,' he wrote to his parents. 'You cannot hear from me very often, but you can always hear me; or perhaps you did not recognise my voice?'[12]

In September 1942 O'Reilly went into training with the *Abwehr* in Bremen. It was initially planned to land him in Ireland by submarine around December 1942 in order to report on shipping movements around Northern Ireland, but the German Foreign Office squashed the scheme for fear of antagonising the Irish government. It was also felt O'Reilly should not be trusted because of his family background and his naive and garrulous nature.

Some three months before Jack was born in 1916, his father, Bernard O'Reilly, an RIC constable stationed in Ardfert, County Kerry, had the dubious distinction of being the policeman who arrested Roger Casement near Banna Strand, shortly after Casement's landing from a U-boat. Although Bernard O'Reilly resigned from the RIC in protest over the conduct of the Black and Tans in 1920, neither he nor his family were ever allowed to forget the arrest of Casement.

In June 1943 Jack O'Reilly transferred to the *Sicherheitsdienst*, the overseas political intelligence service of the Gestapo. His frequent letters home betrayed an intense homesickness. He was dropped by parachute near Moveen, about three miles from Kilkee, in the early hours of 16 December 1943. He walked to Kilkee, carrying a suitcase that was obviously heavy. It contained two radios. He told people he met on the way that he had arrived in Doonbeg by train en route to Kilkee for a holiday. Gardaí quickly heard of the strange man with the heavy suitcase. They called to O'Reilly's home and his mother told them he had arrived home from Germany via Lisbon and Rineanna. Jack called to the Garda station at about 11.00 p.m. that night and made a long statement.

He said he had made friends with a Luftwaffe pilot in Bremen. 'I suggested to him by way of a joke that some time when he would be engaged in operations over England, he could bring me with him and drop me at home but he, as a German, took the joke seriously and pointed out all its difficulties and its effect on himself if he was found out.'[13]

He said he had planned to fly home from Portugal, but when he got to Lisbon, he learned his flight would first stop in England and he would be arrested there. He therefore went back to France and contacted his Luftwaffe friend and persuaded him to take him on a reconnaissance flight and to drop him near the Clare coast. 'I am aware now that I landed irregularly in Éire,' he told the police, 'but I was not aware of any laws or regulations in the matter and in any event in taking the steps I did, I did not consider the consequences of such an action. I had decided to return home by any means.'[14]

Three nights later John Kenny, who was reared in Kilcummin near Killarney, County Kerry, was dropped about 1.5 miles from Kilkee. He had been working in England and decided to go to Jersey to avoid conscription. 'I did not mind being a solider but I certainly did not feel like fighting for "John Bull" so I left England,' he wrote to his uncle.[15] He had been working as a waiter in Jersey for about three weeks when the Germans invaded on 2 July 1940. He went to work as a driver for a German engineering officer and remained there until September 1943, when Jack O'Reilly recruited him.

Kenny was then trained in Berlin with the aim of dropping him in Clare.

On landing in a strong wind, he was dragged by the parachute and suffered a fractured skull when he banged his head on a wall. This required six months' hospitalisation. O'Reilly admitted that Kenny was to help him and they were supposed to make their way to England and engage in political espionage. While Kenny recovered in hospital, O'Reilly was jailed in Arbour Hill, but he managed to escape in July 1944. He made it to Kerry and sought IRA help, but the Republicans did not trust him in view of his father's role in the arrest of Casement. He therefore went home again to Kilkee, where his father reported his presence to the police and collected a £500 reward. This was apparently done in agreement between father and son. The money was banked and given to Jack when he was released from jail at the end of the war.

The British exploited the arrival of O'Reilly and Kenny to insist Irish authorities demand that the Germans surrender their transmitter. Hempel's position had been seriously undermined and he agreed to deposit the transmitter in the vault of a Dublin bank, from where he could only retrieve it with the approval of the Department of External Affairs.

In December 1943 Gray had an opportunity to give vent to their displeasure when the Irish sought permission to purchase an American ship. The two American ships chartered in 1941 had both been lost at sea while carrying wheat to Ireland. Gray noted the Irish government had not protested, even though there was evidence a German submarine had torpedoed one of them. Gray also complained that handing over those two ships had 'had negligible propaganda value in Ireland as the government continuously ignored any obligation to the United States for them'.[16] Influenced by Gray, the State Department replied that any further ships transferred to Ireland would likely meet the same fate because the Germans had demonstrated they were 'in fact making war upon Ireland'.[17]

On a visit to Dublin in late December, 'Spike' Marlin exploited the dropping of the two German spies. 'Hurst stressed to the Irish the tremendous seriousness of the situation from now on so far as the safety and success of our invasion was concerned and how vulnerable we might be from a security standpoint if the Irish did not cooperate fully with us in counteracting espionage,' Nicholas noted. 'He said he thought the incident of the parachutists should be given more publicity in order to place the country on the *qui vive*.'

Colonel Dan Bryan explained, however, that the Irish were cooperating with MI5 in playing down the matter in order to keep Berlin guessing as long as possible. The British had warned G2 to expect arrivals from the two German planes and to keep a lookout for a third. Bryan explained that the Germans had been broadcasting call signals to O'Reilly and Kenny. While the

State Department was giving vent to its displeasure with the Irish, Carter Nicholas was, ironically, hoping the Irish might help by allowing either O'Reilly or Kenny to be used as double agents. With the planned Allied invasion of Europe barely six months away, the oss was anxious to explore all 'means of supplying the Germans with false information'.[18]

'Every possibility of this kind, however remote, must be exhausted as extraordinarily few opportunities present themselves,' Nicholas wrote to Marlin on 30 December 1943. 'Whether a reasonable chance in fact exists and the key to the methods to be followed if one does exist, can be determined only after as many facts as possible are in. Those in charge here of the penetration of Germany consider the next three months critical. Every effort must be made to establish our own sources there.'[19]

After securing exhaustive reports on the interrogation of the two men, the oss dropped the idea of using either of them as a double agent, because each had 'an IRA background and hence an anti-British bias', according to Nicholas. But Marlin did receive interesting information from Kenny about the spy school he attended in Lienitz and the names and descriptions of his fellow trainees.[20]

While Gray was fulminating about the Irish security threat, the Irish were in fact cooperating fully with the Allies on security matters. Gray, in truth, was really more concerned about American domestic political considerations. Consequently the surrender of the German transmitter had no impact on his latest initiative. The State Department sounded out the Joint Chiefs of Staff, the War Department and the oss. John D. Hickerson, the head of the British Commonwealth Affairs Division of the State Department, talked with Carter Nicholas on 29 December. In view of the supposed security considerations in asking for the removal of the Axis diplomats, it is worth quoting Nicholas' account of this meeting at some length:

For fear of trespassing in the matter of State Department policy I avoided arguing that the note should or should not be delivered but sought to make sure the Department was aware of all the facts in our possession which might have a bearing. Mr Hickerson stated that the War Department was aware that the British (presumably MI5) were satisfied with the security situation in Éire. The conversation covered the following ground:

That the only direct method of communicating open to Axis diplomats in Éire was a British controlled cable; that messages sent through this cable were broken; that cable facilities were left open by the English as a *quid pro quo* for the Germans leaving open communications from Bern to London; that while the radio transmitter at the German Legation had been removed only a few days before, the Germans had not been permitted to use it for years and a twenty-four hour watch had been maintained to make sure they didn't; that the British not only did not want Éire but did not want her to grant, at this time at least, the use of air or sea bases either to the United States or to themselves. Mr Hickerson informed me that the British attitude with respect to Éire's entering the war was seconded by our Navy and War Departments.

The conversation turned to reasons for satisfaction with Éire's neutrality, i.e. the arguments on one side of the balance which included—

(a) the large enlistment of Irish in the British forces. Mr Hickerson put this at 250,000, which I think too high, but I did not say so.

(b the advantageous food situation. Practically all of Ireland's agricultural exports go to England. The Irish pound is tied to the British pound and payment is in the form of credit.

(c) the Irish Army, reserves and the local defense forces and coast watching service have been kept mobilised and on the job. Unless we are to assume that the United Nations intended to invade Ireland this was a mobilisation against Germany.

(d) Éire in the war would undoubtedly have meant an activation of the radical elements which as it is have been effectively kept under control.

(e) if Éire were in the war it would probably be bombed and the effect of bombings would undoubtedly be to disrupt the transportation system and the shipment of food to England, to require from the United Nations relief materials for reconstruction, and arms much needed elsewhere.

(f) full cooperation with the British and with us in security measures, and liaison with respect to counter intelligence and affirmative intelligence.

(g) German aviators landing in Éire are all interned. Allied aviators are returned to their bases. Rescued German naval personnel were interned, although international law did not require it.

I told Mr Hickerson that I wanted to be absolutely certain that no information which we had received from the Irish as a result of our liaison should be used against them in the note. He assured me flatly that this was the case. As a matter of fact very little of what had been received had been disseminated to the State Department as it was principally of military interest. Mr Hickerson showed me the draft of the proposed note then before the Joint Chiefs of Staff, and I was satisfied that it contained no information which we had received as a result of our liaison with the Irish.[21]

While Hickerson and Nicholas were talking, a drama involving an Irish ship was playing out in the Bay of Biscay. The *Kerlogue*, a 142-ft-long steamer owned by the Wexford Steamship Company, was returning from Portugal with a cargo of oranges on the morning of 29 December. It was 362 miles south of the Fastnet Rock and 340 miles west of Brest when a German aircraft signalled it to rescue seamen in distress. It led the *Kerlogue* to the aftermath of a naval battle. For the next 10 hours the ship's ten-man crew fished 168 German sailors out of water. Some were in a very bad way, and two soon died and were buried at sea.

The *Kerlogue* was supposed to put in at Fishguard for a navicert before proceeding to Ireland, but in an act of compassion the captain made straight for Cobh, deliberately maintaining radio silence for as long as possible in order to avoid being forced into a British port. About three-and-a-half hours out, the *Kerlogue* radioed Valencia:

> Proceeding Cobh expect arrival 2 am tomorrow morning. Have on board
> 164 seamen survivors, seven men seriously injured, one man dead. Please
> instruct port control Cobh that I request urgent medical assistance. Have
> no food, water or clothing.[22]

The *Kerlogue* ignored an Admiralty order to proceed to Fishguard. The rescued sailors had not violated Irish territory. Under international law they should have been freed as distressed mariners, but Maffey insisted they should be interned. 'A German in Éire is a menace to England, while an Englishman in Éire is no menace to Germany,' he told de Valera.[23] The sailors were duly moved to the Curragh and interned for the duration of the war.

The Joint Chiefs of Staff in Washington had no objection to the proposed note calling for the expulsion of the Axis diplomats. The State Department therefore instructed Gray to relay the proposal to Winant, so that he could sound out the British. Gray explained that it would merely ask the Irish to be 'truly neutral' by expelling the Axis diplomats and thus denying them the espionage advantage they enjoyed in Ireland. The whole thing was really a propaganda ploy to provoke American resentment against de Valera by depicting his government as endangering the lives of Americans by refusing to expel potential spies during the crucial months leading up to the Allied invasion of Europe. 'A threat to the lives of American soldiers will unfailingly excite American resentment,' Gray explained. 'The only choice open to us appears to be whether we shall meet this situation while the war continues, while Anglo-American solidarity is strong, while American obligation to Northern Ireland for facilities is remembered, or wait upon a time and circumstance favourable to Mr de Valera.'[24]

The British were receptive to the latest initiative. 'If the German and

Japanese Ministers remain at their posts in Dublin,' Churchill wrote to Cranborne on 2 February, 'it may be necessary on military grounds to sever all contacts between Ireland and the Continent in the near future for a period of months.'[25] He was responding to a memorandum in which Cranborne outlined the various courses open to the British in dealing with the proposed American note. Rather than adopting a joint approach with the Americans, he suggested Britain sent a note explaining that 'we had been consulted by the United States Government before their approach was made and that we warmly welcomed their initiative and supported the request'. But he was under no illusion about the purpose of the note. 'Although the German Minister in Dublin is probably not in a position to give his Government much useful information,' Cranborne wrote, 'it is intolerable that he should be there at all.' He thought it 'most likely' that de Valera would refuse the American demand and this 'would put himself very much in the wrong with the United States Government and, if it came out, with the American people'.[26]

Even Churchill acknowledged that security was not the prime consideration behind the American note when the War Cabinet met to discuss it. 'We should not be justified, on the advice tendered to him, on basing the demand now proposed direct on Security,'[27] Churchill told his colleagues. He favoured the approach suggested by Cranborne.

If the British were really serious about getting the Axis representatives expelled, however, Maffey suggested that de Valera should first be approached informally, because he could be amenable. Ties between Dublin and Berlin were already strained and there were plenty of grounds for severing diplomatic relations, in view of the earlier bombings, the sinking of Irish ships and dropping of the two spies in County Clare, not to mention the other spies captured earlier. But Maffey noted that de Valera would 'in all probability reject' a formal request. 'No other possibility is to be considered,' he insisted:

At a time when relations with the Axis must be thoroughly strained ought we not give Mr de Valera the opportunity of making the break of his own motion? The presentation of formal notes must create a different atmosphere and a stiffer reaction. Everything should be laid on for the presentation of the notes as soon as the position had been felt out. This 'feeling out' would have to be a one-man job. Up to date we have always felt our way with him. In matters of the release of our airmen and in getting secret service cooperation we have certainly done far better than we should have done by formal requests. We also avoid being told afterwards that things would have been quite different if they had been handled in a different way.[28]

British Intelligence opposed the American Note. 'There would be very little, if any, security advantage in the removal of the German legation,' MI5 warned the Cabinet after consulting with MI6. The British already controlled the cable by which Hempel was communicating with the Continent, and they had been reading his messages since breaking his code in December 1942.[29] In addition, MI5 had gone back over Hempel's earlier messages and had concluded that 'de Valera had played straight with Britain in 1940 and 1941'.[30]

'The actual information which the German Minister has so far been able to collect and telegraph does not suggest that hitherto he has been able to obtain any information seriously likely to hamper or injure our operations,' MI5 concluded. Expelling Hempel would therefore pose a danger because the Germans might replace him with some undercover agent who might pass on a vital message of which the British would not be aware. 'There would be no security in the removal of the German legation,' the British War Cabinet concluded.[31] Moreover, from the security standpoint, messages from Dublin to Tokyo were of such low grade that the British rarely even bothered to read them because they appeared 'to have no intelligence value'.[32]

'The American line is to play for the answer "No".' Maffey reported on 10 February. 'Mr Gray, who has just left my office, tells me that that is what his President wants.' If a 'negative answer with its supposedly beneficial effect in the field of Irish-American politics is what we also prefer', they were going about it the right way.[33]

Knowing that Kearney would be opposed to a formal approach, Gray did not inform him, but Maffey asked the Dominions Office if the Canadians ought to be consulted. 'We have come to the conclusion that it would be a mistake to try to bring in the Canadians at this stage,' he was told in reply. 'For your own information, we are not at all sure that they would be willing to be associated with our approach.' Moreover, consulting the Canadians would involve a delay and would inevitably raise a question about consulting other dominions.[34]

Chapter 26 ∾

IT WILL COME AGAINST
YOU LATER

On 17 February 1944 Gray was instructed to revise the proposed diplomatic note in line with his own suggestions and deliver it to de Valera. It read:

Your Excellency will recall that in your speech at Cork delivered on the fourteenth of December 1941 you expressed sentiments of special friendship for the American people on the occasion of their entry into the present war and closed by saying, 'The policy of the state remains unchanged. We can only be a friendly neutral.' As you will also recall, extracts of this speech were transmitted to the President by your Minister in Washington. The President, while conveying his appreciation for this expression of friendship, stated his confidence that the Irish government and the Irish people, whose freedom is at stake no less than ours, would know how to meet their responsibilities in this situation.

It has become increasingly apparent that despite the declared desire of the Irish government that its neutrality should not operate in favour of either of the belligerents, it has in fact operated and continues to operate in favour of the Axis powers and against the United Nations on whom your security and the maintenance of your national economy depend. One of the gravest and most inequitable results of this situation is the opportunity for highly organised espionage which the geographic position of Ireland affords the Axis and denies the United Nations. Situated as you are in close proximity to Britain, divided only by an intangible boundary from Northern Ireland, where are situated important American bases, with continuous traffic to and from both countries, Axis agents enjoy almost unrestricted opportunity for bringing military information of vital importance from Great Britain and Northern Ireland into Ireland and from there transmitting it by various routes and methods to Germany. No opportunity corresponding to this is open to the United Nations, for the Axis has no military disposition which may be observed from Ireland.

We do not question the good faith of the Irish government in its efforts to suppress Axis espionage against American shipping and American forces in Great Britain and Northern Ireland is, of course, impossible to determine with certainty. Nevertheless, it is a fact that German and Japanese diplomatic and consular representatives still continue to reside in Dublin and enjoy the special privileges and immunities customarily accorded to such officials. That Axis representatives in neutral countries use these special privileges and immunities as a cloak for espionage activities against the United Nations has been demonstrated over and over again. It would be naive to assume that Axis agencies have not exploited conditions to the full in Ireland as they have in other countries. It is our understanding that the German Legation in Dublin, until recently at least, has had in its possession a radio sending set. This is evidence of the intention of the German government to use this means of communication. Supporting evidence is furnished by the two parachutists equipped with radio sending sets recently dropped on your territory by German planes.

As you know from common report, United Nations military operations are in preparation in both Britain and Northern Ireland. It is vital that information from which may be deduced their nature and direction should not reach the enemy. Not only the sources of the operations but the lives of thousands of United Nations' soldiers are at stake.

We request therefore, that the Irish government take appropriate steps for the recall of the German and Japanese representatives in Ireland. We should be lacking in candour if we did not state our hope that this action will take the form of severance of all diplomatic relations between Ireland and these two countries. You will, of course, readily understand the compelling reasons why we ask as an absolute minimum the removal of these Axis representatives whose presence in Ireland must inevitably be regarded as constituting a danger to the lives of American soldiers and to the success of Allied military operations.

It is hardly necessary to point out that time is of extreme importance and that we trust Your Excellency will favour us with your reply at your early convenience.[1]

Gray handed the note to the Taoiseach on the afternoon of Monday, 21 February 1944. That morning Irish newspapers published Cardinal MacRory's Lenten pastoral, in which he complained that some people in Northern Ireland were calling for vindictive treatment of the south over neutrality:

I wonder what these people expect Éire to do? Did they want her to show gratitude for partition, which only a few years previously had unjustly cut up into two portions, against its will, one of the oldest nations in Europe? ... Éire deserves credit, in the circumstances for not having allied herself with the Axis nations, and offered them hospitality and assistance.[2]

Gray opened the meeting by criticising the Cardinal's remarks. De Valera understood Gray's attitude, but said the American Minister should try to appreciate the Cardinal's viewpoint. Eighty per cent of the Irish people were being forced to live with the injustice of partition. Wishing to get the Taoiseach's immediate reaction to the note, Gray waited for de Valera to read it. The Taoiseach showed no anger but looked 'very sour and grim' as he read it slowly, often pausing to re-read certain passages carefully.

'Of course our answer will be no,' he said before he had even finished. 'As long as I am here it will be no.'

When he came to the phrase calling for the removal of the Axis diplomats 'as an absolute minimum', he asked if the document were an ultimatum.

'I have no reason to believe that it is more than a request to a friendly state,' Gray replied. 'As far as I can see there is no "or else" implication in this communication.'

On finishing the note, de Valera's reply was emphatic:

As long as I am here Éire will not grant this request. We have done everything to prevent Axis espionage, going beyond what we might reasonably be expected to do and I am satisfied that there are no leaks from this country; for a year and a half you have been advertising the invasion of Europe and what has got out about it has not been from Éire; the German Minister, I am satisfied, has behaved very correctly and decently and as a neutral we will not send him away.[3]

Gray assumed the Axis representatives were engaged in espionage activities in Dublin, in view of the conduct of their diplomats in other neutral countries. Of course, this was hardly surprising seeing as his own government had sent Marlin to Ireland as a spy under a diplomatic cover. In addition, the Americans were using Irish diplomats on the Continent as spies. Gray argued his government would be lax if it did not try to do something about the potential German spies in Ireland.

After the leaving the Taoiseach, Gray went to Maffey's office and told him what had transpired. They both felt the British Note should be handed over as soon as possible.

Meanwhile de Valera called a meeting of the National Defence Conference, which considered measures to deal with an American attack. As the conference was in session, the British military attaché telephoned to enquire where the Irish authorities wished to take delivery of some motorcycles he had procured for them. The call could have been taken as a reassuring sign, but the Taoiseach continued to attribute the most sinister motives to the American request.

The following afternoon Maffey delivered a short note explaining that British authorities 'warmly welcome the initiative which has been taken by the United States government and that they fully support the request for the removal from Éire of German and Japanese diplomatic and consular representatives'.[4] Although de Valera had remained calm with Gray, he became quite angry with Maffey. 'After perusing it,' Maffey wrote, 'he turned to me, white with indignation, and exclaimed: "This is an ultimatum. This is an outrage".' The Irish had done much from a security standpoint to ensure the Axis diplomats could not pass on information. 'He professed to see in the proceeding nothing but an attempt to push him into the war and deprive Éire of the symbols of neutrality and independence,' Maffey continued. 'It was obvious that he attached tremendous importance to this symbolic factor.'[5]

From Washington, Robert Brennan warned that refusing the American request 'would lose us support, if not sympathy, of friends here because however unfounded, belief that American lives are jeopardised will prevail'.[6] He hoped to get John McCormack, the Majority Leader of the House of Representatives, to intercede with Roosevelt.[7]

Since the country's avowed neutrality bolstered the sense of national independence, de Valera saw the diplomatic notes as a threat to this newly manifested freedom. He therefore turned to Canada for help, because Canadians had long shared the Irish desire to demonstrate dominion independence. As a result, Ottawa might be loath to support any British effort to compel Ireland to abandon its neutrality, as this would undermine dominion rights and negate Canada's own symbolic gesture at the start of the war in waiting for some days before declaring war on Germany.

De Valera discussed the notes with Kearney, who was taken completely by surprise; neither Gray nor Maffey had informed him. Nevertheless he adopted the attitude that they must have been moved by a genuine concern about the espionage threat. The Taoiseach contended there was no evidence to justify ordering the expulsion of the Axis representatives, even if he were so inclined.

According to Kearney, the Taoiseach 'thought the delivery to him of formal notes instead of more or less informal verbal representations which have hitherto been made by the American Minister and British Representative was alarming and significant'. He realised the notes were designed for propaganda purposes, but he thought they were to prepare public opinion for an Allied attack on Ireland. He asked if the Canadian government could use its influence to have the notes withdrawn.[8] 'Even if verbal representation were substituted for formal notes,' Kearney reported, de Valera would not close the Axis missions, but he 'would give assurances that he would take any measures which might be suggested to eliminate any possible espionage'. There would, however, be no question of jumping on the Allied bandwagon. He pointedly told Kearney he would never act as Salazar had done in allowing the Allies to use Portuguese bases in the Azores.[9]

Mackenzie King seemed to toy with the idea of supporting de Valera's request. He attached a short memo to Kearney's telegram: 'I view favourably the suggestion made in this telegram but would like you to think it over and let me know your reaction.'[10]

Before Norman Robertson could reply, there was some hectic diplomatic manoeuvring. On learning that Canada had been asked to intervene, Maffey suggested Churchill should personally contact the Canadian Prime Minister. The Dominions Office quickly despatched a message to Ottawa explaining that the notes were designed to protect British and American troops, and that Canadian service personnel would also be protected by the expulsion of the Axis representatives from Dublin.

Churchill thereby hoped that Mackenzie King would not only reject de Valera's request but also endorse the British and American notes. This was too much for the Canadians, and they promptly told the British *chargé d'affaires*. Robertson reported to Mackenzie King:

> We pointed out that the Canadian government had not been consulted about this new approach to the Irish government, and had only been informed of it after it had taken place. In the circumstances, I thought it extremely unlikely that the Canadian government would be prepared to consider associating itself, formally and belatedly, in the way Mr Churchill had suggested. We would be very glad to see the Irish government compel the withdrawal of Axis diplomatic representatives from Dublin, but the measures taken did not seem very well designed to achieve the end in view.[11]

As allies of Britain and the United States, the Canadians felt compelled to reject de Valera's request. Robertson and his deputy, Hume Wrong, would have been glad to see Dublin expel the Axis representatives, but they thought what was done was not calculated to achieve that end. Hume Wrong astutely perceived that there might be an American domestic political motive behind the Note.[12] 'In the circumstances,' Robertson advised Mackenzie King, 'I think it was a mistake in judgment for the United

Kingdom and United States Governments to present formal notes on this subject to the Irish Government at this time, but I do not think we could act as Mr de Valera's intermediary in attempting to bring about their withdrawal.'[13]

A telegram instructing the High Commissioner in Dublin to tell de Valera that Canada could not intervene was already prepared when a second telegram was received from Kearney. He had not tendered any advice in his first telegram, but now suggested Canada turn down de Valera's request but show good faith by suggesting that all notes on the subject be kept secret. In this way Dublin could be reassured that there were no sinister propaganda motives.

There was no advantage 'in giving publicity to an unsuccessful diplomatic manoeuvre from which none of the Governments concerned get any glory', Robertson advised King.[14] The Prime Minister concurred, so Kearney was instructed to act essentially on the lines of his own advice. 'The question which Mr de Valera has raised with you is not one in which we can intervene at this stage without risk of misunderstanding,' Mackenzie King informed Kearney. 'Even if the notes were withdrawn such harm as has been done would not be undone.'[15]

Canada had 'a good deal of sympathy' with Irish objections to the timing and formal nature of the American and British notes, but Kearney told de Valera on 26 February that 'the Irish government would be well advised to comply'. Quoting from his instructions, Kearney explained:

We have welcomed each indication of Irish sympathy and support and we keep alive the hope that sooner or later Ireland will be able to make some more direct contribution to the winning of this war. In this spirit we would naturally be very glad to see Axis Missions removed from Dublin and are thus in full sympathy with the object of the approach which the United States and United Kingdom have made.

The High Commissioner concluded by advocating that each of the parties involved should come to an arrangement to avoid publicity.[16]

De Valera was very emotional and seemed to think Ireland was going to be invaded, according to Kearney, who suggested Dublin could use the recent dropping of the two German spies as grounds for expelling the Axis. The notes only complicated this, however, de Valera replied, because 'If chief purpose of the United Nations was to guard against espionage,' he argued, 'they would not have departed from the ordinary mode of communication, but would have sought by private negotiations to find additional means to guard against espionage and would have found him most cooperative.'[17]

At the State Department Robert Brennan asked John D. Hickerson of the European Affairs division and Robert Stewart of the British Empire section if Ireland would be invaded if the request were formally rejected. 'They both assured me there was no such intention,' Brennan reported. Steward read a memo reaffirming Roosevelt's 1942 assurance that there was not 'the slightest thought or intention of invading Irish territory, or threatening Irish security'. The note was intended solely to warn that Dublin would be held responsible if any leak was subsequently traced to Ireland. 'The punishment would be, not invasion or any other measures, but anger and curses of millions of American mothers, many of them Irish,' Hickerson explained.[18]

Next morning the Canadian Prime Minister was annoyed to read a recent speech by Churchill. 'It showed they hogged everything for Britain and talked of what had been done in war of air warfare as if Britain alone was represented in the RAF,' King noted in his diary. 'Really there is ground for strong offence on the part of the dominion in his attitude, should we care to take it.'[19] It therefore seemed a particularly appropriate time for John J. Hearne to call on Mackenzie King.

Explaining that de Valera wished to keep his approach to the Canadians as informal as possible, Hearne suggested the British had inspired the American note and he wondered if Ireland would ever get the credit 'for our generous attitude in the United Nations'.

'Credit?' the Prime Minister asked. 'Did you read Churchill's war summary in the House of Commons a few days ago? Not one word about Canada. You would think we hadn't a single soldier in the fight. But I let it go. I supposed he was too preoccupied with the whole war situation to bother about this or that contribution to the main efforts.'

Mackenzie King thought the Americans were 'genuinely afraid' of the threat posed by the Axis representatives in Ireland. 'They want to clear every potential danger out of the way,' he said. 'Mr de Valera took more out of it than was intended.'

What would happen if Ireland refused? Hearne asked.

'I am quite sure that there will be no desire or attempt to take the matter further,' the Prime Minister replied. 'Of course, it could go against you later on.'[20]

'Hearne dwelt particularly upon the significance of the words "an absolute minimum" and also the words "that time of extreme importance"', according to Mackenzie King. He said the note was an effort to dictate to Ireland, but Dublin would not yield to such dictation.

The Canadian Prime Minister, who had already been informed by Kearney of the benevolence of Irish neutrality, argued that the note should be taken on face value, as an effort by the Americans to ensure the safety of their troops.

'In the midst of confusion of the time, the enemy might easily be supplied with information from sources that seemed harmless enough at other times,' he argued. 'The only wise thing was to avoid possible dangers, at all costs and to take account of every contingency.'

'I said I could understand wondering why the United States request should have been preferred in writing, in formal notes, rather than by verbal representations in the first instance,' Mackenzie King added. 'I had been asking myself what the reason for that could be. I had concluded and I thought quite rightly, it was because of the great importance which the U.S. government attached to seeing their forces were protected in every way.' If the motive behind the British and American notes had been to drag Ireland into the war, he believed Canada would have been consulted. The Prime Minister concluded Kearney had read the situation correctly. 'I felt it would be unwise to have publicity given to the notes—unwise alike for all parties concerned.' The Prime Minister continued:

> He then asked if he might say that I would like to be kept informed of any further developments and would I be willing to help in any way. I said that I had no desire of being drawn into the matter beyond that of trying to help to clarify the situation and, naturally, would be gratified receiving any word which the Irish Government would wish to send, but that I would not wish, so to speak, to attempt to intervene in a matter which was one between the government of the United States and the government of Éire, or the British government and the government of Éire.[21]

Although Mackenzie King supported his allies, he had reservations and 'had quite a long talk' next day with Malcolm MacDonald, the British High Commissioner, who seemed to agree that the whole thing involving the notes was 'quite ludicrous'.[22]

Maffey and Gray essentially agreed with the recommendation to withhold publicity, but Churchill disagreed. 'I hope it will come out in public,' he wrote. 'I am sure the House of Commons would support us.'[23]

From the outset Gray realised de Valera might try to make 'political capital' out of the note by depicting it as 'the first step in a conspiracy to crucify Éire with hostile propaganda as a prelude to armed invasion'.[24] The American Minister therefore wished to blur the situation by having the Allies play the role of aggrieved friends who helped the Irish but received nothing in return. He suggested that the State Department be ready to announce, with great fanfare, the release of strategic material for the Irish Sugar Company, so that any suggestion of hostile American intent towards Ireland could be made look ridiculous.

Initially Maffey did not share this concern. 'So far as this country is concerned,' he wrote, 'I for my part cannot believe that Mr de Valera's attempt to confuse the issue and dramatise the situation will carry conviction, even to a mentality notoriously unpredictable.' Describing the Taoiseach as 'a strange mixture of sincerity, hysteria and astuteness', Maffey thought the anxiety was just a passing phase fuelled by de Valera's extreme dislike of Gray. 'Public hysteria abates here as swiftly as it arises if it is not fed,' Maffey observed. 'Mr de Valera may thus find himself "all dressed up and nowhere to go".'[25]

With the Irish Army on alert, there was a great deal of public uneasiness. 'Thousands spent the weekend convinced that an American ultimatum had been delivered, that fighting had begun on the Northern border, and that battleships were assembled off Howth,' Maffey reported.[26] There were unfounded rumours on 26 February that Richard Mulcahy, the new Fine Gael leader, had been arrested and that James Dillon had been shot.[27] De Valera talked about 'extreme danger' as he warned a Fianna Fáil convention in Cavan next day that the Defence Forces should be at the ready. 'No words which I can use', he said, 'would be strong enough to express my conviction of the necessity of maintaining these forces at their maximum strength and efficiency.'[28]

'At any moment the war may come upon us,' he added. 'Until the last shot has been fired in the war, we shall be in danger and at times in great peril. The danger becomes greater as the theatre of war moves more in our direction and the efforts of the belligerents against each other reach their climax.'[29]

On hearing that John Garland, the secretary of the Canadian High Commission, was shocked on reading the American note, Maffey reassessed the situation. Although born and reared in Dublin, Garland had spent thirty years in Canada and was obviously no Anglophobic nationalist. If he was genuinely uneasy, then there were grounds for suspecting other intelligent Irish people would be distressed by what Maffey considered de Valera's 'childish' attempts to spread alarm. 'The touchiness of these Irishmen passes the limits of sanity,' Maffey explained. 'But we knew that before.'[30]

'The British reputation with these people is so tarred and plucked,' Kearney told Maffey, 'that they will never believe that you are not going to take a big stick to them. They cannot believe that they will get through this war without you doing it. When anything like this happens they say "There you are. We told you so".'[31] Maffey urged Kearney to keep in close touch with the Irish in order to 'act as a "lightening-rod role" in this matter'.[32]

Hempel was so anxious about the rumours that he called on Joe Walshe, who blamed the Germans. It was 'all due to those damned parachutists', Walshe said. He told Kearney afterwards that the German Minister was deeply embarrassed.

'Then why does he not resign?'[33] Kearney asked.

'I shall have to do something now to put a stop to the rumours that are circulating,' de Valera told Gray. One possible course would have been to publicise the whole affair, he said, but he did not want publicity.

'That is entirely in your hands,' Gray replied. 'We have no desire to have you crucified by a press campaign and will not give the story out in any immediate future but if you give it out and a storm breaks that is your affair. It is a matter of indifference to us.'[34]

Gray repeated the assurance given to Brennan that the Americans had no intention of invading Ireland. De Valera then had Brennan deliver his formal reply to the American Note on 7 March 1944:

The note of the American Government was handed to me by the American Minister on February 21st. I informed him at once that the request it contained was one with which it was impossible for the Irish Government to comply. The Irish Government has since given the matter careful consideration and I now confirm the reply which I then gave verbally. The Irish Government have also received the assurance of the American Government conveyed to the Irish Minister at Washington and later confirmed by the American Minister here in an interview with me on February 29th that the American Government did not contemplate proceeding to military or other measures because of the reply which had been given. The American Minister quoted in particular the President's personal message to me of February 26, 1942, that 'there is not now nor was there then the slightest thought or intention of invading the territory of Ireland or of threatening the security of the Irish' and added that this attitude was unchanged.

The Irish Government wish to express their appreciation of this assurance. They were indeed surprised that so grave a note as that of February 21st should have been addressed to them. The terms of the note seemed to them altogether out of harmony with the facts and with the traditional relations of friendship between the Irish and American peoples. They doubted that such a note could have been presented had the American Government been fully aware of the uniform friendly character of Irish neutrality in relation to the United States and of the measures which had been taken by the Irish Government, within the limits of their power, to safeguard American interests. They felt moreover that the American Government should have realised that the removal of representatives of a foreign state on the demand of the Government to which they are accredited is universally recognised as the first step towards war, and that the Irish Government could not entertain the American proposal without a complete betrayal of their democratic trust. Irish neutrality represents the united will of the people and parliament. It is the logical consequence of Irish history and of the forced partition of national territory.

Already before America's entry into the war, the policy of the Irish Government toward Britain, America's ally, had been directed toward carrying out the intentions indicated in a statement of policy made by me in Dáil Éireann on May 29th 1935 namely that 'our territory would never be permitted to be used as a base for attack upon Britain.' That policy has during the war been faithfully pursued. From the beginning, by the establishment of strong observation and defence forces, by a wide and rigorous censorship of press and of communications, by an extensive anti-espionage organisation and by every other means within our power, we have endeavoured to prevent the leakage through Ireland of any information which might in any way endanger British lives or the safety of Great Britain. Since the United States entered the war, the same spirit of scrupulous regard for American interests has been shown. American officials have had an opportunity of seeing the measures which have been taken–they have indeed made favourable comments on their effectiveness–and it is satisfactory to observe that in the note itself not a single instance of neglect is alleged and no proof of injury to American interests is adduced. Should American lives be lost it will not be through any indifference or neglect of its duty on the part of this State. As was known to the American officials, it is true that the German Minister had a wireless transmitter, but he had been for a long time debarred from using it and it has been in the custody of the Irish Government for some months.

As regards the two parachutists dropped in Ireland last December, they were apprehended within a few hours. Two other agents dropped here since the war began met with a similar fate. The fifth, who arrived during the first year of the war, remained at large until December 3rd 1941, but the police were aware of his presence here almost from the first moment of landing, and successful activities on his part were rendered impossible. The total number of persons, inclusive of these parachutists, suspected of intentions to engage in espionage, and now held in Irish prisons, is 10 foreign and 2 Irish nationals. These are the facts, and it is doubtful if any other country can show such a record of care and successful vigilance.

The British Government have informed the Irish Government that they welcome the initiative of the American Government in sending the note and that they attached the utmost importance to it. The Irish Government do not wish to comment on this, except to remark that it is perhaps not known to the American Government that the feelings of the

Irish people towards Britain have during the war undergone a considerable change precisely because Britain has not attempted to violate our neutrality. The Irish Government feel sure that the American Government would agree that it would be regrettable if any incidents now should alter that happy result.

The Irish Government are therefore safeguarding, and will continue to safeguard, the interest of the United States, but they must in all the circumstances protect the neutrality of the Irish State and the democratic way of life of the Irish people. Their attitude will continue to be determined not by fear of any measures which could be employed against them but by good will and the fundamental friendship existing between the two peoples.[35]

Chapter 27 ꙮ

| PRESS HYSTERIA

After the Canadians rejected the Irish request to try to get the American and British notes withdrawn, John Dulanty approached the Australian and New Zealand representatives in London to ask their governments to intervene.

Australia's External Affairs Minister, Herbert A. Evatt, replied to High Commissioner Stanley Bruce that Canberra 'would be delighted if the Government of Éire saw its way clear not only to remove the Germans and Japanese representatives but to declare a state of war with both countries'. He had so little empathy with the request that he had difficulty believing de Valera would even have authorised Dulanty to make such an approach, as this was essentially asking for another rebuff. 'In the circumstances we hesitate to intervene in such a matter especially in view of what had already happened,' Evatt added. 'It might be best for you to give no answer unless strongly pressed, and then to give no answer in writing.'[1]

'Dulanty's visit to me was an official one for the purpose of giving me an official message from his Prime Minister for transmission to you,' Bruce telegraphed Prime Minister John Curtin. In the circumstances Bruce felt the Prime Minister should respond, as the Irish were waiting for an official reply. 'Both the United Kingdom and the United States of America Governments are aware of the approach to Australia and are awaiting with considerable interest what reply is returned,' Bruce added. 'Not unusually the hope of both is that the Australian reply will be down similar lines to that of the Canadian Government thus presenting a solid front on this issue.'[2]

Curtin had a strong Irish background. His father, who was from County Cork, had reportedly been involved in the Fenian movement in the 1860s before migrating to Australia, where he became a policeman. He married Kate Bourke, an Irish woman, in Australia and their son, John, the future prime minister, was born in Victoria in 1885. He became a socialist at an early age and abandoned his Catholic religion to join the Salvation Army for a time. He opposed Australian participation in World War 1 and was jailed briefly for resisting conscription. This was the result of his socialist beliefs, however, rather than the influence of his Irish background. As a politician he did not play the Irish card, and he took his time responding to Bruce. While he procrastinated, the press got hold of the American Note.

As Associated Press (AP) was about to break the news, the State Department published the exchange of notes on 10 March 1944. There was little important news next day, so the Irish refusal made front-page news throughout the United States. For the next two weeks the American press tended to portray Ireland as infested with Axis spies.

There was confusion over who was responsible for the leak. The State Department blamed the Dublin government because the Taoiseach had informed his whole Irish Cabinet. The Irish, on the other hand, suspected the Americans. *The Observer* (London) submitted a fairly accurate story to Irish censorship on 4 March, citing sources in Washington. The Irish censor stopped that story, and then the British also blocked it. Brennan reported a reference to a diplomatic note in the *New York Times* on 6 March.[3] There was also a story from London in the *Boston Globe* by Geoffrey Parsons, Jr., about the presence of Axis representatives in Dublin:

> Edouard Hempel, the German Minister, and the Japanese consul Setsuya Beppu and their staffs have the diplomatic privilege of driving freely around Dublin. American gasoline helps them to run their errands for Hitler and Tojo and their legations are heated by British coal or Irish turf transported with the British coal, but Éire sees nothing illogical or ironic in the situation.[4]

On 10 March the *Washington Times-Herald* published a Press Association story from Belfast that the United States had asked for the expulsion of the German Minister from Dublin.[5] As the AP also had the story that day, the State Department decided to publish the notes. Brennan's telegram about the AP account was the first indication Dublin had that the story had actually broken.

'As the press in London and elsewhere has reported, Dublin was full of the most various and fantastic rumours in last week of February, it was quite possible to pick out something approximating the fact from flood of baseless speculation which was current,' according to Walshe. He thought any suggestion of an official leak from Dublin was impressively disapproved by the fact that 'not one single whisper of the story was submitted to or passed by censorship here between 22nd February and 10th March'. If the information were contained in any telegram, this would have been sent from Belfast.[6] Maffey told Kearney the story had broken in the United States, while Gray apparently feared he might have been the source of the story himself. He told Kearney that an American reporter who had been in Dublin might have broken the story and compromised him.[7]

From the outset the de Valera government had full public support at home. 'All of Éire's three million population are behind Mr de Valera,' reported Ralph Woolfe of the *Empire News*.[8]

'Long before America entered the war I tried hard to get de Valera to abandon neutrality and join in,' George Bernard Shaw told the *Daily Sketch* in an interview that was circulated extensively on both sides of the Atlantic. 'I told him that he wouldn't get away with it … But de Valera did get away with it.' Shaw contended this afforded England an opportunity of making a 'magnanimous gesture' to redress 'centuries of grievances'. Any sanctions at this point, instead of changing the Irish attitude towards neutrality, would have the opposite effect, he warned.[9]

Dublin could take some solace from an editorial in *The Observer*: 'What would Allies say if Germany insisted that British and American diplomats should be forced to leave Sweden and Switzerland? We in Britain respected Éire's neutrality in 1940/41 when it was an acute menace to us. To become a party in its breach now when it is no longer more than serious nuisance might undo what history may well regard as one of our most unselfish and most far reaching acts in this war.'[10]

Generally, however, there was little comfort for the Dublin government in any of the Allied newspapers. 'Call for St Patrick!' exclaimed a *Dallas Morning News* editorial. 'The snakes are back in Ireland.'[11] The same day the *Fort Worth Star-Telegram* declared, 'The German and Jap embassies in Éire are nothing less than spy bases from which helpful information can be furnished Hitler and Tojo.' It added, 'A nation either is a friend of the Axis or the United Nations. But not meeting cooperatively with the latter it becomes a friend of the former.'[12] The *Atlanta Constitution* was hysterical as it complained that Ireland had been 'notoriously loose' in dealing with the Axis legations and that 'thousands and thousands of American soldiers will die because of the Irish position'.[13] Although the *New York Times* was not so definite, it warned in an editorial that despite Irish vigilance, Axis agents might possibly pass on information that could 'endanger the lives of many thousands of Allied soldiers, including many of Irish descent'.[14]

In this emotional atmosphere the American press gave currency to wild and ridiculous rumours, many of which had already been discredited. Notwithstanding the repeated explanations that the German Legation consisted of only a half dozen people, the *Christian Science Monitor* declared in an editorial that 'the German diplomatic staff was for long much oversized'. Geoffrey Parsons, Jr., reported in the influential *New York Herald Tribune* that the German Minister had a staff of seventeen, who were 'free to operate with all diplomatic privileges, including the sending of diplomatic pouches to their home capitals. This is something of a problem for Beppu, but for Hempel it is merely a matter of getting pouches to Lisbon.' He actually accused the Irish of manufacturing 'a full-fledged invasion scare' and he accused de Valera of 'doing his best to make good political capital out of the American "aggression" against Ireland'.[15] The old charge about u-boat bases on the Galway coast reappeared in PM Daily, which published a particularly inflammatory series of articles by Michael Sayers and Barnett Bildersee. One headline, 'HOW IRELAND HARBOURS NAZI SPIES', took up most of the front page.[16] They justified the American Note by citing the capture of German agents as proof that spies had been in Ireland. They added that many more had possibly gone undetected. 'Fascism thrives on Éire's neutrality,' the series concluded.[17]

The Fort Worth Star-Telegram carried a particularly distorted editorial in its evening edition on St Patrick's Day, accusing the Irish government of permitting the Axis powers to retain excessively large staffs with nothing to do 'other than spying upon the Allied forces in England and Northern Ireland'. Dublin's attitude had supposedly 'opened a dangerous threat to the Allied invasion of Europe and to the safety of the American troops moved up to participate in that invasion'. In fact, the Irish were accused of actually 'fighting America and Americans' in a covert manner by providing beacons to enable 'Nazi raiders to get their bearings and easily locate targets, such as Coventry, Liverpool and Belfast. The point may be well made that Éire's "neutrality" has served only the Germans and to a lesser extent the Japs.' As a result, the editorial continued, the American Note was 'a logical and reasonable demand' and the most extreme measures, even military invasion, would be justified to secure the removal of the Axis representatives. The poorly informed editorial writer actually stated Ireland had gained her independence through a 'bloodless revolution' with the financial aid of the United States. Now, action was needed. 'Either Éire throws out the Jap and German spies or stands the consequences. Whether blockade or more extreme measures will be necessary to bring Prime Minister de Valera to face realities is for him to decide.'[18] De Valera's Irish Press retaliated by accusing the Fort Worth publisher of exposing himself to 'every cheapjack lie spoken about Ireland'.[19]

Attacks on Irish neutrality were not confined to poorly informed editorial writers on small city newspapers. Sumner Welles, who had resigned from the State Department some months earlier, denounced the Taoiseach in a front-page article in the New York Herald Tribune. 'Eamon de Valera had never been noted for possessing an elastic mind,' Welles complained, as he went on to denounce the Irish for not lifting 'a finger to help' the Allies. The Irish would suffer later. 'Those who will not lend a hand in the supreme effort to make it possible for a real peace once more to exist,' he wrote, 'have no right to expect to be heard by the victors when the war is won.'[20] James Reston, the Washington correspondent of the *New York Times*, wrote that de Valera would never again 'have quite the same political support from the United States that he has always counted on in his ancient battles with the British'.[21]

The Department for External Affairs was obviously concerned about the press campaign in the United States. Brennan was warned to be careful in his public utterances and statements: 'Follow with due reserve line of recognising fairness and correctness of British attitude as regards our neutrality, giving them credit where possible.'[22] With St Patrick's Day approaching, Brennan had opportunities to give the Irish side of the story in interviews with the *Boston Globe*, *Chicago Tribune*, *New York Times* and *Washington Post*. 'Our people, who succeeded in out-witting the British Intelligence from 1918 to 1921—an intelligence corps which up to that time was the best in the world—are not going to be outwitted by any other country today.'

'You can count on that,' Brennan told Hope Ridings Miller of the *Washington Post*.[23] The Germans had no means of transmitting information they might receive in Dublin. 'They have no diplomatic pouch or diplomatic couriers,' Brennan told the *New York Herald Tribune*. 'They have no telephonic communications. They have no wireless transmitter. They can communicate only by cable, which passes through London. Therefore they can transmit no message that the British are unwilling to forward.'[24]

Kearney thought the Irish government was 'dangerously over-confident with regard to its own effectiveness in counteracting Axis espionage'. Intelligence people were in no position to say publicly what they knew at the time, so the Canadian representative felt this issue could not be resolved during the war. Only afterwards, when what the Secret Service knew could be told, would the real situation become apparent. Hence Brennan's arguments were making little impression in the United States. Senator Joseph C. O'Mahoney of Wyoming told him his 'excellent arguments are getting nowhere with the public'.[25]

Former Congressman Martin L. Sweeney, who had been one of the more vocal isolationists before America got into the war, told *PM Daily*, for instance, that fifty Irish citizens had to be dismissed from US construction companies in Ulster because they were pro-Nazi, and some were in communication with the German Legation in Dublin.[26] After more than a decade in Congress, Sweeney had lost his seat in 1942 but still harboured political ambitions. His remarks seemed ominous from the Irish perspective because he had previously been so supportive of Irish neutrality. Brennan suggested it would helpful if the Taoiseach invited the Americans to send 'expert personnel to verify' the security situation in Ireland. He added that this step should be followed by the immediate publication of the invitation.[27]

In a Gallup poll conducted on 15 March, 71 per cent of the American people were aware of the Irish refusal to expel the Axis representatives and two-thirds of those thought the United States should take further action. Of those people, 38 per cent recommended the use of trade sanctions, while 35 per cent thought a degree of force should be used to compel the Irish to be more cooperative. Some 4 per cent advocated declaring war on Ireland and a further 5 per cent suggested the United States 'should go as far as the situation requires'.[28]

Eventually Australia and New Zealand backed the American and British Notes, but privately there were some reservations among the dominions, especially over Churchill's handling of matters. Wellington informed the High Commissioner in London:

> While we would be glad to see the German and Japanese missions moved, I wonder whether at this stage the loss of good will through embarrassment caused to de Valera and his government would be commensurate with any advantage we might be gaining in making a major issue of this particular matter. I would be glad to know what evidence exists regarding espionage activities on the part of the German and Japanese legation in Dublin and also regarding the effectiveness of Éire's security arrangements.[29]

Stanley Bruce was still waiting for a reply from Prime Minister John Curtin when the press reported that Curtin had stated publicly in Canberra that Australia had refused to intervene. 'We said quite definitely that Australia was in accord with the American request,' Curtin said.[30] But nobody had bothered to inform the Irish. Stanley Bruce promptly told Dulanty 'that the Australian Government did not see its way to intervene' because it agreed with the purpose of the Notes.

'When I deplored the fact that the procedure appropriate to intercourse between Governments has been so discourteously ignored by announcing the decision in Canberra without any prior consultation with us,' Dulanty wrote, 'Mr Bruce immediately agreed.'[31] The Australian High Commissioner stopped short of suggesting Canberra would like Ireland to join the war effort, because neither the British nor American Notes had gone that far. Bruce urged that he should not be pressed to take a stronger stand.[32]

In Canada, the Toronto *Globe and Mail* reported on 13 March that Churchill wished to punish Ireland, so there was some uneasiness in government circles. Gordon Graydon, the leader of the Canadian opposition, asked in Parliament about Canada's role in the whole affair. Mackenzie King responded with a statement prepared by Robertson. He said Canada was 'in full sympathy' with the aim of the American Note. He told this to Hearne, and Kearney informed de Valera that 'we would not wish to interfere in the matter'.[33] Privately, however, the Prime Minister noted this reply was 'quite different from what I would have prepared myself if there would have been time'. He thought his reply was 'hardly fair' because the Irish approach had been strictly informal. 'I did cut out from the External Affairs statement some parts that I think would really hurt de Valera and Hearne and which were not needed at this time,' he added.[34] He cut out, for instance, a part that ran: 'The Canadian Government has, moreover, long entertained the earnest hope that the Irish Government and people would come to share our conviction that the permanent interests of Ireland are identified with the victory of the United Nations, and would make of their own motion a direct contribution to the defeat of the Axis power.'[35]

That day, in Boston, the British ambassador Lord Halifax said, 'England will respect Irish neutrality and allow Éire to choose and follow its own course as regards the war.' This was 'the most convincing proof of the complete independence of the Dominion', he explained. 'The British Government never has exerted any pressure on Prime Minister de Valera's government to change its neutrality stand.'[36]

But the following day, 14 March, Churchill sparked fears that Britain was going to retaliate when he told the House of Commons that travel restrictions to and from Ireland were the first step in the policy designed to isolate southern Ireland from the outer world during the critical period now approaching. 'In the corridors of the Dáil, the news came as a complete bombshell,' according to AP correspondent Roger Green. Few doubted that Churchill's speech foreshadowed a blockade.[37]

Kearney happened to arrive at the Irish Department of External Affairs to find Joe Walshe in an agitated state. Churchill must have had 'his tongue in his cheek', Kearney said in an effort to placate Walshe. He added the announcement was possibly intended only 'as a sop to British sentiment', disturbed by Ireland's refusal to expel the Axis representatives.[38]

Churchill had apparently caught even his own people by surprise. Immediately after leaving Walshe, Kearney hurried over to Maffey's office, where he found the British Representative 'obviously worried over the Churchill pronouncement'.[39] Maffey explained he had sympathy for Walshe. 'He can certainly make out a good case based on evidence of friendly interpretation of neutrality (forced landings, secret intelligence, control of Axis legation) and I told him that there was no objection to that case being public stated,' Maffey reported.[40] Next day Walshe offered Maffey 'all co-operation possible to the British Government in any plans to effect closer control of Axis Legation'.[41]

Even though the British press strongly supported the American initiative in relation to the Axis diplomats, some newspapers had reservations about any sanctions against Ireland. The *Daily Herald* warned, for instance, that the British and American public 'should not allow themselves to be goaded into vengeful mood' and opined that the two governments would 'blunder badly if they should take any measure against Éire which was not strictly confined to security purposes'.[42] Any attempt to punish Ireland would not add to security but would revive old hatreds.

The Canadians objected to Churchill going off on a solo run without consulting anybody. 'My own feeling', Normal Robertson wrote, 'is that we would be justified in protesting pretty sharply to the United Kingdom not only because of their failure to communicate but also because of the unwisdom in the common interest of the action that had actually been taken.' Mackenzie King and Cabinet agreed.[43] Ottawa therefore sent telegrams to Australia, New Zealand and South Africa complaining that Churchill had not consulted the dominions before announcing plans to isolate Ireland. If it was simply for security, the dominions had no reasonable cause for complaint, but there was a fear that Britain might have other motives.

'We wish therefore to emphasise that we are concerned over the position that has arisen,' Mackenzie King wrote to the Dominions Secretary. 'We have felt from the first that the approach looking to the removal of the Axis representatives was not made in the form designed to achieve its object, but we at once did what we could to persuade the Irish Government to comply. We have also publicly supported the action taken. We hope that there will be full consultation before any further steps are taken which are likely to have repercussions on the position of Ireland in the Commonwealth.'[44]

The future Canadian Prime Minister, Lester B. Pearson, who was a senior figure at the Department of External Affairs, wrote to Robinson endorsing the stand taken. 'I think it is exactly what was needed,' Pearson wrote.[45]

Archbishop Daniel Mannix of Melbourne, who was from Cork and had emigrated to Australia early in the century, was one of the most influential public figures in Australia. He was appointed coadjutor bishop of Melbourne in 1912 and became Archbishop five years later. He was one of the most vocal opponents of Australian involvement in World War I and was a driving force in the successful fight against conscription. Although detested by many Anglo-Australian Protestants, he was widely recognised as the Irish leader in Australia and had demonstrated a political clout over the decades that politicians could not ignore. He was the main speaker at a big meeting in Melbourne on St Patrick's Day 1944, at which he protested 'against the attempt which has recently been made to infringe upon the neutrality of Éire'. He went on to congratulate 'de Valera and his people for the unhesitating firm and dignified manner in which they have dealt with the unexpected attack upon the rights of their small nation'.[46]

South Africa was the one dominion whose help de Valera had not sought, as Smuts was unlikely to have any sympathy with him. 'I have not been approached in any way by President de Valera and if I had been my answer would have been in similar terms to the replies made by the Prime Ministers of Australia and Canada,' Smuts told Parliament.[47] But Daniel F. Marlan, the leader of the opposition, sent de Valera a telegram of support:

> I desire to convey to you our profound admiration of your determination and courage in resisting the attempts which are being made to interfere with Éire's right of self-determination. We make known to the world that we regard any form of external pressure which may be applied to you as being contrary to and in conflict with the aims and ideals for which the United Nations profess to be fighting. More particularly we regarded such pressure as an attack upon Dominion autonomy in general which we in our own case would not be prepared to countenance. We wish you all success in resisting aggression whatever form it may take.[48]

Marlan accused Churchill of 'trying to cast doubts on whether a Dominion had a right to remain neutral'. He said that Churchill and Smuts were critical of 'Éire because she exercised her full rights as a Dominion. They were filled with rage at Éire and decided to teach her a lesson while the war spirit was still abroad in the world.' Marlan's colleague, Eric Louw, complained that Smuts got involved because de Valera had not asked him to intervene. 'Churchill had not taken any action himself but got President Roosevelt to intervene for him,' Louw added. 'That was cowardly behaviour.'[49]

Gray was 'extremely apprehensive' about Churchill's remarks.[50] Next day, after lunch with the American Minister, Joe Walshe reported that Gray 'is clearly becoming more and more perturbed at the hornets' nest which he stirred up. His main preoccupation is to prove that he was not responsible for the leakage.' Gray asked for Walshe's view of the American Note. 'I said quite frankly that there was a lot of the "big bully" about the end of it.'

'That is the part I had nothing to do with,' Gray said, adding that he was astonished when the last paragraph was added.[51]

'Churchill statement greatly heightened tension when it was tending to quiet down,' Walshe telegraphed Brennan. 'We do not believe that economic sanctions will be taken openly, measures approximating to sanctions may be taken under guise of security measure. Our feeling is, however, that fear that British might be hit harder than us will act as a deterrent to anything like complete cutting off of essential supplies.'[52]

Gray thought de Valera and his Irish-American supporters had been sufficiently discredited by the whole affair, but he was afraid the Irish, both at home and in the United States, would rally in support of the Taoiseach if the Allies exerted pressure on Dublin. Henceforth the American Minister was anxious to avoid the appearance of trying to coerce Ireland. He suggested the State Department authorise him to announce the United States planned no coercive measures against Ireland and to bolster the announcement by releasing much-needed material for the Irish Sugar Company. He also suggested that Churchill should be warned to forestall any possible denunciation of Ireland.

But Secretary of State Hull felt Washington should follow Britain's lead in the matter. He asked Ambassador Winant to sound out London.[53] Churchill had no intention of reassuring the Irish. 'We have followed the American initiative in this matter and have come forward in support,' Churchill wrote to the Dominions Secretary. 'It would be very wrong for them now to explain it all away and leave us out in the open. There is no question of punishing the Irish but only of preventing the German Embassy in Dublin from betraying the movements of our armies. This will entail isolation measures.'[54]

Maffey feared Churchill's policy would backfire if Britain took a hard line while the Americans assured Dublin that they had no intention of adopting coercive measures. On St Patrick's Day Maffey warned the Dominions Office:

Do not imagine for one moment that America will see us through a brawl with the Irish. It has always been my dream here to put Éire out of favour in America while England remained the great gentleman. Today the Irish are mad against America and you will see America back-pedalling for a certainty. They will wake up with a start to the election factors present in the Irish question. The Irish-American associations are already on the move. It would suit American politics to put back into our arms the baby we have put into theirs. If the arms are the arms of our Prime Minister it would suit America best of all.[55]

In view of the quiet benevolence consistently shown by the Dublin government towards the Allies, Maffey believed Churchill's complaints against the Irish were unfair. The Irish could 'make out a good case based on evidence', he warned.

The difficulty in the present situation is that the case against Éire on the score of the Axis Legations is not so strong as we have to make out. The German Legation, as I have often said, is the Symbol, and if I could say to Mr de Valera: 'Keep your Symbol but put it in the zoo,' he would say: 'Now you are talking'. We could be sure, in fact, that Germany would not be much more effectively represented in Dublin by Hempel than Greenland is by the Polar Bear.[56]

The Allied Notes effectively challenged the Irish people's right to neutrality, which was a symbol of their much-cherished independence. 'The Irish see the attack is against the symbol,' Maffey explained. 'When it comes to practical measures for caging the Axis they will cooperate to any length. We spurn this, put in a Note which invites a negative reply and then act on our own.'[57]

Maffey was so worried that Churchill might 'jump the reservation and gum things up' that Gray urged the State Department to advise Churchill simply to play the role of an aggrieved party and not introduce any sanctions. Roosevelt agreed.[58] Ambassador Halifax was told and he duly telegraphed Foreign Secretary Eden that Roosevelt did not want economic sanctions against Ireland. This was a British affair, but the President wanted his views known because of the presence of American troops in Northern Ireland.[59] Privately, Churchill was prepared to admit the measures to isolate Ireland were designed solely for security reasons.

'There is no question of punishing the Irish but only of preventing the German Embassy in Dublin from betraying the movement of our armies,' Churchill wrote on 15 March.[60] He informed Roosevelt on 19 March that Britain was cutting off all Irish shipping to the Iberian Peninsula, but there would be no interference with Ireland's transatlantic shipping, or shipping between Britain and Ireland. 'We have followed Gray's lead in Ireland and it is early days to start reassuring de Valera,' Churchill continued. 'There is not much sense in a doctor telling a patient that the medicine he has just prescribed for his nerve troubles is only coloured water. I think it would be much better to keep them guessing for a while.' Rather than 'allaying alarm in de Valera's circles', the Prime Minister suggested, 'we should let fear work its healthy process. Thereby we shall get behind the scenes a continued stiffening up of the Irish measures which even now are not so bad to prevent leakage.'[61]

Maffey and Kearney thought the whole controversy was turning into 'a net loss' for the Allies because of Churchill's attitude.[62] Cranborne pleaded with Churchill to allow the Dominions Office to reassure de Valera 'that these measures are based on military grounds' and that there would be no punitive action. 'I do hope very much you will give the authority for this,' Cranborne pleaded.[63] But Churchill insisted that there should be 'no soothing of Irish alarms, publicly or privately'.[64]

Chapter 28 ∾

GRAY OPPOSED DIGNIFYING DE VALERA'S ANSWER

D
avid Gray was in a particularly uncomfortable position in Dublin. He was being openly blamed for having inspired the crisis over the American Note by misrepresenting Irish neutrality. Had he informed the State Department about the true state of affairs, Irish officials were convinced the Americans would never have sent the Note. Matters were only made worse by reports filed in the midst of the media hysteria by two American press correspondents.

The first report—written by Frank King of the Press Association and carried in the *New York Times*—stated Gray had said the Irish government did not have the legal power to stop leakage of military information from Dublin to Berlin 'so long as the German and Japanese diplomatic missions remained in Dublin, and so long as they had the diplomatic privilege' of sending couriers back and forth from Ireland with diplomatic pouches.[1] All travel to and from Ireland passed through Britain, so the Germans had no couriers, and they no longer had a diplomatic bag either. The Japanese had only consular, not diplomatic, status. Gray denied the statements attributed to him.[2]

Two weeks later there was further embarrassment when Robert Green, the AP correspondent, reported that Gray told him the Irish had 'deliberately slighted' the United States government by not inviting an American representative to a Red Cross function at which the German Minister and Japanese Consul were guests. The charge was inaccurate because the Irish Red Cross had not sent specific invitations to any foreign representative, but had circularised each mission with a notice about the function. The German and Japanese representatives had purchased tickets, so the United States Legation, which admitted that a notice had probably been received, announced the charge of 'discourtesy was without basis'.[3]

Gray again denied he had been the source of the story. 'I had given no statement or interview to any representative with reference to the matter in question,' Gray explained when a reporter questioned him about the latest story. 'I was not interested in speculating as to why and upon what information Mr Green had written his article.'[4] But the Irish authorities were virtually certain Gray was lying. They had access to the full report that Green telephoned to London. In it he not only reported the misinformation about the Red Cross dance, but also provided accurate details of the conversation between de Valera and Gray on the presentation of the American Note.

'This is an ultimatum,' de Valera was reported to have told Gray as he thumped the table. 'If you read the note again,' Gray reportedly replied, 'you will find there is no "or else" clause and no time limit. It is not an ultimatum. It is only a sincere effort by the United States Government to safeguard the lives of thousands of American soldiers from the very real danger by Axis espionage in Éire.' As de Valera had not talked to Green, Gray must have been the source of the details of the private conversation with de Valera, in the opinion of the *Irish Press*.[5]

Since Gray had already denied the story, T.F. O'Higgins of Fine Gael attacked the government for using its own semi-official organ to attack a foreign diplomat. He also denounced the censor for permitting the editorial to be published. Frank Aiken rather disingenuously replied that the censor had cleared the editorial because it was considered to be questioning the veracity of the reporter rather than the American Minister. Associated Press then got into the act by defending Green with an announcement that Gray gave him the information during an interview at the United States Legation on 18 March. Gray admitted to Roosevelt that he had 'talked off the record' to Green, who then let him down and provoked 'a teapot tempest'.[6]

Gray declined to say anything further publicly. 'Now,' he explained to Roosevelt, 'the opposition has a chance without welching on neutrality to attack Dev in the Dáil for affronting the representative of a friendly power and has taken it in a big way. The way to handle this ugly group of bad hats is to tell them to go sit on a tack.'[7] He was showing signs of frustration, but he still professed a genuine affection for the Irish people. His ire was directed against 'the little group of political racketeers who have captured the country'.

'I have a great deal of sympathy for Mr Gray,' the Canadian High Commissioner reported, 'because I have never found him otherwise than most agreeable and cooperative. He is a very forthright type of person who always speaks his mind.'[8]

The Irish did not blame Churchill so much as Gray for the controversy over the Axis diplomats. 'No other Government in world would have their affairs in hands of [a] frustrated old man who has been so demonstrably hostile and foolish,' the Department of External Affairs advised Brennan. The two interviews that Gray gave journalists during the crisis and subsequently repudiated, as well as his earlier letter to Cardinal MacRory, should have been 'sufficient to brand him a danger to both countries', the Department continued. 'Gray has become a by-word among the ordinary people for dishonest anti-Irish exaggeration. You should not ask for his removal but you could say that he is creating an atmosphere inimical to American interests.'[9]

'All the harm to our relations has been done by the preoccupation of the diplomatic representative here with security matters he knows nothing about,' the Department added in a further telegram the following week.[10] Gray seemed ready to believe the most ridiculous rumours, if they showed de Valera in a bad light. He thought, for instance, the Taoiseach was trying to ingratiate himself with the IRA and would not therefore cooperate with the Americans when it came to dealing with the IRA threat. 'De Valera is not going to spill inside dope to outsiders about the IRA,' Gray wrote.[11] This was absurd because the Irish had already been cooperating with the FBI in such matters, and de Valera had long since crossed the Rubicon in his relations with the IRA during the Emergency.

On the day the American and Irish Notes were published, Carter Nicholas happened to write to Marlin from OSS headquarters in Washington in an effort to establish a more regular flow of reports from the Continent. He was hoping Marlin could persuade Joe Walshe to go to the Continent on an espionage mission for the OSS. When Marlin visited Dublin the following weekend, he found that 'the unfavourable reaction of the American newspapers has caused the Irish a great deal of concern.'[12] Relations between Dublin and Washington had plummeted to an all-time low and were in danger of becoming even worse. Walshe complained bitterly about a report by Geoffrey Parsons, Jr., in the *New York Herald Tribune, stating* that the United States Government was refusing, for security reasons, to say what it knew about the adventures of captured spies.[13] Walshe noted:

I said that if any information which we gave to him in confidence, as part of our secret arrangement for securing the safety of American interests in this country, were used for the purpose of trumping up a case against us, there would be a catastrophic breach, not only in the friendly relationship which had been established between the two Intelligence Services, but also in the wide relations between the two Governments which naturally required a considerable degree of trust in each other. Our anti-espionage activities were completely successful; and, as he himself had acknowledged, so effective that there was no need for him as the American Intelligence special representative to remain at his post in Ireland.[14]

The security precautions taken by the Irish 'were effective and fully satisfactory', Marlin replied. In fact, he said he would resign from the oss if the information supplied by the Irish were used against them. In his own report of the visit, Marlin noted that the Irish authorities had 'offered their prompt cooperation in adopting whatever security safeguards we and the British desire in Éire'.[15]

'The Irish could be of great value to the United States after the war, and that the two countries should maintain their friendly relationship which meant almost more to the Irish than anything else,' according to Walshe. 'In future there was a danger that Europe might be threatened by Russian expansion and Russian ideas—communism—and that in such an eventuality the Irish would fulfil their part loyally in any Western European grouping that might be necessary to protect the common civilization of the United States and Éire.'[16]

While the American Note was essentially a means of discrediting de Valera, Gray had been talking so much about the danger of espionage that even some of his own people thought he had a tendency to see spies under the bed. Even Colonel David K. Bruce, the head of oss operations in the European theatre, had told the Irish that they 'should not take any notice of Gray's idiosyncrasies in this matter'.[17]

Marlin suspected the State Department might not be aware of the co-operation that the Irish had given to the oss. Although Walshe dismissed this in his conversation with Marlin, he telegraphed Brennan a few days later that there must have been no liaison between State Department and the oss. 'Otherwise such a hostile note could not have been written,' he declared. 'This state of affairs particularly dangerous since Gray is recognised even by his best friends a pathological spy maniac. He has produced a new rumour almost every day since the crisis.'[18]

The American Minister was 'an avid listener' to the short-wave radio broadcasts of the Nazi propagandist Lord Haw Haw, according to Walshe. Many people listened to him more as a source of amusement than enlightenment. Haw Haw, whose real name was William Joyce, had been reared in Galway, though he was not remembered with much affection there. He had essentially been run out of town for siding with the Black and Tans during the war of independence. People were entertained by his disparaging remarks, like his sarcastic comments about the Irish Army being unable to beat the 'tinkers' out of Galway. But Gray 'listens to every word Haw-Haw says for evidence of secret wireless though every fool knows that secret transmitter would not be used for transmission of propaganda', Walshe noted. 'Haw-Haw's Irish news comes from Press agencies through Stockholm, Lisbon and Berne.'

Walshe instructed Brennan to tell those he could trust in the United States 'about this state of affairs which could so easily cause disaster between us.'[19] Gray had tried to frustrate cooperation when Walshe approached Marlin about establishing a proper liaison with the oss; Colonel David Bruce came over because Gray was trying to block the cooperation. In a telegram to Brennan, Walshe merely referred to Marlin as 'x'.

> We knew x's position from beginning and I suggested to him that security relations should be put on more official and comprehensive basis, hence conference with Bruce who recognised fully our frankness and real desire to be helpful. All this was done against wishes of David who did his best to prevent it because as he foolishly acknowledged to me after lunch given by him for Bruce, he wanted to be the exclusive channel for reporting to headquarters. x withdrew little later to London headquarters as he felt situation here completely satisfactory and fully acknowledged effectiveness of work being done. x comes over about every six weeks and maintains constant correspondence with our security on Irish matters.[20]

If any of the material given to him were 'used by State Department for bogus plot against us', Walshe warned Marlin that all future cooperation would be jeopardised. Since oss officials had previously expressed satisfaction with the security situation in Ireland and Marlin had reaffirmed that satisfaction, Brennan told Hickerson 'the Irish Government could only conclude that the State Department is not informed of the true state of affairs'.[21]

Carter Nicholas kept Hickerson and the State Department informed about Ireland because the oss was anxious to continue the intelligence cooperation and receive 'further information from the Irish'. On 25 March he gave Hickerson full details of what had been happening in the first two weeks following the publication of the Notes. 'The Irish', he explained, 'had offered us their prompt cooperation in adopting whatever security measures we and the British might want.'

At the time the State Department was preparing a second note for de Valera, so Nicholas was particularly anxious to ensure no information supplied by the Irish in confidence would be used against them. He wished to kill a second note, but felt compelled to limit his objections to security considerations. 'At the end of the conversation,' Nicholas wrote, 'I was satisfied that he was aware of all reasons arguing against the delivery of the second note, although I limited whatever reasons I advanced to those directly affecting our interests.'[22]

The State Department was therefore informed about the true security situation in Ireland, but there were questions about how much they knew at

the White House. William J. Donovan, the head of the oss, was anxious to
make sure the President was aware of the full facts, so he had Nicholas outline
the details of Irish cooperation. Donovan then incorporated this outline
verbatim in a memorandum to Roosevelt on 30 March 1944. He noted that the
information supplied by the Irish included material on

> German agents in Ireland, their training, instructions, equipment
> (including radio equipment) and ciphers; the Irish Republican Army;
> complete lists of Axis nations, persons of Axis origin, Axis sympathizers in
> Éire, their jobs and where possible their views and activities; Axis
> diplomatic and Consular representatives and their known contacts; map
> of Coast Watching System, reports on shipping activities; Axis
> propaganda; submarine activity off the Irish coast to the extent known;
> Irish prisoners of war in Germany and known activities of Irishmen in
> Germany; political groups in Ireland with Fascist leanings or ideologies;
> interviews with persons who have recently left the Continent, including
> the Irishmen recently parachuted by the Germans into Ireland; lists of
> German aviators interned; lists of interviews with survivors of a naval
> action off the Bay of Biscay picked up by an Irish ship.[23]

Donovan went on to outline the extraordinary arrangement that Nicholas
had made in Dublin regarding using the Irish diplomats on the Continent. 'So
far the information contained in these reports has been of use primarily as
confirmation of information from other sources,' he continued. 'However the
potentialities are important.'

'The cooperation in intelligence matters offered and given by the Irish has
been very full. It should be pointed out that we did not offer the Irish
information in return and have given them little,' Donovan explained. 'Since
the delivery of the American Note the Irish offered their prompt cooperation
in adopting whatever security measures may be recommended by us.'[24]

Of course, most Americans knew nothing about the security cooperation.
Senator Joseph O'Mahoney of Wyoming had already suggested to Brennan
that de Valera should invite the United States 'to send expert personnel' to
verify the security situation and publicise the invitation. Brennan asked for
permission to reveal that American security people had already inspected and
approved the security measures in operation in Ireland. 'To make doubly sure,
we suggested early in 1943 the American security Force in Ireland be
strengthened,' he intended to tell the press.[25] But such public disclosures
would have made a mockery of Ireland's supposed neutrality.

'Better to avoid making any public statement about security
collaborations,' the Department of External Affairs promptly replied.[26]

Walshe visited London instead and approached the oss and the British directly with an offer to implement further security measures. Ambassador Winant authorised Marlin to set up a meeting for Walshe with J. Russell Forgan, who was acting head of European operations for the oss in David Bruce's temporary absence. During the ensuing meeting, which was also attended by Marlin and Hugh Wilson, Walshe 'protested vigorously' about the way the Irish government was being treated in the American press.

'Although I agreed with him completely,' Forgan explained afterwards, 'I had to say that if we told the actual facts, all of the wonderful work that his intelligence services had been doing with the Allies would be ruined. He saw the point immediately.' Forgan later admitted the Irish had provided some 'very useful' cooperation to the oss on intelligence matters. 'In general, despite the American news media,' he wrote, 'the Irish worked with us on intelligence matters almost as if they were our allies. They have never received the credit due them.'[27]

Walshe proposed that American and British security officials hold a meeting in Dublin with their Irish counterparts to 'discuss what measures ought to be taken to make Éire safe from Axis espionage'. He also suggested that the British and Americans station agents in Ireland 'to keep in constant touch with Irish authorities on the problems, to receive reports from them, and to make recommendations for improving methods of surveillance'.[28]

On learning of the Irish proposals, Gray objected strongly because he feared the Irish gesture could be used 'as a political means of wiping off the record' the stigma of de Valera's refusal to dismiss the Axis representatives. 'As long as we keep him hooked on his record of refusing our request he cannot do us any great harm either now or in the post war period but he is very apt to catch us napping and wriggle off,' Gray warned.[29]

He was not only worried de Valera might get off the hook but also afraid the Irish leader would seek political revenge on Roosevelt. 'He will probably try to start a political underground movement against you,' Gray advised. 'The time may come when it would be advisable for you to characterise it as an insult to the American people that any foreigner should attempt to inject himself into American politics with racial pressure group methods.' The American Minister was hoping the wartime solidarity in the United States would finally kill ethnic politics in the country by bringing about the complete assimilation of so-called hyphenate groups like the Irish-Americans, Polish-Americans, Italian-Americans and German-Americans. 'This war should have put an end to hyphens,' he wrote.[30]

After discussing Walshe's proposals with British intelligence people, the oss decided against stationing special agents in Ireland until after the invasion of Europe, just in case the Axis representatives in Dublin did somehow manage to betray the Allied plans. This did not mean, however, that the oss was dissatisfied with Irish security at the time. oss agents in Britain actually expressed their satisfaction in even stronger terms than Nicholas had done in Washington. As the agent in the field most involved with Ireland, for instance, Marlin was prepared to be quite definite. Gray complained that Marlin said he was 'completely satisfied' with the Irish situation.[31]

'Hurst was willing to state affirmatively that the oss was satisfied with security conditions in Ireland,' Nicholas wrote. 'I was unwilling to state the same thing in Washington but limited my statement to the fact that all evidence in our possession pointed to this conclusion and that all evidence to the contrary in our possession had been successfully proven false.'[32]

The follow-up note, which Roosevelt approved, was a request to de Valera to reconsider his previous refusal and take steps 'to insure that Irish neutrality shall not be used by the Axis powers to harm the United States'. The note went on to stress that the continued presence of the Axis representatives 'must be regarded as a danger to American lives and military operations for which the Irish Government cannot escape responsibility'.[33]

Irish authorities were understandably annoyed that another note was being prepared. John Belton complained to Marlin that Dublin was afraid the note would actually cite information turned over to the oss. 'Walshe was very anxious about the point,' Carter Nicholas noted, 'particularly as the Irish could not publicly admit to having engaged in so unneutral an act as supplying us with anti-Axis intelligence.'[34]

The oss had already made sure that no such evidence would be cited. Hickerson had assured Brennan, 'we would never dream of using any confidential information we could have got from your people.'[35] Marlin assured Belton in London there was no danger of Irish confidence being betrayed in such a manner, but Belton warned that further intelligence co-operation would be terminated if a second note were delivered.

Although Gray described the new note as 'excellently conceived and drafted', he opposed its delivery because, for one thing, it would not put de Valera more on record than the first note had already done. Secondly, another note would 'give de Valera important help for his political campaign by giving him the opportunity for rousing the country with more emotional and disingenuous appeals'.[36] Thirdly, it would enhance the Taoiseach's 'prestige by dignifying his answer to us with a reply'.

'Another note to him would build him up again with his own people,' Gray wrote to Roosevelt. 'There will be no hope for constructive sane cooperation with anybody while he is master of the Twenty-six Counties but only his own people can deflate him. We should do nothing to prevent that by making a martyr out of him or by giving him more opportunity to defy us. Your idea of the absent treatment is the key idea.'[37]

Maffey joined with Gray in opposing another note. While the 'note possibly has value in relation to internal American politics', he warned the Dominions Office, 'from every other point of view it appears to me undesirable. The first note has done its work. The second will only produce another negative response and will increase de Valera's status and exaggerate Irish sense of their [own] importance. My advice would be to leave well alone.'[38]

Brennan was told he could assure friends of Ireland privately that American security officials were 'satisfied' with the situation. 'We are convinced American Government does not fear serious espionage from here,' the department advised Brennan on 17 April. 'Why do they not place some of their men here if they are? Why do they not insist on closing the border? British are not even thinking of doing it though suggestion made by us.'[39] But Brennan was not to go public with those arguments. 'It would be impossible to make public statement on even general lines of collaboration without risking misunderstanding of our essential neutrality at least by our own people here at home,' the Department explained. De Valera 'fully appreciates your great difficulties and has highest appreciation of way you handled situation. He knows you understand that we may have to suffer much abuse abroad for sake of home paramount consideration.'[40]

While the second note was being considered in Washington, the tripartite security conference suggested by Walshe was convened in Dublin on 2 May 1944. It lasted for three days. Marlin and Hubert Will of x-2 (the counter-espionage branch of the oss) represented the Americans. Winant had authorised their participation without thinking it necessary to inform Gray, who was both surprised and annoyed when the two oss agents called on him. He was irritated that they were taking up any Irish offer of cooperation and things got worse when Marlin stated the Irish situation was not bad from the security standpoint.

Gray cited rumours of pro-Axis activities in Ireland, but Marlin, who was not the most patient of men, summarily dismissed these rumours. He did not bother to explain why the stories could not be true; he just dismissed them as absurd.[41] 'It subsequently appeared that Hurst's consistent and somewhat dogmatic and tactless attitude about these and similar reports was one of the principal causes of the recurrent friction with the Minister,' Nicholas noted.[42]

'Gray was almost paranoid in his suspicions,' according to Marlin, who apparently did not realise until many years later that Gray was really thinking primarily about post-war politics, not the security situation. He was trying to have de Valera ostracised politically. 'My views on security were an embarrassment to Gray,' Marlin realised afterwards.[43] Gray suspected, for instance, that Marlin might be in league with those Irish and Irish-American elements that the American Note was intended to discredit. Consequently he refused to accompany Marlin and Will to the security conference with the British and Irish.

The conference discussed intensification of radio security and details of the secret cooperation between the Irish Army Signal Corps and the British, as well as the existing cooperation between the Irish coast-watching service and the RAF to prevent agents being dropped by aircraft. Security measures for keeping an eye on individuals with Axis sympathies were also reviewed extensively. Of course, this included the German Minister and his staff, who were being carefully observed by their Irish police escort, which kept records of all their contacts. This involved monitoring their telephone calls, censoring their mail and compiling lists of their correspondents.[44]

In the midst of the controversy over the American note, de Valera had taken a stand in relation to Rome and the Vatican, which also probably helped his standing at home. On 12 March Pope Pius XII had appealed for Rome to be spared from the fighting. W.T. Cosgrave, the former Fine Gael leader, called on de Valera to make representations to the belligerents on behalf of the Vatican. The Taoiseach promptly appealed to the belligerents to declare Rome an open city and not fight over 'this great centre of the Christian faith and civilisation'. He sent a note to President Roosevelt through Robert Brennan:

> I request you to listen to the voice of millions from every land praying the belligerents to seek through appropriate intermediary channels, an agreement by which Rome may be saved. Future generations will forget the military considerations which may now seem to dictate the occupation or possession of Rome, but, should the city be destroyed, the fact of its destruction will be remembered forever.[45]

'It is clear to all that, if the city be militarily defended by the one side and the other attacked, its destruction is inevitable,' the Taoiseach warned in similar notes to the Americans, the British and the Germans. 'The destruction of this holy city, which, for almost 2,000 years has been the seat of the sovereign authority of the Catholic Church, and contains the great central temples of the Catholic religion and the great central seminaries and libraries of the Christian faith, would be a major calamity for the human race, robbing man for all time of the noblest memorials of his supreme religious and cultural heritage whose origins are the teaching of Our Divine Saviour, Jesus Christ.'[46] 'I share your concern for the preservation of that ancient monument of our common civilization and faith,' Roosevelt replied. 'If the German forces were not entrenched in Rome, no question would arise concerning the city's preservation,' so it was a matter for the Germans, if they continued to occupy the city.[47]

The Germans expressed an 'urgent desire to preserve the priceless monuments and works of arts of the "open city" of Rome'. Berlin announced that the city was being demilitarised.[48]

There was, however, some resentment in the Allied press. 'It is superb insolence on the part of Mr de Valera to offer advice about the conduct of a war in which his country scorns to participate,' the *Toronto Telegram* complained. 'The fervour of his plea for Rome invites reflection upon the fact that no Gaelic lamentations were heard across the Irish Sea when German bombers—with some brief and undistinguished collaboration from Italy—destroyed or damaged historic English cathedrals and churches.'[49]

Whatever about de Valera's standing in the Allied press, recent events had enhanced his standing at home considerably. All the national newspapers—*The Irish Times, Irish Independent, Irish Press, Cork Examiner, Evening Press* and *Evening Herald*—supported the government's stand, along with twenty-eight other provincial newspapers.

It was just six months since Fianna Fáil lost its overall majority in the Dáil, but when the government lost a minor vote on a Transportation Bill on 12 May 1944, de Valera called another general election. He openly admitted that his aim was to secure an overall majority. 'A strong stable government assured of a majority can meet with confidence the crises as they occur or plan effectively in the knowledge that their plans can be carried through,' he said. 'Only such a government can command respect, either at home or abroad.'[50]

Despite the opposition of Winant, Gray, Maffey, Cranborne and Churchill, the Roosevelt administration had still been considering sending a second note, but the calling of the general election for 30 May scuttled it. 'The development, even aside from other considerations,' Hull advised Roosevelt, 'would appear to make the sending of a further note definitely undesirable.'[51]

Gray realised Fianna Fáil was going to win. He wrote to Hickerson that 'the great mass' of the Irish people would rally to 'de Valera as the man who told America where to get off'.[52]

Fianna Fáil gained seventeen seats in the general election, giving the party a comfortable overall majority. *Time* magazine concluded de Valera had the United States to thank for the resounding victory, because American pressure had simply made the Irish people 'more devoted to their own belligerent neutrality than ever'.[53] According to Robert Smyllie, editor of the *Irish Times*, the American Note provided the Taoiseach with 'a God-given opportunity once more to demonstrate Éire's absolute independence of everybody, including on this occasion the United States and to figure in the eyes of his own followers as one of the greatest statesmen since Abraham Lincoln'.[54]

It was 'a good thing' de Valera was returned with a clear majority, Gray wrote to Roosevelt on 2 June 1944. 'He is in now for five more years and if his mistakes are what we think they are, he will have to liquidate them. There was a danger that he would duck responsibility for a while and let the opposition pay the bills and clean the slate and then come back when they bungled.'[55]

Next day, Rome was declared an open city. The Germans withdrew and allowed the Allies to take the city without a fight on 4 June 1944. Whether de Valera's appeal made any impact on the Germans is a matter for conjecture, but it certainly did not hurt.

| TO THE BITTER END

The Allies had stated that they were bound to feel Ireland had not done everything possible to ensure the security of plans for the Allied invasion of Europe as long as the Axis representatives were allowed to remain, but Gray feared the secret security talks with the British and the Americans might help de Valera to restore his international standing. He was particularly afraid that Marlin might reveal publicly that Irish security was completely satisfactory. 'None of us here has much confidence in Marlin's discretion,' Gray wrote to Marlin's superior, David Bruce.[1] The following week he wrote a further letter suggesting Marlin should be transferred to North Africa, where he could be kept out of Irish-American circles.[2]

Following the successful Normandy invasion, the si division of the oss noted that 'interest in Éire waned rapidly'.[3] The oss decided that Edward Lawler of x-2, the counter-intelligence division, would move to Dublin to take over liaison with G2. Lawler had been a classmate of Carter Nicholas at Harvard Law School, from which they both graduated in 1933.

Marlin had asked to be recalled to Washington, where his wife and seven young children were living. He was supposed to visit Dublin with Hubert Will and Lawler, but Gray objected to Marlin's presence, so he returned to the United States while the other two went to Dublin, which gave the mistaken impression that Marlin had been sent home in some kind of disgrace.

Lawler and Will met with Walshe, Colonel Dan Bryan and Garda Commissioner Paddy O'Carroll. 'We were able to satisfy ourselves that every precaution was being taken insofar as security was concerned and that there were no serious leaks of information to the other side,' Lawler wrote. 'I can truthfully say that we received 100% cooperation from the Irish authorities,' he explained years later. 'The cooperation and information we received from the Irish was every bit as extensive and helpful as it would have been if Ireland had been a full partner with us in the war effort.'[4]

During the discussions, Walshe sought to impress on Will and Lawler that Marlin had done a great job in Ireland. 'But for his patriotism in the interests of America and his complete understanding of this country,' Walshe wrote, 'the liaison between our security officials would never have been established.'[5]

Marlin came on the scene at a time when misunderstandings seemed likely to increase, but he had turned things around, according to Walshe. He wrote to Marlin:

> The new relationship has gone most of the way towards eliminating these misunderstandings, and I most earnestly hope that the part played by your courage and patriotism will be fully understood and appreciated by your own authorities. I know you always held tenaciously, and strongly expressed the view, that we were wrong to be neutral. But some day I hope to convince you that, notwithstanding an increased friendliness in our relations with Britain (one of the astonishing results of the war in this part of the world), we could never resign ourselves to the possibility and consequences of the inevitable re-occupation by British forces.'[6]

'Colonel Bruce understood the situation and held Marlin in the highest esteem,' according to Hubert Will. 'He knows the excellence of Marlin's work in Ireland and how much he contributed to better relations.'[7]

Back in Washington, Marlin wrote up a full report of his Irish activities. 'It was my view that the Irish were prepared to give us every advantage within their neutral position and that they would not permit their country to be used against Great Britain and the United States as a base for espionage,' he wrote. Gray eventually assented to Marlin's establishing an 'open liaison with the Éire authorities. By doing so I was enable to satisfy OSS Washington of the true situation in Ireland, confirmed by the British Secret Service.'[8]

Douglas Gageby, an officer at G2 headquarters and later editor of the *Irish Times*, reported that Emara O'Neill, an employee at the American Legation, told him at the time of the American Note that Marlin had 'made no effort to conceal the fact that he thought it was outrageous. He is said to have written several indiscreet notes to Washington at this time, and it is generally believed among Miss MacNeill's colleagues that his recall to Washington a couple of weeks after the invasion of France was directly due to this.'[9] This was not the case; Gray would never have wished Marlin to go to Washington, where he could influence Irish-American politicians.

John V. Heffernan later wrote to de Valera that Marlin had expressed strong views about the Taoiseach. 'I hate him for ignoring the greatest cause for which free peoples ever fought. He belonged with us, his people belonged with us,' Marlin said. 'Now that you know my patriotic feeling, let me give you my personal opinion. De Valera is the smartest man in the world,' he added, 'Churchill, in his relations with Éire was the dumbest.'[10] Colonel J. L. Hathaway, the American Military Attaché, reported that the Irish Chief of

Staff, Lieutenant General Daniel McKenna, remarked that 'Churchill was the greatest enemy to Ireland since Cromwell'.[11]

Following the Allied invasion of Normandy on 6 June 1944, Maffey exerted strong pressure on de Valera for release of the remaining eight airmen in Gormanston. 'In regard to our interned airmen,' Maffey reported on 10 June, 'he told me in the most explicit manner that he had re-examined the matter with every desire to be helpful—particularly to me personally—but that he found it quite impossible to give way on this point.' But Maffey was insistent. 'Quite unforeseeable complications would accrue if this question produced no more than an impasse,' Maffey warned. He was going to London for consultations and he demanded to know exactly where de Valera stood in the matter.

'Mr de Valera paced about the room uneasily and said that as today was Saturday he would not be able to get in touch with his cabinet before my departure,' Maffey noted. 'I said that we required to have his answer in London at the latest before early on Tuesday morning. I should expect a telephone message in London from Mr Walshe one way or the other on Monday evening. Mr de Valera said he would arrange this.'[12] In effect, the British Representative had issued a virtual ultimatum. Unless Dublin released the remaining Allied internees, Britain was going to exert economic pressure.

'He was obviously badly shaken,' Maffey reported. 'It is so much for a neutral to think that supplies are a kind of manna dropping as the gentle dew from Heaven. Fortune has spoiled Mr de Valera by paying him unfailing dividends for his untiring obstinacy.' The British Representative felt it was 'impossible to forecast' de Valera's decision because '[h]e has the martyr complex and would hungerstrike for a principle. But there are one or two hard-headed men in the Government and we can only wait and see. At any rate the long chapter of arguments and dialectics on this subject is now closed. It may be necessary to give a turn of the screw.'

De Valera duly relented. On 15 June 1944 the eight remaining Allied internees were secretly released and driven to Northern Ireland. The internment camp at Gormanston was closed. Releasing the remaining Allied internees had been a very difficult step, the Taoiseach later told Maffey. 'I consoled him with the platitude that the choice for statesmen does not lie between an easy and a difficult course, but between two difficult courses, and said that I was sure that time would prove him right,' Maffey reported. 'His difficulties in a matter of this kind must not be under-estimated.'[13] Freddy Boland said de Valera was often on the point of releasing the internees, but events stopped him. For instance, when the crew of a RAF plane that landed at Strokestown, County Roscommon, on 4 July 1942 were released, the whole Local Defence Force resigned in protest.

In August 1944 de Valera agreed to an American request that his
government accept responsibility for the care of 500 Jewish children from
France. He also agreed to pass on to Berlin an American message calling on
the Germans not to exterminate inmates in concentration camps.[14]

Those were not the only humanitarian gestures. As mentioned earlier, the
Irish sent a ship of food supplies to Spain in March 1943, and the following
year de Valera had £100,000 sent to India for famine relief in Calcutta. Some
Irish doctors also tried to send medical supplies to France following her
liberation. The medical material was part of $500,000 worth of supplies
which Roosevelt had announced was being sent to Ireland in 1941. But those
had not actually been given to Ireland; instead, they were entrusted to the
Irish Red Cross for the Irish people when needed. Gray therefore took
exception to Ireland sending any of those supplies to the French. If the
supplies were not needed in Ireland, he thought they should be handed back
to the American Red Cross, which could then get the credit for the
humanitarian gesture.

Of course, what the American Minister really feared was that de Valera
would be given credit for the gesture. In fact, Gray wrote to Roosevelt that the
Taoiseach was behind the move as a ploy both to secure credit for
humanitarianism and to ingratiate himself with Charles de Gaulle, the French
leader. 'Now,' Gray explained, 'he wants to get solid with de Gaulle because he
knows de Gaulle is out to make trouble' for the British and Americans.[15]

Even though the controversy surrounding the American Note had done
enormous damage to de Valera's reputation and his potential support in the
United States, Gray was not allowing himself to become complacent. He was
determined not only to frustrate any efforts by de Valera to redeem himself in
American eyes but also to exploit further opportunities to discredit the Irish
leader by getting him to refuse other requests. On 22 September 1944, for
example, Gray formally asked the Taoiseach for an assurance that Ireland
would not give political asylum to any German war criminals, who were
defined as anybody who contributed to the Axis war effort. The request for
this blanket assurance was clearly designed to provoke a rejection from de
Valera, who would inevitably view it as a further challenge to the country's
independence by asking him to surrender its right to grant asylum.

'He was very sour about it,' Gray wrote to the President. 'It put him on the
same spot as our note about Axis missions.'[16] But this time the American
Minister did not make the mistake of allowing de Valera to exploit the request
by depicting it as a threat to Ireland.

'I told him that it was not an ultimatum and that there was no threat in the
background,' Gray explained. He was again hoping the Taoiseach would reject
the request. 'If he should say "no" as he would like, that would be best,' Gray

wrote. But this time a flat rejection seemed unlikely. Instead, the more probable reply was a refusal to make a commitment one way or the other. This, of course, would still amount to a refusal to provide the requested assurance. Gray was therefore satisfied the affair would 'further strengthen our hand against pressure group action'.[17]

While waiting for a reply, Gray expressed satisfaction with the way American policy towards Ireland was panning out. 'I think our tough attitude has increased respect for us,' he explained to the President. 'The Irish despise soft headed "mugs".' The primary aim of this policy had really nothing to do with winning Irish favour, however; rather it was dictated strictly by domestic political considerations in the United States. 'As I have told you before,' Gray continued, 'I think our Irish policy should be conducted primarily with reference to political conditions in America and to the end of protecting the Administration from pressure group attacks on our foreign policy. This you have done and we are in a much better position if there has to be a showdown.'[18]

As expected, de Valera refused to commit his government on the asylum issue. 'The Irish Government', he explained, 'can give no assurance which would preclude them from exercising that right should justice, charity or honour or the interest of the nation so require,' he replied. But he added there was no intention of altering the existing practice of denying 'admission to all aliens whose presence would be at variance with the policy of neutrality, or detrimental to the Irish people, or inconsistent with the desire of the Irish people to avoid injury to the interests of friendly states'.[19] In short, real war criminals were unlikely to be granted political asylum, but he was not prepared to sacrifice his country's freedom to do so by making a prior commitment.

The State Department published the reply, thereby opening the Taoiseach to further ridicule in the American press—this time as a would-be protector of Nazi war criminals. Gray was delighted. 'The Department has handled this War Criminals versus Éire situation extraordinarily well,' he wrote to Roosevelt. 'I detected your fine Italian hand in letting de Valera's reply speak for itself, leaving the matter for the journalistic wolves.'[20]

Even though the aim in tarnishing de Valera's reputation was to undermine his ability to make trouble over partition, Gray believed the Irish leader would still be able to stir things up. In his latest letter to Roosevelt, for instance, he predicted that 'serious trouble will break out in Northern Ireland fomented by de Valera and Cardinal MacRory' after the end of the war, when thousands of demobilised servicemen would return to the Six Counties to reclaim jobs that had been taken up by 30,000 migrants from the south. The latter would inevitably lose their jobs and be forced to return home. This would result in complaints that they were 'being expelled *from their own country*' which, Gray feared, would 'touch the IRA off again'.[21]

Unlike the American Minister, who believed de Valera was instigating trouble over partition for his own political ends, Maffey thought the Taoiseach was trapped by circumstances and with 'good cause for uneasiness'. For one thing, Maffey realised there was no valid justification for the inclusion within Northern Ireland of so many nationalists against their will. Stormont gerrymandered constituencies and imposed unfair restrictions on those nationalists. Hence they had a legitimate grievance, and their calls for help placed de Valera in a thorny position.

'The fabric established by the Act of Partition is not a durable fabric,' Maffey wrote. 'It is certainly not a case of "leaving well alone". The active Catholic minority in the North are well aware that if they stage a blood sacrifice Mr de Valera and his patriots are bound in honour to stand by Irishmen who are only carrying on the fight of Easter 1916.' The British Representative therefore wanted contiguous nationalist areas transferred to the Twenty-six Counties and the remainder to join Scotland. This might not actually settle the problem, but it would at least remove 'the only real Catholic grievance'.[22]

On 10 November 1944 de Valera made it clear that he was not going to be satisfied with anything less than the whole of the Six Counties. The easiest solution would simply be to transfer Westminster's powers relating to Northern Ireland to the Dublin government, which would then allow the Belfast parliament to retain its existing powers. Otherwise, he argued, 'if the difficulties of amalgamating the North and South were insuperable, there should be a transfer of population out of the North so that nothing insuperable remained.' Those who did not want to be part of Ireland 'should be physically transferred to the country to which they wished to adhere'.[23] In short, he was proposing what would later be called ethnic cleansing as a solution rather than the re-partition envisaged by Maffey. The Taoiseach would undoubtedly have been even more opposed to the line of thinking being pursued by Gray, who argued there should be a federation between Britain and Ireland in which the Twenty-six Counties would have similar powers of self-government as the state of New York had within the United States of America. This, he believed, would be beneficial to both Britain and Ireland:

For the benefit of each there should be a federal bond. Each needs federated security and federated trade. How to bring this about is a British problem and an Irish one too, though the Irish don't realise it. Appeasement and 'Wait and See' is to my mind the worst way of going about this. But it is none of our business how the British settle their problem as long as they do not brutalise Ireland and both lose the support of American liberal opinion and strengthen Irish nationalist sentiment in America which is now at a low ebb, thank God.[24]

The IRA was largely sympathetic to Germany, but de Valera cracked down heavily on the organisation, interning more than 1,000 members without trial and using Emergency Powers to have military courts jail almost as many more. Five members of the IRA were executed during the war years. Charlie Kerins, the twenty-four-year-old who was appointed Chief of Staff in the wake of the Stephen Hayes affair, was arrested in June 1944. He was convicted by a military court and sentenced to death for the murder of Detective Sergeant Denis O'Brien in September 1942. De Valera was apparently determined to make an example of Kerins, who was denied the military death by firing squad accorded to four other members of the IRA executed since 1940. Tom Pierrepoint, the British hangman, was brought over to hang Kerins on 1 December 1944.

In the early part of the war Maffey had been able to persuade Gray to see Irish affairs almost through British eyes. Now it seemed Gray had become even more imperialist in outlook than the British Representative. Of course, Gray was acting in what he believed was the best interest of President Roosevelt, who had given the British Prime Minister a virtual veto over America's policy towards Ireland. In the process Gray viewed British and American interests, in relation to Ireland, as inextricably linked. He seemed to be on the same wavelength as Churchill in advocating the isolation of the Irish.

There was a sign of a possible crack in Washington on this approach on 11 September 1944, when the United States invited the Irish government to send representatives to an international conference on civil aviation in Chicago at the beginning of November. The British had decided to have the dominions meet in Ottawa in advance, and the dominion governments were consulted about the necessity of inviting the Irish to participate.

The Australians thought there would be considerable advantage to gaining Irish support in advance of the Chicago meeting because Canberra believed 'the Irish base of Foynes had been of such value to the joint war effort'.[25] But the British expressed strong reservations. Churchill informed the Australian and Canadian Prime Ministers:

It would be impossible for us to advocate an Empire conference at which a member state of the British Empire was present who actually at the moment would be maintaining in Dublin German and Japanese diplomatic representatives and Irish representatives at Berlin and Tokyo. Although Anglo-Irish relations are a matter of concern to the whole Empire, it will I am sure be admitted that the interest of the United Kingdom on account of our very close proximity, is one which must be considered paramount.[26]

Fearing the British approach would ultimately drive Ireland from the Commonwealth, Mackenzie King took issue with Churchill. The Canadian Prime Minister thought the policy might provoke the Irish into 'ending all co-operation with the Allies'. He did not wish to upset Dublin, so he instructed Kearney to tell the Dublin government that 'no constitutional or political importance should be attached to the absence of Ireland from the meeting in Canada'. King suggested 'an easy explanation' for the Irish would be that the conference would be discussing military air service during the war. The Canadian Prime Minister wrote to Churchill that he would agree to the exclusion of the Irish provided there were discussions about wartime air services and that this was made public.[27]

The Irish negotiating team at Chicago included Minister Robert Brennan, his colleague from Canada John Hearne, and Secretary of the Department of Industry and Commerce John Leyden, as well as a number of other civil servants. It quickly became apparent that relations were strained between the British and the Americans, who were advocating freedom of the air on much the same basis as freedom of the seas.

'You have the planes, and the men to fly them,' replied Lord Swindon, the head of the British team. 'None of the rest of us have. If your policy is adopted, the US will be enabled to collar all the air freight and air passenger services in the world and leave the rest of us high and dry.'[28]

Adolf Berle, the head of the American delegation, said that if the conference failed to establish the principle of freedom of the air, it would be failing in its duty to mankind.

Brennan had private meetings with both the British and the Americans, and relations between the two main Allies became more strained. The Americans offered to conclude a bilateral agreement with the Irish, who accepted the offer after consulting Dublin. Churchill was taken aback that the Americans would contemplate such a deal. Having acceded to an American request not to conclude a meat agreement with Argentina, Churchill clearly felt aggrieved that the Americans were ignoring his request in relation to Ireland. 'I am sure we may ask you to postpone these negotiations with the Southern Irish until at least you and I have a chance to talk it over together,' he wired Roosevelt on 27 January 1945.[29]

Although the President ignored the telegram, the State Department confirmed the following week that it was negotiating with the Irish and by the weekend, much to Churchill's indignation, an agreement had been signed with the Irish. The two sides agreed to reciprocal landing rights in an agreement that provided for all American planes bound for Europe to stop at Rineanna, which would be renamed Shannon Airport, in place of Foynes.

'Our special concern with Éire is obvious on political and geographical grounds, and it is indeed much closer than that of the United States with the Argentine,' the Prime Minister cabled Roosevelt on 6 March. He felt the agreement would weaken his hand in relation to Ireland because it would encourage de Valera to play the United States and Britain off against each other. 'I trust therefore that you will be able to take the necessary steps to have the agreement annulled,' Churchill continued.[30]

In a 'Personal and Top Secret' reply, Roosevelt informed Churchill that the agreement would stand. Even though he understood Britain's political concerns, in view of Ireland's wartime record, the President indicated he fully approved of the State Department's action in signing the agreement with the Irish because it related to a post-war matter.[31]

The British were also anxious to keep Ireland out of the United Nations Organisation unless the country was prepared to get on the Allied bandwagon before the end of the war. 'Although the Southern Ireland Government has, in fact, helped us in a number of unobtrusive ways, her general policy of neutrality, her refusal to grant us bases and to remove the Axis Legations, and her unsatisfactory attitude over war criminals, put her quite out of court,' Cranborne advised the British Cabinet on 21 February 1945. He realised that dominions would be likely to take exception to this attitude, which really challenged dominion rights. 'However ill-judged Southern Ireland's behaviour over the war has been, she was entitled, as a Dominion, to stay out, if she thought right,' the Dominions Secretary continued. He actually listed fourteen ways in which the Irish secretly helped Britain and essentially discriminated against the Germans, but he was still determined to block Ireland's admission to the United Nations out of what could only be described as sheer vindictiveness.[32]

Nevertheless the Americans were still not finished with their plans to discredit de Valera. This time Gray advocated asking the Irish government to allow the United States to seize the German Legation in Dublin before Hempel would have time to destroy documents. The British were consulted, and Churchill warmly approved of the idea. He doubted there was 'anything of any value' in the German archives, but then he realised de Valera was unlikely to accede to the request anyway. Indeed, if the Allies seriously wanted the German documents, they would have had someone other than Gray approach the Taoiseach.

Before Gray could act, however, Roosevelt died suddenly on 12 April 1945. That evening Robert Brennan was due to attend a party in Washington. He assumed it would be called off, but to his surprise the host told him that it would go on. 'So off we went to find fifty or sixty people, members of Congress, army and navy officers, newspapers men, etc., in our host's house in Georgetown,' Brennan noted. 'The conversation was entirely about the new situation.' This was something new for Brennan and his wife. 'It was typical of America that any concern with the past is a waste of time,' he wrote. 'FDR was dead. He was now in the past. We may be able to do something about the future.'[33]

The Irish had lost one of their severest critics, but there was no rejoicing in Dublin. Gray was surprised; members of the Irish government were genuinely grieved. Next day he wrote to the late President's widow:

> This is indeed a strange country. All this forenoon members of the government, their wives and leaders of the opposition have been coming in a stream to pay their respects. Mr de Valera made a very moving tribute to the President in the Dáil this morning and moved adjournment till tomorrow. I thought I knew this country and its people but this was something new. There was a great deal of genuine feeling.[34]

President Douglas Hyde, who had been incapacitated by a stroke, took no part in any of the ceremonies, but he did send a formal telegram of condolence to President Harry Truman. The American Legation also told the *Irish Press* that Cambreth Kane, of President Hyde's staff, called at the American Legation to express 'sympathy to the American Minister and Mrs Gray on the death of President Roosevelt'.[35]

Gray took offence, however, when Catholic members of the Government refused to enter a Protestant church for commemoration services. At the time Catholics in Ireland considered it sinful to enter a Protestant church. Gray was disgusted and was further annoyed a few weeks later when the President's secretary, Michael McDunphy, formally called on the German minister to express condolence following the death of Hitler. The American Minister took grave umbrage and formally protested at what he considered 'a serious discourtesy to himself and his country'.[36] But that is getting ahead of the story.

In the days following the death of Roosevelt there was news of the liberation of several German death camps. Details of the Holocaust were published in the British papers, which were available in Ireland. 'Everybody shocked at the horror photographs taken in the German concentration camps at Buchenwald, Belsen and Nordhausen,' Kearney noted in his diary.[37] 'Stories of German atrocities growing. The British Government is sending a Parliamentary Committee to investigate. *Daily Express* is displaying atrocity pictures.'[38]

There was intense public interest in Ireland in the fall of Germany. 'Everybody listens to the radio these days in expectation of announcement of Germany's surrender,' Kearney wrote on 30 April. 'Gray sent me a letter stating that on behalf of the United Nations he was to request the Irish Government to facilitate in taking possession of the German Legation and its contents. It is a request addressed to all neutrals and is for the purpose of securing information such as codes, etc. Should he be successful, he has asked that we send a representative from this office to help seal archives.'[39]

That day Gray formally asked de Valera for permission to seize the German Legation. Reading from a memorandum, Gray said Allied forces were almost in total control of Germany and Ireland had, in effect, recognised the collapse of the Third Reich by withdrawing the Irish *Chargé d'Affaires* to safety in Switzerland. Once Germany had been defeated, title to all German property would be vested in the Allies, so he asked that the Americans be allowed to take control of the Legation early in the hope of getting their hands on German codes before the Legation staff could destroy them. He contended those codes could then be used to save the lives and property of Irish nationals as well as others in the event some U-boats tried to carry on the struggle from the Atlantic, or if there were armed pockets of German resistance.

'As I proceeded,' the American Minister reported, 'Mr de Valera grew red and looked very sour. He was evidently annoyed, but his manners were correct. When I finished, he slapped the copy of the memorandum, which I had presented him, on his desk and said, "This is a matter for my legal advisers. It is not a matter that I can discuss with you now".'[40]

Time was of the essence, Gray argued, but the Taoiseach refused to discuss it further. Next day Walshe told Gray that Hempel would be instructed to hand over his keys once the German surrender had been announced and the Americans could then, and only then, take charge of the legation.

Later that day Gray gave Kearney a copy of the memorandum he used during the interview. Kearney noted:

He said that deV was visibly annoyed. I was surprised to learn that Gray did not make it clear that all neutrals were being approached in the same way as Ireland. Gray remarked that in friendship you get what you give, and suggested that it was time that Ireland showed some acts of friendship. He gave the example of two men fighting in a ditch and one called for help while a third party just look on. Mr deV replied that those topics had been the subject of previous conversation and he did not propose to discuss them further and added something to the effect that Ireland would adopt the correct attitude for a neutral.'[41]

That night, German radio announced Hitler's death.

Chapter 30 ∾

| LOOSE ENDS

The announcement of Hitler's death led to a defiant gesture of Irish independence that caused a sensation of shock and revulsion when de Valera, accompanied by Walshe, went to the German Legation to express condolence to Hempel, who warned the Taoiseach that there could be trouble over the visit.

'I do what I think is right,' de Valera told him.[1]

Although he made no favourable comments about Hitler in the Dáil and made no attempt to have the latter adjourn as a mark of respect, as he had done following the death of Roosevelt, his visit to the German Legation provoked a firestorm of criticism in the Allied press. 'This forbidding fanatic who directs affairs in Éire might have spared us this tomfoolery,' the London *Evening Star* complained.[2] The gesture was 'the silliest act of the whole war', according to Sir Robert Vansittart, a prominent British diplomat. 'I wonder if he went on all fours,' Vansittart added. 'I have never heard of anything so craven in my life.'[3] The Taoiseach was merely observing strict protocol of a non-belligerent state, but this was seen as no excuse. 'Considering the character and the record of the man for whose death he was expressing grief,' the *New York Times* noted, 'there is obviously something wrong with the protocol, the neutrality, or Mr de Valera.'[4]

Even the Canadian press, which had previously been restrained in its comments about Irish policy, was outraged. According to a report sent to Kearney, Canadian editorials were unanimously critical, with comments ranging from 'neutrality gone mad' to expressions of sympathy for the embarrassed Irish people in view of de Valera's 'bad taste'. The *Peterborough Examiner* called him 'a melancholy clown' and the Vancouver *News Herald* accused him of crowning a 'career of infamy and treachery'.[5] The *Toronto Telegram*, which charged the Taoiseach with having 'forfeited any claim to respect from the decent-minded people of the world', went on to suggest Canada withdraw its High Commissioner from Dublin in protest.[6]

The criticism was not reflected in the heavily censored Irish newspapers, but there was a great deal of private criticism in Ireland. 'Nothing which Mr de Valera has done during the years which I have been in Dublin has evoked such widespread criticism and much of it comes from persons who are normally supporters of his own party,' Kearney wrote. Seán MacEntee, his wife Margaret, and their daughter Máire dined with the Kearneys on 4 May. Margaret MacEntee said that de Valera 'might have held his hand—particularly as it was not at all clear that Hitler was head of the German State when he died—nor were the circumstances of his death known'.[7]

Why did the Taoiseach go to such lengths to express sympathy for the death of a man he really despised? John Gunther, the famous author and journalist, thought de Valera was probably 'tweaking' the tail of the British Lion, but a more accurate analogy would probably have been that he was ruffling the feathers of the American Eagle.[8]

Although Gray believed de Valera had reluctantly made the visit at the insistence of Aiken, Maffey thought the gesture was in reaction to Gray's 'most recent assault on his principles, i.e. by the request for possession of the German archives before VE day'. While de Valera's gesture was 'a very unwise step', Maffey thought it was nevertheless 'a conspicuous act of neutrality' that demonstrated de Valera 'was no "bandwagoner"'.[9]

The Taoiseach instructed External Affairs not to defend his actions, and he did not account publicly for his behaviour at the time. But some weeks later Maffey reported that de Valera told him 'that common gentlemanly feeling of sympathy with Dr Hempel in the hour of the country's collapse called for the gesture. He suggested with humourless politeness that he would have done the same by me.'

'Hempel had acted the gentleman throughout,' Maffey noted, but he was not impressed with de Valera's explanation. 'I said', he wrote, 'that nobody would quarrel with a gesture of human sympathy, but this had been a publicised act of a state, admittedly devoid of any element of sympathy.'[10]

The Buchenwald and Belsen death camps had already been liberated, so de Valera could have been in no doubt whatever about the nature of the Nazi regime at the time. Three days before the announcement of Hitler's death, for instance, Walshe told Maffey that Hempel 'was horrified' by the Buchenwald revelations.[11] In that light, de Valera's expression of official sympathy following Hitler's death seemed inexplicable. He could, for example, have delayed on the pretext of waiting for official confirmation of Hitler's death. 'It was even far from certain at the time that Hitler was dead,' according to Maffey, who added, 'It was more than possible that Dr Hempel was delighted to think that Hitler was dead.'[12]

Maffey was probably right in believing de Valera's annoyance at Gray had played a pivotal part in the whole affair. In a letter to the Irish Minister in Washington, for instance, de Valera wrote that it would have been an 'unpardonable discourtesy to the German nation and to Dr Hempel himself' not to proffer an official condolence. Having paid what even Gray described as 'a moving tribute' to Roosevelt little over a fortnight earlier, it would have been insulting to the German Minister if the death of his leader was simply ignored. And the Taoiseach was not about to insult Hempel because he had a much higher regard for him than for Gray. 'During the whole of the war,' de Valera wrote, 'Dr Hempel's conduct was irreproachable. He was always and invariably correct—in marked contrast with Gray. I certainly was not going to add to his humiliation in the hour of defeat.'[13]

'I did what I did as my duty,' he told the Dáil some weeks later. 'I was quite aware when I was doing it that it was capable of being misrepresented, but I am going to do my duty here in this country.'[14]

On 7 May 1945 it was announced that Germany would formally surrender the following day. Some students at Trinity College Dublin, which was still widely identified as an anglophile university, began flying the Allied flags from the flagpole on the roof of the entrance to the college in the heart of the city. When people on the ground took exception to the flying of the Irish tricolour beneath the other flags, the students on the roof reacted by taking down the Irish flag and trying to burn it. They then threw the smouldering remnant from the roof.

On hearing what had happened, a number of students from the nearby National University marched on Trinity College. Some of those who joined the march were carrying Nazi flags. Two of the students—the future Taoiseach Charles J. Haughey and Seamus Sorohan, a future senior counsel—produced a Union Jack and proceeded to burn it. What had started out as a good-humoured incident turned very ugly and a riot ensued as the police baton-charged the crowd.

Later that evening some of the demonstrators went to the office of the United States Consul General and to Maffey's residence and stoned both buildings. Although the attack on the residence of a British representative in Ireland was hardly surprising, the attack on the American building was unprecedented. 'The mentality of such persons is obviously a favourable soil for the seeds of National Socialist resurgence,' Gray wrote to de Valera.[15] It was a measure of the extent to which the normally cordial relations between the United States and Ireland had deteriorated during the war.

The public reaction in Ireland to de Valera's visit to the German Legation following the death of Hitler was slow to develop because the Irish people knew very little about the Holocaust in Europe. When censorship was lifted the following week, people were suddenly confronted with the full horrors of the Nazi reign of terror.

'In the public mind,' Maffey wrote, 'Mr de Valera's condolences gradually took on a smear of turpitude, and for the first time, and at a critical time, a sense of disgust slowly manifested itself and a growing feeling that Mr de Valera had blundered into a clash with the ideals of decency and right and was leading away from realities.'[16]

Vincent Massey, the Canadian High Commissioner in London, thought it was in reaction to the condolence gesture that Churchill delivered a stinging attack on de Valera and Irish neutrality during a victory address over BBC on 13 May 1945. It was just as likely, however, that the Prime Minister was highlighting the contrast between the loyalty of Northern Ireland and what he considered de Valera's rancid indifference to the plight of the Allies. By speaking out strongly in such an historic speech, the Prime Minister would help to further weaken de Valera's ability to cause trouble over partition.

Churchill pulled out all the stops in his speech as he referred to the Irish leader with dismissive contempt. He emphasised the different syllables of de Valera's name in such a way as to conjure up a subliminal suggestion of the Taoiseach as the personification of the devil and evil in Éire by pronouncing the name as if it were 'D'evil Éire'. The Prime Minister said:

> Owing to the action of Mr de Valera, so much at variance with the temper and instinct of thousands of Southern Irishmen who hastened to the battlefront to prove their ancient valour, the approaches which the Southern Irish ports and airfield could so easily have guarded were closed by the hostile aircraft and U-boats. This was indeed a deadly moment in our life, and if it had not been for the loyalty and friendship of Northern Ireland we should have been forced to come to close quarters with Mr de Valera or perish forever from the earth. However, with a restraint and poise to which, I say, history will find few parallels, His Majesty's Government never laid a violent hand upon them, though at times it would have been quite easy and quite natural, and we left the de Valera government to frolic with German and later with the Japanese representatives to their hearts' content.[17]

There was an air of anticipation in Ireland as people waited for de Valera to respond. On 16 May Walshe told Kearney that de Valera would probably stress the part of the speech in which Churchill hoped for better understanding between Britain and Ireland. He also thought the Taoiseach might refer to his visit to the German Minister. Kearney suggested that de Valera might be better not referring to the visit:

> I was amazed to learn that Mr de Valera proposed to involve the religious background and customs in Ireland rather than protocol. I told Mr Walshe

that in my opinion an attempt to justify it on these grounds would be misunderstood abroad and would only make things worse. I suggested that since Mr Churchill, in his speech, had not actually mentioned the visit, I thought that Mr de Valera might profitably remain silent on it. I also told him that the visit was a boost for Mr Gray and a slap in the eye for Maffey and myself, and I also felt sure that this was never intended. From a subsequent remark I gather that Mr Walshe, and probably Mr de Valera, appreciates that a mistake was made, because Mr Walshe said that they could not very well apologise for it. I said I could not imagine Mr de Valera apologising, but at least he could leave the matter alone.[18]

It was generally assumed de Valera would respond with a broadside against Churchill. The Taoiseach began his reply broadcast over Radio Éireann by thanking God for sparing Ireland from the conflagration, which had left much of Europe in ruins. Next he expressed gratitude to the various people who had contributed to the successful efforts to keep the country out of the war. And then he turned to Churchill's speech.

He knew what many people were expecting him to say and what he would have said twenty-five years earlier, but the occasion now demanded something else. With an exquisite touch of condescension, he explained that Churchill could be excused for being carried away in the excitement of victory, but there would be no such excuse for him. Speaking calmly de Valera said:

> Mr Churchill makes it clear that, in certain circumstances, he would have violated our neutrality and that he would justify his action by Britain's necessity. It seems strange to me that Mr Churchill does not see that this, if accepted, would mean that Britain's necessity would become a moral code and that when this necessity became sufficiently great, other people's rights were not to count. It is quite true that other great powers believe in this same code—in their own regard—and have behaved in accordance with it. That is precisely why we have the disastrous successions of wars— World War No. 1 and World War No. 2—and shall it be World War No. 3?

He then turned to praise Churchill for resisting the temptation to violate Irish neutrality:

> It is, indeed, hard for the strong to be just to the weak, but acting justly always has its rewards. By resisting his temptation in this instance, Mr Churchill, instead of adding another horrid chapter to the already bloodstained record of relations between England and this country, has

advanced the cause of international morality an important step.[19]

Kearney listened to the speech in the St Stephen's Green Club, along with ten to twelve Irish people, who were unanimous in their praise of the speech. Dr Kevin Malley thought it was 'the best speech de Valera ever made'. Dr Jack Dunne, who described it 'marvellous', almost got into a fight when a young Dublin solicitor named Doyle began laughing at something de Valera said. Dr Eddie Falvelle thought the speech was good and told Dunne he was 'making an ass of himself'. Desmond Bell, a solicitor, said that he did not like de Valera, or 'for what he stands, but thought he made a great speech'.[20]

The public reaction to the address in Ireland was overwhelming. 'With little exception,' Kearney reported, 'Mr de Valera's broadcast is regarded in Ireland as a masterpiece, and it is looked upon as probably his best effort. It has served to almost still the criticism which his visit to the German Minister provoked, and, in so far as I can judge, on balance, Mr de Valera now stands in higher favour in Ireland than he did before his visit to the German Minister.'[21]

It even stilled the criticism in Canada over the visit to Hempel. John J. Hearne noted that the chief matter of interest relative to Ireland was the reply to Churchill. 'There was no press campaign against Ireland since that historic episode,' he noted. 'The French Canadian newspapers were more friendly than ever.'[22]

'We had him on a plate,' Kearney told Maffey the morning after the Taoiseach's speech. 'We had him where we wanted him. But look at the papers this morning!'[23]

Churchill's remarks had been a great mistake, according to Maffey, because they gave de Valera the opportunity to escape from the consequences of his actions following Hitler's death. In the last analysis, he added, it was not the Prime Minister's speech, but de Valera's reply 'which bore the stamp of the elder statesman'.[24]

Maffey was particularly critical of the suggestion that it would have been natural for Britain to take Irish bases: 'I felt that something was lost in the moral plane by suggesting that we might have seized them. However, where we lost most tricks in the rubber here was in the fact that after five and a half years of war the British Prime Minister, in a historic speech, gave prominence to Mr de Valera, attacked him personally and thereby introduced him to the spotlight and a world radio contest.'[25]

'With the Irish people today Mr de Valera is as great a hero as is the Irishman who scores the winning try at Twickenham,' Maffey added.[26]

While the Dominions Office did not dispute his assessment of the Irish reaction to de Valera's speech, Eric Machtig noted the international perspective of this so-called battle of the broadcasts was quite different. The latest events apparently had a comparatively similar impact to the American Note of February 1944, when de Valera's image at home was enhanced even though his international standing was seriously damaged. The Dominions Secretary had been at the San Francisco Conference to set up the United Nations Organisation at the time. Coming in the midst of the gruesome revelations about the Buchenwald concentration camp, news of de Valera's condolence gesture 'inflicted a profound and enduring shock on the American people'. Consequently, Churchill's 'severe remarks were therefore accepted and even applauded as a salutary rap over the knuckles'. As a result the Dominions Office concluded, 'we have certainly gained in the eyes of the world, whatever may be the effect in Éire itself.'[27]

But de Valera was redeemed in the eyes of his own people both at home and abroad. 'For the Irishman in the homeland and overseas,' Maffey wrote, 'it is once again a case of "Up Dev!"'[28]

Although hostilities had ended in Europe, Japan was still fighting in the Far East, from where there were reports of Irish missionaries having been murdered and imprisoned by the Japanese forces. Maffey was afraid de Valera might try to win favour with the American people by declaring war on Japan over the killing of the missionaries. The British Representative noted that the headline, 'De Valera Breaks with JAPAN', would read well in the United States. But the Taoiseach had no intention of climbing on the Allied bandwagon.[29] In any event, there were still some loose ends to be cleared up with the Germans.

Dublin had to tackle thorny questions of what to do with the 266 interned German airmen and sailors, the handful of captured agents and the staff of the closed German Legation. On 11 June 1945 the State Department instructed Gray to ask the Irish to intern or keep under house arrest all German diplomatic personnel and captured agents.

Gray seemed to be taking satisfaction out of making himself thoroughly disagreeable to the de Valera government. After learning that Michael McDunphy, Secretary to President Hyde, had paid formal condolence to Hempel following the death of Hitler, Gray formally protested and demanded an apology because McDunphy had not called on him following the death of Roosevelt little over a fortnight earlier. 'Until the matter was cleared up to his satisfaction,' Gray threatened, 'he would not call upon the President.'

'The circumstances were entirely different,' President Hyde's office contended.[30] Following Roosevelt's death, 'President Hyde as head of the Irish state cabled a message of sympathy to President Roosevelt's successor in office, President Truman.' This and President Truman's reply were published on 14 April. In the case of Hitler's death, there was no recognisable successor to whom President Hyde could send a telegram, so McDunphy called on Hempel in person. There was therefore no justification to Gray's complaint of discourtesy.[31]

Having deliberately provoked refusals from de Valera for more than a year, Gray adopted a different approach to the issue of the German internees because he was now looking for cooperation. Fearing the request would be rejected, he advocated the Allies do nothing until the Irish approached them to take the internees off their hands. Those men had not been paid their salaries for several months and they were somewhat restless at the Curragh. In fact, in late May there were disturbing signs of an impending mutiny between socialist elements among the naval ratings and their more conservative officers. Gray therefore suggested the Allies should ask for all the Germans to be handed over at once. Otherwise, de Valera would just hand over the internees and then refuse to surrender either the diplomats or the spies, whose crimes were only against the Irish state. The one trump card the Allies had to get all the men was to exploit the 'nuisance value of those disorderly and expensive internees'.[32] While Gray was arguing with the State Department over the timing and form of the approach, the British went ahead and asked for the internees and the spies. De Valera flatly refused to surrender the diplomats, but he did agree to hand over the internees on condition Britain guaranteed that none of the men would be executed nor forced to return to the Soviet Zone in Germany.

The American Minister was bitterly opposed to the latter stipulation, believing that Dublin was trying to split the Allies by having them discriminate against one another.[33] He tried to persuade the State Department to pressure the British to reject de Valera's conditions, but with Roosevelt dead, Gray no longer enjoyed the same influence in Washington. His advice was rejected by the State Department, which instructed him to cooperate with Maffey, who by this time had already agreed to the Taoiseach's conditions.[34]

Arrangements were made for the British to pick up the internees at Rosslare on 11 July, but less than a week before that date Maffey informed the Department of External Affairs that Britain could no longer guarantee that none of the men would be returned to the Soviet Zone. With this, the arrangements fell through.

After further negotiations the British again relented and agreed to the conditions, so in the early hours of 13 August 1945, the day before the Japanese formally surrendered, thereby ending the Second World War, the German internees boarded a British battleship at the North Wall, Dublin. Twelve men were missing: eight had absconded and gone into hiding with Irish friends; the other four were personally granted political asylum by de Valera. Two were ill—one suffering from tuberculosis and the other from cardiac problems—while the other two were Austrians who feared they would be unjustly charged with war crimes in Austria, because they had apparently supported the Nazi takeover in 1938. De Valera quietly authorised them to stay on condition they did not disclose their presence to the authorities in Austria.

Six of the German internees who absconded were turned over to the British at the border on 8 October 1945. Another was repatriated the following month, and the last man was finally captured and handed over in April 1946. By the end of that year de Valera even indicated he might be prepared to surrender the captured spies, much to the surprise of the US State Department.

A difficulty arose, however, over a difference of opinion between de Valera and Gerry Boland, his Minister for Justice. The Germans had already been told they would be allowed to remain in Ireland, so Boland was reluctant to order their repatriation. He not only threatened to resign, but actually submitted a letter of resignation protesting against the proposed forced repatriation. De Valera prevailed upon his Justice Minister to withdraw the resignation and left him to deal with the matter.

Gray therefore discussed the question with Boland, whom he described as 'a man of high character, great courage, and iron nerve combined with what in our view is a somewhat sentimental tenderness towards appeals on compassionate grounds'.[35] The Justice Minister was particularly anxious about the spy Hermann Goertz, who had threatened to commit suicide rather than face deportation.

Although Gray argued that the former spy, who came to Ireland in 1940, could hardly come to any harm seeing that he had been out of Germany when most of the Nazi atrocities were committed, Goertz was terrified of being persecuted by the communists because he had been involved in the bloody suppression of the Spartacist Revolt in Berlin back in 1918. On one occasion when Gray was pressing the issue with Boland, the latter became so agitated that he actually ordered the American Minister from his home.

On 23 May 1947 Goertz was taken back into custody and told he was being deported. Boland's fears were realised when the former spy killed himself by taking a cyanide capsule.

Irish authorities quickly rescinded their deportation order on another of the Germans, Werner Unland, who, together with his British wife, had also been threatening to commit suicide if he were forced to return to Germany. When it became clear the Irish would not deport him, the British dropped their demand, but Gray was never told. Blinded by his own prejudices, he was unwilling to give de Valera any credit for what Maffey acknowledged was 'an always difficult and often generous interpretation of neutrality'.[36]

Chapter 31 ❧

┃ IN PERSPECTIVE

'David Gray in that crisis of human affairs, felt that "those who are
not with us are against us"', Sir John Maffey later explained. 'That
was his stern unshakeable principle. In his diplomacy there was no
room for compromises.'[1] Gray's judgment on Irish matters was at times
seriously distorted. American intelligence agents sent to Ireland saw Irish
policy in a very different light.

De Valera made no apologies for not leading the country into the war in
what would have been a pointless crusade for a small nation. Britain and
France supposedly went to war on behalf of Poland, but the rights of Poles
were essentially sacrificed even before the end of the war. The Taoiseach told
the Dáil in July 1945:

> There are big nations to-day and they have fought for certain principles,
> and we see nations that wanted their freedom, and we see them carved up.
> If the big nations are not able to put into effect their principles because of
> the situation in which they find themselves, what do you think will be the
> position for small nations? Would not I or any other Irishman—anybody
> else who is here—be in a nice position if, as Head of the Government, I
> had led our people into this war to save, say, Poland, and I should have to
> come back and tell our people here: 'I am not able to do the things that I
> asked the young men of this country to go out and fight for?'
>
> These are the things that people ought to bear in mind when they are
> asking small nations to engage in crusades.[2]

Sir John Maffey realised de Valera was benevolently disposed towards the
Allies. 'For the first time in history the British Cabinet have been able to
conduct a long war without any anxiety about Ireland,' Maffey wrote the week
after hostilities concluded. 'When any German activity developed, I was the
first to be informed.'[3]

At the beginning of the war de Valera promised to give Britain all the help he could, short of war. The British were allowed to station an aircraft at Foynes to satisfy themselves that the Irish were not succouring u-boats. Coast-watchers essentially reported to Dublin and the British simultaneously. Their reports were transmitted to one of a number of central points, from where details of sightings were radioed to Dublin. Initially the messages were sent in the clear. In theory the British and Germans were being informed at the same time, but the Germans were too far away to use the information. Later the messages were encoded in a code secretly supplied by the British. The latter were allowed to fly through 'the Donegal Corridor' and to station armed tugboats in Cobh and Killybegs for air-sea rescue purposes.

The Irish secretly shared weather information with the British, who were allowed to set up a radio direction-finding mast on the east coast in the summer of 1941 and later set up a radar station on the south coast, for use against the latest form of submarine activity, plus two direction-finding wireless stations on Malin Head.[4] The British and the Canadians were allowed to open diplomatic missions in Dublin during the war. The British were allowed to station military, naval and air attachés, but the Germans were denied permission to bring in any replacements for their diplomatic personnel during the war. The Irish also arranged for the extinction of trade and business lighting in coastal towns, where such lighting was alleged to afford useful landmarks for German aircraft.

Over 140 Allied planes came down in Ireland during the war. Forty-one were American, and eighteen of those were refuelled and allowed to fly away; a further twenty-one were salvaged and returned by road to Northern Ireland; and all 275 American survivors were promptly released. Of the more than 100 other Allied landings, twenty-nine aircraft were allowed to fly away and seventeen were salvaged and returned by road. In addition, 225 other Allied airmen were promptly let go, but forty-six were interned for a time. Those interned included eleven Canadians, three Poles, a Frenchman, a New Zealander and an American serving in the RAF. The others were from various parts of the United Kingdom. Two were released on compassionate grounds and ten escaped prior to October 1943, when all but eleven of the remainder were secretly released. Three more were handed over on compassionate grounds in the following months, and the remaining eight were secretly freed in June 1944 after the successful Allied invasion of Normandy. All survivors of the eighteen German aircraft that came down on Irish territory were interned for the duration of the war, with the exception of a seriously injured airman, who was handed to the British for repatriation to Germany by the Red Cross in October 1943. Another escaped from the Curragh, but was handed over to the British when he was discovered as a stowaway on a boat bound for Portugal. The situation in relation to seamen was even more unbalanced. No

Allied seaman was interned in Ireland, but 213 German sailors were interned, even though they should have been released under international law as stranded mariners.

De Valera refused to allow the British to occupy the Treaty ports, but he argued that they would not be of much use. Maybe he was trying to rationalise his policy, but in time it became apparent that his argument was valid. In 1943 Gray persuaded Roosevelt and Churchill to ask for bases in order to get de Valera's refusal on record. The American Joint Chiefs of Staff and their British counterparts blocked this request because they were unwilling to take any chance that de Valera would comply, as they concluded that Irish bases would only be a liability.

The Germans were responsible for sinking practically all the Allied ships in the Atlantic, but Allied propaganda seemed to suggest that the Irish government somehow shared responsibility for each of the ships sunk within 500 miles of the Irish coast. The most dangerous area for the Allied shipping in the Atlantic was northwest of Ireland where the shipping funnelled together in the approach to Britain. Lough Foyle provided a base for Allied ships engaged in protection, while the aircraft used bases at Lough Erne and at Eglington, which were superior to any possible bases in the south of Ireland, especially when aircraft based on Lough Erne had the use of the Donegal Corridor. Lough Swilly in County Donegal would have cut a short distance off the turnaround journey for ships based at Lough Foyle, but the Americans dismissed the difference as insignificant. Historian Paul McMahon noted that some thought a base on the Shannon estuary would have provided protection against German capital ships sailing from France. 'It is impossible to exaggerate the importance of this matter,' one naval planner wrote in October 1940, but he exaggerated it grossly. English bases provided much greater protection for the few capital vessels coming from France.[5]

Air bases in Ireland would have allowed the Allies to provide air coverage a little over 100 miles further south and west into the Atlantic, but would have provided no extra protection for ships taking the more popular northerly route. Moreover the extra protection would only have been provided for seamen in that comparatively narrow stretch of remote ocean, and this would have been at the expense of the Irish people. Irish towns and cities would have provided a much easier target for German aircraft than distant ships in the remote expanse of the Atlantic Ocean. For de Valera to put the country's population at risk in those circumstances would have been the height of recklessness and irresponsibility. Some of those who were loudest in criticising Ireland's failure to fulfil a moral obligation to go to war with Germany in support of the democracies were essentially advocating that de Valera should have trampled on democracy at home.

John D. Kearney, the Canadian High Commissioner, accepted that de Valera did give all help short of war. The Allies eventually concluded that Ireland's entry into the war would have been a liability to the Allied cause, with the result that de Valera did essentially provide as much help as possible.

A secret liaison had been established between G2 and MI5, with the approval of de Valera, before the war and this was expanded during the conflict. An argument could be made that the Irish might have provided more help earlier. Colonel Dan Bryan of G2 admitted there was justification for Maffey's statement: 'You have no use in going to these people for certain things while they are convinced the Germans have won the war.'[6]

Sir David Petrie, the head of MI5, afterwards praised the Irish for assisting his organisation's operations in Ireland. 'The one factor indispensable to success was the good-will of the Éire officers,' he wrote.[7] The Irish turned a blind eye to the surreptitious activities of MI6 in Ireland. Through its many agents on the ground, MI6 was able to confirm that there were essentially no grounds for the earlier hysterical reports about Ireland being a centre of German espionage. David Gray, who was notoriously indiscreet, did not learn of this secret Anglo-Irish cooperation until after the United States entered the war. Even he admitted this cooperation went 'beyond what might reasonably have been believed possible'.[8]

The OSS sent three undercover agents to Ireland. Two were promptly uncovered, but unlike the MI6 agents, who were essentially ignored, or the German spies, who were promptly jailed, the Irish offered to cooperate with the OSS agents. 'The Irish worked with us on intelligence matters almost as if they were our allies,' wrote J. Russell Forgan, the deputy head of the OSS for Europe.[9] The OSS had nothing to do with the request to remove the Axis diplomats from Dublin in 1944, because it was just a political ruse. But when the White House considered sending a follow-up note, William J. Donovan, the Director of the OSS, assured Roosevelt that 'the cooperation in intelligence matters offered and given by the Irish has been very full'.

The cooperation was so extensive that both OSS and MI5 were confident the Irish were coping with the German espionage threat. Of course, it was only after the war that anyone could be sure of this. All German agents sent to Ireland were uncovered and all but one arrested during the war. Most were caught within a matter of hours. James J. O'Neill of Wexford, who had been captured by the Germans on a British merchant vessel on which he was a carpenter, got out of the prisoner-of-war camp by offering his services to the Germans. He was sent to work in France with instructions to flee over the Spanish border and to get papers from the Irish Legation in Madrid in order to return legitimately to Ireland, where he was to wait for a while before sending reports to an address in Spain. Instead, however, he offered his services to the British in November 1942. They brought him to Britain before allowing him to return to Ireland.

The presence of Herman Goertz in Ireland was quickly detected, but he remained at large for eighteen months. Willi Preetz was loose for a matter of weeks after he returned to Ireland, having secretly left to join the *Abwehr*. He managed to remain at large for about two months, but his radio transmissions were being monitored. Other *Abwehr* agents—Weber-Drohl, Anderson, Gartner, Tributh, Obed, Schultz, O'Reilly and Kenny—were all arrested within hours of their arrival. The only one who was not actually arrested was Joe Lenihan, who fled into Northern Ireland to offer his services to the British as a double agent.

Unlike World War I when thousands of British soldiers were tied up in Ireland to cope with the threat from Republicans, the de Valera government handled the bulk of that threat during World War II. Members of the IRA may have been ready to help the Nazis, but the de Valera government came down heavily on them by interning 1,130 Republicans without trial, while over 800 were jailed after being convicted in the Central Criminal Court. Five IRA members were executed and two others allowed to die on hunger strike.

At the end of the war de Valera could honestly say Ireland had helped the Allies. Figures for the number of Irish people who served in British forces differ. General Sir Hubert Gough noted that 160,000 gave Irish addresses for their next-of-kin. Some 1,550 Irish people were killed while serving in the British Army and 220 died in the Royal Navy. Many of those who served did so with great distinction.[10] Six men born or reared in the Twenty-six Counties and one born in Northern Ireland won the Victoria Cross (VC), Britain's highest award for gallantry. Harold Ervine Andrews, a native of Cavan, and Donald Edward Garland from County Wicklow won their awards for actions in Belgium early in the war. David Lord of Cork was posthumously awarded his VC for his part in the battle for the 'Bridge Too Far' at Arnhem, in the Netherlands. James Jackman of Dublin won his award at Tobruk in North Africa, while James J. Magennis from the Falls Road, Belfast, won his at Singapore, and Richard J. Kelleher of Tralee won the VC for his bravery in New Guinea.

There were others, too, such as Brendan Eamonn Fergus Finucane of the RAF, who was credited with shooting down thirty-two German aircraft. In June 1942, at the age of twenty-one, Finucane—who was born and reared in Dublin and called 'Paddy' by his British colleagues—became the youngest ever wing commander of the RAF. A month later he was killed when his crippled plane crashed at sea.

It may possibly have been more than mere chance that Churchill singled out others in the victory broadcast in which he lashed de Valera:

When I think of these days, I think also of other episodes and personalities. I do not forget Lieutenant-Commander Esmonde, v.c., d.s.o., Lance-Corporal Kenneally, v.c., Captain Fegen, v.c., and other Irish heroes that I could easily recite, and all bitterness by Britain for the Irish race dies in my heart. I can only pray that in years which I shall not see, the shame will be forgotten and the glories will endure, and that the peoples of the British Isles and of the British Commonwealth of Nations will walk together in mutual comprehension and forgiveness.[11]

All three of those mentioned were actually born in Britain. Esmonde was reared in Ireland and his brother was a sitting member of Dáil Éireann during the war, while Fegen's mother was from County Tipperary, but John Patrick Kenneally, the war hero who was supposedly from Tipperary, had only the most tenuous connection with Ireland. Born and reared in the north of England, his real name was Leslie Robinson. On his eighteenth birthday, in 1939, he joined the Royal Artillery and was stationed in north London. Bored, he fell in with some Irish labourers who persuaded him to desert and accompany them to Glasgow. They gave him the identity card of John Patrick Kenneally of Tipperary, who had returned to Ireland. Under his new identity Robinson enlisted in the Irish Guards and saw action in North Africa, where he was awarded the vc under his *nom de guerre.*

The true picture in relation to Irish policy during the war was distorted in later years by historians who got access to espionage information, which they misinterpreted. It would be some decades before the role of one of the most extraordinary spies, Fritz Kolbe, would be told. He was sent to Berne as a courier for the German Foreign Office on 15 August 1943. A devout Catholic who privately abhorred the Nazi regime, Kolbe approached the British embassy with an offer of help, but he was rebuffed.

'I don't believe you,' the British diplomat said to him. 'And if you are telling the truth, you are a cad.'[12]

Kolbe then went to the Americans and gave Allen Dulles of the oss a number of documents. When those were compared with intercepts of German diplomatic traffic, they were pronounced authentic. Kolbe was given the code name George Wood, and the material he provided was code-named Boston. He made regular visits to Berne, during which he handed over some 2,600 documents.

Some of it had sensational implications. It was from the documents furnished by Kolbe, which were dubbed 'the Boston Series', that the oss first learned that the Germans were getting information from within Roosevelt's Cabinet. Vice President Henry Wallace had been talking indiscreetly to his brother-in-law, a Swiss diplomat, who had been passing on the information to his own foreign ministry, where it was falling into German hands. On the basis of Kolbe's documents, Donovan reported, according to historian Joseph E. Persico, 'that a great deal of information pertaining to Allied activities in England and Ulster comes from the German embassy in Dublin. The Legation which is heavily staffed has succeeded in infiltrating agents into England.'[13] Kolbe informed Dulles that German diplomats in Dublin had identified 600 air installations in England involved in the Allied invasion of Normandy.[14]

Roosevelt was first informed about the Boston Series on 10 January 1944. He was shown fourteen select documents, which included information on the secret transmitter in Dublin. This noted that the Irish were aware of the transmitter and the Germans were keeping it for emergency use while they used the cable to Berne to forward their regular reports. The OSS added in a footnote that the transmitter had actually been removed on 24 December 1943.

Initially the OSS was alarmed about Kolbe's material relating to Ireland. 'The so-called Boston series of cables looked to me at first as though there was a serious leak from Eire,' Carter Nicholas wrote. In November 1943 MI5 prepared an anonymous letter that was passed to Hempel and, much to the delight of MI5, he forwarded the misinformation to Berlin. Most of what MI5 was feeding Hempel would have been 'accurate but unimportant information' in order to establish credence, according to Dennis Wheatley, who was one of those involved in the deception process. Occasionally they included information that would establish 'some really good line of deception'.[15] Kolbe's documents relative to Ireland contained the information that the Germans were, in fact, being fed by British intelligence. Hence those who were not aware of this were initially deceived by the 'Boston Series'.

This kind of information not only fooled the Germans but also the OSS. 'For a considerable time I was alarmed by the apparent evidence,' Nicholas explained. 'Internal SI security in this case led for a time at least to an entirely false conclusion.' When the OSS shared this alarming information with MI5, the British were able to clear up the matter. 'Eventually when I had all the facts on the Boston Series,' Nicholas wrote, 'they tended to prove exactly the opposite—that the situation was even better under control that I had previously thought.'[16]

As the British had been reading all the messages sent from Ireland before they were reaching Berlin since December 1942, when they broke Hempel's code, there were no surprises in this material for those in the know, but some people who were not aware of the broader Irish picture jumped to wrong conclusions. Joseph Persico wrote, for instance:

When FDR learned that agents of the German intelligence service, the *Sicherheitsdienst* (SD), equipped with wireless radios, were parachuting outside Galway, he decided that Irish neutrality had been stretched far enough. He found particularly disconcerting that every move of the U.S. XV Corps, stationed in Ulster and preparing to transfer to England for Overlord, was reported to the German General Staff by Abwehr agents in Ireland.[17]

Persico believed it was this that prompted Roosevelt to send the American Note. The *Abwehr*'s operations in Ireland had been comically inept, and all of its agents had been caught and jailed, as were the two SD agents. Neither O'Reilly nor Kenny—the agents 'parachuting outside Galway'—had supplied the Germans any material. Both were promptly arrested before they got off any message. Moreover, the German Legation had already handed over its transmitter in December 1943, more than two weeks before Roosevelt was even informed of the Boston Series.

Ireland did not really figure in the broader wartime picture, so writers like Persico and Anthony Cave Brown, who were dealing with the wider international scene, were deceived by looking at the Boston Series in isolation. If Carter Nicholas, the head of SI's Eire Desk, was deceived for a time, it was hardly surprising that Persico and Cave Brown would jump to the wrong conclusions.

In 1971 J. Harris Smith caused some sensation with his book, *The O.S.S.*, which asserted that the Irish diplomatic corps assisted the Americans in smuggling espionage material out of Italy. According to Smith, the 'Vessel Project' originated when the Acting Secretary of State at the Vatican, Monsignor Giovanni Montini (later Pope Paul VI), offered to arrange the transfer to the Americans of strategic information from a Vatican source in Japan. Smith added that Michael MacWhite, the Irish Minister in Rome, forwarded the information to Dublin, from where it was transferred to the OSS.[18] The highly prized secret material was in the form of voluminous reports from Japan.

The Irish had furnished Marlin and Nicholas with diplomatic reports from the continent, but the OSS concluded it would be impractical to use any Irish diplomatic bag to transfer material. Before the war Michael MacWhite suspected the Italians were opening the diplomatic bags.[19] After Italy entered the war in June 1940 the Department of External Affairs ordered 'the transmission of secret reports and communication by diplomatic mail-bag to all offices in Europe, excluding Great Britain, should be entirely suspended'. Diplomats wishing to communicate with Dublin 'on secret matters of urgency' were instructed to communicate by means of coded cables.[20] 'Pouches from Vichy, Berlin and Switzerland were all sent to Paris first where they were opened and read by the Germans,' Carter Nicholas noted. 'The plan of using Irish pouches offered us no possibilities of secure transmission of information either into or out of Europe. The idea of installing a courier was rejected by the Irish as impossible.'[21] In the final twenty months of the war the Department of External Affairs only received seven diplomatic bags from Rome. Those took, on average, around fifteen weeks to reach Dublin.[22] The Irish did not trust the diplomatic bag to send sensitive material, so the Americans would hardly have used it.

The supposed involvement of the future Pope and the future President of Ireland was probably leaked as a cover story to justify the oss not releasing details of the Vessel Project, because the oss had been duped. The material for which it paid $500 a month was actually part of a scam being run by a former journalist named Virgilio Scattolini, who had sold bogus Vatican information to various wire services before the war. With the liberation of Rome, he sought to re-establish this lucrative trade with forged documents. The Vessel information was considered so good that some of this raw material was also actually shown to Roosevelt.

Suspicions were roused in February 1945, however, when one of the documents purported to be a report of a meeting that had never taken place. Some of the Vessel messages were found to be embellished reports from Monsignor Paolo Marella, the Vatican's representative in Tokyo. The Allies had broken his code and were already reading his messages, so Scattolini's handiwork could easily have been discovered if the branches of the American intelligence network had checked with each other. The whole thing helps to explain, in part, why some people suggested that oss really stood for Oh So Social, or Oh So Silly.[23]

Smith's distortions were minor in comparison to Gray's plans. He was already in his late seventies when he retired in 1947, but this did not stop him from pursuing what had become a virtual obsession—trying to discredit de Valera. He began writing a book about his Irish experiences. President Roosevelt suggested the idea in 1943. Gray began writing an exposé of the Irish leader's supposed indifference and even hostility towards the Allied cause. Entitled 'Behind the Green Curtain', the manuscript went through several drafts. It was a distorted and vitriolic attack on de Valera, whom he frequently compared to Hitler, or to Nero fiddling while Rome burned.[24] Gray worked on his book for years. When Roosevelt's sons met him, they would frequently ask how the book was coming along, until one day he announced he had decided to abandon the project because their father's ghost had advised him to forget it.

To what degree Gray was influenced by spiritualism is a matter of conjecture. He was probably influenced when the messages tended to confirm his own suspicions, in much the same way as Prime Minister Mackenzie King of Canada was possibly influenced. The Canadian leader was deeply involved in spiritualism and he regularly recorded in his diary the psychical advice he was receiving. He was aware of Geraldine Cummins, but did not meet her until a visit to Britain in November 1947. *Time* magazine later published a sensational report about Cummins contacting Roosevelt's ghost for Mackenzie King, who asked if the late President thought he should retire as Prime Minister.

'Don't retire, stay on the job,' Roosevelt's ghost supposedly replied. 'Your country needs you.' The late American President reportedly went on to warn Mackenzie King 'to watch Asia' as that was where the danger lay. The Berlin airlift was about to begin, but that was depicted as merely calling a Soviet bluff. Roosevelt's ghost then purportedly warned that there would be war in the Far East within a couple of years, though Korea was not specified.[25] Mackenzie King took what Cummins wrote on that occasion and did not even confide it to his diary, but he subsequently noted 'the facts are that Roosevelt did speak strongly against my giving up public life at this time'. On 12 April 1948 he received a letter with a further communication that Cummins received during a session at which the supposed ghosts of Roosevelt's former aides, Pa Watson and Missy Le Hand, reportedly said Roosevelt wished to send a further message to Mackenzie King. 'He had been thinking the matter over since and now wished to say that he felt I was entitled to a rest and that he did not wish to urge that I should stay on,' the Prime Minister noted in his diary. Mackenzie King thought it particularly significant that the letter from Cummins arrived on the third anniversary of Roosevelt's death.[26] Mackenzie King duly stepped down as Prime Minister some months later, in November of 1948.

With the benefit of hindsight and the release of documents, it is clear the Germans would have violated Irish neutrality by attacking Ireland, if only as a diversionary tactic in their attack on Britain, but de Valera realised this was likely and he therefore pursued a policy that was deliberately favourable to Britain. In the circumstances it is inaccurate to call that policy neutrality; it was determined non-belligerency. He promised to keep his country out of the war, but he, unlike Franklin D. Roosevelt, meant what he said, and he fulfilled his promise and thereby conclusively demonstrated Ireland's political independence.

'Éire is more than ever a foreign country,' Maffey wrote in an astute assessment for the new British government headed by Clement Attlee. 'It is so dominated by the National Catholic Church as to be almost a theocratic State.

Gaelic is enforced to show that Éire is not one of the English-speaking nations, foreign games are frowned upon, the war censorship has been misapplied for anti-British purposes, anti-British feeling is fostered in school and by Church and State by a system of "hereditary enemy" indoctrination.'[27]

During the war Maffey demonstrated that he was an astute observer of the Irish scene. It was a pity that Churchill did not heed his advice with an open mind. In the short term Churchill undoubtedly posed the greatest threat to Éire. His hand was stayed by the likely reaction of public opinion in the United States. Ironically, the same fear of de Valera's ability to exploit American opinion prompted both Roosevelt and Churchill to distort the true benevolence of Irish neutrality in order to undermine the influence that Irish-Americans might exert on American foreign policy after the war. Was there any justification for believing that Irish-Americans—having been largely discredited by their opposition to Roosevelt prior to the Pearl Harbour attack—would have the influence to disrupt the White House's foreign policy?

Father Charles E. Coughlin never regained political prominence but another Irish-American, Senator Joseph R. McCarthy, essentially took his place in exploiting the fear of Communism. His red scare tactics led to one of the shoddiest chapters in American history. He engaged in a smear campaign, accusing the Roosevelt and Truman administrations of twenty years of treason in their dealing with the communists. In the aftermath of the McCarthy smears, some politicians were so afraid of being tainted with being soft on Communism that this arguably led to American involvement in the Vietnam War, in which Francis Cardinal Spellman played a seminal political role, which is outside the scope of this book.

To an extent Gray and others were probably right in thinking de Valera would try to turn the Irish partition question into an international issue. Throughout his long career de Valera talked a great deal about Irish unity, but never made any gestures to try to win over the support of the Protestant unionist majority in Northern Ireland. He was essentially demanding a solution on his own terms of unionist capitulation, or ethnic cleansing. In the process he essentially abandoned the nationalist population of Northern Ireland. But Gray was wrong in thinking de Valera would deliberately try to stir up violence. When the IRA later waged its Border Campaign, de Valera again came down heavily on the Republicans by re-introducing internment without trial in 1957.

Churchill, Roosevelt and Gray deliberately discredited de Valera by distorting the true nature of Irish neutrality. They also essentially abandoned the Roman Catholic people of Northern Ireland by supporting a bigoted and neo-Fascist regime that trampled on their rights and treated them, at best, as second-class citizens. The people on both sides of the sectarian divide in

Northern Ireland ultimately suffered when the province erupted in violence in the late 1960s. It was, in a sense, a consequence of the indifference prompted by the distorted ignorance of what actually happened during World War II.

NOTES

Abbreviations used in References

AFIN: American Friends of Irish Neutrality
DAFP: *Documents on Australian Foreign Policy*
DEAC: Department of External Affairs, Ottawa, Canada
DFA: Department of Foreign Affairs, Dublin
DGFP: *Documents on German Foreign Policy*
DIFP: *Documents on Irish Foreign Policy*
FDRL: Franklin D. Roosevelt Library, Hyde Park, New York
FFFI: Fight for Freedom, Incorporated
FRUS *Foreign Relations of United States*
IMA: Irish Military Archives, Rathmines, Dublin
NAC: National Archives of Canada, Ottawa, Canada
NAI: National Archives of Ireland, Dublin
NAUS: National Archives of the United States, Washington, D.C.
NLI: National Library of Ireland, Dublin
OSS: Office of Strategic Services
SI: Strategic Intelligence Division of Office of Strategic Services
TNAGB: The National Archive of Great Britain, Kew, Surrey, England
UCDA: University College Dublin Archives
USSDP: United States State Department Papers
WIR: Western Institute of Research, Laramie, Wyoming, USA

REFERENCES

Chapter 1 Background (PP. 1–11)

1. Dáil, *Private Sessions*, 22 Aug. 1921, p. 30.
2. *Seanad Debates*, 15 (2 Jun. 1932):938.
3. *Dáil Debates*, 41 (29 May 1932):1090–91.
4. De Valera speech, Geneva, 26 Sep. 1932, De Valera, *Peace and War*, pp. 5–14.
5. *News Chronicle*, 27 Sep. 1932.
6. *The Times* (London), 27 Sep. 1932.
7. *New York Times*, 27 Sep. 1932.
8. De Valera, address, 16 Sep. 1935, *Peace and War*, pp. 44–8.
9. Memo presented to Cabinet, 24 Sep. 1935, S.8083, NAI.
10. *Round Table*, 26 (Dec. 1935):131.
11. Maurice Moynihan, *Speeches and Statements*, p. 330.
12. De Valera, address, 12 Oct. 1937, *ibid*, p. 337.
13. Robert Rhodes James, *Churchill: A Study in Failure*, New York, 1965, p. 257.
14. Seán Lester, Diary, 20 May 1937, Stephen Barcroft, 'International Civil Servant', p. 228.
15. *Dáil Debates*, 62 (18 Jun. 1936):2726.
16. De Valera, address, 2 Jul. 1936, *Peace and War*, pp. 54–9.
17. *Ibid*.
18. W.M. Hughes, cabinet submission, 15 Nov. 1938, Australian Government: *Documents on Australian Foreign Policy* (DAFP).
19. Chamberlain, Diary, 23 Jan. 1938, Keith Feiling, *Neville Chamberlain*, p. 310.
20. *Ibid*.
21. FDR to de Valera, 22 Feb. 1938, FDRL.
22. MacEntee to de Valera, 17 Feb. 1938, *Documents on Irish Foreign Policy* (DIFP), 5:222.
23. *Dáil Debates*, 46 (1 Mar. 1933):192.
24. MacEntee to de Valera, 17 Feb. 1938, DIFP, 5:222.
25. Cabinet conclusion, 19(38)6 of 13 Apr. 1938. Carlton Younger, *A State of Disunion*, pp. 307–8.
26. Winston Churchill, *The Second World War*, 1:277.
27. Churchill in House of Commons, Seán Cronin, *Washington's Irish Policy*, p. 60.
28. Viscount Templewood, *Nine Troubled Years*, London, 1954, p. 284.
29. MacDonald in House of Commons, 10 May 1938, Seán Cronin, *Washington's Irish Policy*, p. 64.
30. *Dáil Debates*, 71 (27 Apr. 1938):36.
31. Cudahy to Hull, 2 May 1938, J.L. Rosenberg, 'America and Irish Neutrality', p. 245.
32. Conversation between Inskip and de Valera, 8 Sep. 1938, Deirdre McMahon, *Republicans and Imperialists*, p. 209.
33. De Valera to Chamberlain, 15 Sep. 1938, P150/2809 de Valera Papers, UCDA.

34. Chamberlain to de Valera, 17 Sep. 1938, P150/2809 de Valera Papers, UCDA. Deirdre McMahon, 'Malcolm MacDonald and Anglo-Irish Relations,' MA thesis, UCD, p. 217.

35. De Valera, address, Radio Nations, 25 Sep. 1938, *Peace and War*, pp. 69–75.

36. De Valera open tel. to Chamberlain, 27 Sep. 1938, *The Times*, 28 Sep. 1938.

37. McMahon, *Republicans and Imperialists*, p. 219.

38. Interview with Hessell Tiltmann of *Evening Standard*, *Irish Press*, 18 Oct. 1938.

39. *Ibid.*

40. *Ibid.*

41. De Valera, address, 23 Nov. 1938, see Cudahy, des. No. 173, 25 Nov. 1938. USSDP.

42. Eunan O'Halpin, *Spying on Ireland*, p. 40.

43 *Seanad Debates*, 22 (7 Feb. 1939):978–1005.

44. De Valera, AP interview, 17 Mar. 1939, John Bowman, *De Valera and the Ulster Question*, p. 313.

45. De Valera, address over Vatican Radio, 17 Mar. 1939, Moynihan, pp. 376–9.

46. Roosevelt to Hitler, 14 Apr. 1939, U.S. State Department, *Peace and War: United States Foreign Policy, 1931–1941*, Washington D.C., 1943, p. 457.

47. Robert Brennan, *Ireland Standing Firm*, p. 23.

48. William L. Shirer, *The Rise and Fall of the Third Reich*, p. 474.

49. Hitler, Reichstag speech, 28 Apr. 1939.

Chapter 2 'Friendly to England' (PP. 12–22)

1. James A. Farley, *Jim Farley's Story*, p. 49.

2. Hempel to Foreign Ministry, 31 Aug. 1939, *DGFP*, 7:471.

3. *Dáil Debates*, 71 (29 Apr. 1938):428.

4. *Ibid.*

5. *Dáil Debates*, 164 (28 Nov. 1957):1258.

6. Hempel, to Foreign Ministry, 8 Oct. 1939, *DGFP*, 8:241.

7. *Dáil Debates*, 72 (13 Jul. 1938):699.

8. *Ibid.*, 77 (2 Sep. 1939):2.

9. *Seanad Debates*, 23 (2 Sep. 1939):1030.

10. *Cork Examiner*, 4 Sep. 1939.

11. *Ibid.*

12. *Kerry Champion*, 9 Sep. 1939.

13. Mike Kemble, *On a Sailor's Grave*, pp. 1–9.

14. Nicholas Bethell, *The War Hitler Won*, p. 235.

15. Churchill, 5 Sep. 1939, CP19/3, Martin Gilbert, *Finest Hour*, p. 10.

16. Churchill to First Sea Lord, 5 Sep. 1939.

17. Churchill to Director of Naval Intelligence, 6 Sep. 1939, Enno Stephan, *Spies in Ireland*, p. 45.

18. Maffey, report of conversation with de Valera, 14 Sep. 1939, CAB66/1/34. TNAGB.

19. *Ibid.*

20. *Ibid.*

21. *Ibid.*

22. Eden, memo., 16 Sep. 1939, CAB66/1/34. TNAGB.

23. *Ibid.*

24. Bethell, p. 240.

25. Guy Liddell, Diary, 7 Sep. 1939, KV4/185.

26. Maffey, report of conversation with de Valera, 21 Sep. 1939, Bethell, p. 241.

27. *Ibid.*

28. *Ibid.*

29. Churchill to Deputy Chief of Naval Staff, 24 Sep. 1939, Winston Churchill, *The Second World War*, 1:728–9.

30. Michael R. Beschloss, *Kennedy and Roosevelt*, p. 122.

31. FDR to Churchill, 11 Sep. 1939. Warren F. Kimball, *Churchill and Roosevelt: The Complete Correspondence*, 1:24.

32. Liddell, Diary, 22 Sep. 1939, KV.4/185, TNAGB.

33. Churchill to Deputy Chief of Naval Staff, 24 Sep. 1939, Churchill, 1:729.

34. Michael Kennedy, *Guarding Neutral Ireland*, p. 64.

Chapter 3 Churchill's Dangerous Designs (PP. 23–34)

1. Maffey to Machtig, 4 Oct. 1939, DO130/2, TNAGB.

2. *Evening News* (London), 5 Oct. 1939; *The War Illustrated*, 28 Oct. 1939.

3. Werner Lott, interview by Marese McDonagh, *The Kerryman*, 21 Sep. 1984.

4. Jim Fenton to author, 3 Sep. 1999.

5. WM 16 (39), 15 Sep. 1939, CAB65/1/16, TNAGB.

6. Hearne to Department of External Affairs, 12 Oct. 1939, DFA/P4, NAI; *Life*, 16 Oct. 1939.

7. Robert J. Cressman, *Hyper War: The Official Chronology of the US Navy in World War II*.

8. Churchill, telephone conversation with Roosevelt, 5 Oct. 1940, Warren F. Kimball, *Churchill and Roosevelt*, p. 25.

9. Werner Lott, interview by Marese McDonagh, *The Kerryman*, 21 Sep. 1984.

10. Guy Liddell, Diary, 12 Oct. 1939, KV.4/185, TNAGB.

11. Richard J. Whalen, *The Founding Father*, pp. 263–4.

12. *Ibid*, p. 141.

13. Michael R. Beschloss, *Kennedy and Roosevelt*, 189.

14. Laurence Leamer, *The Kennedy Men*, p. 141.

15. Kennedy to Hull, 11 Sep. 1939, *FRUS, 1939*, 1:421–4.

16. Beschloss, p. 194.

17. James A. Farley, *Jim Farley's Story*, pp. 198–9.

18. Nicholas Bethell, *The War Hitler Won*, p. 244.

19. WM 50 (39), 17 Oct. 1939, CAB65/1/50.

20. WM 51 (39), 18 Oct. 1939, CAB65/1/51.

21. Instruction to Maffey, 20 Oct. 1939, WP 98 (39), CAB66/2, TNAGB.

22. Eden to Halifax, 20 Oct. 1939, Martin Gilbert, *Finest Hour*, pp. 67–8.

23. Maffey, memo of conversation with de Valera, 21 Oct. 1939, WP 98 (39), CAB66/2/48, TNAGB.

24. *Ibid.*

25. Maffey to SSDA, 26 Oct. 1939, WP 97 (39), CAB66/2/47, TNAGB.

26. *Ibid.*

27. *Ibid.*; see also Lord Rugby (Maffey), address, 24 Jul. 1950, at Rugby School, *Kerry Champion*, 29 Jul. 1950.

28. John D. Kearney, memo of conversation with de Valera, 27 Aug. 1943, John D. Kearney Papers, NAC.

29. *Irish Press*, 30 Sep. 1939.

30. Gilbert, pp. 67–68.

31. Churchill to Eden, 21 Oct. 1939. FO 800/310, TNAGB.

32. Gilbert, p. 68.
33. WM 58 (39), 24 Oct. 1939, CAB65/1/58, TNAGB.
34. *Ibid.*
35. *Ibid.*
36. *Ibid.*
37. Churchill to Eden, 26 Oct. 1939, Paul Canning, *British Policy*, p. 255.
38. Maffey to SSDA, 26 Oct. 1939, WP 97 (39), CAB66/2/47, TNAGB.
39. Cudahy to FDR, 27 Oct. 1939, FDRL.
40. Canning, p. 255.
41. Chamberlain to Maffey, 20 Oct. 1940, q. in Maffey to de Valera, 27 Jan. 1942, P150/2617, de Valera Papers, UCDA.
42. Lord Rugby (formerly Sir John Maffey), address, 24 Jul. 1950, q. *Kerry Champion*, 29 Jul. 1950.
43. Republican Publicity Bureau, *War News*, 28 Oct. 1939, NLI.
44. Owen Bowcott, 'Britain feared 1940 invasion of Ulster by IRA', *The Guardian*, 19 Jun. 2002.
45. *Ibid.*
46. Hempel for Foreign Ministry, 13 Nov. 1939, *DGFP*, 8:405–6.
47. Naval Staff, 'Intelligence Organisation in Eire', presented to cabinet by Churchill, 21 Nov. 1939, CAB66/3/31, TNAGB.
48. *Ibid.*
49. Cabinet Conclusions, 23 Nov. 1939, CAB65/4/19.
50. *Ibid.*
51. *Ibid.*, WM 75 (39), 8 Nov. 1949, CAB65/2/9, TNAGB.
52. Paul McMahon, *British Spies and Irish Rebels*, p. 290.
53. *Ibid.*
54. Robert Fisk, *In Time of War*, p. 119.
55. Report of the Committee to Review The Offences Against the State Acts, 1939–1998, 4:20–22.

Chapter 4 Irish-Americans, FDR and the European War (PP. 35–46)

1. Donald Warren, *Radio Priest: Charles Coughlin, the Father of Hate Radio.*
2. Cudahy to Roosevelt, 25 Sep. 1939. FDRL.
3. Robert Shogan, *Hard Bargain* (N.Y., 1995), p. 92.
4. *New York Times,* 5 Sep. 1939.
5. *Irish World,* 9 Sep. 1939.
6. *Gaelic American,* 9 Sep. 1939.
7. *San Francisco Leader,* 9 Sep. 1939.
8. Martin E. Marty, *Modern American Religion*, Chicago, 1990 and 1996, 2:279.
9. William V. Shannon, *The American Irish*, p. 314.
10. *Ibid.*, p. 315.
11. *Social Justice,* 30 Jan. 1939.
12. Seymour A. Hersh, *The Dark Side of Camelot,* p. 63.
13. *New York Times,* 31 May 1995.
14. Theodore Irwin, *Inside the Christian Front*, p. 5.
15. *Time,* 24 May 1939; John Roy Carlson, *Under Cover*, New York, 1943, p. 61.
16. *The Tablet*, 10 Sep. 1939, Charles J. Tull, *Fr. Coughlin and the New Deal*, Syracuse, N.Y., 1965, p. 219.
17. *Social Justice,* 1 Sep. 1939, Avro Manhattan, *The Vatican in World Politics*, p. 384.

18. *New York Times,* 2 Oct. 1939.
19. *Ibid.*
20. Profile, Monsignor John A. Ryan's papers, Catholic University of America.
21. *Ibid.,* 16 Oct. 1939.
22. Gallup Poll, pp. 184–5.
23. Thomas H. O'Connor, *The Boston Irish,* Boston, 1995, pp. 203–4.
24. Michael R. Beschloss, *Kennedy and Roosevelt,* p. 170.
25. *Ibid.,* p. 198.
26. Eunan O'Halpin, *Defending Ireland,* p. 172, and Paul Canning, *British Policy,* p. 260.
27. Bechloss, p. 200.
28. Laurence Leamer, *The Kennedy Men,* p. 122.
29. Michael Sayers and Albert E. Kahn, *Sabotage,* p. 152.
30. *New York Times,* 15 Jan. 1940.
31. *Ibid.,* 31 May 1995.

Chapter 5 Diplomatic Changes in Dublin (PP. 47–57)

1. Cudahy to FDR, 1 Mar. 1938, FDRL.
2. FDR to Cudahy, 9 Mar. 1938, *ibid.*
3. FDR to Cudahy, 8 Jan. 1934, *ibid.*
4. Cudahy to FDR, 6 Apr. 1938, FDRL.
5. Harold Ickes, *Diary,* 2 (26 Jun. 1938):403.
6. Cudahy to FDR, 15 Sep. 1939, *ibid.*
7. *Ibid.*
8. FDR to Cudahy, 17 Oct. 1939, Cudahy Papers, Milwaukee.
9. Cudahy to FDR, 28 Oct. 1939.
10. Cudahy to Margaruite Lehand, 17 Nov. 1939, FDRL.
11. *Ibid.*
12. *Ibid.*
13. Cudahy to Roosevelt, 7 Dec. 1939, FDRL.
14. Cudahy Des. 307, 7 Dec. 1940. NAUS.
15. Cudahy to Roosevelt, 7 Dec. 1939, FDRL.
16. *Ibid.*
17. *New York Times* and *Globe and Mail,* 26 Dec. 1939.
18. Cudahy to F. Ryan Duffy, 26 Jan. 1940, Cudahy Papers, Milwaulkee.
19. Cudahy to FDR, 25 Jan. 1940, *ibid.*
20. *Ibid.*
21. Mackenzie King, Diary, 12 Feb. 1940.
22. Memo for Mackenzie King, 29 Dec. 1939; Mackenzie King to de Valera, 30 Dec. 1940, NAC.
23. Mackenzie King, Diary, 24 Feb. 1940, NAC.
24. Hearne to DFA, 31 Mar. 1944.
25. Cudahy Des. 2060, 26 Nov. 1945.
26. *Ibid.*
27. Gray to FDR, 21 Mar. 1940. FDRL.
28. *Ibid.*
29. Gray to FDR, 8 Apr. 1940.
30. *Ibid.*

31. *Ibid.*
32. *Ibid.*
33. *Ibid.*
34. *Ibid.*
35. Gray to Roosevelt, 15 Apr. 1940, *ibid.*
36. *Toronto Telegram*, 23 Apr. 1940.

Chapter 6 Spy Scare (PP. 58–68)

1. *News Review*, 2 May 1940, Robert Cole, *Propaganda, Censorship and Irish Neutrality*, Edinburgh, 2006, p. 25.
2. Guy Liddell, Diary, 26 Apr. 1940, KV.4/186, TNAGB.
3. Hugh Trevor-Roper, 'The man who put intelligence into spying', *Sunday Telegraph*, 9 Apr. 1995.
4. De Valera broadcast, RTÉ, 8 May 1940, Maurice Moynihan, *Speeches and Statements*, p. 434.
5. Liddell, Diary, 8 May 1940, KV.4/186, TNAGB.
6. Maffey, memo, 10 May 1940, John Bowman, *De Valera and the Ulster Question*, p. 220.
7. De Valera in Galway, 12 May 1940, *Irish Press*, 13 May 1940.
8. Hempel, tel. 239, 15 May 1940, DFA/P3, NAI.
9. Warnock to Hempel, 31 Dec. 1958, DFA/P3, NAI.
10. *Ibid.* p. 110.
11. *Ibid.*, pp. 155–6.
12. De Valera to Chamberlain, 15 May 1940, P150/2548, de Valera Papers, UCDA.
13. Chamberlain to de Valera, 18 May 1940, P150/2548, de Valera Papers, UCDA.
14. Liddell, Diary, 15 May 1940, KV.4/186, TNAGB.
15. Churchill to Roosevelt, 15 May 1940, in Warren F. Kimball (ed.), *Roosevelt and Churchill*, 1:37.
16. Gray to FDR, 16–21 May 1940, Gray Papers.
17. *Ibid.*
18. *Ibid.*
19. Hull to Gray, tel. 18, 22 May 1940, *FRUS, 1940*, 3:161.
20. Minutes of meeting between Walshe, Archer and Machtig, 23 May 1940, DFA/A3, NAI.
21. WP 183 (40), 30 May 1940, CAB66/8, Paul Canning, *British Policy*, p. 269. CAB66/8, TNAGB.
23. War Cabinet 147 (40), 30 May 1940, CAB65/7, Martin Gilbert, *Finest Hour*, p. 433.
24. Gray to FDR, 31 May 1940, Gray Papers.
25. *Ibid.*
26. Ismay to Churchill, 29 May 1940, Canning, p. 271.
27. Churchill to Ismay, 31 May 1940, Gilbert, p. 433.
28. Hempel to Foreign Minister, 25 May 1940, *DGFP*, 9:432.
29. Hempel to Foreign Minister, 23 May 1940, *ibid.*, 433–4.
30. Memo of conversation with Warnock, 21 May 1940, *DGFP*, 9:401–2.
31. Hempel to Foreign Ministry, 17 Jun. 1940, *DGFP*, 9:601.
32. *Dáil Debates*, 120 (19 Apr. 1950):716.
33. Woermann to Hempel, 1 Jun. 1940, Enno Stephan, *Spies in Ireland*, p. 113.
34. *DGFP*, 9:525.
35. Hempel to Foreign Ministry, 17 Jun. 1940, *DGFP*, 9:602.
36. Dublin to Warnock, 17 Jun. 1940, DFA/P3, NAI.

Chapter 7 Restraining Churchill (PP. 69–79)

1. De Valera, speech, 1 Jun. 1940, *Irish Press*, 3 Jun. 1940.
2. William L. Langer and S. Everett Gleason, *The Challenge to Isolation*, 2:524, 717–8.
3. Kennedy to Hull, 17 Jun. 1940, *FRUS, 1940*, 3:162.
4. Churchill to Roosevelt, 13 Jun. 1940, and Roosevelt to Churchill, 13 Jun. 1940.
5. Gray to Duff Cooper, 30 May 1940, Gray Papers.
6. WM 141 (40), 27 May 1940, CAB65/736.
7. Gray to FDR, 6–12 Jun. 1940, Gray Papers.
8. Gray to FDR, 6–11 Jun. 1940, Gray Papers.
9. Gray to FDR, 19–25 Jun. 1940, Gray Papers.
10. Gray to FDR, 6–11 Jun. 1940, Gray Papers. Some of Gray's letters to Roosevelt were written over a number of days as he waited to see off the next diplomatic pouch. He called them 'diary letters'.
11. *Ibid.*
12. Guy Liddell, Diary, 18 Jan. 1940, KV4/185, TNAGB.
13. Robert Fisk, *In Time of War*, pp. 121–2, and Paul McMahon, *British Spies*, p. 317.
14. Gray to Roosevelt, 6–11 Jun. 1940, Gray Papers.
15. FDR, speech in Charlottesville, Virginia, 10 Jun. 1940.
16. Gray to FDR, 6–11 Jun. 1940, Gray Papers.
17. Mary MacSwiney to de Valera, n.d., Jun. 1940, Mary MacSwiney Papers, P48a/257 (5), UCDA.
18. Gray to FDR, 6–11 Jun. 1940.
19. WM 168 (40), CAB65/7/63, TNAGB.
20. Massey to Mackenzie King, 15 Jun. 1940, 822–39C, DEAC.
21. Mackenzie King, Diary, 16 Jun. 1940, NAC.
22. Mackenzie King, Diary, 4 Jun. 1940, NAC.
23. Mackenzie King, Diary, 16 Jun. 1940, NAC.
24. Mackenzie King to Craigavon, 16 Jun. 1940, 822–39C, DEAC.
25. *Ibid.*
26. Craigavon to Mackenzie King, 19 Jun. 1940, 822–39C, DEAC.
27. Hearne to Dublin, tel., 13 Sep. 1940, DFA/P4, NAI.
28. MacMahon, p. 323.
29. WM 168 (40) of 16 Jun. 1940, CAB65/7/63, TNAGB.
30. MacDonald, report of meeting with de Valera, 17 Jun. 1940, CAB65/7/68.
31. *Ibid.*
32. *Ibid.*
33. Gray to FDR, 19–25 Jun. 1940, Gray Papers.
34. *Ibid.*
35. MacDonald, report of meeting with de Valera, 17 Jun. 1940.
36. Hempel to Foreign Ministry, 21 Jun. 1940, *DGFP*, 9:639–640.
37. Hempel to Foreign Ministry, 19 Jun. 1940, *DGFP*, 9:638.
38. Gray to FDR, 19–25 Jun. 1940, Gray Papers.
39. Bevin to Churchill, 18 Jun. 1940, PREM 4/53/2/118.
40. Churchill to Ernest Bevin, 18 Jun. 1940, Brian Girvin, *The Emergency*, p. 107.
41. Winston S. Churchill, *Secret Session Speeches*, New York, 1946, 20 Jun. 1940, p. 12.
42. WM 173 (40), 20 Jun. 1940, CAB65/7/68. TNAGB see also Cadogan, Diary, 20 Jun. 1940, *The Diaries of Sir Alexander Cadogan*, ed. David Dilks, London, 1971, p. 305.

43. Paul Canning, *British Policy*, p. 280.

44. Chamberlain to Ida Chamberlain, 21 Jun. 1940, John Bowman, *De Valera and the Ulster Question*, p. 228.

45. Caldecote to Londonderry, 21 Jun. 1940, DO35/100008/9, TNAGB.

46. Gray to Roosevelt, 19–25 Jun. 1940, Gray Papers.

47. *Ibid.*

48. *Ibid.*

Chapter 8 A Last Desperate Effort (PP. 80–90)

1. Gray to Roosevelt, 19–25 Jun. 1940, Gray Papers.

2. *Ibid.*

3. Chamberlain, memo, 25 Jun. 1940, WP 223 (40), CAB66/9, TNAGB.

4. MacDonald, memo, 21–22 Jun. 1940, PREM 3/131/1, TNAGB.

5. *Ibid.*

6. WM 182 (40), 25 Jun. 1940, CAB65/7/77, TNAGB.

7. Machtig to Maffey, 4 Jul. 1940, DO130/12, TNAGB.

8. Kennedy to Secretary of State, tel. 1847, 26 Jun. 1940.

9. Chamberlain, memo, 'Éire: Negotiations with de Valera', 25 Jun. 1940, WP 223 (40), CAB66/9, TNAGB.

10. WP 285 (40), 25 Jul. 1940.

11. MacDonald, report of meeting with de Valera, 25 Jun. 1940, PREM2/131/1, TNAGB.

12. *Ibid.*

13. *Ibid.*

14. MacDonald report, 27 Jun. 1940 in Maffey, tel. 65, WP 233 (40), CAB66/9/13, TNAGB.

15. Keith Feiling, *The Life of Neville Chamberlain*.

16. *The Observer* (London), 30 Jun. 1940.

17. Cabinet meeting of 28 Jun. 1940, WM 180 (40), TNAGB.

18. Gray to Roosevelt, 28 Jun.–5 Jul. 1940, Gray Papers.

19. Mackenzie King, diary, 24 May 1941, NAC.

20. *Dáil Debates*, 120 (19 Apr. 1950): 714.

21. Brooke to Gray, 8 Feb. 1956, J.L. Rosenberg, 'America and the Neutrality of Ireland', p. 144.

22. Chamberlain to de Valera, 29 Jun. 1940, q. in SSDA, memo, 29 Jun. 1940, WP 233 (40), TNAGB.

23. Mulcahy, memo, 2 Jul. 1940, Mulcahy Papers, P7a/210, UCDA.

24. Cosgrave to de Valera, 9 Jul. 1940, de Valera Papers, P150/2597, UCDA.

25. De Valera to Cosgrave, 13 Jul. 1940, de Valera Papers, P150/2597, UCDA.

26. Cosgrave to de Valera, 16 Jul. 1940, de Valera Papers, P150/2597, UCDA.

27. Mulcahy, memo., 5 Jul. 1940, Mulcahy Paper; Gray to Roosevelt, 28 Jun.–5 Jul. 1940.

28. *Ibid.*

29. *Ibid.*

30. MacDermot to author, 16 Oct. 1974.

31. Chamberlain to Ida Chamberlain, 7 Jul. 1940, q. John Bowman, *De Valera and the Ulster Question*, p. 239.

32. Gray, Des. NO. 32, 23 Jul. 1940, Box 56, PSF, FDRL.

33. Maffey, report of conversation of 17 Jul. 1940, WP 274 (40), TNAGB.

34. Walter Warlimont, *Inside Hitler's Headquarters, 1939–1945*, p. 106.

35. *Daily Express*, 4 Jul. 1940.

36. *Toronto Globe and Mail*, 8 Jul. 1940.

37. Hempel to Foreign Minister, 1 Jul. 1940, *DGFP*, 10:89–90.

38. Churchill to Ismay, 30 Jun. 1940, Winston Churchill, *The Second World War*, 2:172.

39. *The Times*, 5 Jul. 1940.

40. WM 194 (40), 5 Jul. 1940, CAB/65/8/6, TNAGB.

41. *Ibid.*

42. Bernard L. Montgomery, *Memoirs*, p. 65.

43. De Valera, statement, 4 Jul., *Irish Press*, 5 Jul. 1940.

44. Aiken, NBC interview, 4 Jul. 1940, US *Congressional Record*, 86:4928.

45. *New York Times*, 6 Jul. 1940.

46. *Ibid.*

47. Walshe, memo, 6 Jul. 1940, DFA/P3, NAI.

48. Draft of Churchill to FDR, 5 Jul. 1940, Warren F. Kimball, *Churchill and Roosevelt*, p. 54.

49. Kennedy to Hull, 5 Jul. 1940, *FRUS, 1940*, 3:56; see also Colville diary, 5 Jul. 1940, John Colville, *The Fringes of Power*, p. 185.

50. Maffey, report of conversation with de Valera, 17 Jul. 1940, WP 274 (40), TNAGB.

51. *Dáil Debates*, 120 (19 Apr. 1950):716; Ribbentrop to Hempel, 11 Jul. 1940, *DGFP*, 10:184.

52. *Dáil Debates*, 120 (19 Apr. 1950):716.

53. Robert Shogan, *Hard Bargain*, pp. 92–3.

Chapter 9 'In Imminent Danger' (PP. 91–101)

1. *Daily Mail*, 23 Jul. 1940.

2. Donal Ó Drisceoil, *Censorship in Ireland, 1939–1945*, p. 204.

3. *Ibid.*

4. Robert Fisk, *In Time of War*, p. 131.

5. Helen Kirkpatrick Milbank, interview by Anne S. Kaper, 3–5 Apr. 1990, Press Club Foundation, see http://wpcf.org/oralhistory/kirk.html.

6. *Ibid.*

7. J. Carolle Carter, *The Shamrock and the Swastika*, p. 196.

8. Maffey to Machtig, 15 Jul. 1940, DO130/32, TNAGB.

9. Walshe, memo of conversation with Maffey, 15 Jul. 1940, de Valera Papers, p150/2571.

10. Dominion Office to Maffey, tel. 106, 16 Jul. 1940, CAB66/10/5 TNAGB, also DFA/A5, NAI.

11. Maffey, report of conversation with de Valera, 17 Jul. 1940, WP 274 (40), CAB66/10/5, TNAGB.

12. *Ibid.*

13. De Valera to W.T. Cosgrave, 13 Jul. 1940, Mulcahy Papers, UCDA.

14. Maffey, report of conversation with de Valera, 17 Jul. 1940.

15. Eunan O'Halpin, *Spying on Ireland*, pp. 113, 225.

16. *Ibid.*

17. Caldecote, memo, 'Relations with Éire', 18 Jul. 1940, WP 274 (40), CAB66/10/5 TNAGB.

18. *Ibid.*

19. Dulanty, No. 51, 9 Aug. 1940, DFA, A5, NAI; W.P. Crozier, *Off the Record*, pp. 179–80.

20. *The Times*, 17 Jul. 1940.

21. Walshe to Gray, 9 Aug. 1940, Aengus Nolan, *Joe Walshe*, p. 167.

22. Estero to Washington, 21 Jul. 1940, DFA/P2, NAI.

23. Hempel to Foreign Ministry, 31 Jul. 1940, *DGFP*, 10:379–80.

24. Hempel to Foreign Ministry, 31 Jul. 1940, *DGFP*, 10:379–80. *Ibid.*

25. Estero to Vichy legation, 20 Jul. 1940, DFA/P12/1, NAI.

26. Gray to Hull, No. 40, 6 Aug. 1940, NAUS.

27. See memo by Edgar P. Allen of Division of Control, 16 Aug. 1940, *FRUS, 1940*, 3:164–5.

28. Roosevelt to Gray, 15 Aug. 1940, Gray Papers.

29. Gray to Roosevelt, 25 Aug. 1940, Gray Papers.

30. Gray to Roosevelt, 26 Aug. 1940, Gray Papers.

31. The *Irish Times*, 27 Aug. 1940.

32. Estero to Warnock, tel. 111, DFA/P3, NAI.

33. Warnock, tel. 62D, 14 Sep. 1940, P3/DFA, NAI.

34. Boland to Archer, 5 Oct. 1940, IMAR.

35. Col. Archer to Adjutant General, S. 231, IMA.

36. F.H. Boland to Col. Liam Archer, 5 Oct. 1940, 363/4, IMA.

37. Paul Mayhew to Christopher Mayhew, 8 Oct. 1940.

38. Boland, memo, 18 Nov. 1940, 363/4d, DDI.

39. Paul Mayhew to Basil Mayhew, 4 Jan. 1941, IMA.

40. John H. Kelly to O.D. Skelton, 9 Oct. 1940, NAC.

41. The *Irish Times*, 23 Oct. 1940.

42. The *Irish Times*, 24 Oct. 1940.

Chapter 10 Irish-Americans and the Third Term (PP. 102–112)

1. Laurence Leamer, *The Kennedy Men*, p. 142.

2. *Ibid.*, p. 149.

3. *Newsweek*, 19 Aug. 1940.

4. *Ibid.*

5. *Daily Express*, and *News Chronicle* , q. *New York Times*, 8 Aug. 1940.

6. Harold Ickes, *Diary*, 10 Aug. 1940, 3:296–7.

7. Hull to Cudahy, 13 Aug. 1940, Cudahy Papers, Milwaukee.

8. *Time*, 19 Aug. 1940.

9. Ickes, *Diary*, 10 Aug. 1940, 3:296–7.

10. *Irish Press*, 27 Jul. 1940.

11. *New York Times*, 14 Aug. 1940.

12. Section 14 (a) Act of 28 Jul. 1940 (public NO. 671, see Attorney General Robert H. Jackson to Roosevelt, 27 Catholic 1940.

13. Roosevelt to Gray, 21 Catholic 1940, FDRL.

14. *Chicago Tribune*, 6 Catholic 1940.

15. *Irish World*, 24 Catholic 1940.

16. Walsh to Roosevelt, 19 Catholic 1940, FDR Papers.

17. Gray to Walsh, 22 Catholic 1940, FDRL.

18. Gray to Roosevelt, 4 Sep. 1940, Gray Papers.

19. *Time*, 16 Sep. 1940.

20. Gray to Joe Walshe, 25 Jul. 1940, DFA/P10, NAI.

21. Gray to FDR, 2 Oct. 1940, Gray Papers.

22. Presidential recordings, 8 Oct. 1940, R.J.C. Bulow, 'The Story Behind the Tapes', *American Heritage Magazine*, Feb./Mar. 1982.

23. John T. Flynn, *Country Squire in the White House*, New York, 1940, p. 113

24. Thomsen to Foreign Ministry, 7 Catholic 1940, *DGFP*, 10:427.

25. Hans Thomsen, to Foreign Ministry, 4 Nov. 1940, *Ibid.*, 11:463–4.

26. *New York Times*, 28 Oct. 1940.

27. Irwin F. Gellman, *Secret Affairs*, p. 172.

28. Ted Morgan, *FDR: A Biography*, pp. 557–8.

29. Gray to Kennedy, 30 Oct. 1940.

30. FDR to Kennedy, 17 Oct. 1940, q. *ibid.*, p. 153.

31. Michael R. Beschloss, *Kennedy and Roosevelt*, p. 215.

32. Ibid., pp. 215–6; and *New York Times*, 28 Oct. 1940.

33. Beschloss, p. 216.

34. Beschloss, p. 221.

35. *Ibid.*, p. 219.

36. Rose Kennedy, *Times to Remember*, p. 294.

37. Beschloss, p. 220.

38. *New York Times*, 31 Oct. 1940.

39. Beschloss, p. 221.

40. James McGregor Burns, *Roosevelt: The Soldier of Freedom*, London, 1970.

41. *Gaelic-American*, 2 Nov. 1940.

42. San Francisco *Leader*, 2 Nov. 1940.

43. *Social Justice*, 4 Nov. 1940.

44. *The Tablet*, 26 Oct. 1940.

45. Edgar Eugene Robinson, *The Vote for Roosevelt: The Presidential Vote, 1932–1944*.

Chapter 11 Churchill's Outburst (PP. 113–123)

1. Hansard, 365 (5 Nov. 1940):1243.

2. Hempel to Foreign Ministry, 7 Nov. 1940, *DGFP*, 11: 493.

3. *Ibid.*, p. 494.

4. Gray to Secretary of State, tel. 99, 10 Nov. 1940, *FRUS, 1940*, 168–70.

5. Walshe to Gray, 12 Nov. 1940, DFA/P48, NAI.

6. Walshe to Gray, memorandum, n.d. DFA/P48, NAI.

7. *Dáil Debates*, 81 (7 Nov. 1940):585.

8. *New York Herald Tribune*, 7 Nov. 1940.

9. *New York Times*, 10 Nov. 1940.

10. Churchill told Defence Committee on 31 Oct. 1940, Martin Gilbert, *Finest Hour*, p. 881.

11. Cosgrave, memo, 11 Nov. 1940, Mulcahy Papers.

12. T.F. O'Higgins to Cosgrave, 11 Nov. 1940, Mulcahy Papers, UCDA.

13. Dillon, memo, 19 Nov. 1940, Mulcahy Papers, UCDA.

14. War Cabinet Conclusions, WM285 (40), 8 Nov. 1940, CAB65/10/5, TNAGB.

15. *The Leader*, 16 Nov. 1940.

16. Paul O'Dwyer, Memoirs, MS, p. 38.

17. *Ibid.*, pp. 38–9.

18. *Ibid.*, pp. 39–40.

19. *Ibid.*, p. 41.

20. US *Congressional Record*, 76th Congress, 2nd Session 1940, Appendix, 86:A6590–91.

21. Gray to Hull, 10 Nov. 1940, *FRUS, 1940*, 3:169.

22. *Ibid.*, p. 170.

23. S.W. Roskill, *White Ensign*, p. 228.

24. *New York Times*, 9 Nov. 1940.

25. *Ibid.*

26. *The Economist, Irish Press*, 7 Nov. 1940.

27. *The Observer*, 10 Nov. 1940.

28. The *Irish Times*, 13 Nov. 1940.

29. Canada, *Commons Debates*, 1941, 1 (12 Nov. 1940):26–7.

30. Kelly to SSEA, 15 Nov. 1940, 832–39C, DEAC.

31. Hearne, memo, included in Skelton to Mackenzie King, 18 Nov. 1940, 822–39C, DEAC.

32. Walshe, report of meeting with Maffey, 13 Nov. 1940, de Valera Papers, P150/2571, UCDA.

33. *Ibid.*

34. Maffey to SSDA, 20 Nov. 1940, CAB104/183, TNAGB.

35. Maffey to Machtig, 19 Nov. 1940, DO130/12, TNAGB.

36. Maffey to Churchill, 25 Nov. 1940, Terence de Vere White, 'Lord Rugby and Mr. de Valera', The *Irish Times*, 23 May 1975.

37. Churchill to Dominion Secretary, 22 Nov. 1940, Churchill, *History of the Second World War*, 2:690.

38. Welles to Gray, 19 Nov. 1940, *FRUS, 1940*, 3:171.

39. Interview in Eamon de Valera, *Ireland's Stand*, pp. 29–33.

40. Frank Pakenham Longford and Thomas P. O'Neill, *De Valera*, p. 375.

41. Gray to Hull, telegram no. 105, 24 Nov. 1940, *FRUS, 1940*, 3:172.

42. Gray to de Valera, 25 Feb. 1942, FDRL.

43. Gray to FDR, 30 Nov. 1940, Gray Papers.

44. Gray to Hull, tel. 105, 24 Nov. 1940, *FRUS, 1940*, 3:172.

45. Gray to FDR, 30 Nov. 1940, Gray Papers.

46. *Ibid.*

47. De Valera to Brennan, 4 Dec. 1940, Longford and O'Neill, p. 376.

Chapter 12 The Economic Screw (PP. 124–134)

1. *Washington Evening Star*, 30 Nov. 1940, *San Francisco Leader*, 21 Dec. 1940.

2. John Colville, *The Fringes of Power*, p. 305.

3. *Ibid.*, p. 306.

4. Churchill to Roosevelt, 13 Dec. 1940.

5. *New York Times*, 8 Dec. 1940.

6. Washington to DEA, 9 Dec. 1940, DFA/A2, NAI.

7. Press Conference 150, 17 Dec. 1940.

8. *PM Daily*, 7 Jan. 1941.

9. FDR, Fireside Chat, 29 Dec. 1940.

10. Gray to Hull, 7 Jan. 1941, *FRUS, 1941*, 3:215.

11. Walshe, memo, 3 Jan. 1941, DFA/A21, NAI.

12. DEA to Legation, Berlin, No. 254, 19 Dec. 1940.

13. *Ibid.*

14. Walshe, memo, 3 Jan. 1941, DFA/A23, NAI.

15. *Ibid.*

16. Terry de Valera, *A Memoir*, Dublin, 2004, p. 177.

17. Kelly, telegram no. 37, 27 Dec. 1940, NAC.

18. *Irish Times*, 4 Jan. 1941.

19. *Ibid.*
20. Kelly to Sec. of State for External Affairs, 16 Jan. 1941, 822–39C, DEAC.
21. Mulcahy, memo of Defence Conference meeting, 29 Jan. 1941, Mulcahy Papers, UCDA.
22. Walshe, memo, 6 Jan. 1941, DFA/A21, NAI.
23. WM 1 (41), 2 Jan. 1941, CAB65/17/1, TNAGB.
24. Churchill to Cranborne, 3 Jan. 1941, PREM 3/128/4, Paul Canning, *British Policy*, p. 305.
25. Liam Archer to J.P. Walshe, 7 Jan. 1941, DFA/A8, NAI.
26. *The Economist*, 18 Jan. 1941.
27. AP report, 8 Jan. 1941, Marin Mitchell, *Atlantic Battle and the Future of Ireland*, p. 9; also *Time*, 37(20 Jan. 1941):39.
28. *The Times*, 10 Jan. 1941.
29. Maffey to Cranborne, 19 Jan. 1941, DO130/17, TNAGB.
30. Maffey to Cranborne, 22 Jan. 1941, DO130/17.
31. Kelly to Secretary of State for External Affairs, 14 Jan. 1941, 822–39C, DEAC.
32. Kelly to Secretary of State for External Affairs, 16 Jan. 1941.
33. Skelton to censor, 20 Jan. 1941, Ryan Touhy, 'Exercising Canada's Autonomy in Foreign Relations', p. 54.
34. Churchill to SSDA, 17 Jan. 1941, CAB120/506 TNAGB.
35. Churchill to Cranborne, 21 Jan. 1941, PREM3/131/4, q. Canning, p. 306.
36. Churchill to Cranborne, 31 Jan. 1941, PREM3/131/3, Winston Churchill, *History of the Second World War*, 3:645.
37. Maffey to Cranborne, 19 Jan. 1941, DO130/17, TNAGB.
38. Published 13 Jan. 1940, *Gallup Poll*, p. 260.
39. Maffey, memo of conversation with de Valera, 20 Jan. 1941, DO 130/17, TNAGB.
40. Maffey to SSDA, 22 Jan. 1941, DO 130/17, TNAGB.
41. De Valera, radio address, 29 Jan. 1941, q. Eamon de Valera, *Ireland's Stand*, p. 41.
42. Mulcahy, memo of conversation with de Valera, 30 Jan. 1941, Mulcahy Papers, UCDA.
43. Gray to Secretary of State, tel. 14, 25 Jan. 1941, *FRUS, 1941*, 3:217–8.
44. Gray telegram, 25 Jan. 1941, *FRUS*, 1941, 3:217–8.
45. Gray to FDR, 4 Feb. 1941, FDRL.
46. FDR to Gray, 6 Mar. 1941, FDRL.
47. Gray to Eleanor Roosevelt, 10 Feb. 1941, Gray Papers.

Chapter 13 Distinguished Visitors (PP. 135–145)

1. Laurence Leamer, *The Kennedy Men*, p. 157.
2. Michael R. Beschloss, *Kennedy and Roosevelt*, p. 235.
3. *Ibid.*
4. Gordon Beckles, *America Chooses!*, pp. 80–82.
5. Gerald Campbell to Cadogan, 17 Mar. 1941, *FRUS*, *1941*, 3:267.
6. *New York Times*, 9 Feb. 1941.
7. Leonard Baker, *Roosevelt and Pearl Harbor*, New York, 1970, p. 739.
8. *New York Times*, 10 Mar. 1941.
9. British Security Coordination, *The Secret History of British Intelligence in the Americas, 1940–1945*, p. 85.
10. *New York Times*, 10 Mar. 1941.
11. *Irish Echo*, 24 May 1941.

12. Quoted in Cranborne, memo., 19 Mar. 1941, WP 64 (41), TNAGB.

13. Mulcahy, notes of Fine Gael front-bench meeting, 4 Mar. 1941, Mulcahy Papers, UCDA.

14. Quoted by Dillon, *Dáil Debates*, 82 (2 Apr. 1941):1444.

15. Account related by Robert Kinter, Harold Ickes, *Diary*, 3:439–40.

16. Harold Nicolson, *Diaries and Letters, 1939–1945*, London, 1967, 2:143.

17. Gray to Roosevelt, 4 Feb. 1941, Gray Papers.

18. Nicolson, 2:143.

19. Cranborne to Churchill, 17 Feb. 1941, Robert Fisk, *In Time of War*, p. 258.

20. Menzies, Diary, 21 Feb. 1941.

21. Menzies, Diary, 22 Feb. 1941. see http://www.oph.gov.au/menzies/irelandandtheusa.htm#2link

22. Gray to FDR, 4 Feb. 1941.

23. Gray to FDR, 31 Dec. 1940, FDRL.

24. Maffey, tel., 24 Feb. 1941, FO371/29108, TNAGB.

25. Maffey, tel., 26 Feb. 1941. *Ibid.*

26. Gray to de Valera, 3 Mar. 1941.PSF1, FDRL.

27. Gray to Welles, 7 Mar. 1941, 841D.00/1306, USDP. NAUS.

28. Hempel instructed to approach de Valera again about receiving arms on 24 Feb. 1941, *DGFP*, 12:153–3.

29. *Dáil Debates*, 81 (20 Feb. 1941):2319.

30. Walshe to de Valera, 14 Jan. 1943, DFA/A2, NAI.

31. Walshe to de Valera, 19 Feb. 1941, *Ibid.*

32. Donovan's report in Winant's telegram to Hull, No. 932, 11 Mar. 1941.

33. *PM Daily*, 18 Apr. 1941.

34. Donovan's report to Knox, in Winant's telegram to Hull, des. 932, 11 Mar. 1941.

35. *Ibid.*

36. *Ibid.*

37. Menzies to A.W. Fadden, telegram, 4 Mar. 1941.

38. Maffey to Machtig, 13 Mar. 1941, DO130/17, TNAGB.

39. Walshe, memo, 14 Jan. 1943, DFA/A2, NAI.

Chapter 14 Aiken Mission in Context (PP. 146–156)

1. Dan Bryan Papers P91/103, UCDA.

2. Joseph Louis Rosenberg, 'The 1941 Mission of Frank Aiken to the United States: An American Perspective', *Irish Historical Studies*, 22:(Sep. 1980):165.

3. *Boston Traveler, The Tablet,* 5 Apr. 1941.

4. *New York Times,* 25 Mar. 1941.

5. John Cudahy, 'Cudahy Support Ireland on Bases,' *New York Times,* 2 Feb. 1941.

6. *Life,* 31 Mar. 1941.

7. San Francisco *Leader,* 29 Mar. 1941.

8. San Francisco *Leader,* 4 Jan. 1941.

9. *Gaelic American,* 29 Mar. 1941.

10. *New York Daily Mirror,* 16 Apr. 1941.

11. Acheson, memo of conversation, 2 Apr. 1941, *FRUS, 1941,* 3:224.

12. Foreign Office to Washington, 2 Apr. 1941.

13. Winant to Hull, 6 Apr. 1941, 740.0011 EurWar1939/9664 (RG59).

14. Robert Brennan, *Ireland Standing Firm: My Wartime Mission to Washington,* p. 47.

15. Hull, *Memoirs*, 2:1352–3.
16. Speech in Boston, 15 Apr. 1941, Aiken Papers, P104/3569, UCDA; speech in San Francisco, 6 May 1941, *The Leader* (San Francisco), 17 May 1941.
17. Text of speech in Boston, 18 Apr. 1941, Aiken Papers, UCDA.
18. *Christian Science Monitor*, 17 Apr. 1941.
19. *Philadelphia Public Ledger*, 19 Apr. 1941.
20. *New York Times*, 24 Apr. 1941.
21. Gray to Hull, 1 May 1941, SDP.
22. *PM Daily*, 24 Apr. 1941.
23. Hull, memo, 19 Apr. 1941, 741.41D/121, NAUS.
24. Wayne S. Cole, *America First: The Battle Against Isolationism, 1940–1941*, Madison, Wisconsin, 1953, p. 157.
25. *FRUS, 1941*, 3:226–7.
26. Gray to Secretary of State, 1 May 1941, *Hfrus, 1941*, 3:230–31.
27. Longford and O'Neill, *De Valera*, p. 381.
28. Gray to Secretary of State, 1 May 1941, *FRUS, 1941*, 3:231.
29. Walshe, memo of dinner, 22 Apr. 1941, DFA/A2, NAI.
30. *New York Herald Tribune*, 28 Apr. 1941.
31. Mulcahy, memo of 9 May 1941 and details of meeting with de Valera on 17 May, memo, 20 May 1941, Mulcahy Papers, UCDA.
32. Maffey to Machtig, 15 May 1941, FO 371/29108, UCDA.
33. Eden, memo, 9 May 1941, *Ibid.*
34. Cranborne to Eden, 16 May 1941, *Ibid.*
35. Cadogan to Machtig, 30 May 1941, *Ibid.*
36. Section censored from *Irish Independent*, 19 May 1941, Aiken Papers, P04/3573, UCDA.
37. *New York Daily News*, San Francisco *Leader*, 3 May 1941.
38. Press conference, 20 May 1941, *Complete Press Conferences of Franklin D. Roosevelt*, 17:335.
39. Charles Lindbergh, 24 May 1941, *Wartime Journals*, p. 495.
40. Philadelphia *Daily News*, 30 May 1941, Sayers and Kahn, *Sabotage*, 197–8.
41. Frank Pakenham Longford and Thomas P. O'Neill, *De Valera*, p. 381.
42. Memo of convesation between Cudahy and von Ribbentrop, 5 May 1941, *DGF*, 12:704–10.
43. Hewel's diary, David Irving, *Hitler's War*, p. 395.

Chapter 15 Bombing and Conscription Crises (PP. 157–168)
1. Brian Barton, *The Blitz*, p. 106.
2. *Ibid.*, p. 129.
3. E.J. Garland to SSEA, 22 Apr. 1941, File 1,000–40, DEAC.
4. De Valera speech, Castlebar, 19 Apr. 1941, Moynihan, p. 458.
5. Walshe, memo of meeting with Hempel, 17 Apr. 1941, 210/189, DFA.
6. Hempel, interview, *Sunday Press*, 8 Dec. 1963.
7. *Ibid.*
8. William Percival Crozier, *Off the Record*, p. 325.
9. Guy Liddell, Diary, 21 May 1941, KV 4/187, TNAGB.
10. Bevin, Memo, 21 May 1941, WP 107 (41), CAB66/16/30, TNAGB.
11. Morrison, Memo, 22 May 1941, WWP 108 (41), CAB66/16/31, TNAGB.
12. Sir John Andrews, tel., 22 May 1941, DO35/1109/WX37/4, TNAGB.

13. *Ibid.*
14. Machtig to Maffey, 23 May 1941, DO35/1109/WXX37/4, TNAGB.
15. Gray to Secretary of State, tel. 54, 24 May 1941, *FRUS, 1941*, 3:235–6.
16. *Ibid.*
17. *Irish Weekly and Ulster Examiner*, 21 May 1941.
18. *News Chronicle, New York Times*, 28 May 1941, p. 1.
19. *New York Times*, 25 May 1941.
20. *Ibid.*, 26 May 1941.
21. *Ibid.*, 27 May 1941.
22. The *Irish Times*, 24 May 1941.
23. Cabinet meeting, 26 May 1941, WM 53 (41), CAB65/18/21, TNAGB.
24. Mackenzie King, memo or conversation with Hearne, 23 May 1941, Mackenzie King, diary, NAC.
25. MacDonald to Dominion Office, 26 May 1941, DO35/1109/W37/7, TNAGB.
26. *Ibid.*, 24 May 1941, Mackenzie King Papers, NAC.
27. Mackenzie King, telegram to Churchill, 25 May 1941, in SSEA to Dominion Secretary, 25 May 1941, NAC.
28. A.W. Martin, *Robert Menzies*, Carlton, Victoria, 1993–1999.
29. Gray to Roosevelt, 28 May 1941.
30. *Ibid.*
31. De Valera to Gray, 25 May 1941, FDRL.
32. De Valera to Churchill, 25 May 1941, Moynihan, *Speeches and Statements*, p. 459.
33. Frank Pakenham Longford and Thomas P. O'Neill, *De Valera*, p. 386.
34. Maffey, tel. 206, 25 May 1941, WP 113 (41), TNAGB.
35. Wickham, memo, WP 111 (41), CAB66/16/35, TNAGB.
36. Eunan O'Halpin, *Spying on Ireland*, p. 106.
37. Alexander Cadogan, *The Diaries of Sir Alexander Cadogan*, ed. David Dilks, London, 1971, p. 381.
38. Machtig to SSDA, 26 May 1941, DO35/1109/W37/7, TNAGB.
39. Cadogan, 26 May 1941, p. 381.
40. Winant to Hull, tel. no. 2123, 26 May 1941, *FRUS, 1941*, 3:239.
41. *New York Times*, 28 May 1941.
42. Harold Nicolson, *Diaries and Letters, 1939–45*, London, 1967, p. 167.
43. *Ibid.*
44. *Round Table*, Dwyer, *Irish Neutrality and the USA*, p. 128.
45. The *Irish Times*, 6 Jun. 1941.
46. Gray to Roosevelt, 9 Jun. 1941, Gray Papers, WIR.
47. Dwyer, *Guests of the State*, pp. 73–82.

Chapter 16 Spies and Ghosts (PP. 169–179)

1. Walshe, memo, 15 May 1945, DFAA/A2, NAI.
2. Gray to FDR, 9 Jun. 1941, FDRL.
3. *New York Times*, 28 Jun. 1941.
4. FDR, *Complete Press Conferences of Franklin D. Roosevelt*, 17(27 Jun. 1941):414.
5. Gray to FDR, 9 Jun. 1941.
6. *Dáil Debates*, 74 (16 Feb. 1939):686.

7. *Ibid.*, 84 (17 Jul. 1941):1867.
8. *Ibid.*, 1911.
9. *Ibid.*, 1913–14.
10. *Ibid.*, 1883.
11. Gray to Roosevelt, 28 Jul. 1941, FDRL.
12. Ross McGillycuddy to Gray, 10 Jul. 1941, enclosed in Gray to FDR, 11 Jul. 1941, FDRL.
13. His brother, Patrick, was elected to the Dáil, as were two of Patrick's children. Brian Lenihan would serve in various ministries under Seán Lemass, Jack Lynch and Charles Haughey from the 1960s to the 1980s, rising to the position of Tánaiste in the late 1980s, when his sister, Mary O'Rourke, would join him in Cabinet, and would become deputy leader of Fianna Fáil in the 1990s. Brian's sons, Brian and Conor, would become ministers in the governments of Bertie Ahern and Brian Cowen.
14. Statement by Patrick Lenihan, 29 Jul. 1941, IMA.
15. Paul McMahon, *British Spies*, p. 399.
16. Boland to W.C. Hankinson, 4 Feb. 1943, DFA/A60, NAI.
17. Gray to Roosevelt, 28 Jul. 1941, FDRL.
18. Gray to FDR, 11 Catholic 1941.
19. FDR to Gray, 2 Catholic 1941.
20. Roosevelt to Gray, 21 Catholic 1941.
21. Gray, memo of conversation with John Winant and Myron Taylor, 27 Sep. 1941, Gray Papers.
22. Maffey to Dominions Office, 14 Oct. 1941, DO130/17, TNAGB.
23. Gray to FDR, 21 Oct. 1941, FDRL.
24. MacRory to Gray, 20 Oct. 1941, Gray Papers.
25. Gray to FDR, 21 Oct. 1941, FDRL.
26. W.P. Crozier, Diary, 2 Oct. 1941, *Off the Record*, p. 239.
27. Gray to FDR, 21 Oct. 1941, FDRL.
28. Kearney to SSEA, 27 Catholic 1941, NAC.
29. King to Kearney, 29 Catholic 1941, NAC.
30. *Ibid.*, 28 Catholic 1941.
31. Kearney, Notes, Sep. 1941, John D. Kearney Papers, NAC.
32. Walshe to Gray, 11 Sep. 1941, DFA/P48, NAI.
33. Donovan to Roosevelt, 12 May 1941, FDRL.
34. Kearney to Norman A. Robertson, 17 Oct. 1941.
35. Kearney to Robertson, 20 Feb. 1942.
36. Gray to FDR, 15 Feb. 1942, FDRL.
37. Geraldine Cummins, *Unseen Adventures*, pp. 9–10.
38. Gray to FDR, 15 Feb. 1942, FDRL.
39. Transcript of séance, 7 Nov. 1941, *ibid.*
40. Gray to FDR, 30 Apr. 1940, FDRL.
41. Transcript of séance, 8 Nov. 1941, *ibid.*
42. Gray to FDR, 15 Feb. 1942, FDRL.
43. Transcript of séance, 8 Nov. 1941, *ibid.*
44. Transcript of séance, 8 Nov. 1941, *ibid.*
45. *Ibid.*
46. Gray to FDR, 15 Feb. 1942, FDRL.

Chapter 17 Irish-Americans Against the War (PP. 180–191)

1. Joseph P. Hurley, address to National Council of Catholic Women, 30 Apr. 1941, *No Blarney from Hitler.*

2. Hurley, broadcast on CBS, 6 Jul. 1941, Fight for Freedom, Inc., (FFFI) Papers, University of Chicago.

3. Francis E. McMahon, radio address, WBYN, 28 Aug. 1941, FFFI Papers.

4. British Security Coordination, *The Secret History of British Intelligence in the Americas, 1940–1945,* p. 85.

5. *Washington Post,* 15 Sep. 1941.

6. HSC8–58, TNAGB.

7. *No Blarney from Hitler,* HCA 8—56, TNAGB.

8. BSC report, 18 Oct. 1941, Thomas E. Mahl, *Desperate Deception,* p. 39.

9. Minutes of Executive Meeting of AFIN, 18 Sep. 1941, AFIN Papers.

10. *Ibid.*

11. Denis Devlin to Michael McGlynn, 9 Jun. 1941, AFIN Papers.

12. *Christian Science Monitor,* 17 Sep. 1941.

13. MacDermot, radio address, WJSV, 17 Sep. 1941, HCA8–56, TNAGB.

14. *Ibid.*

15. *Neutrality News,* 22 Sep. 1941, HSC8–857, TNAGB.

16. Report of Irish-American Alliance Organisation meeting, 29 Sep. 1941, FFFI Papers.

17. *Boston Globe,* 27 Sep. 1941.

18. *Boston Globe,* 27 Sep. 1941.

19. *Ibid.*

20. *New York Times,* 18 Oct. 1941.

21. *Boston Herald,* 27 Sep. 1941.

22. *Irish Echo,* 27 Sep. 1941.

23. McGlynn to Brennan, 2 Oct. 1941, DFA/P6, NAI.

24. *Gaelic American,* 25 Oct. 1941.

25. McMahon to 380 priests, 10 Oct. 1941, FFFI Papers.

26. *Ibid.*

27. *Boston Post,* 9 Jan. 1942.

28. Michael Sayers and Albert E. Kahn, *Sabotage,* p. 157.

29. *Washington Daily News,* 21 Oct. 1941.

30. *Ibid.,* 31 Oct. 1941.

31. *Ibid.*

32. *Washington Post,* 26 Oct. 1941.

33. HCA 8/58, TNAGB.

34. *Irish Echo,* 15 Nov. 1941.

35. Minutes of meeting, 8 Oct. 1941, q. in AFIN, statement, 14 Nov. 1941, AFIN Papers.

36. Terence O'Donnell, *The Case for American-Irish Unity,* p. 6.

37. Frank Murphy, *Catholicism and the Crisis,* Washington, D.C., 1941, pp. 2–4.

38. *Irish Echo,* 22 Nov. 1941.

39. *Gaelic American,* 29 Nov. 1940.

40. *Boston Post,* 26 Nov. 1941.

41. *Chicago Sun,* 7 Dec. 1941.

42. Mahl, p. 40.

43. AFIN, statement, 13 Dec. 1941, AFIN Papers.

Chapter 18 In a World at War (PP. 192–202)

1. Churchill to de Valera, 8 Dec. 1941, de Valera Papers, P150/3023, UCDA.
2. Walshe, memo, 30 Mar. 1950, Department of An Taoiseach, s.14782.
3. *Ibid.*
4. Terry de Valera, *A Memoir,* Dublin, 2004, p. 201.
5. De Valera, memo, 8 Dec. 1941, de Valera Papers, P150/3023, UCDA.
6. Walshe, memo, 30 Mar. 1950, Department of An Taoiseach, s.14782.
7. De Valera to Churchill in Maffey to SSDA, 10 Dec. 1941, DO 130/17, TNAGB.
8. Cranborne to Maffey, 9 Dec. 1941, DO 130/17, TNAGB.
9. Roosevelt to Churchill, 8 Dec. 1942, *FRUS, 1941*, 4:732–3.
10. Maurice Moynihan (ed.), *Speeches and Statements,* pp. 461–2.
11. Gray to Roosevelt, 17 Dec. 1941, FDRL.
12. Gray to FDR, 17 Dec. 1941, FDRL.
13. Cranborne, memo of conversation with Gray, 16 Dec. 1941, DO 130/17, TNAGB.
14. Cranborne, memo of conversation with Gray, 16 Dec. 1941, DO 130/17, TNAGB.
15. Gray to FDR, 17 Dec. 1941, FDRL.
16. Cranborne, memo of conversation with de Valera, 17 Dec. 1941, DO 130/17, TNAGB.
17. *Ibid.*
18. *Belfast Telegraph,* 29 Jan. 1941.
19. Report of the landing, 27 Sep. 1941, G2/X/0872, IMA.
20. Estero to Hivernia, tel. 89, 5 Dec. 1941, DFA/P4, NAI.
21. Hibernia to Estero, tel. 95, 17 Dec. 1941, *ibid.*
22. FDR to de Valera, 22 Dec. 1941, *FRUS, 1941*, 3:251–2.
23. Maffey, memo of conversation with de Valera on 23 Dec. 1941, dated next day, DO 130/27 TNAGB.
24. De Valera, broadcast to USA, 25 Dec. 1941, Moynihan, p. 464.
25. Gray to FDR, 1 Jan. 1942, Gray Papers, WIR.
26. *Ibid.*
27. *Ibid.*
28. *Ibid.*
29. Maffey to Machtig, 1 Jan. 1942, DO130/27. [This letter was misdated 1 Jan. 1941.]
30. Maffey to Machtig, 27 Jan. 1941, DO130/27, TNAGB.
31. *Ibid.*
32. Kearney to N.A. Robertson, 20 Feb. 1942, NAC.
33. R. Carter Nicholas, A *Short History of S.I. Activities with Respect to Éire,* p. 4.
34. *Ibid.,* p. 3.
35. O'Mara to Commissioner P. Carroll, 20 Jan. 1942, DFA/A23, NAI.
36. Chief Superintendent Thomas Collins to Commissioner, DFA/A23, NAI.
37. Nicholas, p. 3.
38. Lt. N. Hewett, report, 22 Jan. 1942, DFA/A8, NAI.
39. Comdt P. Power to CSO, G2, 30 Jan. 1942, DFA/A8, NAI.
40. De Valera speech, *The Irish Times,* 13 Jan. 1942.
41. John W. Blake, *Northern Ireland and the Second World War,* Belfast, 2000, p. 272.
42. Gray to Roosevelt, 11 Aug. 1941, Gray Papers.

43. Cordell Hull, *Memoirs*, 2:1354.
44. De Valera, statement on American landing, Eamon de Valera, *Ireland's Stand*, pp. 59–60.
45. Nicholas, p. 4.
46. Gray to FDR, 27 Jan. 1942, Gray Papers.
47. *Irish Press*, 27 Jan. 1942.
48. Kearney to Robertson, 20 Feb. 1942, CDP.

Chapter 19 Beyond Reasonable Belief (PP. 203–213)

1. William L. Shirer, 'Will Hitler Take Ireland?' *The Nation*, 31 Jan. 1942, pp. 132–4.
2. *Daily Herald*, 6 Feb. 1942.
3. Gray, memo., n.d., CP 229, DFA.
4. Wolfe to David Gray, 10 Jan. 1942, CP229, DFA.
5. Kearney, des. 39, 24 Feb. 1941, 1841–40, DEAC.
6. Col. T. McNally to Adjutant General, 8 Jan. 1942.
7. Kearney to SSEA, tel. 2, 11 Feb. 1942, file 841–40, DEAC.
8. Kearney to SSEA, tel., 19 Feb. 1942, file 841–40, DEAC.
9. Report of discussion in Taoiseach's Office with Cashman of Department of Defence, 23 Feb. 1942, File PM 7333P, Department of External Affairs.
10. *The Irish Times*, 11 Feb. 1942.
11. Walshe to de Valera, 17 Feb. 1942, DFA/A25, NAI.
12. *Ibid.*
13. Gray to FDR, 16 Feb. 1942, Gray Papers.
14. Gray to FDR, 15 Feb. 1942, FDRL.
15. Gray to FDR, 15 Feb. 1942, FDRL.
16. Paul McMahon, *British Spies*, pp. 358–9.
17. Gray to FDR, 16 Feb. 1942, Gray Papers.
18. FDR to George C. Marshall, 27 Feb. 1942, FDRL.
19. Machtig to Maffey, 16 Feb. 1942, DO 130/27, TNAGB.
20. FDR to de Valera, 26 Feb. 1942, *FRUS, 1942*, 1:759.
21. *The Spectator*, 31 Mar. 1942.
22. Gray to Maffey, 16 Mar. 1942.
23. *Dáil Debates*, 85 (11 Mar. 1942):2396–7.
24. Gray to Secretary of State, Des. 320, 23 Mar. 1942, NAUS.
25. Gray to Secretary of State, 21 Mar. 1942.
26. FDR to Welles, 21 Apr. 1942.
27. T. Ryle Dwyer, *Guests of the State*, p. 111.
28. Gray to FDR, 8 May 1942.
29. Barry to author, 23 May 1975.
30. Gray to Churchill, 11 May 1942, Gray Papers.
31. J.L. Rosenberg, *America and Irish Neutrality*, p. 127.
32. Quoted in Col. Dan Bryan to DFA, 20 Jul. 1942, DFA/A8, NAI.
33. Gray to FDR, 20 May 1942, FDRL.

Chapter 20 FDR's Cold Shoulder (PP. 214–224)

1. Report of telephone conversation between Gray and Dillon, 19 Apr. 1942, DFA/A8, NAI.
2. Gray to FDR, 20 May 1942, FDRL.

3. Gray to William J. Donovan, 6 Jun. 1942, Gray Papers, WIR.
4. Gray to FDR, 6 Jun. 1942.
5. Gray to Secretary of State, 7 Jul. 1942, *FRUS, 1942*, 1:762.
6. *Ibid.*
7. Gray to Secretary of State, 26 Aug. 1942, *FRUS, 1942*, 1:766.
8. Maffey to Cranborne, 31 Aug. 1942, DO 130/27, TNAGB.
9. Gray to FDR, 11 Sep. 1942.
10. *The Irish Times*, 28 Sep. 1942.
11. Gray to Cardinal MacRory, 7 Oct. 1942, Gray Papers, WIR.
12. Gray to FDR, 19 Oct. 1942.
13. MacRory to Gray, 23 Oct. 1942, NAUS.
14. Gray to FDR, 19 Oct. 1942.
15. Donal Ó Drisceóil, *Censorship in Ireland*, pp. 222, 226.
16. Gray to de Valera, 29 Oct. 1942, NAUS.
17. Gray to State Department, 3 Nov. 1941, Seán Cronin, 'Neutrality under Fire', *The Irish Times*, 31 Aug. 1982.
18. Gray to FDR, 6 Nov. 1942, FDRL.
19. Gray to Duke of Abercorn, n.d., Gray Papers, WIR.
20. Robert Cole, *Propaganda, Censorship and Irish Neutrality in the Second World War*, Edinburgh, 2006, p. 111; Ó Drisceoil, p. 199.
21. See Michael Adams, *Censorship*, pp. 81–8.
22. Gray to State Department, 6 Nov. 1942, Cronin, *Washington's Irish Policy*, p. 124.
23. De Valera, speech in Navan, *Irish Press*, 13 Jan. 1942.
24. Maffey, memo of conversation with de Valera, 24 Jan. 1941, DO 130/27, TNAGB.
25. Gray to Hayes, 11 May 1947, Gray Papers, WIR.
26. Joseph Connolly, *Memoirs of Senator Joseph Connolly*, p. 404.
27. Gray to FDR, 16 Sep. 1942.
28. FDR to Gray, 16 Sep. 1942.
29. *Ibid.*
30. Gray to FDR, 8 Oct. 1942.
31. Paul McMahon, *British Spies*, p. 387.
32. Gray to FDR, 29 Nov. 1942.
33. *Ibid.*
34. Gray to FDR, 11 Dec. 1942.
35. *Ibid.*
36. Gray to Walshe, 22 Dec. 1942.
37. Randolph Churchill, 'Irish Neutrality', US Congressional Record, 91:A4988.
38. Gray to FDR, 28 Dec. 1942, FDRL.

Chapter 21 OSS Agents in Ireland (PP. 225–235)

1. W.J. Donovan to FDR, memo. 212, 4 Feb. 1943, FDRL.
2. R. Carter Nicholas, *Short History of S.I. Activities with Respect to Éire*, p. 11.
3. *Ibid.*
4. Nicholas, p. 12.
5. Marlin to author, 4 Jun. 1985.
6. O'Ruirc, interviewed by author.

7. Blenner-Hassett, personal report, 26 Jan. 1943, OSS Papers.

8. *Ibid.*

9. Nicholas, p. 13.

10. Blenner-Hassett, report, 26 Jan. 1943, OSS Papers.

11. *Ibid.*

12. Welles, memo of conversation with Brennan, 29 Oct. 1942, *FRUS, 1942*, 1:768.

13. Nicholas, pp. 81–2.

14. Welles, memo of conversation with Brennan, 25 Oct. 1942, *FRUS, 1942*, I:772–3.

15. Robert Stewart, memo, 27 Mar. 1944, NAUS.

16. Marlin, 'Activities Since Arrival in Éire', 4 Sep. 1942–21 Nov. 1942.

17. William A. Kimbel to Major David Bruce, 25 Nov. 1942, OSS Papers.

18. Nicholas, p. 15.

19. *Ibid.*, p. 20.

20. Cole, *Propaganda, Censorship and Irish Neutrality*, p. 113.

21. *Ibid.*, p. 114.

22. Memo., 18 Jan. 1943, DFA/A60, NAI.

23. Marlin interviewed by author, 24 Nov. 1983.

24. Marlin to author, 4 Nov. 1984.

25. Marlin to author, 4 Jun. 1985.

26. Marlin interviewed by author, 24 Nov. 1983.

27. Walshe, memo, 23 Jun. 1944, DFA/A60, NAI.

28. Blenner-Hassett, personal report, 26 Jan. 1943, OSS Papers.

29. *Ibid.*

30. *Ibid.*

31. Nicholas, p. 25.

32. Blenner-Hassett, 'Report on the Present State of Éire', 26 Jan. 1943, enclosed in Francis P. Miller to W.J. Donovan, Record Group 226, File 1196/1, OSS Papers.

33. *Ibid.*

34. *Ibid.*

35. *Ibid.*

36. Nicholas, pp. 25–6.

37. Maffey, memo, 21 Aug. 1945, DO130/56, TNAGB; see page 344.

Chapter 22 Getting Maximum Cooperation (PP. 236–246)

1. Walshe to Brennan, tel. 109, 27 Mar. 1944, DFA/A53, NAI.

2. Nicholas, *A Short History of S.I. Activities with Respect to Éire*, p. 31.

3. Gray to Walshe, 19 Mar. 1943, Nolan, *Joseph Walshe*, p. 230.

4. *Ibid.*, pp. 33–4.

5. Paul McMahon, *British Spies*, pp. 367 and 412.

6. *Ibid.*, p. 413.

7. J. Carolle Carter, *Shamrock and Swastika*, p. 187.

8. Dan Bryan to author, 12 Dec. 1983.

9. Marlin to author, 24 Nov. 1983.

10. Marlin to Quigley, 4 Nov. 1984, Quigley Papers.

11. Marlin to author, 24 Nov. 1983.

12. Marlin to author, 4 Jun. 1985.

13. Nicholas, p. 26.
14. Ibid., pp. 29–30.
15. Maffey to Machtig, 2 Apr. 1943, DO130/33, TNAGB.
16. Nicholas, p. 46.
17. Martin Quigley, *A U.S. Spy in Ireland*, p. 74.
18. *Ibid.*, p. 68.
19. *Ibid.*, pp. 75–6.
20. *Ibid.*, p. 68.
21. *Ibid.*
22. Quigley, *pp.* 75–6.
23. *Ibid.*, p. 65.
24. Quigley report, 2 Jun. 1943.
25. *Ibid.*
26. Report of 24 Jul. 1943, *ibid.*, p. 146.
27. Quigley, report, 4 Jul. 1943, *ibid.*, pp. 122–8.
28. Quigley, report, 17 Jul. 1943, *ibid.*, pp. 136–41.
29. Quigley, report, 12 Jul. 1943, *ibid.*, pp. 128–36.
30. Quigley to author, 3 Jan. 1978.
31. Quigley, p. 105.
32. Quigley to author, 3 Jan. 1984.
33. Quigley, p. 92.
34. Nicholas, p. 59.
35. *Ibid.*, p. 96.
36. Quigley to author, 3 Jan. 1984.
37. Carter Nicholas to Sherman Wallace, Nicholas, p. 57.
38. *Ibid.*, p. 60.
39. *Ibid.*, p. 61.
40. *Ibid.*, p. 62.
41. Quigley to Francis P. Miller, 16 Nov. 1943, Quigley, pp. 203–5.
42. Report of 25 Sep. 1943, *ibid.*, p. 168.
43. Quigley, report, 2 Oct. 1943, *ibid.*, pp. 174–8.
44. Quigley, report, 16 Nov. 1943, *ibid.*, p. 204.
45. Quigley to Francis P. Miller, 16 Nov. 1943, *ibid.*, pp. 203–5.
46. Quigley, report, 13 Nov. 1943, *ibid.*, p. 199.
47. *Ibid.*, pp. 202–5.
48. *Ibid.*
49. *Ibid.*
50. Martin S. Quigley, *Great Gaels*, p. 16.

Chapter 23 Without so Much as 'Thank You' (PP. 247–257)

1. Kearney to SSEA, 12 Aug. 1943, 1841–40, DEAC.
2. Crash file G2/X/1127, IMAR.
3. Gray to Hull, tel. 52, 19 Apr. 1943, NAUS.
4. Kearney to Norman A. Robertson, 15 Feb. 1942, NAC.
5. Gray to FDR, 13 Feb. 1943, FDRL.
6. *Ibid.*

7. Attlee to Eden, 5 Mar. 1943, FO371/36002, TNAGB.
8. Kearney to Robertson, 29 Mar. 1943, NAC.
9. Gray to Welles, 15 Mar. 1943, Gray Papers.
10. B.H. Liddell Hart, *History of the Second World War*, p. 405.
11. Hibernia to Estero, tel. 25, 3 Apr. 1943, DFA/94, NAI.
12. Kearney, Diary, Vol. 1, 9 Apr. 1943, NAC.
13. Canada, Debates of House of Commons, 1943, 3 (12 Apr. 1943):2046.
14. Churchill to Eden, 11 Apr. 1943, CAB120/506, TNAGB.
15. Churchill to Roosevelt, 11 Apr. 1943, Warren F. Kimball, *Complete Correspondence*, 2:186–7.
16. FDR to Churchill, 19 Apr. 1943.
17. Churchill to Attlee, 5 May 1943, CAB120/506, TNAGB.
18. Gallup, *The Gallup Poll*, pp. 323, 363.
19. Hadley Cantril (ed.), *Public Opinion*, p. 378.
20. Gray to FDR, 13 Feb. 1943, FDRL.
21. *New York Times*, 4 Apr. 1943.
22. *Ibid.*, 5 Apr. 1943.
23. Gray to FDR, 5 Apr. 1943, FDRL.
24. Gray, memo, 14 May 1943, *FRUS*, 1943, 3:138.
25. *Ibid.*, pp. 134–5.
26. *Ibid.*, p. 141.
27. Gray, memo of conversation with de Valera, 3 Jun. 1943, PSF2, FDRL.
28. FDR to Hull, 15 Jun. 1943, FDRL.
29. Hull to FDR, 29 Jun. 1943, *FRUS, 1943*, 3:143.
30. Dillon, speech, Monaghan, 30 May 1943, *Sunday Dispatch*, 3 Oct. 1943.
31. *Dáil Debates*, 91 (9 Jul. 1943):569.
32. *Ibid.*, 572–3.
33. Cudahy to Gray, 25 May 1943, Gray Papers, WIR.
34. Avro Manhattan, *The Vatican in World Politics*, p. 384.
35. Gray to Cudahy, 25 Aug. 1943, Gray Papers.
36. Gray to Col. T.A. McInerny, 14 Sep. 1943, Gray Papers, WIR.
37. W. Averell Harriman to author, 1 Jul. 1971.
38. Gray to FDR, 26 Aug. 1943, Gray Papers.
39. Gray, draft letter, 16 Aug. 1943, *FRUS, The Conferences in Washington and Quebec*, 621–3.
40. *Ibid.*
41. Gray to Hull, 21 Apr. 1943. Gray Papers.
42. Frank Pakenham Longford and Thomas P. O'Neill, *De Valera*, p. 405.
43. Gray, memo, 16 Aug. 1943, Gray Papers.
44. Machtig to Maffey, 20 Aug. 1943, DO 130/32, TNAGB.
45. SSDA to Maffey, 3 Sep. 1943, DO130/32, TNAGB.

Chapter 24 Living the Life of Riley (PP. 258–268)

1. Robert I. Cannon, *The Cardinal Spellman Story*, p. 208.
2. Gray to Roosevelt, 5 Apr. 1943, Gray Papers.
3. See Kearney account of two meetings with MacRory, Kearney, Diary, 15 Jan. and 12 Apr. 1945.
4. Gray to Roosevelt, 5 Apr. 1943, Gray Papers.
5. F.H. Boland, memo, 4 Feb. 1943, DFA/A26, NAI.

6. Michael Rynne, memo, 11 Apr. 1943,DFA/A50, Aengus Nolan, *Joseph P. Walshe*, p. 246.
7. Maffey to Walshe, 12 May 1943, DFA/A50, NAI.
8. *Toronto Star*, 9 Jun. 1943.
9. Bruce N. Girdlestone, *Memoirs of Internment*, MS, p. 44.
10. H.J. Eustace to John D. Kearney, 29 Jun. 1943, Raph Keefer, *Grounded in Eire*, p. 231.
11. Memo for de Valera, 5 Jul. 1943, DFA 241/341, IMA.
12. Maffey to Boland, 9 Jun. 1943.
13. Memo for de Valera, 5 Jul. 1943, DFA 241/341, IMA.
14. Kearney memo of conversation with de Valera, 27 Aug. 1943, NAC.
15. Maffey memo of conversation with de Valera, 11 Sep. 1943, DO130/32, TNAGB.
16. G2/x/0758, Irish Army Archives; T. Ryle Dwyer, *Guests of the State*, pp. 60, 74.
17. Maffey, memo of meeting with de Valera, 9 Oct. 1943, DO130/32 TNAGB.
18. Walsh, memo of meeting with Maffey, 11 Oct. 1943, DFA/A2. NAI.
19. Maffey, memo of meeting with de Valera on 9 Oct., with Walshe on 11 Oct., and with de Valera on 13 Oct. 1943, DO130/32 TNAGB.
20. *Ibid.*
21. Girdlestone, MS, p. 50.
22. Gray to Hull, 13 Sep. 1943, *FRUS, 1943*, 3:146.
23. Maffey, memo of conversation with Norman Archer, 24 Aug. 1943, DO130/32, TNAGB.
24. Maffey to Gray, 5 Sep. 1943, DO130/32, TNAGB.
25. Maffey to Erich Machtig, 7 Sep. 1943, DO130/32. TNAGB.
26. *Ibid.*
27. Gray to Maffey, 9 Sep. 1943, Gray Papers.
28. Gray to FDR, 17 Sep. 1943, FDRL.
29. George C. Marshall to FDR, 11 Aug. 1943, *FRUS, 1943*, 3:143–4.
30. Hull to Winant, 18 Sep. 1943, *FRUS, 1943*, 3:147–150.
31. Gray to Hull, 28 Sep. 1943, *ibid.*, p. 153.
32. Maffey to SSDA, 23 Sep. 1943, DO130/32, TNAGB.
33. Maffey to Machtig, 4 Oct. 1943, DO130/32, TNAGB.
34. Gray, memo, 22 Sep. 1943, Gray Papers, WIR.
35. Hull to Gray, 5 Oct. 1943, *FRUS, 1943*, 3:156.
36. Gray to FDR, 20 Oct. 1943, FDRL.
37. Gray to Hull, 1 Oct. 1943, *FRUS, 1943*, 3:155.
38. Gray to Stettinius, 22 Oct. 1943, NAUS.
39. Maffey to SSDA, 8 Oct. 1943, DO130/32, TNAGB.
40. Kearney to Norman A. Robertson, 15 Oct. 1943, NAC.
41. Eunan O'Halpin, *Defending Ireland*, p. 191.
42. Churchill to Cranborne, 2 Nov. 1943, CAB120/506, TNAGB.
43. Gray to Secretary of State, 9 Nov. 1943, *FRUS, 1943*, 3:160–1.
44. Hull to Winant, 13 Nov. 1943, *Ibid.*, 162.
45. Lidell, Diary, 23 Nov. 1943, KV.4/192, TNAGB.

Chapter 25 As an Absolute Minimum (PP. 269–279)

1. Eden to John Winant, 17 Dec. 1943, DO 130/32, TNAGB.
2. Gray, memo of conversation with Kearney, 12 Nov. 1943, Gray Papers.
3. Donal MacCarron, *Landfall Ireland*, p. 130.

4. Walshe, memo of meeting with Hempel, 15 Dec. 1943, A26/DEA, NAI.
5. Kearney, Diary, 29 Dec. 1943, NAC.
6. Gray to Secretary of State, 13 Dec. 1943, *FRUS 1943*, 3:165.
7. *Ibid.*
8. J.P. Walshe to de Valera, 15 Dec. 1943, DFA/A2, NAI.
9. O'Reilly's statement, 17 Dec. 1943, taken by Superintendent James Dawson, Kilrush, IMA.
10. O'Reilly to his parents, 27 Jul. 1941, IMA.
11. O'Reilly, statement, 17 Dec. 1943, to Superintendent James Dawson.
12. O'Reilly to his parents, 20 Jan. 1942, IMA.
13. O'Reilly, statement, 17 Dec. 1943, to Superintendent James Dawson.
14. *Ibid.*
15. John Kenny to his uncle, 3 Aug. 1944, IMA.
16. Gray to Secretary of State, 18 Dec. 1943, *FRUS, 1943*, 3:166.
17. Hull to Gray, 30 Dec. 1943, *FRUS, 1943*, 3:168–9.
18. Nicholas, *A Short History of S.I. Activities with Respect to Éire*, p. 65.
19. *Ibid.*
20. *Ibid.*, p. 72.
21. *Ibid.*
22. Message from Kerlogue, 31 Dec. 1943, G2/X/1269, IMA.
23. Maffey to Machtig, 8 Jan. 1944, DO 130/43, TNAGB.
24. Gray to Winant, 7 Jan. 1944, Gray Papers, WIR.
25. Churchill to Cranborne, 2 Feb. 1944, CAB120/506, TNAGB.
26. Cranborne, memo, 1 Feb. 1944, WP 69 (44), CAB66/46/19, TNAGB.
27. WM 15 (44), 4 Feb. 1944, CAB65/45/10, TNAGB.
28. Maffey to DO, 6 Feb. 1944.
29. Eunan O'Halpin, *Spying on Ireland*, p. 247.
30. *Ibid.*, p. 239.
31. *Ibid.*, p. 248.
32. *Ibid.*, p. 232.
33. Maffey to Machtig, 10 Feb. 1944, DO 130/43, TNAGB.
34. Machtig to Maffey, 15 Feb. 1944, *ibid.*

Chapter 26 It Will Come Against You Later (PP. 280–291)

1. Roosevelt to de Valera, 21 Feb. 1944, *FRUS, 1944*, 3:217–8.
2. *The Irish Times*, 21 Feb. 1944.
3. Gray to Hull, 21 Feb. 1944.
4. Gray to Hull, 23 Feb. 1944, *FRUS, 1944*, 3:224.
5. Maffey, tel. 26 to DO, 22 Feb. 1944, FO 371/4594, TNAGB.
6. Brennan, tel. 58, received 23 Feb. 1944, DFA/A53, NAI.
7. Brennan, tel. 60, 24 Feb. 1944, *ibid.*
8. Kearney to SSEA, 23 Feb. 1944, 126 (s), NAC.
9. Kearney to SSEA, 24 Feb. 1944, 126 (s), DEAC.
10. Mackenzie King, memo, 24 Feb. 1944, *ibid.*
11. Robertson to King, 25 Feb. 1944, *ibid.*
12. Hume Wrong, memo. for Mackenzie King, 24 Feb. 1944, *ibid.*
13. Robertson to King, 25 Feb. 1944, *ibid.*

14. Robertson, memo for King, 25 Feb. 1944.
15. SSEA to Kearney (No. 4), 25 Feb. 1944, *ibid.*
16. Kearney to SSEA, 11 Mar. 1944, *ibid.*
17. Robertson, memo to Mackenzie King, 25 Feb. 1944, *ibid.*
18. Brennan, tel. 63, 26 Feb. 1944, NAI.
19. WLM King, Diary, 27 Feb. 1944, NAC.
20. Hearne, report of conversation with Mackenzie King, 3 Mar. 1944, DFA/A53, NAI.
21. Mackenzie King, memorandum re. US and UK Notes to Government of Éire re. Germans and Japanese Missions, 27 Feb. 1944, Mackenzie King, Diary, NAC.
22. Mackenzie King, Diary, 29 Feb. 1944, NAC.
23. Churchill to Cranborne, 27 Feb. 1944, CAB120/306, TNAGB.
24. Gray to FDR, 21 Feb. 1944, FDRL.
25. Maffey to SSDA, tel. 28, 24 Feb. 1944, FO 371/4594, TNAGB.
26. Maffey for Machtig, 28 Feb. 1944.
27. Winant to SS, des. 1797, 4 Mar. 1944.
28. *Irish Press*, 28 Feb. 1944.
29. *The Irish Times*, 28 Feb. 1944.
30. Maffey to Machtig, 26 Feb. 1944, DO 130/43, TNAGB.
31. *Ibid.*
32. Kearney, tel. 14, 28 Feb. 1944.
33. Maffey to Dominion Office, 1 Mar. 1944, FO 371/4594, TNAGB.
34. Gray to SS, 1 Mar. 1944, *FRUS, 1944*, 3:230–1.
35. De Valera to Roosevelt, 7 Mar. 1944, in Stettinius to Gray, 8 Mar. 1944, *FRUS, 1944*, 3:232–3.

Chapter 27 Press Hysteria (PP. 292–302)

1. Evatt to Bruce, tel. 32, 9 Mar. 1944, *Documents of Australian Foreign Policy* (DAFP).
2. Bruce to Curtin, tel. 38 [A], 9 Mar. 1944, *DAFP*.
3. DEA to Brennan, tel. 77, 15 Mar. 1944.
4. *Boston Globe*, 6 Mar. 1944.
5. Brennan, tel. 94, 13 Mar. 1944, DFA/A53, NAI.
6. DEA to Brennan, tel. 77, 15 Mar. 1944, *ibid.*
7. Kearney, Diary, 11 Mar. 1944, NAC.
8. DEA to Brennan, tel. 65, 12 Mar. 1944, DFA/A53, NAI.
9. Shaw, *Daily Sketch* interview, *The Irish Times*, 14 Mar. 1944.
10. *The Observer* (Dublin) to Brennan, tel. 65, 12 Mar. 1944, DFA/A53, NAI.
11. *Dallas Morning News*, 14 Mar. 1944.
12. *Fort Worth Star-Telegram*, 14 Mar. 1944.
13. *Atlanta Constitution*, 13 Mar. 1944.
14. *New York Times*, 12 Mar. 1944.
15. *New York Herald Tribune*, 11 Mar. 1944.
16. *PM Daily*, 14 Mar. 1944.
17. *PM Daily*, 20 Mar. 1944.
18. *Fort Worth Star-Telegram* (evening), 17 Mar. 1944.
19. *New York Times*, 30 May 1944.
20. *New York Herald Tribune*, 22 Mar. 1944.
21. *New York Times*, 11 Mar. 1944.

22. DEA to Brennan, tel. 65, 12 Mar. 1944, DFA/A53, NAI.
23. *Washington Post*, 17 Mar. 1944.
24. *New York Herald Tribune*, 18 Mar. 1944.
25. Brennan to DEA, tel. 119, 25 Mar. 1944.
26. *PM Daily*, 14 Mar. 1944.
27. Brennan to DEA, tel. 119, 25 Mar. 1944.
28. Hadley Cantril (ed.), *Public Opinion*, p. 378.
29. Dulanty, Secret Report No. 4, 16 Mar. 1944, DFA/A53, NAI.
30. *New York Times*, 13 Mar. 1944.
31. Dulanty to Walshe, Secret Report No. 3, 13 Mar. 1944, DFA/A53, NAI.
32. Bruce to Curtin, Cablegram 40, 14 Mar. 1944, *DAFP*.
33. Hansard (Canada), *Debates*, 11 (13 Mar. 1944):1405.
34. Mackenzie King, Diary, 13 Mar. 1944, NAC.
35. Ryan Touhey, *Exercising Canada's Autonomy*, p. 102.
36. Brennan, tel. 96, 14 Mar. 1944, DFA/A53, NAI.
37. *Irish Press*, 15 Mar. 1944.
38. Kearney to SSEA, 28 Mar. 1944, NAC.
39. *Ibid.*
40. Maffey to DO, tel. 47, 15 Mar. 1944, FO 371/42679, TNAGB.
41. Maffey to DO, tel. 50, 16 Mar. 1944, *ibid.*
42. Winant to Hull, 14 Mar. 1944, *FRUS, 1944*, 3:237–9.
43. Robertson to King, 15 Mar. 1944, RG25. File 398, vol 781.
44. SSEA to Dom. Sec. (No. 43) 20 Mar. 1944, Files 126(s), DEAC.
45. Pearson to Robertson, 22 Mar. 1944, Touhey, p. 104.
46. Mannix to de Valera, 21 Mar. 1944, DFA/A53, NAI.
47. *Cape Times*, 16 Mar. 1944, *ibid.*
48. DEA to Brennan, tel. 85, 17 Mar. 1944, *ibid.*
49. *Cape Times*, 17 Mar. 1944, *ibid.*
50. Gray to Secretary of State, 15 Mar. 1944, NAUS.
51. Walshe to de Valera, 16 Mar. 1944, DFA/A2, NAI.
52. DEA to Brennan, tel. 82, 16 Mar. 1944, DFA/A53, NAI.
53. Hull to Winant, 14 Mar. 1944, NAUS.
54. Churchill to Dom. Sec., 15 Mar. 1944, FO 371/4594, TNAGB.
55. Maffey to Machtig, 17 Mar. 1944, DO130/43, TNAGB.
56. *Ibid.*
57. *Ibid.*
58. Gray to Roosevelt, 24 Mar. 1944, FDRL.
59. Halifax to Eden, 17 Mar. 1944, FO 371/4594.
60. Churchill to SSEA, 15 Mar. 1944, CAB120/506, TNAGB.
61. Churchill to Roosevelt, 19 Mar. 1944, *FRUS, 1944*, 3:243.
62. Kearney, Diary, 22 Mar. 1944, NAC.
63. Cranborne to Churchill, 23 Mar. 1944, CAB120/506, TNAGB.
64. Churchill to Cranborne, 24 Mar. 1944, *ibid.*

Chapter 28 Gray Opposed Dignifying de Valera's Answer (PP. 303–314)

1. *Irish Press*, 13 Mar. 1944.

2. *Irish Press*, 14 Mar. 1944.

3. Statement issued by Aaron Brown, *Irish Press*, 24 Mar. 1944.

4. *The Irish Times*, 24 Mar. 1944.

5. DEA to Brennan, tel. 106, 24 Mar. 1944, DFA/A53, NAI.

6. Gray to Roosevelt, 24 Mar. 1944, FDRL.

7. *Ibid.*

8. Kearney to SSEA, 28 Mar. 1944, 120(s), DEAC.

9. DEA to Brennan, tel. 114, 6 Apr. 1944, DFA/A53, NAI.

10. DEA to Brennan, 14 Apr. 1944, *ibid.*

11. Gray to Hull, 11 Apr. 1944, USNA.

12. Marlin Report, 22 Mar. 1944, in Nicholas, *A Short History of S.I. Activities with Respect to Éire*, pp. 75–6.

13. Washe to de Valera, 18 Mar. 1944, DFA/A53, NAI.

14. *Ibid.*

15. *Ibid.*

16. Nicholas, p. 103 insertion.

17. Walshe to de Valera, 18 Mar. 1944, DFA/A53.

18. DEA to Brennan, tel. 96, 22 Mar. 1944, A53.

19. *Ibid.*

20. DEA to Brennan, tel. 109, 27 Mar. 1944, *ibid.*

21. *Ibid.*

22. Nicholas, *A Short History of S.I.*, MS, p. 81.

23. Donovan to FDR, 30 Mar. 1944, FDRL.

24. *Ibid.*

25. Brennan to DEA, tel. 135, 4 Apr. 1944, DFA/A53, NAI.

26. DEA to Brennan, tel. 114, 6 Apr. 1944, *ibid.*

27. Forgan to author, 6 Nov. 1970, Forgan Papers, Hoover Institution for War, Peace and Revolution.

28. Nicholas, MS, pp. 89–90.

29. Gray to FDR, 14 Apr. 1944.

30. Gray to FDR, 14 Apr. 1944.

31. Gray to David Bruce, 17 Jun. 1944, Gray Papers.

32. Nicholas, p. 85.

33. Hull to Winant, 4 Apr. 1944, *FRUS, 1944*, 3:246–9.

34. Nicholas, p. 86.

35. Brennan to DEA, tel. 145, 8 Apr. 1944, DFA/A53, NAI.

36. Gray to Hull, 8 Apr. 1944, *FRUS, 1944*, 3:254–5.

37. Gray to FDR, 14 Apr. 1944, Gray Papers.

38. Maffey to Machtig, tel. 76, 6 Apr. 1944, FO 371/42680, TNAGB.

39. DEA to Brennan, tel. 123, 17 Apr. 1944.

40. DEA to Brennan, tel. 141, 26 Apr. 1944.

41. Dan Bryan to J.P. Walshe, 13 Oct. 1946, DFA/A60, NAI.

42. Nicholas, p. 98.

43. Marlin to author, 23 Sep. 1983.

44. Hubert Will, memo for Col. David Bruce, 15 May 1944, Nicholas, pp. 88, 94–98.

45. De Valera to Roosevelt, 15 Mar. 1944, *New York Times*, 20 Apr. 1944.

46. *The Irish Times*, 25 Mar. 1944.
47. Roosevelt to de Valera, 3 Apr. 1944, *New York Times*, 20 Apr. 1944.
48. DNB quoted, *Toronto Globe and Mail*, 20 Apr. 1944.
49. *Toronto Telegram*, 31 Mar. 1944.
50. *New York Times*, 12 May 1944.
51. Hull to FDR, 17 May 1944, *FRUS, 1944*, 3:256–7.
52. Gray to Hickerson, n.d., received 10 May 1944, 123 Gray, David/113, NAUS.
53. *Time*, 43(12 Jun. 1944):30.
54. Robert M. Smyllie, 'Unneutral Neutral Éire', *Foreign Affairs*, 24 (Jan. 1946):324.
55. Gray to FDR, 2 Jun. 1944.

Chapter 29 To the Bitter End (PP. 315–326)

1. Gray to Bruce, 10 Jun. 1944, Gray Papers, WIR.
2. Gray to Bruce, 17 Jun. 1944, *ibid.*
3. Nicholas, *A Short History of S.I. Activities with Respect to Éire*, p. 100.
4. Ed Lawler to author, 5 Apr. 1985.
5. J.P. Walshe, memo, 23 Jun. 1944, DFA/A60, NAI.
6. J.P. Walshe to E.R. Marlin, 29 Jun. 1944, *ibid.*
7. J.P. Walshe, memo, 23 Jun. 1944, *ibid.*
8. Marlin's report, 16 Jul. 1944, Nicholas, pp. 102–3.
9. F.J.D. Gageby to CSO, G2, undated, DFA/A60, NAI.
10. John V. Heffernan to de Valera, 1 May 1946, *ibid.*
11. Hathaway, memo of meeting with McKenna, 19 May 1944, in Gray to Secretary of State, Des. 876, 19 May 1944, NAUS.
12. Maffey, memo of conversation with de Valera, 10 Jun. 1944, DO 130/43, TNAGB.
13. Maffey to Machtig, 8 Jul. 1944, DO130/43, TNAGB.
14. Gray to Winant, 23 Aug. 1944, Gray Papers.
15. Gray to FDR, 2 Oct. 1944, FDRL.
16. *Ibid.*
17. *Ibid.*
18. *Ibid.*
19. *New York Times*, 16 Nov. 1944.
20. Gray to FDR, 18 Nov. 1944.
21. *Ibid.*
22. Maffey, memo of conversation with de Valera, 10 Nov. 1944, DO130/43, TNAGB.
23. *Ibid.*
24. Gray to FDR, 18 Nov. 1944, FDRL.
25. Australian Government to Dom. Sec., tel. 248, 26 Sep. 1944, ADP.
26. Churchill to Curtin, tel. D1478, 1 Oct. 1944, *DAFP.*
27. SSEA to Kearney, No. 31, 4 Oct. 1944, NAC.
28. Robert Brennan, *Ireland Standing Firm*, pp. 88–91.
29. Churchill to Roosevelt, tel., 27 Jan. 1945, Warren F. Kimball, *Complete Correspondence*, p. 520.
30. Churchill to Roosevelt, tel., 6 Mar. 1945, *ibid.*, p. 544.
31. Roosevelt to Churchill, tel., 16 Mar. 1945, *ibid.*, pp. 571–2.
32. Cranborne, memo, 21 Feb. 1945, WP 104 (45), CAB66/62/9.
33. Brennan, p. 93.

34. Gray to Eleanor Roosevelt, 13 Apr. 1945, Gray Papers, WIR.
35. *Irish Press*, 14 Apr. 1945.
36. Memo, 'Complaint by American Minister', Jun. 1945, S.13647, Taoiseach Dept, NAI.
37. Kearney, Diary, 20 Apr. 1945, NAC.
38. *Ibid.*, 21 Apr. 1945.
39. Kearney, Diary, 30 Apr. 1945.
40. Gray, memo of conversation with de Valera, 30 Apr. 1945, FDRL.
41. Kearney, Diary, 1 May 1945, NAC.

Chapter 30 Loose Ends (PP. 327–335)

1. Carolle J. Carter, 'America's Neutral Ally, 1939–41', *Éire-Ireland*, 7:12.
2. *Toronto Globe and Mail*, 5 May 1945.
3. San Francisco *Leader*, 19 May 1945.
4. *New York Times*, 4 May 1945.
5. SSEA to Kearney, 18 May 1945, 822–39C, DEAC.
6. *Toronto Telegram*, 4 May 1945.
7. Kearney, Diary, 4 May 1945.
8. John Gunther, *Procession*, London, 1965, p. 107.
9. Maffey, memo, 21 May 1945, DO130/56, TNAGB.
10. Kearney, Diary, 22 Mar. 1945, NAC.
11. Maffey to Eric Machtig, 27 Apr. 1945, DO 130/56, TNAGB.
12. Maffey, memo of conversation with de Valera, 6 Jul. 1945, DO130/56, TNAGB.
13. De Valera to Robert Brennan, 21 May 1945, P150/2676, UCDA.
14. *Dáil Debates*, 97 (19 Jul. 1945) 2755–6.
15. Gray to de Valera, n.d., Box 2, Gray Papers.
16. Maffey, memo, 21 May 1945, DO 130/56, TNAGB.
17. Churchill's speech, 13 May 1945, Winston Churchill, *Victory*, pp. 132–8.
18. Kearney, Irish Diary, 16 May 1945, NAC.
19. Maurice Moynihan, *Speeches and Statements*, pp. 474–5.
20. Kearney, Irish Diary, 16 May 1945, NAC.
21. Kearney to Norman A. Robertson, 22 May 1945, 822–39C DEAC.
22. Hearne, annual report for 1945, Hearne to DEA, 22 Mar. 1946, DFA/359/1, NAI.
23. Kearney, Irish Diary, 19 May 1945, NAC.
24. Kearney to Norman A. Robertson, 22 May 1945, 822–39C DEAC.
25. Maffey, memo re, de Valera's broadcast, 21 May 1945, DO 130/56, TNAGB.
26. *Ibid.*
27. Machtig to Maffey, 18 Jul. 1945, DO 130/58, *Ibid.*
28. Maffey, memo re. de Valera's broadcast, 21 May 1945, DO 130/56, *Ibid.*
29. *Ibid.*
30. Memo, 'Complaint by American Minister', Jun. 1945, S.13647, Taoiseach Dept, NAI.
31. *Ibid.*
32. Gray to Stettinius, 13 Jun. 1945, *FRUS, 1945*, 3:789.
33. Gray to Stettinius, 5 Jul. 1945, *Ibid.*, 796.
34. Grew to Gray, 7 Jul. 1945, *Ibid.*
35. Gray to Secretary of State, 28 May 1947, NAUS.
36. Maffey, interview with T. de Vere White, *The Irish Times*, 4 Jul. 1962.

Chapter 31 In Perspective (PP. 336–347)

1. Maffey, interview with T. de Vere White, *The Irish Times*, 4 Jul. 1962.
2. *Dáil Debates*, 97 (18 Jul. 1945):2742–3.
3. Maffey, memo, 21 Aug. 1945, DO130/56, TNAGB.
4. Cranborne, memo, 21 Feb. 1945, WP 104 (45), CAB66/62/9, TNAGB.
5. Paul McMahon, *British Spies*, p. 330.
6. *Ibid.*, p. 405.
7. Eunan O'Halpin (ed.), M15 *and Ireland*, p. 17.
8. Gray to Secretary of State, Des. 320, 23 Mar. 1942, NAUS.
9. Forgan to author, 6 Nov. 1970.
10. *The Irish Times*, 5 Sep. 1946.
11. Churchill's speech, 13 May 1945, Winston Churchill, *Victory*, pp. 132–8.
12. Joseph E. Persico, *Roosevelt's Secret War*, p. 251.
13. Anthony Cave Brown, *Body Guard of Lies*, p. 543.
14. Persico, p. 305.
15. Dennis Wheatley, *Deception Planners*, p. 189.
16. Nicholas to Sherman Wallace, 20 Feb. 1945.
17. Persico, pp. 305–6.
18. R. Harris Smith, *The O.S.S*, p. 84.
19. MacWhite to Dublin, 17 Dec. 1938, Crowe *et al.*, *DIFP*, 5:283–3.
20. F.H. Boland, memo, 18 Jun. 1940, 2001/20/52, NAI.
21. Carter Nicholas to Sherman Wallace, memo, 18 Oct. 1945, p. 66.
22. DFA/333/18, NAI.
23. Nelson D. Lankford in David K. Bruce, *OSS Diary*, p. 205.
24. 'Behind the Green Curtain', MS, Gray Papers. An earlier copy of the MS can be found in the FDR Library.
25. *Time*, 24 Dec. 1951.
26. Mackenzie King, Diary, 12 Apr. 1948, NAC.
27. Maffey, memo, 21 Aug. 1945, DO130/56, TNAGB.

BIBLIOGRAPHY

UNPUBLISHED MATERIAL:

Manuscript Collections
Aiken, Frank, Papers, UCD Archives, Dublin.
American Friends of Irish Neutrality Papers, St John University, N.Y.
Brennan, Robert, Papers, National Library of Ireland, Dublin.
British State Papers (Cabinet Papers, Foreign Office and Dominions Office), National Archives of
    Great Britain, Kew, England.
Bryan, Dan, Papers Archives, University College Dublin.
Canadian Diplomatic Papers, Department of External Affairs and National Archives of Canada,
    Ottawa.
Cudahy, John C., Papers, Milwaukee County Historical Society, Milwaukee, Wisconsin, USA.
de Valera, Eamon, Papers, University College Dublin.
Forgan, J. Russell, Papers, Hoover Institution on War, Revolution and Peace, Stanford, California.
Friends of Freedom Committee Papers, University of Chicago.
Gray, David, Papers, Laramie, Wyoming, and FDR Library, Hyde Park, N.Y.
Irish Department of Foreign Affairs Files, National Archives of Ireland.
Irish Military Archives, Cathal Brugha Barracks, Dublin.
Kearney, John D., Papers and Diaries, National Archives, Ottawa, Canada.
King, William Lyon Mackenzie, Diary, National Archives, Ottawa, Canada (http://king.
    collectionscanada.ca/EN/Default.asp).
Liddell, Guy, Diary, National Archives, Kew, England.
McGarrity, Joseph, Papers, National Library of Ireland, Dublin.
MacSwiney, Mary, Papers, UCD Archives, Dublin.
Mulcahy, Richard, Papers, UCD Archives, Dublin.
oss Papers, National Archives, College Park, Maryland, USA.
Quigley, Martin S., Papers, Georgetown University, Washington, D.C.
Roosevelt, Franklin D., Papers, FDR Library, Hyde Park, N.Y.
—*Complete Presidential Press Conferences of Franklin D. Roosevelt*, volumes 16–23, New York, 1972.
US Department of State, Papers, Department of State and National Archives, Washington, D.C.

Author received correspondence from

Acheson, Dean
Avon, Earl of (former Sir Anthony Eden)
Barry, Tom

Boland, Frederick H.
Boland, Kevin
Brady, Charles

Brookeborough, Lord
Bruce, David K.
Bryan, Colonel Dan
Clissmann, Helmut
Cosgrave, Liam
Cudahy, Katherine
Dillon, James
Farley, James A.
Fleishmann, George
Forgan, J. Russell
Girdlestone, Bruce
Hancock, W.K.
Harriman, W. Averell
Kearney, John D.
Keefer, Ralph G.
Kelly, James A.
Lawler, Edward J.

Longford, Earl of
MacCormack, John
MacDermot, Frank
MacDonald, Malcolm
MacEntee, Seán
McGlynn, Michael
Marlin, Evin R. 'Spike'
Mayhew, Christopher
Mollenhauer, Kurt H.
Moynihan, Maurice
Neymeyr, Konrad
O'Dwyer, Paul
Quigley, Martin S.
Stewart, Robert B.
Verity, Hugh
Wolfe, Roland L.

Contemporary Newspapers and Periodicals

Atlanta Constitution
Chicago Tribune
Cork Examiner
Daily Express (London)
Daily Herald (London)
Daily Mail (London)
Dallas Morning News
Economist, The
Evening News (London)
Fort Worth Star Telegram
Gaelic American
Globe and Mail (Toronto)
Irish Echo (New York)
Irish Independent (Dublin)
Irish Press (Dublin)
Irish Times (Dublin)
Irish World (N.Y.)
Kerry Champion

Kerryman
Letter from America
Manchester Guardian
Milwaukee Journal
Nation
New York Herald Tribune
New York Times
Newsweek
The Observer
Round Table
San Francisco Chronicle
San Francisco Leader
Social Justice
Sunday Telegraph
Tablet, The (Brooklyn)
Times, The (London)
Toronto Globe and Mail
Toronto Telegram

Diaries, Memoirs and Documents

Australian Government. *Documents on Australian Foreign Policy, 1937–1945*, Canberra, 1975–1983. (http://www.info.dfat.gov.au/historical)

Brennan, Robert. *Ireland Standing Firm: My Wartime Mission in Washington*, Dublin, 2002.

British Security Coordination. *The Secret History of British Intelligence in the Americas, 1940–45*, N.Y., 1999.

Bruce, David K. OSS *Against the Reich: The World War II Diaries of Colonel David K.E. Bruce*, ed. by Nelson Douglas Lankford, Kent, Ohio, 1991.

Canada. *Hansard, House of Commons, 1939–1945*.

Cantril, Hadley, ed. *Public Opinion, 1939–1946*, Princeton, N.J., 1951.

Churchill, Winston S. *The End of the Beginning: War Speeches of the Rt Hon Winston S. Churchill*, Compiled by Charles Eade. VOL. 3. London, 1952.

—*The Second World War*, 6 vols., Boston: Houghton, 1948–53.

—*Victory: War Speeches of the Rt Hon Winston S. Churchill*, Compiled by Charles Eade, VOL. 6. London, 1946.

Colville, John. *Fringes of Power: The Incredible Inside Story of Winston Churchill During WW II*, London, 1985.

Connolly, Joseph. *Memoirs of Senator Joseph Connolly (1885–1961): A Founder of Modern Ireland*, ed. by J. Anthony Gaughan, Dublin, 1996.

Crozier, William Percival. *Off the Record: Political Interviews, 1933–1943*, ed. by A.J.P. Taylor, London, 1973.

Cummins, Geraldine. *Unseen Adventures: An Autobiography covering Thirty-four Years Work in Psychical Research*, London, 1951.

Dáil Éireann, *Debates*, Volumes 77–97 (http://historical-debates.oireachtas.ie/index.html).

de Valera, Eamon. *Speeches and Statements by Eamon de Valera, 1917–1973*, ed. by Maurice Moynihan, Dublin, 1980.

—*Ireland's Stand: Being a Selection of Speeches by Eamon de Valera during the War*, Dublin, 1946.

—*Peace and War: Speeches by Mr de Valera on International Affairs*, Dublin, 1944.

Farley, James A. *Jim Farley's Story: The Roosevelt Years*, N.Y., 1948.

Gallup, George. *The Gallup Poll: Public Opinion, 1935–1971*, vol. 1, 1935–1945, N.Y., 1972.

Girdlestone, Bruce N. 'Memoirs of Internment at Curragh', MS.

Gray, David. 'Behind the Green Curtain,' MS.

Hachey, Thomas E., ed. *Confidential Dispatches: Analyses of America by the British Ambassador, 1939–1945*, Evanston, IL., 1974.

Hull, Cordell. *The Memoirs of Cordell Hull*, N.Y., 1948.

Ickes, Harold L. *Secret Diary of Harold L. Ickes*, N.Y., 1953–1954.

Irwin, Theodore. *Inside the Christian Front*, N.Y., 1940.

Kearney, John D. Diaries, MS, National Archives of Canada, Ottawa.

Kennedy, Rose Fitzgerald. *Times to Remember*, N.Y., 1974.

Kimball, Warren F., ed. *Churchill and Roosevelt: The Complete Correspondence*, Princeton, 1984.

Liddell, Guy M. Diary, National Archives of Great Britain, Kew, England.

MacDonald, Malcolm. *Titans & Others*. London, 1972.

Mackenzie King, William Lyon. Diaries, National Archives of Canada, Ottawa (http://king.collectionscanada.ca/EN/default.asp).

Mansergh, Nicholas, ed. *Documents and Speeches on British Commonwealth Affairs, 1931–1952*, 2 vols. N.Y., 1952.

Menzies, Robert. *Afternoon Light: Some Memories and Events*, London, 1967.

Montgomery, Bernard L. *Memoirs of Field Marshall Montgomery*, N.Y., 1958.

Moynihan, Maurice, ed., *Speeches and Statements of Eamon de Valera, 1917–1923*, Dublin, 1980.

National Archives of Ireland. *Documents on Irish Foreign Policy*, Crowe, Catriona, with Ronan Fanning, Michael Kennedy, Dermot Keogh and Eunan O'Halpin, eds., *Documents on Irish Foreign Policy*, Vol.5, 1937–1939, Dublin, 2006.

Nicholas, R. Carter. 'A Short History of s.i. Activities with Respect to Éire', MS.

O'Halpin, Eunan, ed. *MI5 and Ireland, 1939–1945: The Official History*, Dublin, 2003.

Quigley, Martin. *A U.S. Spy in Ireland*, Dublin, 1999.

Smuts, Jan Christiaan. *Selections from the Smuts Papers, Volume 6, December 1934—August 1945*, ed. Jean Van Der Poel, Cambridge, 1973.

Stuart, Francis. *The Wartime Broadcasts of Francis Stuart*, ed. Brendan Barrington, Dublin, 2000.

United Kingdom. *Confidential Dispatches: Analyses of America by the British Ambassador, 1939–1945*, ed. Thomas E. Hachey, Evanston, IL., 1974.

U.S. *Congressional Record, 1939–1945*.

U.S. Department of State. Foreign Relations of the United States: The Conferences at Washington and Quebec 1943, Washington, D.C., 1970.

—Foreign Relations of the United States: Diplomatic Papers, 1940, 1941, 1942, 1943, 1944, and 1945, Washington, D.C., 1958–1969.

—*Documents on German Foreign Policy, 1918–1945* (Series D) 13 vols, Washington, D.C., 1949–1954.

Warlimont, Walter. *Inside Hitler's Headquarters, 1939–1945*, N.Y. 1964.

Secondary Works

Adams, Michael. *Censorship: The Irish Experience*, Montgomery, Alabama, 1968.

Alcorn, Robert Hayden. *No Bugles for Spies: Tales of the OSS*, London, 1963.

Andrew, Christopher. *Secret Service: The Making of the British Intelligence Community*, London, 1985.

Barcroft, Stephen A. 'The International Civil Servant: The League of Nations Career of Seán Lester', Ph.D. Dissertation, Trinity College Dublin. 1973.

Barton, Brian. *The Blitz: Belfast in the War Years*, Belfast, 1989.

Beckles, Gordon. *America Chooses!* London, 1941.

Bell, J. Bowyer. *The Secret Army: The IRA, 1916–1979*. Cambridge, Mass.: MIT Press, 1983.

Berger, Alexander. *Les Prisonniers de L'Ile Verte*, Paris, 1966.

Beschloss, Michael R. *Kennedy and Roosevelt: Uneasy Alliance*, N.Y., 1980.

Bethell, Nicholas. *The War Hitler Won: The Fall of Poland, September 1939*, N.Y., 1973.

Bowman, John. *De Valera and the Ulster Question, 1917–1973*, Oxford, 1982.

—*Allegiance*, Dublin, 1950.

Boyce, George. 'From War to Neutrality: Anglo-Irish Relations, 1921–1950', *British Journal of International Studies* 5, no. 1 (1979): 15–36.

Brown, Anthony Cave. *The Last Hero: Wild Bill Donovan*, N.Y., 1982.

—*Bodyguard of Lies*, London, 1976.

Calder, Jack. 'I Flew Into Trouble', *Maclean's* Magazine, August, 1942.

Canning, Paul. *British Policy Towards Ireland, 1921–1941*, Oxford, 1985.

Cannon, Robert I. *The Cardinal Spellman Story*, N.Y., 1962.

Carroll, Joseph T. *Ireland in the War Years, 1939–1945*, Newton Abbot, 1975.

Carson, William Arthur. *Ulster and the Irish Republic*, Introduction by David Gray, Belfast, 1957.

Carter, J. Carolle. *The Shamrock and the Swastika: German Espionage in Ireland in World War II*, Palo Alto, 1977.

Charmley, John. *Churchill's Grand Alliance: The Anglo-American Special Relationship, 1940–1957*, N.Y., 1995.

Coogan, Tim Pat. *Ireland in the Twentieth Century*, London, 2003.

—*Eamon De Valera: The Man Who Was Ireland*, N.Y., 1995.

—*The IRA: A History*, N.Y., 1995.

Cooper, Diana. *The Light of Common Day*, Boston, 1959.

Cressman, Robert J. *Hyper War: The Official Chronology of the US Navy in World War II*, Washington, 2007 (http://www.ibiblio.org/hyperwar/USN/USN-Chron/USN-Chron-Intro.html).

Cronin, Seán, ed. *Washington's Irish Policy, 1916–1986: Independence, Partition, Neutrality*, Dublin: Anvil Books, 1987.

—'Neutrality Under Fire', *Irish Times*, 30 August–2 September 1982.

—*The McGarrity Papers: Revelations of the Irish Revolutionary Movement in Ireland and America, 1900–1940*. Tralee, Ireland: Anvil, 1972.

Doherty, Richard. *Irish Men and Women in the Second World War*, Dublin, 1999.

Duggan, John P. *Herr Hempel at the German Legation in Dublin, 1937–1945*, Dublin, 2003.

—'Germany and Ireland in World War II', *Irish Sword*, no. 75–76 (1993): 93–8.

—*Neutral Ireland and the Third Reich*, Dublin, 1985.

Dunne, James. 'The Cushiest Prison Camp of the War', *Sunday Mirror*, 21–28 November 1976.

Dwyer, T. Ryle. *The Squad and the Intelligence Operations of Michael Collins*, Cork, 2005.

—*Across the Waves*, Cork, 2002.

—*Guests of the State: The Story of Allies and Axis Servicemen Interned in Ireland during World War II*, Dingle, 1994.

—*De Valera: The Man & The Myths*, Dublin, 1991 and 2007.

—*Eamon de Valera: The Man and the Myths*, Dublin, 1991.

—*Strained Relations: Ireland at Peace and the USA at War, 1941–45*, N.Y., 1988.

—*De Valera's Darkest Hour: In Search of National Independence, 1919–1932*, Cork, 1982.

—*De Valera's Finest Hour: In Search of National Independence, 1932–1959*, Cork, 1982.

—*Eamon de Valera*, Dublin, 1980.

—*Irish Neutrality and the USA, 1939–47*, Dublin, 1977.

—'The United States and Irish Neutrality, 1939–1945', Ph.D., Thesis, North Texas State University, 1973.

Feiling, Keith. *The Life of Neville Chamberlain*, London, 1946.

Ferriter, Diarmaid. *Judging Dev: A Reassessment of the Life and Legacy of Eamon de Valera*, Dublin, 2007.

Fisk, Robert. *In Time of War: Ireland, Ulster, and the Price of Neutrality, 1939–45*, Dingle, 1983.

Foot, M.R.D., and Langley, J.M. *MI9*, London, 1980.

Forde, Frank. *The Long Watch: The History of the Irish Merchant Marine in World War II*, Dublin, 1981.

Gelb, Norman. *Dunkirk: The Complete Story of the First Step in the Defeat of Hitler*, N.Y., 1989.

Gellman, Irwing F. *Secret Affairs: Franklin Roosevelt, Cordell Hull, and Sumner Welles*, Baltimore, 1995.

Gilbert, Martin. *Winston S. Churchill: Volume Six, Finest Hour, 1939–1941*, London, 1983.

Girvin, Brian. *The Emergency: Neutral Ireland 1939–45*, London, 2006.

—and Geoffrey Roberts, eds. *Ireland and the Second World War: Politics, Society and Remembrance*, Dublin, 2000.

Gray, David. 'Introduction', in *Ulster and the Irish Republic*, by William A. Carson, i–ix. Belfast 1957.

Gray, Tony. *The Lost Years: The Emergency in Ireland, 1939–45*, London, 1997.

—*Mr Smyllie, Sir*, Dublin: Gill & Macmillan, 1991.

Hawley, Heather J. 'John D. Kearney and Irish-Canadian Relations During World War II', MA Thesis, University of New Brunswick, 1999.

Hearden, Patrick J. 'John Cudahy and the Pursuit of Peace', *Mid-America: An Historical Review*, 68(April/July, 1986):99–114.

Hersh, Seymour A. *The Dark Side of Camelot*, Boston, 1997.

Hull, Mark. *Irish Secrets: German Espionage in Wartime Ireland, 1939–1945*, Dublin, 2003.

Irving, David. *Hitler's War: and the War Path*, Guildford, 2000.

Keatinge, Patrick. *The Formulation of Irish Foreign Policy*. Dublin, 1973.

Keefer, Ralph. *Grounded in Éire: The Story of Two RAF Fliers Interned in Ireland During World War II*, Montreal, 2001.

Kemble, Mike. *On a Sailor's Grave (No Roses Grow): Maritime Disasters of the Second World War*, Bognor Regis, 2005.

Kennedy, Michael. *Guarding Neutral Ireland: Coast Watching Service and Military Intelligence, 1939–1945*, Dublin, 2008.

—*Ireland and the League of Nations, 1919–1946: International Relations, Diplomacy, and Politics*, Dublin, 1996.

—and Joseph Morrison Skelly, eds. *Irish Foreign Policy, 1919–66: From Independence to Internationalism*, Dublin, 2000.

Keogh, Dermot, and O'Driscoll, Mervyn. *Ireland in World War Two: Neutrality and Survival*, Cork, 2004.

Keogh, Dermot. 'De Valera, Hitler and the Visit of Condolence: May 1945', *History Ireland* 5, no. 3 (1997): 58–61.

—*Ireland and the Vatican: The Politics and Diplomacy of Church-State Relations, 1922–1960*, Cork: Cork University Press, 1995.

—*Twentieth-Century Ireland: Nation and State*, New York, 1995.

—'Eamon de Valera and Hitler: An Analysis of International Reaction to the Visit to the German Minister, May 1945', *Irish Studies in International Affairs* 3, no. 1 (1989): 69–92.

—*Ireland and Europe, 1919–1948*, Dublin: Gill & Macmillan, 1988.

Keogh, Niall. *Con Cremin: Ireland's Wartime Diplomat*, Cork, 2006.

Kimball, Warren F., *Forged in War: Roosevelt, Churchill and the Second World War*, N.Y., 1997.

Langer, William L., and Gleason, S. Everett. *The Undeclared War: The World Crisis of 1937–1940 and American Foreign Policy*, Volume 2, N.Y, 1952.

—*The Challenge to Isolation: The World Crisis of 1937–1940 and American Foreign Policy*, Volume 1, N.Y. 1952.

Leamer, Laurence. *The Kennedy Men, 1901–1963: The Laws of the Father*, N.Y., 2001.

Lee, Joe. *Ireland, 1912–1985: Politics and Society*, Cambridge: Cambridge University Press, 1989.

Liddell Hart, B.H. *History of the Second World War*, N.Y., 1971.

Lindbergh, Charles. *The Wartime Journals of Charles A. Lindbergh*, N.Y., 1970.

Longford, Frank Pakenham, and O'Neill, Thomas P. *Eamon De Valera*, London, 1974.

Lyons, F. S. L. *John Dillon: A Biography*, London, 1968.

MacCarron, Donal. *Step Together! The Story of Ireland's Emergency Army as Told by Its Veterans*, Dublin, 1999.

—*Landfall Ireland: The Story of Allied and German Aircraft which came down in Éire in World War Two*, privately published.

MacDonald, Malcolm. *Titans & Others*. London, 1972.

McEvoy, Fred. 'Canadian-Irish relations during the Second World War', *Journal of Imperial and Commonwealth History*, 7:206–26.

McMahon, Deirdre. *Republicans and Imperialists: Anglo-Irish Relations in the 1930s*, New Haven, 1984.

McMahon, Paul. *British Spies and Irish Rebels: British Intelligence and Ireland, 1916–1945*, Woodbridge, 2008.

Mahl, Thomas E. *Desperate Deception: British Covert Operations in the United States, 1939–1944*, London, 1998.

Manhattan, Avro. *The Vatican in World Politics*, London, 1949.

Manning, Maurice. *James Dillon: A Biography*, Dublin, 1999.

Meacham, Jon. *Franklin and Winston: An Intimate Portrait of an Epic Friendship*, N.Y., 2003.

Mitchell, Arthur, and Pádraig Ó Snodaigh, eds. *Irish Political Documents, 1916–1949*, Dublin, 1985.

Morgan, Ted. *FDR: A Biography*, N.Y., 1985.

Nolan, Aengus. *Joseph Walshe: Irish Foreign Policy 1922–1946*, Cork, 2008.

Nowlan, Kevin B. and Thomas Desmond Williams, eds. *Ireland in the War Years and After, 1939–51*, Dublin, 1969.

O'Donnell, Terence. *The Case for American-Irish Unity*, Washington, D.C., 1941.

O'Donoghue, David. *Hitler's Irish Voices: The Story of German Radio's Wartime Irish Service*, Belfast, 1998.

Ó Drisceoil, Donal. *Censorship in Ireland, 1939–1945: Neutrality, Politics and Society*, Cork, 1996.

O'Driscoll, Mervyn. *Ireland, Germany and the Nazis: Politics and Diplomacy, 1919–1939*, Dublin, 2004.

O'Halpin, Eunan. *Spying on Ireland: British Intelligence and Irish Neutrality During the Second World War*, Oxford, 2008.

—*Defending Ireland: The Irish State and Its Enemies Since 1922*, N.Y., 1999.

—'Intelligence and Security in Ireland, 1922–45', *Intelligence and National Security* 5, no. 1 (1990): 50–83.

Packard, Jarrold M. *Neither Friend Nor Foe: The European Neutrals in World War II*, N.Y., 1992.

Persico, Joseph E. *Roosevelt's Secret War: FDR and World War II Espionage*, N.Y., 2001.

—*Piercing the Reich*, London, 1979.

Quigley, Martin. *Great Gaels in Peace and War*, N.Y., 1944.

Raymond, Raymond James. 'American Public Opinion and Irish Neutrality, 1939–1945', *Éire-Ireland* 18: 20–45.

—'David Gray, The Aiken Mission and Irish Neutrality, 1940–41', *Diplomatic History* 9: 55–71.

—'John Cudahy, Eamon de Valera, and the Anglo-Irish Negotiations in 1938: The Secret Dispatches to Washington', *International History Review* 6: 232–64.

Robinson, Edgar Eugene. *The Vote for Roosevelt: The Presidential Vote, 1932–1944*, N.Y., 1970.

Rosenberg, J. L.'The 1941 Mission of Frank Aiken to the United States: An American Perspective', *Irish Historical Studies*, 22:(September 1980):162–177.

— 'America and the Neutrality of Ireland, 1939–1941', Ph.D. dissertation, University of Iowa, 1976.

Roskill, S.W. *White Ensign: The British Navy at War, 1939–45*, Annapolis, 1962.

Sayers, Michael, and Kahn, Albert E. *Sabotage: The Secret War Against America*, N.Y., 1942.

Seanad Éireann, Debates, volumes 23–30 (http://historical-debates.oireachtas.ie/index.html).

Shannon, William V. *The American Irish: A Political and Social Portrait*, N.Y., 1963.

Share, Bernard. *The Emergency: Neutral Ireland, 1939–45*, Dublin, 1978.

Shirer, William L. *The Rise and Fall of the Third Reich*, N.Y., 1960.

Shogan, Robert. *Hard Bargain: How FDR Twisted Churchill's Arm, Evaded the Law, and Changed the Role of the American Presidency*, N.Y., 1999.

Smith, Bradley F. *The Shadow Warriors: O.S.S. and the Origins of the C.I.A.*, N.Y., 1983.

Smith, R. Harris. *The O.S.S.: The Secret History of America's First Central Intelligence Agency*, Berkley, 1972.

Smyllie, Robert M. 'Unneutral Neutral Éire', *Foreign Affairs*, 24:316–26.

Stacks, John F. *Scotty: James B. Reston and the Rise and Fall of American Journalism*, Boston, 2003.

Stafford, David. *Churchill and Secret Service*, London, 1995.

Stephan, Enno. *Spies in Ireland*, London, 1953.

Touhey, Ryan. 'Exercising Canada's Autonomy in Foreign Relations: The King Government and the Irish Question in World War II', MA Thesis, University of Ottawa, 1999.

Tully, John Day. 'Identities and Distortions: Irish Americans, Ireland, and the United States, 1932–1945', Ph.D. Dissertation, Ohio State University, 2004.

Turner, John Frayn. *V.C.'s of the Royal Navy*, London, 1956.

Warren, Donald. *Radio Priest: Charles Coughlin, the Father of Hate Radio*, N.Y., 1966.

West, Nigel. *MI5: British Security Service Operations, 1900–1945*, London, 1981.

Whalen, Richard J. *The Founding Father: The Story of Joseph P. Kennedy*, N.Y., 1964.

Wheatley, Dennis. *The Deception Planners: My Secret War*, London, 1980.

White, Terence de Vere. 'Lord Rugby Remembers', *Irish Times*, 3–5 July 1962.

Willis, Claire. *That Neutral Island: A Cultural History of Ireland During the Second World War*, London, 2007.

Willis, Gary. *The Kennedys: A Shattered Illusion*, London, 1981.

Younger, Calton, *A State of Disunion: Arthur Griffith, Michael Collins, James Craig, Eamon de Valera*, London, 1972.

INDEX